MW01194030

HOW THE SPANISH EMPIRE WAS BUILT

HOW THE
SPANISH EMPIRE
WAS BUILT

A 400-YEAR HISTORY

Felipe Fernández-Armesto
and Manuel Lucena Giraldo

REAKTION BOOKS

IN MEMORIAM
RAFAEL DEL PINO Y MORENO

Published by
REAKTION BOOKS LTD
Unit 32, Waterside
44–48 Wharf Road
London N1 7UX, UK

www.reaktionbooks.co.uk

First published in English 2024
Translation © Felipe Fernández-Armesto and Manuel Lucena Giraldo 2024

Translated from the Spanish *Un Imperio De Ingenieros*:
© 2022, Felipe Fernández-Armesto and Manuel Lucena Giraldo
© 2022, Penguin Random House Grupo Editorial, S.A.U.
Travessera de Gràcia, 47-49. 08021 Barcelona,
for *Un Imperio De Ingenieros*
© 2022, Ricardo Sánchez Rodríguez, for the maps

This book has been published with the support of the
Rafael del Pino Foundation

Printed and bound in Great Britain by TJ Books Ltd, Padstow, Cornwall

A catalogue record for this book is available from the British Library

ISBN 978 1 78914 840 4

CONTENTS

PREFACE

Engineers solve problems. Historians pose them. The latter are happiest in the face of unanswerable questions: answers are spoilers, and when a problem is solved its charm has fled. For engineers, however, problem-solving is a professional obligation, and a principal source of pleasure. In consequence, the disciplines attract opposites: sometimes, magnetism results. The authors of the present book have counted engineers among the intellectuals they most admire and the friends they most value. Rafael del Pino y Moreno, to whose memory the book is dedicated, was among the most admirable of intellectuals and the most generous of friends. His work as an engineer complemented his career as a businessman and funded his contributions as a philanthropist. His labours, perhaps more than those of any other single individual, helped lay the infrastructure of the Spanish economy – the roads, bridges and communications hubs that have made Spain what it is today. He understood how vital infrastructure is to every other kind of political, social and economic success. Just as Spain would not thrive and prosper in peace without the networks he helped to build, so the Spanish Empire of the beginning of the sixteenth century to the end of the nineteenth would not have functioned without the efforts of the engineers related in the pages that follow – some of whom were professionals, though most, especially in the early centuries, came from other vocations in the Church or the armed forces. Rafael del Pino was their successor, and his work reproduced, within Spain, some of the benign effects theirs achieved on an imperial scale. The authors could not think of a worthier dedicatee, or of a more fitting tribute, within the compass of what they are able to offer, to his memory.

Questions that interested him occupy the pages that follow. The Introduction addresses the problem of how to make a pre-industrial empire work. 'Enter the Engineers', the first chapter, is an attempt to track the careers and opportunities amid unpredictable contingencies that turned bandits, soldiers and friars, mild or militant, practical and pious, into engineers able to solve problems of absolute urgency. Beginning with Chapter Three, we turn to the role of communications in sustaining empire. 'Making Ways' and 'Troubled Waters', Chapters Three and Four respectively, concern roads, rivers, itineraries and pathways, through mountains, plains, forests and deserts in four continents. Life was about networks. It still is. Engineers laid them in the Spanish global monarchy on an unprecedented scale.

The price of success for empires was and remains to have enemies. In Chapter Five, fortifications, more numerous than any state had ever constructed before, appear both as symbolic of power and demonstrative of weakness. The subsequent chapter is focused on urban infrastructure because, if cities were at the heart of the Roman Empire, so it was for that of Spain, which followed Roman precedents. Shipyards, mines, theatres, gardens and public works of every kind integrated human diversity and confronted nature. The costs were huge but, as we argue, worthwhile for their effects on the loyalties of distant subjects and the cohesion of the state. The history of hospitals and sanitation demands a chapter of its own, Chapter Six, in which we draw attention to one of the most conspicuous, unusual – for the time – and costly elements of imperial infrastructure. In Chapter Seven we attempt to cover the importance of social and economic infrastructure in the public sphere, by highlighting their astonishing use as outposts in extending and supporting the imperial model. The final chapter, 'The Last Century', is more than an epilogue: in nineteenth-century Cuba, Puerto Rico and the Philippines – Spain overseas – we find instantiations of the theme of the book as a whole: a global state, which managed to encompass an amazing range of cultures and environments, thanks to the impact of the work engineers accomplished.

INTRODUCTION
Making Empire Work

Behold, I have divided unto you by lot these nations that remain, to be an inheritance for your tribes, from Jordan, with all the nations that I have cut off, even unto the great sea westward. (JOSHUA 23:4)

'Look on my works,' Ozymandias urged, as Shelley imagined him, 'and despair!' Shelley's sonnet – perhaps the most perfect, in sonority, pace and rhythm, ever contrived in English – appeared in 1818, when the Spanish Empire was in apparent collapse and romantic ruins in evident vogue. Ozymandias's invocation to despair is ironic. The inscription on the pharaoh's pedestal, intended to intimidate successors with the grandeur of his achievements, bore only 'two vast and trunkless legs of stone'. 'Half sunk, a shattered visage' was all that remained of the image that once, presumably, looked over surrounding monuments, where now 'the lone and level sands stretch far away.'[1]

Shelley's purpose was to expose the pretensions of tyranny and the evanescence of empire.[2] Although a new British empire was taking shape in India, the early modern instantiation of English imperialism had collapsed by the 1780s, with the loss of the thirteen colonies that became the United States. France's effort in North America vanished as early as 1763. The French Revolutionary and Napoleonic Wars inflicted an instant end on what France had retained in Saint-Domingue, as well as enduring agony on the Dutch, Spanish and Portuguese empires. As for the 'republican empire' that threatened the Indigenous peoples of much of North America, the prospect was by no means universally pleasing. In the 1830s Thomas Cole painted a minatory series titled *The Course of Empire* to deter fellow citizens from pursuing imperial glory: the America he imagined passed from the

9

simplicity of savagery and pastoralism to the self-indulgence of the 'consummation of empire' and thence to inevitable decline and fall, such as the Romans and their modern successors had experienced.[3]

Yet to the authors of this book and, we hope, to our readers, Ozymandias's message conveys more than despair. Though the desert, as Shelley's imaginary traveller described it, reclaimed terrain from the buildings and feats of engineering with which the pharaoh tried to smother it, Ozymandias's strategy for engineering an empire was surely correct. If civilization is a process of the modification of nature for human purposes,[4] empire takes environmental adaptation a stage further – refashioning landscape for political ends, laying infrastructure to link disparate communities into a single polity or at least into a bundle, variously neat or ragged, with common ties of belonging and of allegiance.

Imperial Engineering

The mythic engineer Yu the Great founded, in legend, the Chinese Empire by dredging rivers and scoring the land with canals. The floods, which formerly impeded production, subsided. Communications multiplied along the canals. Yu cleft passes from mountain ridges, making paths straight and rough places plain. The story is fanciful, but the sequence is credible. Many genuinely historical episodes reproduce it. While Yu's expertise encompassed roads as well as canals, his focus was on hydraulics, anticipating the 'hydraulic empires' that Karl Wittfogel and Karl Butzer identified as the dominant new polities of the Bronze Age.[5] The mace-head of an Egyptian king of the fourth millennium BC shows the ruler digging a canal – identifying kingship with flood control. A just judge, according to an Egyptian proverb, was 'a dam for the sufferer, guarding lest he drown', whereas a corrupt one was like a flood.[6] From Larsa in Mesopotamia, the archive of a contractor named Lu-igisa, which has survived from around 2000 BC, reveals the nature of his job: to survey land for canal-building, organize the labourers and their pay and provisions, and supervise the digging and the dredging of accumulated silt. Procuring labour was the key task – 5,400 workers to dig a canal and 1,800 on one occasion for emergency repairs. In return, Lu-igisa had the potentially profitable job of controlling the opening and closing of the locks that released or shut off the water supplies. He was bound by oaths that were enforced by threat of loss. 'What is my sin,' he complained to a higher official when he lost control of a canal, 'that the king took my canal from me and gave it to Etellum?'[7] As well as landscape modifications for managing the water supply and waterborne communications, public works included warehouses and sometimes factories, like those that underlay the Palace of Knossos and perhaps inspired the legend of the Minotaur's labyrinth, as well as markets and meeting-places, bridges and, of course, temples.

For early modern Spanish imperialists, who knew little of China or of Bronze-Age imperialisms, the effective model of empire was, of course, the most copious of all in engineering: that of Rome.[8] Engineering was the Romans' ultimate art. They discovered how to make concrete, which made unprecedented feats of building possible.[9] Everywhere the empire reached, Romans and the elites they recruited as allies and confederates invested in infrastructure. They built roads, sewers and aqueducts. Amphitheatres, temples, city walls, public baths and monumental gates arose at public expense, alongside the temples that civic-minded patrons usually endowed. The biggest courthouse in the empire was in London, the widest street in Italica in southern Spain. Colonists in Conimbriga, today's Coimbra, on the coast of Portugal, where salt spray corroded the mosaic floors, demolished their town centre in the first century AD and rebuilt it to resemble Rome's. Rome exported Mediterranean amenities – the building patterns of villas and cities, along with wine, olive oil, mosaics – to the provinces. Romans were brutal conquerors, who razed cities, enslaved peoples, decimated rebels and revelled in triumphs designed to humiliate defeated enemies. Yet they established a Pax Romana that resentment and resistance might have dissolved. Had they imitated Ozymandias, however, and said, 'Look on my works,' the effect would be reassuring: demonstrating the benefits of capitulation or collaboration in an enterprise that nurtured prosperity, extended the range of commerce, and provided relative security for the food supply and for imperial defence.[10] Provincial leaders visited Rome, swore oaths of loyalty at the Capitoline temples, inscribed Roman laws on their city gates and proudly said, like Paul of Tarsus, 'Civis Romanus sum.'

Infrastructure then, was, for ancient empires, in a sense, the great, secret (or at least imperfectly observed) ingredient of success. To some extent, engineering has never ceased to make key contributions to how empires work. By a reasonable standard, for instance, the world's most successful empires have been engineers' creations: not only have China and the United States absorbed vast communities by conquest or other forms of ascription, but they have convinced most of their subject peoples to rethink their own identities and re-designate themselves – whether Hakka or Peng-min, or Pawnee or Mandingo or Italian or Polish or whatever – as Chinese or American as the case may be. Of course, such success has its limits: Tibetans, by and large, and many Muslims in western China reject the opportunity, as do some inveterate secessionists, Puerto Rican nationalists and the Nation of Islam in the United States. But the success of both imperial enterprises in this respect seems conspicuous, especially if one compares the Chinese and u.s. past with the way colonial experience eroded metropolitan identity in most modern European empires.

The United States has upheld what we might almost call a tradition of imperial excellence in engineering.[11] In a land severed by wide, surging rivers and vast inland seas, more than 600,000 bridges have done more for the Union than all the federal generals of the Civil War. Many are now abandoned or decayed – victims of the cult of private enterprise, which is never selfless enough to repair them – but it is inconceivable that the United States could exist without them. Manhattan bristles like a porcupine with skyscraper-spines, but causeways pierce it by the Brooklyn Bridge, opened in 1883, and George Washington Bridge, 1,834 and 1,450 metres long, respectively (over and only a little under 5,000 ft each). The Seven-Mile Bridge, inaugurated in 1912, connects mainland Florida with the Keys. In 1868 the Harpersfield Bridge across the Grand River in Ohio was the first with ferro-concrete supports. The railways, communications-bearers now even more under-appreciated than the old bridges, wrenched commerce and civilization into the interior and pinned the coasts, thanks to the state-sponsored surveys that preceded them from the 1840s. State universities, endowed originally at public expense, produced the engineers who laid down the infrastructure; they are now kept short of funds, but no effort was spared by their founders to give America the economic advantages that public higher education confers. Many American cities even today seem sandwiched between monuments of state or civic majesty – the local or regional university and the State House or City Hall.

There seems, then, to be a connection between infrastructure and empire. Empires are not, save in a very general sense, like machines:

they are too human for that. But they have articulated parts that material infrastructure binds and politics lubricate. The exact nature of the link between empire and engineering depends on how one understands the terms. For present purposes, in this book, under the heading of 'engineering' or 'infrastructure' we include all public works that contribute to economic effectiveness by facilitating communications, enhancing public health and providing for defence. By the 'Spanish Global Monarchy' we mean those parts of the Spanish Empire that have traditionally been called *ultramar* – in the Americas and the Philippines (and subtropical Africa for the brief relevant period). Spanish dominions in Europe and the North African littoral also have a rich engineering history, but the problems of communications and control that they represented were of a different order.

The Problems:
Identifying and Explaining Empires

'Empire' is a more problematic term even than 'engineering' and 'infrastructure'. A few years ago – it must have been in 2006 or 2007 – one of the authors of the present work was in Cambridge, Massachusetts, dining with David Armitage (renowned author of *The Ideological Origins of the British Empire*), Chris Bayly (the acclaimed global historian who wrote *Imperial Meridian* as well as *The Birth of the Modern World*), Leonard Blussé (whose *Strange Company* is one of the most brilliant works ever written on the Dutch Empire) and Shruti Kapila, who had not yet attained her present renown as a historian, but was teaching a course on the global history of empires. The conversation naturally focused on empire and, equally naturally, generated almost comprehensive disagreement, except on one point: none of those present, we concurred, was able to define 'empire'. The effect might have been dispiriting: here were supposed experts on the subject in hand who were obliged to confess that they literally did not know what they were talking about.

Indefinability, however, is a revelatory feature of empire, which we do well to acknowledge. Historians of the early modern period, when the Spanish Empire flourished, typically use the word to designate at least thirty states of widely differing characteristics: a vast, uniformly administered conglomerate, such as the Qing Empire; a highly decentralized state like Japan, expanding yet traditionally compact and homogeneous; small, ethnically distinct monarchies in Southeast Asia, such as those of the Burmese and Khmer; huge, disparate tributary hegemonies, such as that of Russia in Siberia or of the Mughals beyond their heartlands; religiously defined supremacies, like that of the Safavids or Ottomans; precarious maritime networks like the dynastic web of the Sa'id of Oman, or the new European empires that burst into the Atlantic and Indian oceans; short-lived conquest states, such as the Aztecs, the empire of Mwene Mutapa in East Africa and the brief but brilliant trans-Saharan empire of Mulay Hassan of Morocco; traditional nomad dominions over terrorized subject-peoples, such as those of the Uzbeks or Comanche; and dynastic portfolios of mutually independent states, like that of the Austrian Habsburgs. The Spanish Empire – or 'monarchy', as most Spaniards preferred to call it – was anomalous, but so was almost every so-called empire with respect to most of the others.

Although 'empire' is indefinable for our period, it is intelligible as a term denoting a state with a typical but variable profile. Typically, an empire is a conquest state (though obedience can be negotiated as well as or rather than imposed); it tends to be large, at least in relation to its predecessor- and successor-polities; although there are ethnically compact instances, empire usually brings together diverse communities and cultures in a framework of common or at least partly shared identity and allegiance; it often embodies, in the minds of its own elites, values universally applicable that confer legitimacy or justify expansion.

Most people probably assume that strength is another typical feature. It is tempting to suppose that empires must be powerful in order to coerce subject- and victim-peoples into submission. The assumption may be valid for post-industrial empires that can dispose of formidable resources for communicating and enforcing their rulers' wills. Early modern empires, however, had no such resources. They laid, at times, heavy hands on the subjects they could reach easily. But they stretched feeble fingertips towards those at the peripheries. The bigger the empire, the weaker it could be towards its frontiers. In remote parts of the Spanish monarchy, local authorities were effectively exempt from imperial control because of how long it took for the metropolis to communicate with them: it took, depending on conditions, between 59 and 153 days to complete a voyage by sea from Cádiz to Veracruz;[12] writers of royal commands had to reckon on about six months from Madrid to Mexico City, perhaps ten months to Santiago de Chile and as much as a year to Manila.

The most impressive feature of the Spanish monarchy – its enormous reach – was a source of weakness, for it spread tenuously along effectively indefensible frontiers and vulnerable routes, with resources thinly distributed. No document captures the nature of the empire better, perhaps, than the *probanza de méritos* – a legal dossier in support of a claim to rewards for service to the crown – compiled in Ormuz in the Persian Gulf in 1588 by the Portuguese captain Jerónimo de Quadros for submission to King Philip II. The petitioner was in charge of one of seven forts that the monarchy precariously maintained along the coastal underbelly of the Safavid empire, on what must have been one of the world's most perilous edges. It is a bulky document, full of testimonials confirming the heroism of the petitioner's sacrifices for the crown in campaigns up and down the western shores of the Indian Ocean. The covering letter is revelatory. The writer begins by explaining that he must rebuild his fort every year after the rains, 'because it is made of mud'. He explains how his garrison of seven Portuguese and forty native mercenaries is inadequate for the tasks that fall to his lot: manning and rebuilding the fort; fighting off bandits and Persian assailants, protecting caravans that want to trade with Ormuz. He complains of the difficulty of renewing his supplies of weapons, and it emerges at once that he is not speaking, or even thinking, of firearms but of the arrows his men rely on. Finally, he avers that his most serious deficiency is of the opium his men demand to keep them going. Imperial paladins faced difficulties so tremendous that they could face them only with the aid of narcotics.[13] To understand early modern empires, one must begin by acknowledging their most problematic characteristic: weakness.

One of the biggest problems of the history of the world is therefore, 'How did pre-industrial empires function?' In their weakness, how did they harness loyalty, galvanize support, procure service, collect tribute or tax, disarm resistance, forge workable institutions of government and enlist obedience? How did these huge, ill-articulated ogres survive in competition with one another and in defiance of the tug or drift of history towards nation-states and communal self-determination? How in some cases did they endure and even grow against the odds? Without quislings and collaborators empire was

– and probably, to a lesser extent, still is – impossible. But how are quislings made or found? How are collaborations negotiated and secured?

The Spanish Example

Our contention is that the Spanish Empire presents the best opportunity to examine these problems, not because it was a typical empire, but, on the contrary, because it was unique in pertinent ways. It was, until well into the eighteenth century, the world's only great empire of land and sea. The Qing, the Mughals, the Ottomans, Tsardom and other, lesser conglomerates stuck largely to the traditional vocation of conquest-states: expansion landward, across contiguous territory, with the aim of controlling the production of fiscally exploitable resources. Meanwhile, new maritime empires arose – seaborne or perhaps, as Charles Verlinden used to say, 'seaboard' entities, clinging to shores and ports and routes, sometimes developing coastal regions to grow marketable crops, but concentrating on the control of peculiarly profitable trades rather than of production.[14] On a big scale, in the eighteenth century, maritime empires shifted their centres of gravity landward. Portugal, for instance, incorporated the Novas Conquistas in the hinterland of Goa and followed up the late seventeenth-century colonization of Minas Gerais in Brazil with penetration into Amazonia. The English acquired the riches of Bengal, while extending their North American colonies, formerly confined to the coastal rim east of the Appalachians, into the Ohio Valley. The Dutch, who already had experience, on a small scale, in island settings in the Indian Ocean, of controlling production of goods of high value per unit of bulk, began to penetrate ever more deeply into Java. For Spain, there was nothing new in landward strategy. The Spanish Empire acquired its dual character, maritime and landward, when Cortés conquered Mexico in 1519–21 or even, perhaps, when the appropriation of parts of the Isthmus of Panama began earlier in the same decade.

The Spanish Empire is also a suitable case study because of its long reach. Except perhaps for the Dutch Empire (briefly, towards the mid-seventeenth century, when Netherlanders' outposts stretched from Deshima to Manhattan and from the Spitsbergen – now Svalbard – whaling post to the Cape Colony), Spain's was the most widely spread empire in the world, scattered at its climax from Mallorca to

Milan and from the Upper Missouri to the Beagle Channel. It was therefore – in the face of the tyranny of distance and the vagaries of *temps-distance* – the hardest to run centrally.[15] It was surely, moreover, the most environmentally diverse state of its day, encompassing the Andes and the Great Basin, and every biome from desert to ice. More than any other empire – if the present authors are right – it demonstrated vitality in the face of its own weakness. To maintain such a big and diffuse domain from a small, naturally ill-favoured homeland, of which about a third is mountain or desert, with a population small by comparison with that of such rivals as Britain and France, was an unprecedented achievement, paralleled, to some extent, by Portugal and the Netherlands, and on a much smaller scale, perhaps, by Sweden and Denmark, but strictly unequalled.

Finally, the Spanish record in sustaining imperial growth in competition with rivals – who were increasingly, as time went on, more powerful than Spain and in command of greater resources – is uniquely impressive, especially in view of the problems of defending overextended frontiers and maintaining communications with pre-industrial technology. Almost at a gulp Spain gobbled the most productive parts of continental America – Mesoamerica, the Isthmus, most of the Andean world, and the Paraguay and Paraná valleys – in the first half of the sixteenth century, effectively without opposition from European rivals. The acquisitions included – miraculously, according to some early colonial reminiscences – two of the world's most dynamic and aggressive empires of the day, the Aztecs and Inca. When European rivals bestirred themselves, they failed to do more than peck at Spanish pickings, even though internecine struggles divided the defenders, who were few and largely unsupported by professional soldiery. For the rest of the century, rival powers managed only sporadic forays, largely confined to piratical exploits, flitting and stinging on the edge of the Spanish Main, like insects irritating the hide of some great beast. Elizabethan 'projectors' – planners and prophets of a supposedly better future – raged at England's inability to challenge Spanish dominance.[16] Not until 1607 would a lasting English presence in the New World begin to take shape, when a fragile colony settled at Jamestown in Virginia. Viable Dutch and French mainland colonies were even longer delayed and except on the Guiana coast were never securely established. Meanwhile, Spanish arms enjoyed almost uniform success in America and Europe, hardly faltering in the latter continent until the

1630s at sea and the 1640s in land warfare, while in the former Jamaica was the only significant forfeiture, falling to English invaders in 1654. Only twice in the interim did pirates – English in 1589, Dutch in 1628 – disrupt the convoys that linked the moieties of the monarchy across the Atlantic. Piet Heyn's coup in 1628 was the only occasion on which most of a fleet and its cargo passed into enemy hands.[17]

The Problem of Durability

This extraordinary tally of success occurred in spite of perceived decline.[18] From the 1590s, Spanish population fell – markedly so, relative to France, England and the Dutch provinces that painfully pried themselves from the Spanish monarchy, achieving effective independence by 1620. In the same period prophets of doom foretold, erroneously but sincerely, the eclipse of the Spanish monarchy, bemoaning the apparent withdrawal of divine favour and the fragility of an empire that, in principle, might have reprised the grandeur that was Rome. Revenues from the New World fell almost uninterruptedly from the second decade of the seventeenth century and did not begin to recover, fitfully, before the 1660s.[19] The tax yield of Castile, the main source of cash to keep the monarchy going, suffered from depleted population and economic depression. The costs of the Thirty Years' War, which Spain joined, with some reluctance, in 1628, were barely supportable. Provincial and aristocratic loyalties faltered – evidence of a critical change, because the strength of the monarchy had long relied on the availability of an aristocracy defined by a relationship of mutual obligation with the monarch, and on warrior and administrative classes animated by an ethos of service to the crown. In 1640 secessionist revolts broke out in Catalonia, Andalusia, Naples and Portugal, and although only the last was successful, the burden of contending with rebels limited Spanish effectiveness on other fronts. Those fronts were numerous: defending the southern Netherlands with no ready access to the theatre of war and without adequate harbours for shipping; facing allied French and German Protestant foes along the 'Spanish Road' that led from Italy to Flanders; striving to confine the Ottomans in the Mediterranean and to defend North African enclaves; fending Muslim enemies off in the Philippines; and coping with the defence of American dominions too vast to be safely cordoned and too diffuse to be garrisoned on interior lines.

Yet none of these afflictions could stop the Spanish Empire growing overseas in the New World and the Philippines – the areas that made the Spanish monarchy 'global' in the sense intended in this book, and in which, as we hope to suggest, infrastructure was vital for securing allegiance. Expansion resumed towards the end of the seventeenth century with the reoccupation of New Mexico – which Spaniards conquered in 1598 but from which they withdrew in the 1680s in the face of disenchantment among some natives – and the submission of the last independent Maya kingdom in 1697.

New settlements in New Mexico gave rise to new needs: opening communications towards the Pacific, the Gulf of Mexico and the Mississippi Valley, exploring the great plains and the Utah Basin, excluding French interlopers and pacifying the huge arc of frontier to the north of the new limits of the empire. New Mexico seemed like a poor colony, but Spanish settlements electrified the frontier folk, as surely as booty and payola from Rome transformed neighbouring barbarians, or the wealth and magnetism of China affected the Jurchen or Manchus. A horseborne revolution changed ecologies, polities and economies. Among the Apache, White men's wealth, appropriated through raiding or ransom, traditional links of kinship and hierarchy broke down in favour of war leaders who arose to dispute the power of shamans and hereditary chiefs. Unlike the sedentary Pueblos, the Apache, who were hard to pin down, were difficult to domesticate. The Comanche presented a further set of problems. With an economy based on bison and lifeways reliant on horses, they reorganized their society for war, in a confederacy unattainable by the fissile Apache and vastly outnumbering all neighbouring peoples put together. Like steppe-land or Sahelian imperialists in the Old World, they could control great swathes of territory and terrorize subject- and victim-peoples into tributaries or slaves.[20]

Spanish policy hovered between contradictory strategies: playing 'barbarians' off against one another, like medieval Byzantines, or attracting them into peaceful submission or co-operation in the manner of Confucian mandarins with steppeland nomads; intimidating them into quiescence, or forcing them into peace; or exterminating them in the style of English colonists with their unwanted Indians. Common to all these options were efforts to enhance frontier security by seeking allies to the north beyond Apache and Comanche territory. Spain's empire therefore reached into Texas and Arizona, while expeditions emerged like tentacles to prod the plains. Hide paintings by Pawnee artists, for instance, record an expedition of 1719 from New Mexico into Nebraska, with the aim of detaching the natives from their French paymasters; but the negotiations failed and the paintings show the misfortunes of the Spaniards, surrounded by hostile bowmen and French agents.[21] With the Ute, on the other hand, Spanish efforts were successful and an alliance was formed in 1730.

Arizona was attractive at first only as a route towards the Pacific. Natives, variously coy and hostile, protracted the agony of missionaries who formed the Spanish front line. From 1732, however, Spanish efforts were continuously sustained and by mid-century the territory was a reliable, albeit costly and unruly, outpost.[22] Texas, meanwhile, demanded attention to control the Apache and fend off the French. Neither enemy proved tractable, and missions were equivocal in effect, spreading deadly disease along with allegiance to Church and crown,[23] but in the second half of the century the policy of 'attraction' yielded positive results, which can be admired, for instance, in a plan of the settlement of San Juan Bautista, on the Rio Grande, of 1754, where between the arcaded and well-ordered streets processions of Native Americans and Spaniards file with their armed escorts and attendant musicians to meet the mission folk in the main square and erect cele-bratory crosses at its corners.[24] In 1778 Bernardo de Gálvez claimed that peaceful attraction had done more – and at less cost – to pacify Indigenous peoples than warfare, and that dependency was more easily created by gifts of foodstuffs and tools than enforced by violence.[25]

In 1786 Spain made peace with the Comanche, setting the frontier between the two empires at the Arkansas River. Common enmity against the Apache was the decisive influence. The impact was invalu-able: other communities joined the Spanish monarchy or withdrew from war. The relief made the Arizona frontier stranger. The popula-tion of New Mexico leapt from about 9,600 in 1769 to about 20,000 towards the century's end.

Meanwhile, in 1763, despite the inglorious record of Spanish arms in the Seven Years' War, the treaty that ended hostilities with England enormously extended Spanish dominion by assigning most of formerly French Louisiana to Spain. The great province, which had struggled to attract settlers and show profits, benefited at once. Under Spanish rule, the population doubled to 40,000 and exports through New Orleans multiplied. In Florida, in the same period, the proximity of lands occupied by Britain exposed the Spanish frontier to constant threat of erosion or collapse. But the Indigenous population, despite British bribery and intimidation, remained surprisingly loyal to Spain.[26] The loss of the province in the treaty of 1763 was therefore only temporary and the Spaniards recovered it in 1784.

Florida was of value to Spain not for its people or products, but because its harbours bordered the Gulf Stream route from the Caribbean back across the Atlantic. Similarly, on the Pacific coast, California was of interest only because it guarded the current-assisted route from the Philippines to New Spain. Control became critical in the second half of the eighteenth century when the Pacific – formerly a 'Spanish lake' – became contested by Britain, France and Russia. In 1768 José de Gálvez, the king's representative in New Spain, decided that Spain had to incorporate the whole of California.[27] The project proved another great Spanish success. By 1780 a chain of missions reached as far as San Francisco. The colony wrenched the Indigenous population out of nomadism and created a new economy based on farming and ranching. Growth was spectacular. In 1783 grain production stood at 22,000 toneladas (roughly, tons); in 1800 at 75,000. Over the same period, livestock quadrupled. Missions housed veritable industries, producing leather (exported to New England), wood products, building materials, farming implements, wagons, soap and sails. Although Spain could never muster enough manpower to extend colonization further north, the monarchy was fairly successful in keeping Russian and English interlopers at bay south of the 42nd parallel.

While the colonization of California was under way, the American War of Independence – which pitched most of Britain's mainland colonies against their mother country – was an equivocal opportunity for a monarchy disinclined to validate rebellion and apprehensive of empowering an ambitious new neighbour. But, even before intervening directly, Spain resolved to do 'all we can to aid the colonists'.[28] When the war ended, Spain seemed to have attained all her objectives. The British menace had receded, in retreat between Canada and Belize. Florida was recovered. Louisiana and California seemed secure. Frontiers with native states were largely pacified. Although most growth was in North America, in the rest of the hemisphere Spain had achieved a comparable record of success. Adjustments of the frontiers with Portugal had involved some concessions, but had brought the Colonia del Sacramento under Spanish control; and in the southern cone the great parlamento that Ambrosio O'Higgins celebrated in 1793, reputedly with 261 Mapuche chiefs, extended the imperial frontier from the Bío-Bío to the Beagle Channel.[29]

The Spanish empire in America reached its greatest extent in July 1796, when a Spanish agent, John Evans, who represented the Missouri Company, lowered the British flag and raised that of the king of Spain over a Mandan village in South Dakota, towards the edge of what he called 'montañas rocosas' (rocky mountains, though he was way east of what we now call the Rockies).[30] Though a conscientious servant of Spanish interests, Evans was no typical subject of the Bourbons but a Welsh nationalist, born near Caernarfon and baptized a Methodist, who belonged to a conspiracy dedicated to separating Wales from England or, at least, founding a new Welsh colony beyond English influence in the New World. The inspiration for this romantic endeavour was the chivalresque legend of Prince Madoc, who supposedly conquered an empire in the ocean in the twelfth century. People were disposed to believe such effusions. In the reign of Elizabeth I, whose ancestry was Welsh, projectors of warfare against Spain invoked the Madoc myth to justify imperial ambitions.[31] In Evans's circle a further myth of Welsh-speaking North American Indians, commonly identified, for no good reason, with the Mandans, was treated as proof of Madoc's enterprise. Thus Evans, last of the great explorers of America for Spain, upheld the tradition of forebears who had sought such illusions as the terrestrial Paradise, the Fountain of Youth, El Dorado, the City of the Caesars, the Land of Cinnamon, the cities of Cibola or the realms of Amazon queens.

Establishing the Spanish Empire: Securing Collaborators

In the latitudes Evans explored, Spanish dominion lasted only for a few months and in much of the rest of the hemisphere it was only patchily effective. Yet it was robust and amazingly durable wherever Spaniards could engineer infrastructure that served their subjects (or at least their subject-elites) well. Of course, other influences were also at work, which we can review quickly. First was what we call the stranger-effect: the propensity of some cultures to value the stranger so highly as to confide authority to him. Spaniards were lucky to encounter such cultures in much of the Andean world and most of

Mesoamerica, where it was routine among the Maya for outsiders to inaugurate dynasties. In modern Western societies, the propensity is hard to understand, since our attitude to strangers is like that of the peoples who resisted the Spaniards. We mistrust them. We reject them. We call them 'illegals'. We impose on them bureaucratic or fiscal burdens. If we admit them, we make them unwelcome and typically assign them low status and demeaning work. In other times, however, and in other parts of the world, people have not, in these respects, behaved like us. Sacred rules of hospitality oblige people in some cultures to greet strangers with their best gifts and goods and women and even actual deference. When Spaniards found themselves treated this way in parts of the Americas, they felt godlike, and with reason: the anthropologist Mary W. Helms has collected many instances of cultures in which the value of visitors from afar increases with the distance they seem to have travelled, because they bring with them the aura of the divine horizon.[32] This does not necessarily mean that people mistake them for gods, but it does explain why their persons are regarded as special, even sacred. Though the notion is remote from modern Western sensibilities, I think the most hardened, secular-minded Westerner can understand it, if he or she thinks of how we add value to goods according to the distance they traverse. At any American grocer's shop – allowing for relatively modest differences in production and delivery costs – domestic Parmesan alternatives command a much lower price than the kind imported from Italy, not because they are worse, but because they are familiar. The exoticism of the foreign product imparts prestige. So it is, in many cultures, with people. In Christendom in the past, pilgrims profited from a similar effect, acquiring prestige with their neighbours, on returning home, in rough proportion to the remoteness of the shrines they visited.[33]

To defer to the stranger – given an appropriate cultural context – is often a highly commendable, rationally defensible response. The stranger is useful as an arbiter or judge because he or she is uninvolved in existing factional and dynastic conflicts and can bring an objective eye to matters of dispute. For the same reasons, strangers make first-class bodyguards or close counsellors for existing rulers – which is how many European intruders (and even runaway Black slaves, who sometimes ascended to positions of power in Indigenous society without any of the advantages commonly said to be decisive in the case of European conquistadores) began to acquire eminence in American and Asian polities in the early modern period. The stranger is often sexually attractive, perhaps for evolutionary reasons or perhaps for sheer novelty. In the Caribbean, Gonzalo Fernández de Oviedo thought that the women he encountered 'were very chaste with their own men, but gave themselves freely to Spaniards', in what sounds like an act of sexual hospitality instanced in many other cultures.[34] In any case, the stranger typically represents an excellent choice of marriage partner for powerful or ruling families by virtue of arriving untainted by any previous associations with local rivalries. To this day all over the world where monarchies still exist, heirs typically marry foreigners or, increasingly nowadays, social outsiders, for this very reason.

The proliferation of stories of stranger-kings in many parts of the world – stories, that is, of individuals whom polities have entrusted with kingship after arrival from afar or return from long and distant exile – demonstrates the value of strangers as rulers. Even in Europe, many royal dynasties have traced their origins to stranger-founders, and legends multiply the instances. Such cases are very frequent in the Pacific and in parts of Southeast Asia.[35] That touch of the divine horizon, moreover, makes the arriviste from afar a good candidate for sanctity. Many conquistadores in the New World really were holy men, friars who arrived with little or no military support but commanded their hosts with surprising, if sometimes precarious, success. Others were treated as if they were holy men. Typically, Spaniards were arbitrators wherever they were welcome. And it is in the nature of the arbitrator to gain power every time his mediation is invoked. The use of strangers as marriage partners was of particular help, as it enabled Spaniards to attain positions of honour, with access to native services, in Indigenous societies; and *mestizaje*, whom other colonists tended to avoid, forged links between Spaniards and natives while multiplying the ranks of individuals from whom the Spanish monarchy could recruit administrators, soldiers and priests.

Even when the stranger-effect failed to function, wore off or diminished, a second influence favoured Spanish dominance: the traditional enmities of neighbouring peoples made the principle *divide et impera* apply. The fall of Tenochtitlán was procured by an Indigenous alliance, in which Tlaxcalteca and Huexotzinca played the major roles and in which the Spaniards formed, by objective standards, a minor component.[36]

In Peru, Pizarro relied on Huari and Cañari allies. They took the opportunity to vent their hatred of the Inca who had only lately indemnified their hegemony against resistance in massacres of near-genocidal proportions. The Huarochirí manuscript, compiled in San Damián probably in the 1590s, recalls how the Checa transferred their amity from the Inca to the Spaniards because the former had reneged on his promise to dance annually at the Checas' main shrine – a vivid image of how political relationships worked in the pre-Hispanic Andes, as well as an indication of the resentments that shaped internecine warfare.[37] In Yucatán, the Pech, Xiu and Cocom lineages and their allies were more anxious to continue their age-old hostilities than to oppose the Spaniards, whom they tried, often with success, to manipulate in their own interests. The Pech, for instance, represented themselves as 'Maya conquistadores' and enlisted Franciscans in their persecution of Xiu enemies in Mani in 1562.[38]

The dynamics of Indigenous rivalries never wholly abated. In the first months of the establishment of a permanent Spanish presence in Mesoamerica the enemies of Aztec hegemony unleashed two terrible massacres: in Cholula, where Cortés admitted to the slaughter of 3,000 people, and Tenochtitlán, where, in his leader's absence, Pedro de Alvarado jeopardized the Spaniards' tense relations with their Aztec hosts by presiding over the slaughter of Tenochca nobles during the Feast of Toxcatl, which called for human sacrifices, among whom the Spaniards hoped not to figure. In some ways, the massacres are intelligible as the reactions of a fearful band, faced with apparently overwhelming odds, in an unfamiliar environment, resorting to terror in the absence of any other source of security. The main reason for the massacres, however, was that the Spaniards' native allies demanded them as a form of vengeance wreaked on their traditional adversaries. Overwhelmed by the sheer numbers of Tlaxcalteca warriors who surrounded them, and perhaps intimidated or bamboozled by the native interpreter who was in a position to control all negotiations, the Spaniards had no choice but to defer to their more powerful partners.[39]

Similar episodes occurred throughout the colonial period. In 1828, for instance, when the Spanish Empire was effectively over in the mainland New World, a war party, in which native Moquelemnes greatly outnumbered their Spanish comrades, pursued hostilities in the vicinity of San José, California. When the native 'auxiliaries' demanded 'justice' – by which, they explained, they meant the murder of their prisoners, the massacre of the menfolk in the enemy camp, and the enslavement of their women and children – the Spanish commander was disinclined to endorse such illegal brutality. But his sergeant took him aside to warn him that there was no chance of disobliging the Moquelemnes and surviving. 'If it were my own father,' he declared, 'I'd kill him myself.'[40]

The historiography of Latin America has obscured the real workings of colonial rule by projecting a myth of a subverted indigenous world, a history trenched by transforming ruptures, and native peoples deprived of initiative by defeat, culture shock and demographic collapse. But profound continuities, including the persistence of historic hatreds and the power of some incumbent elites, survived the Spaniards' intrusion. Like all successful and enduring empires, Spain's was a joint enterprise of an empire-wide elite and local and regional wielders of power.

Establishing Empire:
The Role of Infrastructure

No alliance is permanent and no collaboration irrefrangible. Although the dynamics of Indigenous societies favoured the growth of the Spanish Empire, there had to be something to grow: the security of Mesoamerican and Andean heartlands had to be perpetuated by other means. To keep collaboration going, the new order over which Spain presided had to reward the well-disposed. Like every major pestilence, the demographic disaster that befell early colonial society benefited the survivors, not only by redistributing existing resources but by encouraging the introduction of new economic expedients. Native chiefs could become ranchers. Indigenous communities could set up silk-weaving or leather-crafting or pig-farming enterprises. Peasants could farm cochineal on previously marginal or useless land or grow cacao for export. In many places, missions were successful examples of capitalist entrepreneurship, in which Indigenous residents, at the cost of enduring clerical paternalism or scowls from a divine termagant, could share economic benefits. None of these activities was possible until Spaniards introduced the relevant products or opened appropriate markets. All new chances of enrichment occurred in the context of the wider economic world to which Spain introduced

America. While injected money lubricated exchange, inter-regional trade linked native civilizations, formerly unknown to one another, and reached across the Atlantic and Pacific Oceans. None of this was of much benefit to peasants whose labour was coerced, peons who subsided into dependence on haciendas or native aristocrats who failed to keep up with the pace of change. But a framework emerged in which prosperity crammed sufficient elites, native and newcomer, into close relationships of mutual benefit.

The temptations of colonial prosperity were inseparable from the advantages public works conveyed, especially for communications, defence and the distribution of vital resources. The Spanish Empire was heir to pre-Hispanic states that sometimes had prodigious engineering feats of their own to their credit. The big empires – the Aztec *Grössraum*, the Inca conglomerate – practised what, with apologies to Alfred W. Crosby, who coined the term in another context, we call 'ecological imperialism': taking advantage of the environmental diversity their hegemonies encompassed to shift consumer products across ecological boundaries. In some ways, the Aztec system was the exchange of goods between communities to ensure that the products of moist forests, coastlands and lowlands were available in arid or mountainous regions and vice versa. Tenochtitlán – a lake-bound mountain-metropolis at an altitude where many of the vital commodities, such as cotton and cacao, would not grow – topped a pyramidal structure in which tribute circulated, with advantages accruing to militarily dominant states. The Inca, similarly but even more spectacularly, dominated an environment of breathtaking diversity, covering 30 degrees of latitude. The empire stretched from the Amazon rainforest in the east to irrigable deserts, coastal fisheries and offshore guano-islands in the west, across high mountains, where grazing for llamas stacked above arable terracing, and climates contrasted from side to side of every valley, according to the slant of the sun and the fall of the rain. The rulers shifted maize, fish, coca and forest products upslope, potatoes down. Much of the Inca world was settled at altitudes too high for maize, but the Inca stockpiled it in warehouses higher than its zone of cultivation, where it could feed armies, pilgrims and royal progresses while supplying maize beer for ritual purposes. They systematically shifted populations towards valleys suitable for maize. They engaged in what we now think of as state-sponsored science, developing new strains, adapted for high yields.[41]

Environmental modification, moreover, was part of local tradition in many of the places Spaniards invaded. In the river-streaked deserts of Peru and the North American southwest, or in the seasonally rainy forests of Central America, ditches and canals provided drainage or irrigation or both alternately as required and provided space for aquaculture. The large cities, ceremonial centres and palace complexes of many Indigenous civilizations required substantial water-supply systems, such as the 760-metre-long (2,500 ft) canal that served Machu Picchu, and the creation of market spaces, such as those depicted in the Codex Mendoza.[42] At Tambomachay, near Cuzco, aqueducts, canals and waterfalls flowed through terraced levels from thermal springs to supply the so-called 'Bath of the Inca'.

On the slopes of the mountains that erupt like a gigantic rash along the spine of the Americas, terracing upheld soil for tillage. In lake-bound or lakeside communities like Tenochtitlán, or in the teeming wetlands of Tabasco, say, or the Petén, people dredged for earth. Indigenous civilizations did not use wheeled vehicles and most had no beasts of burden; so roads were typically rudimentary – beaten tracks for shunting peddlers, envoys and armies. The Inca, who could exploit llamas for transporting modest weights of goods or equipment, were the exceptional builders of paved roads.

The Inca maintained a road network that spanned more than 30,000 kilometres (18,650 mi.), with teams of runners capable, on favoured routes, of covering 240 kilometres (150 mi.) a day. Between Huarochirí and Jauja they climbed passes 5,090 metres (16,700 ft) high. Way stations studded the system at altitudes of up to 3,960 metres (13,000 ft). Here workers were rewarded with feasts and pain-numbing doses of maize beer. Armies found refreshment. Prodigious bridges linked the roads. The famous Huaca-cacha ('Holy Bridge'), secured by cables as thick as a man's body, stretched 76 metres (250 ft) high above the gorge of the Apurimac River at Curahuasi. According to the eloquent Indigenous seventeenth-century critic of Spanish misrule, Felipe Guamán Poma de Ayala, maintenance – a collective annual obligation of nearby communities – was more reliable under the Inca rulers than their successors. The roads streaked the empire with a uniform look that impressed Spanish travellers of the early colonial era and helped to create the impression that the Inca were homogenizers and centralizers whose roads were like grapples, holding the empire in a single grip. And the Inca did have what one might call a signature style – a kind of architecture that shaped the way stations, warehouses, barracks and shrines that they built along the roads and at the edges of their empire. The habit of stamping the land with buildings that proclaimed their presence or passing was a tradition they learned from the Huari and Tiahuanaco. In part, the network was designed for strategic purposes, to speed Inca commands and carry Inca armies with relative speed and efficiency up and down the empire's great length. The extensively excavated way station at Huánuco Pampa was fitted with warehousing for maize and beer to keep a force of thousands refreshed. The network also linked sacred sites. The management of the sacred landscape of the Andes, the maintenance of shrines and the promotion of pilgrimages were all part of the value the empire added to lives lived in its shadow.[43]

Spanish colonists and administrators, despite Felipe Guamán's strictures, were even more assiduous than previous elites in constructing and maintaining infrastructure. They had to be: they had more subject-elites to satisfy, more territory to link, wider frontiers to defend, more cities to serve and a wider world with which to communicate. They had to make roads and explore maritime and riverine routes to destinations beyond the reach or interest of their predecessors. Historians have long acknowledged the importance, scope and durability of engineering in the Spanish global monarchy and have dedicated much research to the subject. The present work would have been impossible without the pioneering efforts of the civil engineer Pablo Alzola y Minondo, who wrote *Las obras públicas en España* (Public Works in Spain) at the end of the nineteenth century, or, nearly a hundred years later, the work of his fellow professional Manuel Díaz-Marta, especially his *Ingeniería española en América durante la época colonial* (Spanish Engineering in America in the Colonial Era), and José Antonio García Diego. Nicolás García Tapia's studies of Spanish engineering in the Renaissance provide essential background; fundamental, too, were the works of Ignacio González Tascón, culminating in his magisterial survey *Ingeniería española en ultramar* (Spanish Engineering in the Monarchy Overseas) (1992). The contributions of Ramón Serrera Contreras, Horacio Capel and their students also require mention, as many have appeared on the 'Geocrítica' website of the University of Barcelona; the *Historia de la ciencia y de la técnica en la corona de Castilla* (History of Science and Technology in the Lands of the Crown of Castile), edited by Luis García Ballester, José Luis López Piñero and

José Luis Peset, and *Técnica e ingeniería en España* (Technology and Engineering in Spain), under the general editorship of Manuel Silva Suárez, have also been important.[44] It would not be possible to survey our subject but for the investment in organizing work and facilitating publications by the Centro de Estudios Históricos de Obras Públicas y Urbanismo – without mentioning all the papers and monographs we refer to in the pages that follow.

All former work, excellent though it is, leaves the present authors with a task worth pursuing. The focus of previous studies has been on the history of science and technology, and of engineering in particular. Existing work fits, on the whole, into a heroic historiographical framework: the long and still unaccomplished struggle to acquaint the world with Spain's might – indeed, in some respects, her central place – in the 'modern' history of science and related disciplines or vocations. Otherwise, work on engineering in the Spanish Empire has been concerned with cataloguing, describing and evaluating public works and those who made them, or with individual themes to which they relate, such as defence, urbanization and economic performance, or with engineering as a response – to use Arnold Toynbee's language – to the challenges of the environments to which Spanish colonialism had to adjust, or with engineering education, decision-making and finance. While we do not intend to neglect any of these areas of enquiry, our hope is to focus on infrastructure as the scaffolding, as it were, on which empire was erected. The contexts we have constantly in mind are political, and we want to see Spanish imperial history in a global dimension, with the broad problems of how pre-industrial empires functioned. In short, our subject is how engineering contributed to making the global monarchy work.

Although the present authors have not done much of it, the subject could almost be studied by way of fieldwork. Unlike the achievements of Ozymandias, the engineers who helped build the Spanish Empire have left much of their work intact or visible. Along u.s. Route 85 you can still drive part of the *camino real de Tierra Adentro* that ran from Mexico City into the far north of New Mexico. Historical pilgrims can visit fragments of it along the way, such as, for instance, the crossing along the Jornada del Muerto where, in 1598, Gonzalo de Villagrá experienced fifty days of despair amid livid dunes, 'scabrous lands and barbarous nomads', while his mount's eyes 'boiled in their sockets'.[45] Heritage trails in Florida and Texas give tourists similar glimpses of the paths that Spaniards stamped between ports and missions. Around the Caribbean, today's yachtsmen can sail between the dozens of formidable forts that still line Spain's 'lago de piedra'.[46] Alexander von Humboldt decried the Spaniards for destroying some ancient waterworks, but many of those they replaced or created still function, like the aqueduct of Chapultepec and the fountains it feeds. One can still saunter among bridges and boulevards built for the health and convenience of citizens, like La Flor de la Canela in Lima, flinging to the breeze, as she sashayed over the bridge across the Rímac River, scents from her breast and from blossoms in her hair. We hope to recapture such historical experience: at least, we intend to recount it.

I

ENTER THE ENGINEERS

Amateurs and Professionals in the
Making of Infrastructure

> Out of heaven he made thee to hear his voice, that he might instruct
> thee: and upon earth he shewed thee his great fire; and thou heard-
> est his words out of the midst of the fire. (DEUTERONOMY 4:36)

'Institutions resemble eternity,' said the engineer and forestry expert
Agustín Pascual, at the start of his inaugural lecture as a member
of the Real Academia Española, on 30 April 1876. Pascual spent much
of the rest of his speech covering a long but lesser stretch of time,
while he compared old notions, inherited from medieval Castilian
laws and enshrined in the codes of the *Fueros* and *Partidas*, with
'Dasonomy' – the newly modish German ideas on how to compute
the value of forests according to their exploitable potential.[1]

Empires may not resemble eternity, though they aspire to do so,
but they sometimes seem to resemble forests, with their long series of
what ecologists call climaxes and renewal. In reality, unseen, unsuspected contingencies launch empires. As with economies, which (if
some theorists can be believed) tend to manage themselves until governments interfere, empires usually evince spontaneity, unpredictability
and indeterminacy at their inception – and Spain's at least as much as
any other. Historians congratulate themselves on a job well done if
they succeed convincingly in misrepresenting contingencies as causes.
That is why, in traditional historiography, empires start with epic deeds.
After the great victories, however, with which empires supposedly
begin, what happens next? What we might call a moment of technology
follows the moment of triumph. Engineers arrive in the aftermath of
conquest, along with the bureaucrats and revenue inspectors. For most
of the period under review, technology chiefly meant two things: on the

one hand the knowledge, procedures and means by which humans reshape nature; on the other, the management of resources. Before the late eighteenth century, it was unusual for a Westerner to espouse the romantic idea that primeval nature, unimproved by human hands, was 'sublime' or 'picturesque' enough to be worth painting.

The engineer's vocation, on the contrary, according to an eighteenth-century Spanish definition, was 'to remedy with art the deficiencies of nature'.[2] Human agency – according to orthodoxies from those of the ancient Greeks onward – could enhance God's work.[3] Not until the nineteenth century did engineers achieve prominence in both of the roles that 'technology' designated, creative and managerial, as agents dedicated to applying to the full the astonishing and apparently unstoppable discoveries of science.

America's 'Indies' in Perspective

When the Capuchin friar Francisco de Ajofrín crossed the Atlantic in 1763, the element of surprise with which earlier travellers sought to compare the Old and New Worlds had vanished. 'Travellers', he wrote,

> who go no further than Veracruz or Campeche say that America is an inferno of intolerably high temperatures. Others, who know only Chile or the Andes, complain because the intensity of the cold recalls Norway or Greenland. The truth about America, however, is that you find every clime and every temperature there.[4]

Ajofrín felt no need to find analogues for what a pineapple or an Aztec temple looked like, or, conversely, to look for American locations with olive-like or orange-like trees to host potential urban settlements or Enlightenment-style projects for re-shaping the landscape on rational lines. America, for him, was neither an actual marvel nor a prospective utopia. Its kingdoms and provinces formed a recognizable outcrop of the Spanish monarchy.

A look at the global context in which the empire was built will help us understand the long process that linked much of America into an enlarged and refashioned 'Western world'. Around 1400, an observer from outer space, despite the objectivity and clarity of a distant standpoint, would have had difficulty in discerning which of the great powers of Eurasia would be most likely to establish a global empire. China and the Muslim states that overlapped Europe and Asia were well equipped materially, and had attained a high level of social and political sophistication, with tried and tested power to continue to expand by land and sea. As Samuel Johnson pointed out in the 'philosophical novel' *The History of Rasselas, Prince of Abyssinia*, which he wrote in a week in 1759 to finance his mother's funeral, the same wind that took European invaders to Africa or Asia to found colonies or impose laws offered similar opportunities for conquests in the opposite direction.[5] Maritime western Europe was barely a beginner in such ambitious projects. Power and wealth had once been concentrated at the eastern end of the Mediterranean; until the Ottoman conquest of Constantinople in 1453, the Roman imperial tradition – which owed so much to engineers – remained in Byzantine hands. Around the year 1000, when Paris had perhaps 7,000 inhabitants, some Islamic capitals numbered their populations in hundreds of thousands. Over the next three or four hundred years, Atlantic-side technologies improved (especially for ploughing and milling), while business methods matured and cultural values emerged that favoured risky capital management and investment in maritime ventures. In 1348 the Black Death shifted the demographic balance in favour of the West. Western Europe ceased to be 'the underdeveloped back yard of the Islamic Near East'.[6]

If we take into account the impressive size and solidity of China in around 1400, the prosperity of the cities, the skills of the artisans and engineers, the quality of consumer goods, and the sophistication of arts and thought, we can appreciate how little the Chinese must have thought of the diminutive and disunited seaboard cities of western Europe – so remote as almost to form China's antipodes. Current debate on the extent of Chinese predominance at that time emphasizes how well placed the empire was for global take-off; but, as we now know, the splendours of superpower status would be long delayed. The abandonment of overseas expansion after the 1420s and the shift of resources to frontier security (which the Great Wall symbolizes) proved to be a fatal combination. Slowed rates of technical innovation and social change followed. China had activated a 'high-level equilibrium trap',[7] where existing productivity was a disincentive to progress. It would take force – exerted from outside by industrializing powers in the nineteenth century – to spring the trap.

At the western extremity of Eurasia, in around 1450, a combination of chance and effort was beginning to favour maritime expansion, especially in the Iberian peninsula. But those beginnings were hesitant. The conflict of ideas mattered. The Spanish Empire, which the rest of Europe later came to see as a trailblazer, self-defined in terms of sacred history and Catholic militancy, was both a precedent and a point of comparison for imperial successors. Historians tend to present the English or British Empire, for instance, as the unpredictable outcome of private initiatives, without any systematically imperialist strategy.[8] Scholars of the Spanish Empire in recent decades have taken a diametrically opposite line. Yet the reality in Spain's case, too, was of improvisation. The Old World precedents for making viable cities, roads, bridges, ports, manufactures and mines were inadequate for the adventures on which Spanish engineers embarked with the acquisition of empire. Neither Castile nor Portugal launched transatlantic operations from the best-equipped centres in terms of shipping and commerce, which were concentrated respectively in Oporto and Bilbao. Those cities, committed to such reliable, stable and predictable enterprises as trade with northern Europe and to North Atlantic fisheries, 'left higher-risk maritime adventures to poor folk from further south. The transatlantic prospect only captured the northerners' attention when it began to yield dividends.'[9] The necessary conditions coalesced with amazing suddenness in the 1490s. The founding of the empire started with voyages that stumbled on America by mistake in an attempt to find a short route to Asia. Almost every subsequent adjustment of the frontier took Spaniards further into the unforeseen: Mexico was conquered by a 'man on the spot' in defiance of orders; while Peru surprised its conquerors by its riches, most subsequent acquisitions were equally surprisingly poor. Fantasies plucked from fiction – a fountain of youth here, a city of gold there, or a land of Amazons, or giants, or the speculative location of the realms of Sheba or Solomon, or imaginary riches elsewhere – led to the absorption of vast tracts of American mainland. The conquistadores of New Mexico expected to find themselves near the shores of the Pacific. The geographical ignorance that impelled Columbus continued to inspire subsequent paladins. Engineers had to turn every surprise into an opportunity, every fantasy into a real frontier.

Almost throughout the existence of the Spanish Empire, engineers were primarily devoted to solving problems posed by the unexpected, unwanted and often hostile features of unfamiliar environments overseas, where catastrophes seemed ever imminent. The first Spanish engineers in America had no option but to resort to experiment. Engineering units did not specialize: they all covered everything that belonged to the role they fulfilled and the needs they served. In return they received liberties and privileges. They fitted into the body politic, like a limb or organ, rather than resembling part of a machine. In the Renaissance, engineers did not belong to schools; their art passed from father to son. They formed a vertical estate or order of society, rather than being a self-organizing corporation or a group within a social class as would be the case in later periods. An engineer's formation was practical and empirical. He matured under the aegis of a master and the tutelage of a guild. Although much of his work was for war, he might equally be found repairing a palace after an earthquake, sketching out an urban project, building a redoubt or lighting a public square to celebrate a prince's birth. In the early modern world, indeed, the term 'engineer' covered a multitude of designations, including, commonly, that of a master craftsman or a specialized artisan.

The Engines of Engineering

According to figures that Nicolás García Tapia has collected on the formation and career paths of engineers, this group can be separated into four categories: theorists, artists, soldiers and practitioners.[10] In the first category, which comprised almost 10 per cent of engineers working in Spain in the sixteenth century, were mathematicians, cosmographers or humanistically trained scientists – ambivalent professionals whose practical forays extended little beyond manipulating plumb lines or measuring boundaries. The artistic types – or perhaps we should call them artificers – who responded to demands for the reconciliation of beauty and utility, formed a quarter of the total. Not infrequently, they were architects well versed in surveying. Warrior-engineers might be naval personnel, engaged in shipbuilding or instrument making, or gunners concerned with foundry or firearms-design, the formulation of gunpowder or the construction of fortifications; mining engineers brought expertise in digging mines and building bridges to cross rivers and ravines. Part of the Italian elite, who, as we shall see, contributed disproportionately to the infrastructure of empire, and their Spanish-born heirs were in this group.

More than a quarter of the total were classed as practitioners of level-finding, machining, clockmaking, locksmithery, carpentry, building, smelting and mining. They might equally calculate the incline of a slope as make devices to raise or lower water, or open a mine, raise weight or melt a metal.

The biggest single category emerged from the profession of soldiering and the context of war. From the seventh century the office of *ingeniator* had been linked with war. In fifteenth-century Spain the name of engineer was regularly bestowed on military and sometimes on civil personnel. According to the early seventeenth-century lexicographer Sebastián de Covarrubias, engineering was definable as the profession of those who 'construct works with which to attack and defend against enemies', or who make contrivances with movable parts, also called 'machinery'. Francisco de Contreras, an expert builder of waterwheels, served as a military engineer, as did the architect Cristóbal de Rojas, who applied for official designation as an engineer on the strength of his work on the defences of Cádiz. The interconnectedness of the soldiering and engineering professions was crucial and an aspect of a wider phenomenon: the growing role of technicians of all kinds in the functioning of states in peace and war alike – and also of the quest for improved efficiency. One further example must suffice. Cristóbal de Rojas was already an engineer when he approached Philip II with a request to be appointed captain in the army so as to elicit obedience from the soldiers who had work to do under his direction in building fortifications. Conversely, soldiers often became engineers out of calling or compulsion, such as Cristóbal de Zubiaurre, the designer of pumps for fountains, pleasure gardens and horticulture in Valladolid.[11]

Meanwhile, new scientific ideas with engineering applications transformed engineers' ways of life by inspiring applications for war and peace. Scholastic or Hermetic theorizing gradually yielded to what we would now recognize as real, rational science. On both sides of the Atlantic, the process by which knowledge was defined – or 'formed' or 'constructed' – changed. The impact can be observed in the history of engineering in two ways: in old ideas dismantled, and the growing demand for solutions to present problems in urbanization, production and war.

From the start of the Renaissance, engineers aspired to be thought of as artists, pursuing a liberal vocation distinct from that of a rude mechanic. Abrahán de los Escudos, recorded in 1480 as 'the king's and queen's engineer', clashed with the town councillors of Burgos when he refused to pay taxes on the grounds that his royally conferred status as a gentleman exempted him. When his property was impounded, he appealed to the Catholic monarchs, who ordered restitution: he was well to do, owning real estate, with a horse and a servant. Correspondingly, there were plenty of artisans or common workers who wanted to upgrade as engineers or who risked reputation and riches on undertakings beyond their capacity. They could descend rapidly into destitution and even stoop to crime. Martín de la Haya was unable to supply some fountains in Burgos with water because he miscalculated differences in altitude, relying, despite the severe reprimands of the mathematical scholar Andrés García de Céspedes, on estimates made with the naked eye. The supposed superiority of empirical over theoretical learning – a classic assumption in the history of technology – often masks social conflict. Another of Philip II's engineers, Juan Francisco Sitoni, a citizen of Milan, claimed descent from a noble Scots family named Seton. The lofty tone of his wit and rhetoric might therefore be thought to proceed from his elevated background; professionally, however, his work was poor.[12]

This shortage of qualified personnel and the surfeit of incompetents is intelligible given that, at home in Spain, engineers were anyway in short supply, while would-be adventurers abounded. In the European dominions of the Spanish monarchy a common affliction was the so-called 'worm of the Indies' – a nagging temptation to think that opportunities in the New World offered escape from the restrictive ambience of home. The dream of 'making it', to use a later term, in the Americas was so alluring that almost anyone who felt deserving but inadequately rewarded at home might petition repeatedly for leave to go there. The case of that well-known veteran of the Battle of Lepanto, Miguel de Cervantes Saavedra, comes to mind. When he was back in Madrid on 17 February 1582, he wrote to Antonio de Eraso, of the Council of the Indies, whom he had met in Lisbon, to thank him for taking an interest in the writer's frustrated efforts to secure an American appointment. Eight years later, through the good offices of his sister Magdalena, Cervantes applied for a post in the fiscal administration in Cartagena and a judicial role in La Paz. In barely a fortnight the Council's decision came back: 'Look at home [in Spain] for a job.'[13] Cervantes vented his rancour with a vengeful pen: in 1613 he published *El celoso extremeño* (The Zealous Extremaduran), one of his 'exemplary novels' about a down-and-out called Felipe de Carrizales, who leaves Seville 'clad in a Straw shroud' and makes for the Indies, 'a last refuge for Spain's roofless, a temple for her malcontents, a sanctuary for her worst criminals, a safe-haven for gamblers, a utopia for whores, a blight for many, and a blessing for few'.[14] The hero returns home rich, only to fall victim to a disappointing marriage to an undeserving wench.

Qualified engineers, however, were rarely desperate enough to hazard the transatlantic trip. The lack of engineers was so acute in Spain that Philip II was willing to overlook the crimes of Vicenzio Locadello, condemned for highway robbery in Italy, if he were willing to take a job.[15] Yet, although the shortage of professionals raised the social status of engineering as a profession, in Spanish America the dangers of the environment and the distance from home acted as disincentives for recruitment. The crown, moreover, lost important former sources of recruits by eliminating the Jewish and Muslim communities that supplied engineers in the fifteenth century, such as Abrahán de los Escudos in Burgos, or Yuza, a 'Moorish engineer' from Guadalajara, employed on a project for delivering water to the municipal fountains of Valladolid.[16] While the numbers of engineers, relative to need, stagnated or fell, the demand increased in the growing empire. Where and how could the monarchy make up the deficiency?

The Church was a vital recourse. As in so many jobs of public utility in the early modern Spanish monarchy – including teaching, the arts, public administration and empire-building – the clergy supplied much-needed specialists in engineering, reducing costs to the public purse. Expanded vocations led Fray Alonso Sánchez Cerrudo, designer of the mill that served the monastery of El Escorial, and Fray Juan Vicencio Casale, who was responsible for fortifications in Portugal, to become expert technicians.[17] Many other clerics, missionaries in the New World, became engineers for the greater glory of God, such as the Franciscan Francisco de Tembleque, who built the Cempoala aqueduct to be, for an extended time, the longest in New Spain. The epitype of the friar-engineer was Fray Ambrosio Mariano Azaro de San Benito, of Neapolitan birth, who, prior to discerning his religious vocation, took part as an engineer in the victory over the French at Saint-Quentin in 1557. He paid a visit to the Council of Trent, sought employment at the court of Poland, and spent two years in prison, accused of a crime of which he was innocent, before becoming a hermit. He then encountered St Teresa of Avila, during her visit to Andalusia. She convinced him to join the Order of Discalced Carmelites. He took pleasure in charging no fee when he undertook hydraulic projects for Philip II, to the equal pleasure of the king and the chagrin of other engineers.[18]

Equally important was recruitment from the monarchy's vast dominions outside Spain. The elite of the engineering profession in the late sixteenth century, by universal acclaim, was supplied from among a group of technicians who came from the monarchy's Italian lands and whom the crown tended to favour. Some of the most famous of Philip II's engineers, who contributed to the history of public works in America, were of Italian provenance – among them the dynasts of the Antonelli family and the Sicilian Tiburcio Spanocci. While Spanocci was at work designing defences for the Strait of Magellan in 1581, Juan Bautista Antonelli – his co-worker on projects of fortification in the Caribbean – was earning a hefty salary of 1,800 ducats a year and the grant of farmland in Murcia to keep him busy in retirement. (Only a few engineers, however, achieved riches, rents and properties. Fortune – that fickle goddess of the Renaissance – did her work as usual. The Toledan gentleman Blasco de Garay, for instance, endured such poverty that he had to sell his sword to buy food, until Charles V rewarded him with a pension of 100,000 maravedíes (somewhat less than an ordinary seamen's wages) for improving the design of boats driven by oars.)

The Engineering Frontier

Conquerors, adventurers, friars, engineers and architects – whoever crossed the Atlantic ventured on a New World that was measureless and unknowable. The best resources for managing uncertainty were the engineer's habitual and defining recourse to sound judgement and the value of experience. In 1703 the Seigneur de Bezin came to Spain with this recommendation from the court of France: 'His chief activities have been in sieges. He is the son of an engineer of great skill and worked with his father before becoming one himself. Thus, as he has accumulated experience from boyhood, he seems that he could be of useful service to the crown.'[19] Experience could be put to the test in various places, with varying traditions and tools. In the Americas, the Spaniards unveiled, there were no horses, mules or draught animals; no iron or gunpowder; the wheel was unexploited; the dome was unknown. The Incas' impressive achievements, often compared with those of the Romans, included a network of roads linked by rope bridges over deep ravines through mountains that defied description. But the public works that were needed for the future were different – unprecedented in the region. Construction materials were often hard to locate. There were so many culturally incommensurate Indigenous peoples to deal with that it was impossible to predict how contact with them would turn out. Would it be possible, for instance, to employ, as workers or peons in the newly founded expanded cities, captives from non-sedentary tribes or, say, from among the northern Mexican Chichimeca, who were known as 'eaters of dog meat'?

The workforce in Spain's overseas possessions relied on indios – to use the normal term for Indigenous people – who paid tribute in the form of labour corvées according to a system inherited from the pre-conquest past, of *mitas*, or rotation in service, or on slaves from Africa or elsewhere. Frequently, slaves with technical skills were freed to found dynasties in Maroon or indigenous kingdoms or to form guilds or similar fraternities in colonial cities. Convicts also appeared among the workers on public projects, as did penniless migrants who had to work to eat, so-called *blancos de orilla*, or 'beached whites'. In the early decades of the sixteenth century, even conquistadores, including Cortés himself, had to take a hand. In Veracruz, according to the soldier-chronicler Bernal Díaz del Castillo:

Having sketched out the church and main square and waterfront and all the things that were suitable for making a town, we built a fort from foundations to roofs and finished it with a guard-room that wanted planking, and we made embrasures and watchtowers and barbicans and all with such haste that we all took part in the work, including Cortés, who was the first to start levelling the ground, lifting the stones, and excavating the foundations, and all the officers and men, and we worked hard to finish the job fast. Some of us worked at the foundations while others made the walls or carried water or made bricks and tiles in the kiln or gathered food; others again did carpentry while the smiths worked on bolts and nails, and thus we worked at it all non-stop from the top man to the lowest in rank, as did the indios who helped us.[20]

Construction work would have been impossible without collaboration across ethnic and cultural chasms. Among the results in Mexico were such phenomena as Tequitqui – the survival of native styles that fused with European influence to produce an unprecedented new look. In 1585 work on the cathedral of Mexico City employed Spaniards, Flemings, free indios and both African and Chichimeca slaves. The first stone had been laid twelve years earlier. Indigenous journeymen, carvers and skilled artisans worked under the orders of Spanish masters of works, who needed interpreters in four languages, at least, to communicate their ideas and negotiate with indio foremen. Native stonecutters would only obey 'captains' of their own who served as intermediaries with Spaniards and creoles. The Chichimeca slaves were prisoners of war despatched from the northern front, while the Blacks included Mexican-born and imported slaves, commonly from what are now Sierra Leone and the underside of the West African bulge. Whether formally enslaved or not, workers were not easy to control. They could be mildly recalcitrant, like thirty-year-old Pedro, a Black who was 'a recent arrival, halfway to learning Spanish', who periodically went absent 'because he was married and his custom was to go off every so often to the place where he kept his wife'.[21]

The problems of mobilizing manpower were matched by those of supplying construction materials. Wood was the first requisite, as the military engineer Francisco de Requena pointed out. He was posted to Guayaquil in 1774 before penetrating the Amazon rainforest in command of an expedition to map the border with Portuguese territory. In his judgement the best woods were balsa for pumps, canafistula for keels, cinnamon for fastenings, native cherrywood for open-air structures, palo maria or native laurel to support rigging and lignum vitae for bolts and dowels. These were all resistant to the principal pests: termites, deathwatch beetle, other kinds of buzzing and boring insects, and shipworm.[22] Essential ropes and cables were made by twisting the native fibres that made possible the stunning rope suspension bridges of Peru. Agave and the maguey cactus provided fibre for cord of every kind of strength, from those used in bridges to those for nets or traps. The roots of the same plants provided cleansing agents that could serve as shampoo, while the leaves could provide extracts suitable for bleaching cloths and dressing wounds, to say nothing of that celebrated beverage, pulque. Not all ropework was made from cacti; lianas and other vinelike tendrils were also exploited, as were tough grasses.

When iron nails, commonly imported, especially from Basque or Catalan factories, were unavailable, strong cattle horns were substituted unless local manufacturers could step in, such as the Catalan Capuchin missionaries in eastern Venezuela, who had their own ironworks from the beginning of the eighteenth century until the wars of independence.

Lime was a basic requirement for mortar and cement. Supply was hard to regularize. The Aztecs used it with profligacy; the Inca did not know of it. In Peru the first limekiln was erected at a monastery in 1545 by the mason and bricklayer Toribio de Alcaraz, who had a contract with Luis de León, a town councillor of Arequipa, to supply labour. The lime was extracted by firing from calceous rocks, or, frequently in America, by titration from seashells or white coral, as Fr Bernabé Cobo recalled:

> [In] the Chancay valley in this diocese of Lima they extract a liquid from a substance found in some creeks at the sea's edge and convert it into a kind of granule from which they make lime so white that it is transported here to Lima to whitewash the buildings. In the province of Nicaragua and other seaboard regions where lime is in short supply they use seashells to make a kind of lime of a whiteness that excedes all others.[23]

In Manila the lime from white coral and oyster shells was so superior that it displaced other types. In Chile, Peru and New Granada the normal practice was to prefer shells over calceous rock. Marine lime can still be seen binding fortifications in Veracruz and Acapulco, where in 1800 the kilns produced 'vast quantities from white corals harvested at sea', according to the scientific traveller Alexander von Humboldt. In Cartagena, engineers and workmen used cement made by titrated coral mixed with sand from the seashore and, for extra strength, a measure of bull's blood. A glance at surviving structures reveals bricks and stones that look seriously eroded; but the mortar or cement shows scant sign of wear. 'Marine lime', in Fr Cobo's assessment, 'sets as firm as brass.'[24]

Over to God

The hardships of arranging transport combined with the high cost of building materials ensured that builders used whatever was closest to hand. Around Lake Titicaca, for instance, adobe furnished the substance of walls and coated the arches of cloisters, while rough stonework supplied buttresses, and exposed walls and towers were of ashlar. Doors had architraves of brick or stone. Roofs were of hardwood or native pine or perhaps of reed thatch in the humblest churches. Private houses – little Babels where Spanish families dwelt in households and among extended families in which whites, Blacks and indios mingled – were built of whatever was readily available. In Panama, despite the ready riches, there were no great mansions or palaces because manpower was scarce and inexpert while materials were costly. Houses were normally of wood covered with tiling, though some were of stone and lime. Iron for nails and locks was so valuable that it was always recycled. Lime came from local deposits of shell. Masters and workers reckoned the cubic capacity of walls, 'boards, footings, planks, sets, beams, pallets, struts, supports, and bracings, as well as the stone bases for columns and pilasters and the stonework for sofits, support walls, and reinforcements'.[25] Two-storeyed dwellings were typical, with the lower floor sometimes functioning as shop or store while the upper formed a residence. The commercial spaces were often rented out at a handsome return owing to the briskness of business and the restricted compass of the built-up area. Frontage was narrow – 12 metres (40 ft) on average – and elevation modest. At the beginning of the seventeenth century Panama had 332 houses of uniform height, tiled over low upper storeys, 44 houses classed as small and 112 reed cottages. There were only eight stone buildings – the town hall and six rich men's homes.

In and around Quito, construction was so chaotic that the council had to specify where to dig for mud to make adobe bricks so as to protect the town centre from the excavations opened at random by citizens in search of building material. Throughout American cities, the commonest form of dwelling – the house built around a courtyard, which functioned for the home much as a main plaza for a city, to define traversable space, separate classes and make activities visible – formed readily articulated blocks. In later times, external corridors became habitual and courtyards arrayed in succession made it possible to augment the space, intensify its use and fill the fabric of the city. In 'lordly Lima' where at the start of the seventeenth century there were perhaps 4,000 buildings, one could admire little urban palaces with colonnades and gardens undivided by courtyards; there were two-storeyed homes with attractive balconies, terraced houses aligned on

the street or sometimes arrayed behind an open yard; and of course
there were shacks in low-class alleys and culs-de-sac, built of adobe,
brick or wood with a bit of stone and wattle, which – consisting of slats
of wood and cane daubed with mud – was earthquake-resistant. A city
such as Tunja in New Granada, of some eminence, although below the
rank of capital, had 251 houses within the official city limits in 1610: 88
classed as tall and 163 as low built. Prosperous encomenderos – rent-
iers who lived off grants of Indigenous labour or tribute – decorated
their homes with painted joinery, grand entranceways and scutcheons
of aristocratic pretension.[26]

The idea that cities should be enhanced by ennoblement was the
outcome of a long history of urban development linked, in Spain,
with the Reconquista. Following Castilian tradition, local public
works were the responsibility of town and city councils. The weight-
iest edifices belonged to important institutions of government: the
audiencias – organizations that both dispensed justice and oversaw
administration – the Council of the Indies or the king or their representatives, as the case might be. From the sixteenth century data-compiling
exercises, known as *Relaciones geográficas*, were laboriously executed
from time to time; these long questionnaires were intended to help the
government function, for example, by informing measures to define
jurisdictions, establishing frictionless connections between potentially
rival centres of authority and describing a network of urban centres that
formed the framework of Spanish colonization. Between 1530 and
1812 the crown issued at least 33 decrees and instructions for comprehensive data-gathering. Questionnaires might cover fewer than 10
items on occasion, up to 355 in one instance in 1604. They demanded
reports, inter alia, on fortifications, roads, boundaries and the numbers
and natures of churches, hospitals, places of education, houses, gardens, parks, water dispensaries, mills and ports.[27] The responses often
included local maps, measurements of the distances in leagues between
urban nuclei, accounts of navigable communications by waterway,
and even three-dimensional drawings of mountain ranges and other
topographical obstacles.

Engineering works were always preceded by plans that involved
disciplined collaboration and shared effort. In the eighteenth century
the formalized rules known as the *ordenanzas de ingenieros* made explicit
the necessity of relying on data gathered on the spot. At the same
time, whether it was a matter of building a bridge or erecting a school

or oratory, or responding to a flood or an earthquake, every project reflected the loyalty owed to God and King.

In consequence, among our major sources for understanding the history of Spanish engineering in the early modern period are the documents known as *arbitrios* – proposals for modifying the environment, submitted to the authorities by individual *arbitristas* – the Spanish equivalent of English 'projectors' – on a plethora of matters. Many *arbitrios* focused on maximizing resources and coping with war – in response to rulers' conflicting priorities, poised between the demands of warfare and the hazards of bankruptcy. If a proposal for reform got anywhere, reward for the proposer would follow. Whether designing a diving suit or sketching a gadget for pumping water out of a mine, the projector could and did hope that royal good sense would grant him recompense of one sort or another. Though such designs have had a bad press and have drawn the derision of novice writers and ill-disposed thinkers, the *arbitristas* were fascinating figures of great resonance in the history of Spanish technology. They show how far apart were the ambitions that animated the monarchy and the resources that sustained it. Yet their work genuinely constituted the raw material of which colonial policy was made. Paradoxically, as it turned out, it was often best to do nothing and to leave nature unmodified, especially when projects were for cleaving new roads or culling vast forests for timber – for a rampart of forest, for instance, could be worth more to the state than a beach-head attractive to an enemy. Such was the case with the Orinoco delta and the hinterland of Guyana, where permission to cut down the forests was unwaveringly withheld, in order to maintain a supposedly protective cordon of dense vegetation against enemy attack.[28]

The importance of seeing the monarchy as a whole was a constant feature of the projects and of official responses to them. The bottom line was always decisive. Section 16, on public works, of Book IV of the *Laws of the Indies* (*Recopilación de leyes de los reinos de Indias*) of 1681 reprints a royal order of 1563 addressed to Vaca de Castro, governor of Peru: 'Should it be necessary to build roads and bridges in those provinces, let us know the anticipated cost, and specify the communities and individuals, both Spanish and indio, who can expect to benefit, and apportion the cost among the beneficiaries proportionately.' The appearance of this important provision in law demonstrates the crown's concern to deter city councils from undertaking inessential or unjustifiable public works or, even worse, projects shrouded in suspicions of corruption or initiated as pretexts for eluding labour regulations or laws against the maltreatment or exploitation of indios. In cities run by *audiencias*, the tribunals that combined judicial and administrative functions, the president of the court had to authorize all projects. If there were no funds to pay a superintendent of public works, a councillor would have to do the job.

The costs of projects might fall to the crown or be shared with encomenderos and indio communities, as appropriate, but contributions might also be levied by way of tolls on bridges or payments for the use of other facilities, or ad hoc sales taxes, the so-called *derecho de sisa*. In 1562 the city council of Havana resorted to such a measure to pay for an aqueduct, after failing to impose a charge for anchorage in the harbour. 'There is', they averred, 'no better way to obtain the money than by charging a levy on certain products, namely wine, soap, and meat, from all of which in total an annual revenue of 400 ducats can be expected.'[29] Charges on grain, wine, spirits and vinegar cropped up in places as far apart as Mexico City and Cuzco. But there was no end to fiscal inventiveness. Midway through the eighteenth century the costs of supplying water to the settlement and shrine of Nuestra Señora de los Remedios, adjoining Mexico City, were met from the proceeds of eight days' bullfighting in the Plaza de Santa Isabel.

However financed, public works always required meticulous prior surveying. Water supply, drainage, roads, bridges and buildings all demanded levelled sites in environments widely threatened by topographical irregularities, which, as the Conde de Floridablanca, the monarchy's chief minister, observed on one occasion, when he heard that a terrible flood had shifted an entire mountain, sometimes sounded fantastic. The first step was to take measurements with such instruments as were available to prepare a sketch or outline a proposal. Levellers and surveyors generally came only a step behind the conquistadores. The former assessed the viability of a project; the latter tackled the practicalities of turning it into reality, compartmentalizing space in terms of allotments of various sizes, yardage and footage.

The most renowned of them all was perhaps the expert in geometry and land measurement Alonso García Bravo. He was one of the companions of Cortés and took roles in the design of the towns of Veracruz and Antequera before becoming 'the surveyor who laid out the street plan of Mexico City'.[30] It was probably he who revised the initial design for the first Spanish city to be founded on the American mainland, late in 1509 by Martín Fernández de Enciso: Santa María la Antigua del Darién, alongside the Atrato River. García Bravo also had a hand in the layout of Acla and as late as 1528 he was at work finalizing the foundation of Antequera, where the main square was at the midpoint between the rivers Atoyac and Jalatlaco, which crossed the valley, and where an inbuilt incline moderated the ferocity with which the sun's rays struck.

Instruments leant a formal, technical appearance to builders' and engineers' plans. In the sixteenth century a stride level, an aligning device mounted on a wooden tripod, preferably of pine, with metal feet, served for measuring distance and altitude. A plumb line registered departures from true on a horizontally placed scale. The scale could be up to 4 metres (13 ft) in breadth and when set up might need as much as 65 metres (20 ft), or 5.6 metres (18 ft) of space between the feet at ground level; so the problems of transporting and wielding the bigger versions were formidable. Yet surveyors were keen on it. A rival instrument was the water level, a form of which was described in 1573 by the Polish geometer Olbrycht Strumieński. It could be set on the level thanks to a reservoir of water in a calibrated compartment and, at both ends, had sights (often improved with lenses) and alidades for measuring angles. Swivelling on an armature fitted with a compass, it could be used to measure angles and facilitate triangulation when deployed in conjunction with a sighting device, linked to it by rope, chain, twine or waxed liana tendrils, at a distance of about 40–45 metres (44–50 yards). Despite inaccuracies caused by temperature changes and the consequent shrinkage or expansion of the materials, until the eighteenth century the design of public works relied on what, at the end of the day, were measurements made with taut rope. Only astronomers and the magi of geodesy dispensed mathematics sublime enough to guarantee exactitude, such as the Mexican Joaquín Velázquez de León obtained with a theodolite between 1773 and 1775 while working on a scheme for improving drainage in the valley of Mexico. The creole sage demonstrated that the required canal should be 52.63 kilometres (32½ mi.) long – a correction to the 52.38 kilometres estimated by old-fashioned technology.[31]

In public works as in private, therefore, accuracy of measurement was an aspiration rather than an aim. Hence there had to be techniques for compensating by adjusting the results. Rather as seamen of the late eighteenth century worked out celestial readings by hand and eye to check the enlightened chronometers they carried on board to determine longitude, so surveyors positioned their levels at two points and bisected the difference. 'By making allowance for the equal and opposite errors in both sightings the true level can be fixed at the midpoint between both readings.'[32] Meanwhile, even before the theodolite perfected the process, there had also been improvements in the reliability of water levels or their replacement with airtight, calibrated glass phials of water – an invention of the Frenchman Melchisédec Thévenot in 1666 – as well as inclinometers, which provided measurements of angles at the horizon against an inclined plane, and ever more sophisticated refinements of the principle of the quadrant, including sextants and octants.

Rag Paper

Most surviving engineering projects from the period under consideration were inscribed on paper made of fabric, especially linen. In his *Treatise on the Origin and Art of Writing Well* (*Tratado del origen y arte de escribir bien*) of 1768, Fray Luis de Olod noted that the best paper, sent regularly to destinations all over the Americas, came from Orusco (Madrid), Capellades (Barcelona) and La Riba (Tarragona).[33] Spain's history of paper-making began with the Moors, with a centre of production at Játiva. Little by little a relationship grew between the size, format and type of paper and the nature of the designs it bore. An anonymous eighteenth-century manuscript, *The Art of Colour-Washing a Plan* (*Arte de lavar un plano*), mentions seven paper sizes, from the 'great eagle' of 24 × 35 inches, to the Cerlier (12 × 16), for all eventualities. The papers were opaque; for tracings, sheets made from hemp or Mexican maguey fibres were used, variously waxed with turpentine or oil or varnished with resin; or copies were made with a device known as the *marion* ('It should be very serviceable to engineers and architects,' according to a report of 1879), which transferred the images onto a blueprint with the outlines showing against the background in white.[34] Mechanical copiers were unavailable until the late nineteenth century. The usual set-up for making plans and drawings was to fix opaque paper of suitable weight to a dampened surface so that no wrinkles would appear. It was important to verify that the paper had left the factory with its surface properly prepared with paste, otherwise the ink would not be absorbed and the drawing would be patchy. Applications of juniper gum, ground mastic or even clean, boiled, ground eggshells would deal with any such problem.

Drawings were done in pencil, and any unwanted specimens erased with bread white, boiled and left for a few days to harden. Pencils made with a single stick of colour were most prized as the danger of breakage increased with the number of sticks employed. The manuscript specifies that 'to make a coloured pencil, one must take cinnabar or vermilion and liquid gum, white lead, and very fine white gypsum, and make a mash of them, forming them into long, round sticks that can be used to draw with.' The business of making pens to turn pencil drawings into finished designs was enormously complex and gave rise to interminable debates. In 1778 the essayist Gabriel Fernández opined that the best pens were made from the outermost feathers of the right wing of a bird – crow for making delicate lines and goose for drawing margins or frames. Others swore by tame duck quills, or turkey or even vulture. Pens had to be tough, with cylindrical stems, of the desired breadth of nib, clean and translucent. Prejudice in favour of the right wing was general, but some heterodox theorists advocated the left. Río de la Plata was an important region for the manufacture of pens. In 1796, 11,890 goose quills were exported from Buenos Aires.[35]

Once the plan was drawn in outline, it had to be colour-washed with fine brushes. The celebrated 'colourist's art' demanded magisterial skill in handling colours, brushes and techniques of dilution and application. There were three types of black ink, for printing (lampblack with gum arabic); 'China' (as Spaniards said, or in English usage 'Indian') ink for fine work; and regular. Inks for outlining and writing were kept in tin wells. Generally, inks for washing a plan or completing a drawing were laborious and complicated to prepare. Shades of purple were obtained from indigo, and of yellow normally from minerals or resins. Red came from cinnabar, red lead or Levantine lacquer, or from American primary products, such as annatto (derived from achiote shrubs), cochineal or logwood. Lily petals treated with alum supplied greens, as did lime or vinegar with the addition of calcium tartrate or compounds of potassium.

As practices became processual and common sense gave way to regulated procedures, engineering projects, too, submitted to the changes under way. In the sixteenth and seventeenth centuries there were no standardized scales, colour codes, symbols or types. In 1568 an attempt was made to impose the Castilian yard as the only permitted standard of measurement. It became normal to put north at the top of maps and plans, to include a scale and to use the colour yellow to indicate an unrealized project. But no universal protocol was forthcoming until the foundation of scientific and technical organizations with their respective academies, such as those of military engineers in 1711, mathematicians in 1720 and *guardamarinas* – midshipmen – in 1717.

The first set of regulations for military engineers, endorsed by Philip V in July 1718, contain in their opening section 28 articles with criteria for making maps or plans or describing them in writing. Maps had to be wider than they were long, with north at the top (indicated, too, by a representation of a compass in the upper margin). Scales had to be set out in Spanish or French leagues, Italian miles and Castilian yards. Specified symbols signified the fitness of roads and whether they were metalled, the state of lands (whether fallow or cultivated), the whereabouts of roads and of standing water, the presence of navigable rivers with indicators of the direction of the current, and the locations of bridges: whether of stone or of less durable materials, and whether made of wood, or with pontoons or boats and whether constructed by the suspension method. The same applied to places, with rules that governed the data to be submitted on each of them, from the imperial capital down through subordinate or provincial capital cities and towns, other communities with and without walls, villages, hamlets, castles, royal properties, places of commerce, monasteries, mills, workshops, manufactories or 'dwellings and all kinds of rural houses'.[36]

In 1803 new ordinances called for longitudes to be included in the maps or a grid with degrees and minutes shown at intervals of ten. To the list of 75 symbols norms for use were added, applicable to colours, cartouches, frames, shading, highlights and insets. According to the scheme suggested in *The Art of Colour-Washing a Plan*, arsenals should be in scarlet or vermilion, canals in indigo, springs in crimson and bridges in 'colours as close as possible to their real ones'. The publication in 1849 of a collection of conventional symbols by three professors of the Army School of Engineering, Antonio Sánchez, Ángel Rodríguez and Francisco de Albear, the last of whom worked on the aqueduct of Havana, shows that there was less congruence on such matters than was hoped for. 'If there is no adequate collection of these symbols, the consequence, as in Spain at present, is that every organization and even every individual invents or adopts such scheme as seems suitable at the time, so that bickering and confusion leads to serious errors.'[37] An innovation the authors proposed was to include a symbol for the newly laid iron tracks of the railroads.

The Centre of the System:
The Imperial Bureaucracy

Engineering is crucial to the launch and development of a world empire such as Spain's because of the role of infrastructure. In pre-industrial times, when there was no clear delimitation of the areas of responsibility of proprietors, officials and the organs of the state, or of where the limits lay between the obligations of king or crown and government or administration, the practical boundaries of state action were fixed by the way technical units in the service of the state operated and by the goals they set themselves.

Like most rulers, Spain's were always seeking 'order' and there-fore practising intervention, usually to slight effect. It is worth recalling that on 22 August 1489, three years before the Spanish discovery of America, Ferdinand and Isabella wrote to the town authorities in San Sebastián, after a destructive conflagration, to complain that 'before burning down, the houses were wooden and building standards were unregulated.'[38] Yet, though the dwellings obviously had to be rebuilt in stone, even after major fires in 1278, 1338, 1361, 1397, 1433 and 1489, the residents were unwilling. The clamour for state-devised 'order' reached the New World in 1503, when the Casa de Contratación was founded in Seville to regulate trade as a result of the need to overcome the pioneering mania Columbus had induced, which itself was a conse-quence of inflated expectations arising from the surprising revelation of America on the horizon of the western world. Just as the people of San Sebastián responded reluctantly to the imposition of their own interests, so shippers, merchants and settlers in America grudgingly and imperfectly submitted or at least adapted to regulation.

Europe's encounter with the Americas upset a lot of existing theory, but the need to control and guide the erratic and investment-intensive business of transoceanic trade was ineluctable.[39] Starting from the model of Portugal's Casa da India, and the similar institutions for regulating Portuguese trade with West Africa, the Sevillan organi-zation was 'a commercial exchange, a department of government, a ministry of trade, a school of navigation, and a customs house' all in one. By bringing together all the elements of the puzzle of transoceanic communications, the Casa de Contratación made it possible to establish cartographic norms and coordinate mapping; gradually or fitfully, after thousands of corrections and modifications, something like a standard Atlantic chart emerged: 'There was too much land and too much sea to rely on dead reckoning to find one's way or to chart the routes without well-observed latitudes.'[40] Navigators had to look skyward, read the language of the stars and, especially beyond sight of the Pole Star, find new guides in the heavens to survive on a hostile ocean. The hydrographic department of the Casa was a big part of the array of influences that introduced technocracy alongside the other elements – legislative, executive, judicial – of the powers of government. Among the Casa's many areas of interest, the primordial objective was to clear presumptions people had of America in favour of what was really there, imposing genuine observations, however unprecedented they seemed and however defiant of imagination.

Direct experience became determinative. A royal order of 1527 stated that:

Anyone who presumes to become a pilot must submit to questioning before qualified witnesses to determine whether he has at least six years' experience of voyaging to America, whether he has been in Central America, Mexico, Hispañola and Cuba, and whether he possesses a sea chart and knows how to use it, and whether he can explain the use of rhumb lines and knows the points of danger on the coasts and the shallows and the places of shelter, and where water, wood and other necessities for the voyage can be taken on board, and whether he owns an astrolabe to measure the altitude of the sun, and whether he has a quadrant to observe the Pole Star, and knows how to manage both instruments in calculating latitude and in adding or subtracting to find the angle of declination of the sun and the variation in the position of the Pole Star, together with knowledge of duration of the hours of daylight and night.[41]

With ships that arrived in Seville came people, goods, curiosities, ideas and emotions that radiated from there to the four winds. The rapid spread of the institution's influence seems palpable when one reflects that when it started, the Casa was a place where traders' representatives, supervisors and practical navigators mingled to arrange commerce with a handful of islands and a fragment of coast. The very word 'America' did not yet exist: Martin Waldseemüller and Mathias Ringmann invented it three years later to pay homage to Amerigo Vespucci, from their remote and ignorant place of observation in Saint-Dié in Lorraine. A further institutional adaptation to an unexpected situation followed in 1524, with the founding of the Council of the Indies (Consejo Real y Supremo de las Indias) with its nucleus of jurists and theologians. By then, Charles v had become Holy Roman emperor; Ferdinand Magellan and Juan Sebastián Elcano had completed their circumnavigation of the world; the Aztec Empire had been refashioned as New Spain; and few doubted, as Chancellor (future Cardinal) Gattinara said to Charles in 1519, that 'God has set you on the road to universal monarchy.'[42] Under the authority of the Council ('the head and mind that must govern the whole orb of the Indies'), during the reign of Philip II (1556–98), the Casa's network of bureaucrats, traders, jurists, seamen and cosmographers kept 41 bishoprics, 15 *audiencias* and 35 American regional governments in touch with the mind and person of the king – to say nothing of the great array of economies that were now in communication with each other and with Spain.[43]

Apart from royal courts, were there any machines more complex or any systems more intricate before the Industrial Revolution than a ship in full sail? The most conspicuous products of Spanish engineering in the sixteenth century were the ships built and outfitted in Vizcaya or Santander. Juan Escalante de Mendoza stated in his *Itinerario de navegación de los mares y tierras occidentales* (Sailing Directions for the Seas and Lands of the West) of 1575 that, while Venetians had great carracks that were fine for warfare, the French had good vessels of low tonnage that were ideal for slipping in and out of port, the Dutch barges were best for hauling heavy cargoes through shallow channels, the small English ships were commendably manoeuvrable and the powerful Portuguese warships could sail to India, the Castilians managed a bit of everything, with their ships, big and small, 'fit for every sea in the world'.[44] There were caravels of slim design and with triangular sails; square-rigged heavy cargo ships; and multi-purpose galleons, with long bowsprits, three masts, streamlined hulls, poops and ample gunports, which formed the convoys that came to dominate the Indies run. It required exceptional talent and training for their captains, pilots and masters to cross the high seas, by contrast with most of their coastbound counterparts who specialized in cabotage. Managing a ship is comparable to governing a city.[45] It seems appropriate, therefore, that the Spanish Empire, an empire of ships, was also an empire of cities.

The City Settings

When the conquistador vanguard reached the great cities of Mesoamerica and the Andean region, conquest became an engineering problem, just as it was in the urban and fortified arenas of most European wars. According to Ignacio González Tascón, 'Nine years into the reign of Moctezuma the water level in the lake that surrounds Mexico City rose so high that the city was swamped and the inhabitants took to canoes and boats, without knowing how to cope or how to stem so great a flood.'[46] It was probably to illustrate the second of his reports, despatched from Mexico City to Charles v on 30 October 1521, that Hernán Cortés sent a map of the city depicting the walkways and the barrier or dyke that protected it from flooding. In later times the refashioning of the city's water supply and flood defence systems would inspire projects for canals, cisterns and ditches named after saints, like the barrier of San Lázaro, completed in 1556. The saint's intercession was inadequate in this case, however, as the floods returned in 1580, 1604 and 1607. On St Matthew's Day, 1629, 30,000 indios died in a deluge 'that swept the city away, without leaving anything intact, in a surge so powerful and violent in the squares, streets, homes, and houses of religion of this city that it reached a height of two yards'. The number of Spanish inhabitants fell to four hundred and the flood did not recede, except from the main square and that of Santiago Tlatelolco, until 1634, when the suffering citizens thanked the Virgin of Guadelupe for retrieving the situation.[47] Desperate remedies were proposed, including that suggested by the town scribe, Fernando Carrillo, who urged every householder to build a rubble pavement outside his house so as to convert the streets into canals at need. Evidently, however, as we shall see, a comprehensive new drainage system was required.

Cities, which still embody the most conspicuous evidence of Spain's presence overseas, were the essential milieu for Spanish colonizers. The background of the medieval Reconquista, where newly founded cities focused the war effort on each new frontier, helps to explain how readily the conquistadores established strongholds – which sometimes existed, at first, only in their founders' imaginations and which they shamelessly called 'cities'. There were two purposes to fulfil: at first, rather like landing a craft on a hostile beach, the cities served as supply, recuperation centres, headquarters for decision-makers and starting points for raiding or tribute-gathering. Secondly, from the time of the conquest of Mexico in 1521 they became nuclei for stabilizing and spreading Spanish colonies – symbols of Spanish power and reach, large-scale laboratories for the engineers. The jurist Juan Solórzano y Pereira acknowledged as much in 1648, more than half a century before John Locke said something similar with reference to England. Both maintained that whoever seeks, finds and occupies land does so in response to a law of nature; and nature repays them for their diligence and skill. For both thinkers pure and applied knowledge were indissolubly linked, as were events in Europe and America.[48] Distance, however, occluded their vision, as it did for most of their successors in the age of Enlightenment. As the Benedictine Benito Jerónimo Feijoo wrote in his *Teatro crítico universal* (Critical Survey of the World) (1726–40), 'Our comprehension suffers from the same defect as our vision: what is remote looks less than it really is. No man, however big he be, looks other than a pygmy at a distance.'[49] He was thinking of the problems of evaluating remote cultures fairly; but for present purposes we can take his words as a reminder of the need to recover from the past, and re-evaluate with close inspection, the work of the makers of the infrastructure of the Spanish global monarchy.

2

THE OCEANIC SCAFFOLDING
Maritime Communications

Thy way is in the sea, and thy path in the great waters, and thy footsteps are not known. (PSALM 77:19)

'Seaborne empires' – thanks to J. H. Parry, the great historian of what his Harvard students called 'fish and ships' – became a much-used term in the 1960s to denote the new imperial states founded, mainly from Atlantic-side Europe, across the early modern world.[1] Spain's was one of them, but exhibited striking anomalies.

The Portuguese Empire that took shape in the fifteenth and sixteenth centuries exemplifies the normal pattern of imperialism. Instead of investing precious resources in acquiring territory landward, the Portuguese left turnover of the commodities they wanted in the hands of existing producers or of small, specialized and often merely sojourning groups of colonists. The pepper of Malabar, the cinnamon of Ceylon or the nutmeg and mace of Ternate and Tidore remained with the local sultanates; supply of the slaves of Africa – give or take a few *razzie* by Portuguese raiders – was left to the predatory states and traditional markets of the regions; African gold and Japanese silver continued to be acquired from the merchant middlemen who handled it, and the logwood of Brazil from harvesters who normally employed native labour. Even major new kinds of exploitation, such as that of sugar, which became the main product of Brazil, required only shallow colonization, confined to strips of coastline – prompting the quip that was often on the lips of Charles Verlinden, the outstanding Belgian historian who first proposed the Atlantic as a proper unit of historical study, that the 'seaborne' empires should rather be called 'seaboard empires'.[2]

'Seaboard' is an appropriate epithet. Whereas traditional land-based imperialism proceeded by conquering contiguous regions in order to control production, the newly widespread kind of maritime enterprise set out to control ports and routes in order to monopolize key trades. It was not entirely innovative. Precedents in antiquity included the Phoenician and Greek networks of trade between coastal communities across the Mediterranean. In the Middle Ages, the Venetian and Genoese empires, and that of the House of Barcelona, reproduced the same sort of model. Though its nature and extent are much disputed, the Chola 'empire' of the twelfth century united bases in India with Southeast Asian ports. Nor was early modern maritime imperialism exclusively European in origin. The Omani network of the seventeenth century – which resembled that of the medieval House of Barcelona in forming loose, largely dynastic links between remote communities that shared little by way of institutions or allegiance or even identity – was impressive while it lasted, seizing much of the Portuguese operation in East Africa, with outposts as far south as Zanzibar.[3]

Still, historians have tended to concur in calling the maritime imperial phenomenon new, because it had never before been seen on so vast a scale, around the world, crossing and re-crossing spaces between oceans and continents. It is also fair to endorse historians' common practice of treating seaboard empires as typically European, inasmuch as most of the initiative in linking distant seaboards came from European Atlantic-side states. In the sixteenth and seventeenth centuries, the empires of France, England, Portugal and the Netherlands, together with the smaller enterprises of similar kinds founded or extended in the seventeenth century by Denmark, Sweden and the Duchy of Courland, to say nothing of the failed imperial efforts launched from Scotland, all conformed to the 'seaborne' or 'seaboard' model. The French, English, Dutch and Portuguese did not begin to emulate Spain and move to acquire large landward territories until the very late seventeenth or the eighteenth century.[4]

Spain's empire conformed to the seaboard model, but only in part. By a mixture of luck and judgement (of which the judgement was not always that of Spaniards so much as of their native collaborators or allies) Spain became the heartland of the world's first great empire of land and sea, uniting the characteristics of territorial and maritime empires – establishing control of valuable routes at sea while also acquiring vast amounts of space landward and dominating the products that Spanish convoys shipped. The first permanent Spanish presence in the continental New World was in Central America – Castilla del Oro, as they called it – from 1513, but that was tentative and patchy. The conspicuous shift to expansion inland is best dated, barely a generation after Columbus's first transatlantic voyage, and without forethought, from the moment in 1521 when Spaniards became the unpredicted successors of Aztec hegemony in much of Mesoamerica. Further huge dilatations of the frontiers occurred with the acquisition of most of the Andean world and the Río de la Plata region from the 1530s to the 1570s, and fairly extensive holdings in the Philippines and parts of North America from the 1570s onwards. In a sense, Spain also had a landward empire in Europe, as a result of the inheritance of the Holy Roman emperor Charles V, who was also Charles I of Spain, and who relied on Spanish money and manpower to help defend dominions scattered from Sicily to Friesland and from Franche-Comté to Moravia. On his abdication in 1556 he left the Netherlands to his son, Philip II of Spain; the axis of the empire in Europe became the 'Spanish road' that carried armies from Milan to Maastricht.[5] Even Spain itself is obviously – as it appears at a glance on the map – an unusual kind of Atlantic realm, with a lot of land in relation to relatively little coastline, owing to the excision of Portugal, like a fragment torn from Spain's fringe. Madrid, the capital city for most of the duration of Spain's global empire, is as far from the sea as it is possible to get.

Nevertheless, it is impossible to understand Spain except as a maritime country, or the global Spanish monarchy except as a seaborne empire. The peninsula juts into the ocean as if fleeing from the continent. The sea is almost as prominent in Spain's literature as in those of England or the Netherlands – more so, by any standard, than in those of France or Italy.[6] Sea flavours are never far from Spanish palates. Madrid may be remote from the coast, but it has Europe's largest fish market. The very precocity – compared with the tardiness of rival European imperialists – with which conquistadores engorged huge tracts of land on the farther shores of oceans depended on maritime communications. The routes across the Atlantic and Pacific were the bones, as it were, around which the continental empire put on flesh. The crucial infrastructure of the monarchy stretched across seas. Some of the lifeblood pumped into the Spanish monarchy originated outside the system of navigation Spain established: contraband from other powers' American and African colonies and cargoes of slaves, brought by agreement with foreign powers and traders direct from African ports, made vital contributions. Local and regional cabotage, of course, supported transoceanic trade: some was on a large scale, such as Peruvian silver carried to Panama or Yucatec cacao to Veracruz; some was conducted in flotillas of small vessels – including canoes of a kind long traditional before Spaniards arrived in the New World – that plied the coasts up and down the Atlantic mainland. A document that English pirates captured in 1595 demonstrates the modest yet necessary nature of this traffic: cargoes of maguey, clay pots, fish from Santa Marta, and half a dozen melons ('but what with the groundings of the canoes they were eaten or went bad') on a canoe: 'if she is not in Cartagena, we fear for her survival. May our Lord provide the remedy!'[7] But the shipping that linked Spain to the western and eastern extremities of the monarchy was a tightly organized operation, of what would now be called a command economy, under bureaucratic control and state protection, of sailing between specific ports along narrow corridors defined by winds and currents.

Decoding the Winds

To a remarkable extent, Columbus laid the broad outlines of transatlantic communications on his first two crossings, in 1492 and 1493. A good deal of splenetic energy has been wasted on pointless bickering over what, if anything, Columbus can properly be said to have discovered. It is obviously appropriate to speak of him 'discovering the New World' to the Old – alerting, first, people in the Azores and the Iberian peninsula and then, by way of the rapid publication of his findings, the rest of Latin Christendom, to the fact that there was land in the ocean to the west, beyond what was already known to his contemporaries from experience or record. Complaints that the existing inhabitants had already 'discovered' America should be evaluated in combination with a further fact: no existing inhabitants, as far as we know, were aware that they inhabited a 'New World' – a vast landmass, distinct from the other landmasses of which the land surface of the planet is composed. Indeed, most native peoples knew only tiny fragments of their hemisphere and nothing of the world beyond. In a sense, therefore, Columbus initiated a new process of discovery of their own world to Native Americans, too. But the undisputed and really important discovery was of routes which, for the first time, linked America to the Old World in reliable, commercially exploitable ways, and made possible the exchanges of life forms and forms of culture that have shaped global history ever since. No predecessor anticipated Columbus in that respect. The question arises, 'How did he do it?'

The answer – here, as well as to almost every question about maritime communications – is, as a famous winner of the Nobel Prize in Literature might say, blowing in the wind. The history of the world, as conventionally written, has too much hot air and not enough wind – for winds and currents have been the inescapable matrix of long-range and large-scale exchanges of culture for most of the past. Even industrialization has not entirely liberated shipping from the influence of the wind, though steam engines and internal combustion engines have shifted a lot of major commerce to land routes. The wind bloweth where it listeth, and before the industrial era, winds were decisive – if not determinant – in setting limits to what was possible for would-be travellers and traders, conquerors and colonists, missionaries and merchants. You could only go where winds and currents took you and could only get there as fast as they permitted with as much or as little security as they sanctioned.[8]

The systems of winds and currents in the Atlantic and Pacific ocean were therefore limiting and conditioning – almost determinant – for the shape and effectiveness of the Spanish global monarchy. The North Atlantic system, which was the first to be explored from Europe, is roughly circular, operating clockwise: the northeast trade winds spring from the African Atlantic at around 30–35 degrees north, as cold air warms and rises and the cooler air that replaces it at surface level is drawn towards the south. Gaining heat in tropical latitudes, the wind curls westward, with greater velocity in winter than summer. Above about 30 degrees north, high pressure over the western hemisphere normally drives the wind in the opposite direction, from west to east. At around 60 degrees north, a series of currents along the Arctic edge creep eastwards from the shores of Scandinavia and along those of Greenland, as far south as Newfoundland: these were important for Norse navigators in the Middle Ages and for the modern Danish North Atlantic empire, but played virtually no role for Spain. The Gulf Stream connects the zones of east and west winds on the western edge of the ocean: hence the Spanish monarchy colonized

Florida, a province of no economic value in the early modern period, to secure its harbours against predators. At irregular intervals, associated with ill-understood changes in atmospheric pressure, the direction of the westerlies can undergo reversal in spring.

Between the North and South Atlantic systems a zone of light, variable winds or atmospheric inertia lies like the filling of a sandwich. Below about 10 degrees south, however, the winds circulate in a way very like that of the northern hemisphere. Southeast trades reach for the western hemisphere from the South Atlantic at around 30 degrees south. Above that approximate latitude reliable westerlies lead back across the ocean. Strong currents run from north to south along the Brazilian coast, and south to north along that of Africa. Off the West African bulge, a quasi-monsoonal effect can drag ships towards shore. Towards the southern extremities of the ocean, with great intensity below about 38 degrees south, the 'roaring forties' constitute a world-circling corridor of high winds, always blowing from west to east, as if dragged by the motion of the Earth.

The Pacific reproduces the Atlantic pattern, with even greater regularity: clockwise rotations on either side of the equator, separated by doldrums. Peculiar to the Pacific is the strength of the currents that flow from Japan near the northern edges of the ocean as far as California – vital for Spanish imperial communications, as we shall see, linking the Philippines and Spain's China trade to America. Similarly, the Humboldt Current, which thrusts northward along the Pacific coast of South America, exceeding the current along the Atlantic coast of Africa, is so strong that shipping has to stand well out to sea to outflank it. The oscillations that reverse the direction of wind and current in the southern moiety are much more frequent in the Pacific, albeit equally unpredictable, occurring, on average but without any regularity, twice a decade.

Modern scrutineers often express bafflement that it took predecessors so long to crack the code of the winds. A great part of the explanation is to be found in ancient, long-sustained mistrust of a following wind, which no seaman now fears except on a lee shore. Astonishingly to today's yachtsmen who love to sail with the wind at their backs, most voyages of maritime exploration before Columbus, outside the limits of monsoonal systems, were made into the wind. Ancient Greek and Phoenician navigators, for instance, crossed the breadth of the Mediterranean against the prevailing westerlies.

Polynesian island-hopping across the South Pacific was achieved in the face of the southeast trades. Norse transatlantic crossings in the Middle Ages were assisted by currents, but occurred in a belt of prevailing westerly winds. The reason for this apparently counter-intuitive pattern is not hard to understand: by sailing against the wind, navigators improved their chances of returning home. If you sail with the wind in a fixed-wind system, you may make stunning discoveries, but how will you find a wind to take you and the news home?[9]

Hence the vastly longer history of long-range open-sea navigation in the Indian Ocean than in the Pacific and Atlantic. Where monsoons blow, you can stand on the shore and feel the direction of the wind change regularly at half-yearly intervals. Wherever the wind takes you, you know that it will turn homeward eventually. In fixed-wind systems, such as those that faced Atlantic seamen, there is no such guarantee. Stand on the Atlantic shore of North America and you will feel the wind unremittingly at your back, inhibiting you from venturing far. Take up a corresponding position on the coasts of Europe, and the wind will be persistently in your face, limiting the reach of any attempted outward voyage. In the forty years preceding Columbus's attempt, at least eight voyages westward from the Azores were commissioned in Portugal: none got very far. But for real conners of the winds and currents there were ways round the obstacle. You could seek far-northerly currents, as the Norse had done, or wait for occasional spring easterlies, as John Cabot was to do on his way to Newfoundland, or exploit the rare and unreliable North Atlantic Oscillation, which, at unpredictable intervals, reverses the normal pattern of the winds. These options, however, were obviously unsatisfactory: they led to destinations profitable for nothing except cod fishing, or they incurred unacceptable uncertainties.

Columbus's great merit was to discover – the word seems apt – a new approach, with a following wind, starting from the Canaries in the zone of the northeast trades. On his first crossing, he set his course due west, probably because he believed that the Canaries were on the same latitude as the great trading ports of Fujian for which he was putatively bound. In consequence, he did not get the full benefit of the trade winds. The absence of contrary winds on the outward journey seems – if some of the early sources can be trusted – to have aroused unrest among crewmen, who did not, of course, think the world was flat or that they would topple off its edge; they did fear, however, that they would never find a homeward wind. To read the account of mutinous murmurings recorded in a sixteenth-century account purportedly by Columbus's younger son is to share the anxieties that deterred voyages with the wind.[10]

The experience of the first crossing, however, alerted Columbus to the advantages of letting the wind bear him. After some hesitation, he set off on his return from the New World early in 1493 by heading north from the Caribbean in search of the westerlies of the North Atlantic. Later the same year, when he headed back to his 'Indies', he took full advantage of the northeast trades, setting a course to the southwest and making his landfall in the Antilles with impressive speed only thirty days out of sight of land: subsequent journeys rarely bettered this record. By exploiting the most favourable winds in both directions, he had unveiled the pattern of the Atlantic wind system, which is roughly circular and clockwise. The only major uncharted element in the system was the Gulf Stream, which provided fast access from the islands Spain began to colonize to the belt of westerlies. Voyagers in Columbus's wake discovered it and, from early in the second decade of the sixteenth century, made it part of the standard route to and fro across the ocean – a route that remained unimproved for the rest of the age of sail. Even for communicating with their North American colonies in the seventeenth century the English preferred to stick to the Spanish route for reliability and speed, rather than continuing with the approach Cabot had pioneered, back and forth along northerly latitudes with rare and unreliable spring easterlies outbound.

The decipherment of the Pacific winds was an even bigger job, owing to the vastness of the ocean, but, in a sense, an easier one thanks to prior Atlantic experience. Except on the monsoonal edges of maritime Asia, the Pacific winds roughly reproduce the Atlantic pattern, as we have seen: clockwise above the equator, anticlockwise below it, with a zone of doldrums in between, and the fierce 'roaring forties' circling the globe towards the extreme south. One might therefore expect pilots from Spanish America to attempt a similar strategy to that of their Atlantic counterparts: seek a route of return far to the north of their outward track. The theory, indeed, did not elude them; but the vastness of the ocean deterred them from exploiting it in practice. From Magellan's first crossing in 1520 it took two generations of persistent effort to work out the pattern of winds and currents and establish a reliable route from Spain's outposts in the Philippines, and the vital markets of China and Japan, to Mexico and Peru and back.

A viable eastbound route was not hard to find. In 1527 one of the conquerors of Mexico, Álvaro de Saavedra, demonstrated that it was possible to get to the fringes of Asia in a few weeks by using the prevailing northwesterlies to skirt the doldrums to the north. But having completed the journey he could find no way back. Less than a decade later, Hernando de Grijalva – a restless seagoer, credited with the discovery of the Revillagigedo Islands – led a similar effort, disfigured by shipwreck, from Peru, where Cortés had sent him to help the conquistadores. Ending in disaster, the expedition seemed to confirm that the Pacific was a one-way ocean, traversable only from east to west.

Navigators needed three more decades of experience before they could break the impasse. By 1564 the most knowledgeable of them was Andrés de Urdaneta. For a figure of primordial importance in the history of the world, he is woefully under-celebrated. Despite leaving plenty of writings of his own he remains maddeningly elusive. His career began in 1525, when he was a teenager besotted with cosmography, in a follow-up voyage to Magellan's. He was independently minded, which he demonstrated by challenging his superiors' competence and surviving shipwreck in the labyrinth of the Strait of Magellan: he located the rest of the fleet and rescued his fellow castaways. He returned home with the daughter a native concubine bore him in an unverified part of the Indies, and with an impressive journal of the voyage.

He spent most of the rest of his youth as a pilot, evincing a growing distaste for command, perhaps because he was beginning to discern a religious vocation. In 1553 he took vows as an Augustinian brother, proceeding to the priesthood four years later. He seems to have found the cloister comfortable. When officials begged him to resume transpacific exploration he declined to do so, until orders from the king pried him from retirement in 1560. 'Although I am now over fifty-two years of age and in poor health,' he wrote, 'having in mind the great zeal of Your Majesty in all that concerns the service of our Lord and the spread of our holy Catholic faith, I am ready to face the labours of this voyage, trusting solely in the help of God.'[11] On Urdaneta's recommendation, in order to forestall accusations that Spain was intruding in waters reserved by agreement to Portuguese explorers, the purpose of the voyage was defined as evangelization of the Philippines, not exploitation of opportunities for trade.

'Next to faith in the help of our Lord,' ran the orders addressed to the commander of the expedition, 'it is confidently believed that Fray Andrés de Urdaneta will be the chief agent in discovering the return route to New Spain, because of his experience, his knowledge of the weather in these regions, and his other qualifications.'[12] Urdaneta realized that timing was the key to success. It was vital to leave the Philippines with the benefit of the summer monsoon and then to make a rapid transition northward to catch the Japan current, continuing as far as necessary to meet the North Pacific current before turning east for home. With a suitable turnaround time in Manila the feat was possible. In November 1564, the attempt began; in February, they set sail for the Philippines, launching the return voyage on 1 June 1565. The quest for a west wind took the ships beyond 30 degrees north. The journey of 17,700 kilometres (11,000 mi.) was the longest ever recorded on the open sea without a landfall. It took four months and eight days to get to Acapulco. Everyone aboard was nearly prostrate with scurvy and exhaustion. Urdaneta's subordinate, Alonso de Arellano, actually preceded him to Mexico by two months, having got separated from the flagship by a storm. But mastery of the Pacific had at last been achieved by daring of the same kind that crossed the Atlantic: sailing with the wind at one's back.

Decoding the wind systems made the Atlantic and Pacific navigable and exploitable. In a sense, the wind did transatlantic pilots' navigating for them, getting them from one shore to another. Finding a particular harbour, of course, required greater precision. Theoretical treatises by academic experts of the sixteenth century have misled historians into thinking that ocean-going was a scientific undertaking. There is little evidence that the *pilotos pláticos* – so-named by Spanish officials and considered the empirically sound, experienced course-plotters who guided the ships – ever respected the experts or read their works, or attended the classes in scientific navigation that, from the early sixteenth century, were offered in Seville by experts designated by royal decree. Although it is hard, in the age of GPS, to imagine technology-free route-finding across thousands of miles of open sea, seasoned navigators did not need to know a lot of maths or astronomy to find their way. Long-schooled 'feeling' could substitute for ratiocination. To sea folk who really know their medium, seascapes are like landscapes – more mutable but similarly recognizable from swells, wave patterns, the sense and smell of the wind and the presence of species of fish and fowl. Reliance on sophisticated technologies has alienated modern Western navigators from the tradition of the *pilotos plácticos* but you can still find individuals in Polynesia with an unerring sense of where they are at sea, even when they are bereft of instruments, hundreds of kilometres from land.

In any case the science that the great historian of navigation Pierre Adam called 'primitive celestial navigation' does not rely on technology – just on a good eye and a sense of the passage of time.[13] Columbus and his famous imitator Amerigo Vespucci both made a great show of manipulating the most complicated direction-finding aids of their day: the astrolabe, which, when sighted on the sun or Pole Star, gave a reading of latitude on an adjoining scale; and the quadrant, which resembled a scaled-down astrolabe, designed for use at sea. Its fixed arm was relatively stable compared with the astrolabe's quivering plumb line that would never stay still for long enough to facilitate a reading on a plunging vessel. Columbus and Vespucci cultivated such instruments merely to impress onlookers: there is no evidence that either explorer ever took a reading – much less an accurate one – at sea with either gadget.[14] A sixteenth-century engraving of Vespucci shows him as he wanted us to see him: fiddling with his instruments, communicating with the heavens, like Christ in the Garden of Gethsemane, while his disciples – the ignorant crewmen – sleep nearby. The scene is shamelessly fictitious. Nor is it adequate to suppose, as a formerly influential school of historians did, that Columbus was an expert in navigation by 'dead reckoning': setting a course by the compass, adjusting for leeway and timing (by sand-clock, celestial indications and sheer innate skill) how far along it your ship went.[15] In reality, both Columbus and Vespucci relied on a modified form of primitive celestial navigation: at night, when the sky was clear, they timed the passage of the guard stars around the Pole and subtracted from 24. They then read their positions off printed tables of latitude according to hours of daylight. We know this because the errors in the readings they claimed to make correspond exactly to misprints in the tables.[16] Not until well into the seventeenth century could a transatlantic traveller confidently expect to cross the ocean under the guidance of instruments of navigation, rather than relying on the feelings of a pilot squinting at the sun and the stars or responding to the motion of the winds and waves. But even when latitude was verified by quadrants (and by the sextants of greater precision that replaced them in the eighteenth century), longitude remained the province of rough-and-ready estimates until the development of reliable chronometers on the pattern invented in England by John Harrison in the 1760s.

Marine charts, too, were surprisingly slow to register an impact.[17] Columbus and Vespucci both promised to provide charts for transatlantic navigators, but there is no evidence that either ever complied with the promise, despite repeated reminders from their royal patrons. Vespucci was commissioned, apparently on the strength of his self-recommendations, to collate data from returning pilots and keep a master-version of an Atlantic chart up to date. This so-called *padrón real*, if it ever existed at all, is unlikely to have been of much use until well into the seventeenth century, when shore-based surveys began to provide reliable data on latitudes, distances and anchorages.[18]

Meanwhile, traditional seamen continued to prefer written sailing directions of the kinds pilots had kept since antiquity, regarding maps as landlubber's aids. Without means of finding longitude, gauging latitude accurately, measuring the speed of a ship or checking for leeway, no one ever knew, save very roughly, where a ship was on the open sea. The pilots' cluelessness was the target of the sarcastic humour of Eugenio de Salazar, a former governor of the Canary Islands, who was a passenger to Santo Domingo in 1574, on his way to take up a post as a judge of the court. After a sufficient lapse of time on the open sea, America started as a smell:

> The pilot and seamen started to sniff and sense land, like asses scenting grass. At such times it was a sight to see the pilot fixing on a star, hoisting Jacob's staff, jiggle the plumb-line, and establish true North, and at the end of it all announce our whereabouts to within 1,000 leagues; and then to see him measure the declination of the sun at noon, with his astrolabe to hand, raising his eyes to the sun and trying to get it between the sights of his astrolabe – and how he could never manage it. And then he'd turn to his handbook and, eventually, throw the problem open to debate with his colleagues . . . And what annoyed me most was the way they affected secrecy with the passengers over what exact degree or part thereof they decided on, and how far they reckoned the ship had sailed. Gradually, however, I came to appreciate the real reason for their reticence: they were never remotely accurate and didn't know what they were doing. What

a lark to hear them at it, as one asked another, 'How many degrees do you think, sir?' 'Sixteen,' one replies. Another says, 'Just about twenty' and another, 'Thirteen and a half.' Then they ask, 'How far do you make it from land, sir?' One suggests, 'I put us forty leagues from land.' 'A hundred and fifty,' says another, and 'This morning,' claims a third, 'my finding was ninety-two leagues.' And, be it three leagues or three hundred, none of them ever agrees with another or with the facts.[19]

In Peril on the Sea

Winds shaped ships as well as empires. Because Spanish ships on transoceanic routes worked with the wind, they were uniformly square-rigged – a pattern Columbus set on his first voyage, when, while in the Canaries, he converted his only mixed-rigged vessel to square sails. Over the colonial period, commercial and naval ships became bigger and faster, with progressively more ample and efficient sail power, but the major innovation that oceanic conditions induced occurred relatively early, with the development in the sixteenth century of the galleon: cutting down the superstructures that encumbered warships made vessels lighter and more streamlined; lengthening the hull increased volume without affecting speed, and narrowing it enhanced the streamlining (though this was not a uniform feature for shipbuilders who valued stability over speed for high-sea sailing). By the late seventeenth century – though galleons might come in almost any size from about 500 tons upward – it was common for them to approach or even attain 2,000 tons. In the eighteenth century, when Spanish communications could no longer rely on naval supremacy in competition with the upstart powers of northern Europe, and especially with the overwhelmingly mighty Royal Navy, it became increasingly prudent to shift the carriage of important cargoes, such as secret papers and American silver, away from convoys of galleons to faster and smaller single ships. The build of galleons, which were primarily naval vessels, influenced merchant ships, which nevertheless remained diverse and were built chiefly for large capacity: while they had galleons to protect them, they did not need to be manoeuvrable or fast.

The number of sailings in the Atlantic was prodigious: they exceeded one hundred for the first time in a single year in 1520, and thereafter only intense piracy or severe repression could restrain the numbers as the colonies expanded and generated production and demand for the rest of the century. Typically, the annual total included twenty or thirty big commercial ships. From the second decade of the seventeenth century numbers slackened, owing to worsening security on war-ravaged seas, fluctuations in production of silver and other commodities of New World origin, and the growing independence of New World economies that supplied ever more of what they needed for themselves.[20] The Pacific was a different proposition. Spain had relatively few productive colonies or large markets on the west coast of the Americas; most of those there were, in the Andean region, communicated with the Atlantic via Panama or Cartagena or the rivers that drained into the Orinoco or River Plate. The Manila galleons sailed annually, except when disasters impeded them, but never numbered more than four and were normally limited to two by official regulations designed to prevent the drainage of silver from Mexico and Peru.

Even with the benefit of gadgets and charts, getting across the ocean and back under sail was fraught with hazard. In the first fleet to reach the Caribbean from Europe on Columbus's first voyage in 1492, the biggest vessel, the *Santa María*, struck ground on the shore of Hispaniola and had to be abandoned. For the rest of the age of sail, storms and the inscrutability of longitude – as a result of which ships frequently came unexpectedly on shores, shoals and rocks – made shipwreck frequent. Although Spanish ships tried to avoid carrying valuable wares in the hurricane season, the weather in the Caribbean is full of surprises, and anyone who has experienced the hurricanes that arise in the Caribbean every summer and fall and hurtle onto the shores of the mainland from Mexico to Maryland and sometimes beyond would expect them to account for many wrecks. In fact, early modern ships were adept at riding storms and most wrecks occurred on the homeward voyage when ships made fast crossings with strong westerlies behind them and came unexpectedly on lee shores. A quick count of recorded wrecks in the sixteenth century shows that over a hundred foundered close to home on the Spanish coast, and about fifty on or off the Azores. Of outward-bound ships a dozen or so never made it beyond the Canaries. In the West Indies, Havana, as the most favoured port, registered no more than fifty wrecks among incoming ships. At most, around fifty other lost ships in New World locations can be ascribed unequivocally to storms.

Human agency – variously greedy or irresponsible – exacerbated danger. Because shipping was costly and usually in short supply, the temptation to overload was almost irresistible. A few spectacular incidents can stand in for the whole story. In 1622 the galleon *Nuestra Señora de Atocha*, bound for Spain from Havana with the Gulf Stream, foundered on the Florida coast. Treasure-seekers recovered cargo worth U.S.$600 million in 1969. In 1711 on the same route the *Santísima Trinidad* hardly got out of harbour before going down in a hurricane. In October 1641, a late hurricane drove the *Nuestra Señora de la Pura y Limpia Concepción*, carrying three times her proper tonnage, onto reefs off what is now the Dominican Republic. The incident haunted generations of treasure-seekers until in 1978 a resourceful team recovered $400 million in booty from the wreckage. In 1593 and 1594 the Manila galleons' voyages were frustrated by failures of seaworthiness, adverse weather and delayed repairs. The *San Agustín* set out in 1595 to replace them and repair the losses, but a sudden storm wrenched her from her anchorage, never to be seen again, in San Francisco Bay while the crew were reprovisioning on their way to Acapulco.

Weather was an impartial enemy. Other, human foes targeted Spanish shipping. War and piracy hardly ever gave honest seafarers a respite. In a sense, piracy is a primitive form of exchange, heavily tilted in favour of one party in the transaction. It made sense for pirates to leave the major investment costs of exploiting the New World to Spain, and reap a share of the profits through threats or violence. Those who started as pirates doubled as smugglers and often, when they could, sought contracts for legitimate or at least informally licensed trade, especially as suppliers of slaves. Some piracy was in the hands of people who had been made, or chose to be, outcasts from their home communities – the 'villains of all nations' or *hostes humani generis* who formed their own anarchical societies, with their own ships, their own precariously elected tyrants and their own rough justice, and who 'declared War against the World'.[21] Most piracy, is best understood as warfare, waged against Spain mainly by French, Dutch and English predators, sometimes as part of regular operations but more often in defiance of the laws of war, to make a profit from prizes and raids. As the historian John Elliott wrote, 'Trade and piracy were liable to be synonymous in this lawless Caribbean world of the later seventeenth and eighteenth centuries, and buccaneers, merchants and planters became fickle accomplices in the enterprise of stripping the Spanish empire of its assets.'[22] War and piracy, indeed, were inseparable, as navies bred men unfit for any vocation except violence, who, on demobilization, frequently continued, unofficially, their previous ways of life. In the eighteenth century the British Navy might have employed nearly 50,000 men in wartime and released more than 30,000 whenever hostilities subsided. Pirates and polities recruited each other's crews. The human jetsam of shore life – fugitives from justice, enslavement, exploitation, debt or their own families – swelled pirate bands.

Because Spanish transoceanic ships were effectively confined to fixed wind-corridors, pirates always knew roughly where to pick them off. The museums and archives of Europe and, to a lesser extent, the United States, are full of evidence of successful predation: thousands of documents and artefacts captured at sea or in raids on land. More remarkable, however, is the success of Spanish countermeasures: the fortification of harbours and the arming and organizing of fleets. The need for improved security became obvious from 1522, when two shiploads of the first rich pickings of the conquest of the Aztecs fell into the hands of the French corsair Jean Flandrin. The crown immediately resolved to create a naval task force for the protection of New World commerce. From 1524, four ships were available annually to escort merchants willing to pay for the service. By 1526 Spanish officials determined that a strategy of safety in numbers was ineluctable, ordering returning ships to form convoys, 'which, as occasion demands, shall be such as seems to us best for the security of the fleet, with the forces needful to defend the ships and boats and inflict punishment on the enemy'.[23]

The spread of colonies, the growth of trade and the vastly increased output of silver from the 1550s required two convoys a year from 1569. An armed escort fleet – the Flota de Nueva España – left Seville every April or May for Veracruz, where it took under its wing assembled vessels from all over Mesoamerica, including those bearing the royal share of the output of the silver mines of Zacatecas. Every August the Flota de Tierra Firme performed the same sort of operation at Portobelo or Nombre de Dios on the Panamanian coast, usually stopping at Cartagena to unload goods intended for Venezuela, Ecuador and what is now Colombia. Nothing, of course, mattered as much as the crown's consignments of silver: although the cash value never remotely equalled the amount the royal treasury raised from taxation, especially in the fiscally productive realm of Castile, the silver made a huge psychological difference to the viability of the Spanish monarchy. As long as it arrived, year in, year out, creditors were reassured and the loans that kept armies in the field and navies afloat kept coming. The galleons remained on patrol in the Caribbean throughout the winter, guarding the treasure as it accumulated in port and protecting the internal commerce of the Spanish Main. In March, the two fleets met in Havana to accompany the commercial and official shipping home. Individual ships made the journey – especially if fast despatches needed to be transmitted – but the menace of piracy made lone merchant ventures rare: in some years there were almost none, and never more than fifty in a single year.

The convoy system was costly and slow. It involved tying up private capital for long spells and committed the crown to enormous outlays. But it worked. It seems astonishing, in retrospect, that Spain's enemies hardly ever succeeded in disrupting the convoys. On only one occasion was the silver fleet captured in its near entirety, in 1628, when Piet Hein, a Dutch seadog who conceived a raid on the Spanish Main as a coup in the war of the United Provinces against Spain, waylaid the Flota de Nueva España as it approached Havana. His victory was a triumph of surprise. Though the Flota de Tierra Firme eluded him, he captured almost the whole of his quarry intact – five galleons and sixteen merchantmen. His haul was reputedly big enough to sustain the Dutch war effort, which lasted for twenty more years, and is still celebrated in a rhyme (versions vary) that every Dutch child knows:

Piet Hein, Piet Hein,
Zijn naam is klein.
Zijn deden bennen groot:
Die heeft gewonnen de Zilverfloot.[24]

Piet Hein in name
Though small in fame
Is magnified by his feat:
For he has seized the silver fleet!

The episode was all the more worthy of renown for being, in practice, unrepeatable. The Spaniards were not caught off guard again until 1656, when war with England excited the ambitions of Admiral Blake to attempt a blockade of Cádiz. He pinned the escort fleet for a year in harbour, but bad weather compelled him to abandon the blockade early in September, just as the Flota de Tierra Firme of six vessels, which had tarried in Havana for the escort that never arrived, hove into view. The Flota had eluded an English patrol off Havana but appears to have failed to recognize Blake's as enemy vessels. Since Hein's escapade, Spanish crews preferred to fight to the end or scuttle their ships rather than surrender precious cargoes: after a long fire-fight the flagship of the returning viceroy of Peru went down in a blaze, as did another big merchantman, and three Spanish ships escaped altogether. But the English hauled off two prizes and over 45 tons of silver. Blake's further effort the following year ended empty-handed but was even more disastrous for Spain as almost the entire cargo was lost. For the rest of the colonial era however, only stragglers from the flotas ever fell into hostile hands.

Ships were hard to snare intact at sea; and the vastness of the Spanish Main constituted an effectively indefensible frontier, which raiders could attack by concentrating forces while Spanish defenders remained dispersed. Pirates therefore preyed with greater ease on port towns and shipping in harbours than on vessels abroad. Such raids did not always yield prizes: in 1708 an English cannonball dispatched one of the richest treasure-ships ever, the *San José*, in Havana harbour: divers' recovery of some of her treasure in 2015 provoked an interna-tional cause célèbre, with the Spanish state disputing the divers' right to the spoils. Ransom and loot from on shore were more regular rewards for raiders. Terror was a handy tactic for raiders who lived off ransom and payola. A famous and characteristic episode, among many hundreds, occurred in 1683, when a Dutch pirate flotilla of 13 vessels and over 1,300 men seized hostages in Veracruz and beheaded them one by one when Spain refused ransom. The same band – or what was left of it after bloody internecine conflicts – repeated the method, with equally little success, in a raid on Campeche a few years later. Spanish pirates responded in kind. For instance, in bloody and incendiary incursions in English and Dutch islands of the Caribbean, Juan Corso was perhaps in his day more celebrated or calumnified than his English and Dutch counterparts, Henry Morgan and De Graaf. He was the arch-exponent of no quarter in engagements at sea and no mercy when looting on land.

In some ways the Pacific was a better hunting-ground for pirates than the Atlantic. Shipping was rarer, but less well protected because of the difficulty of access of the vast and remote ocean. From the establishment of a colony in the Philippines in the 1570s until well into the eighteenth century it remained a 'Spanish lake', largely because no one else wanted it.[25] Only when whaling, harvesting other ocean products, scientific interests and the prospects of trade with burgeoning Spanish colonies in Pacific-side America enticed other powers to compete for supremacy did Spain face a challenge. Meanwhile, any pirate who got into the Pacific by braving Cape Horn or the Strait of Magellan or the belt of storms that guard the approaches from the southwest could roam with every prospect of impunity. Francis Drake scooped up two bonanza-scale cargoes during his circumnavigation of the globe in 1578–9. In 1587 Thomas Cavendish, attempting to repeat the feat, seized the *Santa Ana* off Lower California. In 1709 Woodes Rogers, the rescuer of Alexander Selkirk (whose romantically inspiring 'solitude' as a castaway made him the reputed model for Robinson Crusoe), levied a ransom on Guayaquil and seized the *Nuestra Señora de la Encarnación*. Anson took the *Covadonga* before it could retrieve Manila from Acapulco in 1743 in an act of war; ten years later George Compton invaded the Pacific in a spirit of raw and undisguised piracy, massacring the crew of the grounded *San Sebastián* on the Californian Channel island of San Clemente. By then, British and French navigators were ranging the ocean, as they adumbrated global strategies, developed scientific interests and identified Pacific resources. Meanwhile British and Russian expansion, in North America and Siberia respectively, drew rival empires to the ocean's shores; the growth of Spanish colonies increased the market opportunities.

Spanish naval supremacy waned worldwide: after the 1630s, Spain was never again the preponderant Atlantic superpower she had been in the sixteenth century; and from the second half of the seventeenth century the Dutch, French and English usually outgunned her at sea. But Spanish defensive measures remained efficacious and the balance of victory and defeat in naval encounters continued to favour Spain. Capturing the hazards of taking on the Spanish monarchy, an English shanty – a modification, perhaps, of a storm-disaster shanty of the late seventeenth century – laments, in the version one of the present authors recalls hearing in boyhood, the apparently fictional adventure of the good ship *Benjamin*. It tells of a cruise 'away to Spain, for silver and for gold to gain' that lost nearly five hundred men. When the survivors returned home to Blackwall,

Oh, my boys, oh, oh,
the mothers there were crying for their sons
and the widows wailed for their loved ones
that died on bold *Benjamin*-oh.[26]

In spite of the convoy system's resilience, it was unsustainable: too costly, too cumbersome for an era in which free trade was challenging mercantilism and capitalism was subverting command economies. Seville, moreover, with its silty river access, was no longer an appropriate headquarters for regulating the comings and goings of big ships. In 1717 Cádiz replaced Seville. When war with Britain resumed in 1739, convoys became inoperable: every armed ship was needed to defend Spain's own coasts. The crown fell back on a system of every man for himself: merchants could sail to and from the New World at their own risk. Commerce shifted for a while out of the accustomed routes, towards the mouth of the River Plate or around South America directly to Chile, Peru or the Philippines. The convoy system resumed around the middle of the century, at the behest of merchants in Mexico and Peru – but not for long. Free-trade theory conquered the Spanish elite, as it did the *bien-pensants* of most of Enlightenment Europe, and in 1765 a royal decree opened nine ports all over Spain to direct trade with Cuba, Santo Domingo, Puerto Rico, Trinidad and Margarita. In 1778 a further measure of liberalization increased the number of authorized ports to 13 in Spain and 24 in America, though for a decade more Venezuela was reserved to the monopoly of a joint-stock company based in Guipuzcoa. The effects of liberalization were modest: Cádiz exported over three-quarters, by value, of goods bound for the Americas from Spain in the next two decades. No other port attained 10 per cent. In imports, the dominance of Cádiz was even more emphatic, with over 84 per cent of the value passing through that port.[27]

The Shipboard Experience

The dangers of shipwreck, war and piracy were insufficient to deter transatlantic shippers and voyagers. Perhaps therefore we should not blench at the abominable conditions in which they had to travel. The sheer length of the voyages was daunting. The first leg, from the mouth of the Guadalquivir to the Canaries, took twelve days on average. Columbus had managed it in six on his first crossing, and seven the following year – but his speed was rarely equalled by the heavier vessels that followed. About thirty days was normal for the next leg, from the Canaries to the Caribbean. Landfall in the Antilles was followed by a laborious journey north to Santo Domingo, Puerto Rico or Havana. The Caribbean was, relatively speaking, a more daunting proposition than the Atlantic. To reach Veracruz would add, typically, 23 days to the average voyage. One had to allow up to 116 days if one's destination was Panama.[28] The return voyage needed exceptional luck to achieve the never-surpassed record of 1494 of 35 days; one attempt, from Havana to Cádiz in 1591, registered 37 days. But the normal allowance in the second half of the sixteenth century and the early seventeenth – represented by the average length of the voyages of 53 convoys for that period studied by Pierre and Huguette Chaunu – was of just over 67 days. Of course, erratic conditions could cause huge departures from the norm: up to 162 days in 1553, and 98, for example, in 1611.[29]

Sickness was rife, especially in the forms of scurvy, malnutrition and thirst, on long voyages, and was exacerbated by insanitary conditions, especially on vessels employed in trading slaves. The voyage from Manila to Acapulco was inherently injurious to health. It commonly involved four months at sea, without renewal of supplies, and could last up to eight months in adverse conditions. The ships passed through menacingly cold and horribly torrid latitudes. They were reservoirs of infection. Depending on the size of the flotilla, between 300 and 600 souls made the journey each year that sailings took place: at least 100 could expect to die en route. Up to 150 deaths was not abnormal. On a notorious voyage in 1657, an epidemic of some pustulent disease carried off the entire personnel – 450 people – of one vessel, and half the other's complement of 400.

Scurvy was an enemy at least as merciless as pirates and almost as hard to counter as storms. Lassitude, chest pains and short breath were early symptoms, followed by swollen, livid limbs; hypersensitivity to touch and to pain; retracted, putrid gums and loose teeth – these ominous afflictions 'continuously increasing' in the victims, as a mid-eighteenth-century promoter of exploration, Henry Ellis, reported, 'till at length Death carried them off, either by a flux or a dropsy'.[30] On voyages of more than a couple of months, shortage of vitamin C was bound to affect significant numbers of crew. Spain's seamen, however, had the advantage of access to many ports and harbours in which other nations' ships were interlopers and whose efforts to gather fresh supplies were fraught with hazard. Spanish physicians in the New World, moreover, had privileged opportunities to observe scurvy and could borrow from the pharmacopoeia of ethnobotany. In the 1560s the Franciscan Fray Juan de Torquemada vividly described the horror of treating men in agony, who could not bear to be touched or clothed, and who, unable to chew, wasted for want of solid food. He recommended a native remedy: a couple of ingestions of wild pineapple, 'and God gave this fruit such virtue that it reverses the swelling of the gums and makes them grip the teeth and cleans them, and expels all the putrescence and pus from the gums'. As early as 1569, Sebastián Vizcaino – who reconnoitred much of the Californian coast – noted that on transpacific voyages 'there was no medicine, or any human cure against this disease; or if there was such a cure it was fresh food alone and plenty of it.'[31]

The shipboard day was rigorous and its consolations few. Among those available elsewhere, gambling was forbidden (though it is doubtful whether the prohibition was observed other than by zealots who would have abstained in any case). Fishing was practised, of course, but usually profitlessly. Sodomy was punishable by death.[32] Apart from music-making and conversation, the only other diversion was religious devotion, punctuated by miserable meals. As the routines of shipboard life varied little in the age of sail, the most graphic account of an ocean crossing – by Eugenio de Salazar, whom we have already cited – can serve to evoke virtually the entire colonial period.

Salazar described his first sensations aboard ship. 'I have set sail for my sins. They stuck us in a cabin three hands high and five across, where, when we felt the force of the waves, our stomachs so sickened that we all – fathers and son, old and young – turned all sorts of different colours.' Supplies were piled among the passengers:

> There's so much rigging and so many ropes coiled here and there that we look like a lot of trussed hens and capons on the way to market wrapped in netting. There are trees in this city – not the sort that exude healthful resins and aromatic oils, but rather mucky pitch and reeking tallow.

Astonishingly, the pilot seemed imperturbable, 'seated with great authority on his bench. He presumes, like Neptune, to command the sea and her waves. I have never seen a scoundrel so deserving of his gains as these sailors are.'[33]

The passage of time was marked not by the modern practice of sounding bells but by the lilting of boys. It was one boy's work to mind the sand-clock that measured time in 'glasses' – each of a half-hour's length. Including spares, each ship would carry several of these, for the careful measurement of time was essential to computing the speed of the vessel and therefore the accuracy of navigation. A traditional lilt announced each turn of the clock. After the first half hour of every watch, for instance, the cry rang out:

> One glass has gone.
> Another's a-filling.
> More sand shall run
> If God is willing.
> To my God let us pray
> To make safe our way
> And His Mother, our Lady, who prays for us all
> To save us from tempest and threatening squall.

During the night the boy would exchange calls with the members of the watch to make sure all were alert. At the seventh turn of the glass, the boy in charge sang out a warning to the next watch to be ready to change at the next turn. After eight glasses, or four hours as in modern practice, he called, '¡*Al cuarto, al cuarto, señores marineros!* On deck, on deck, gentlemen, mariners of goodwill, on deck, quickly on deck, all those of Mr pilot's watch, for it's time now. Wake up! Wake up! Wake up!' Important members of the watch, whose vigilance was vital to the safety of the ship, including the boy at the glass, would rotate roles at intervals during the four hours' turn of duty. There were 'good morning' and 'goodnight' lilts, the first at daybreak, the second at the lighting of the ship's lantern, each accompanied by an appropriate prayer:

> Blessed be the light so good.
> And blessed be the Holy Rood,
> And blest
> the Lord of verity,
> And the Holy Trinity,
> Blessed be our souls – God save them –
> And blessed be the God Who gave them.

Blessed be the light of day,
And God Who with it lights our way,
greeted the dawn.

Night was heralded with a more general hope for a safe voyage,
with a reassuring word of report:

The watch is set.
The glass runs yet,
Safe on the seas,
If God decrees.[34]

The changes of watch, the lilting of the boys, made shipboard life
reassuringly conformable to predictable rhythms. The other great
fixed points were the daily common meal and the services of prayer.
Meals intervened without bringing much relief from tedium. Only a
small fire was ever lit in the galley because of the terrible incendiary
risk. Hot food was rarely served except to the sick. Salazar, who was a
master of lugubrious humour, described table service for the shipboard
elite, seated at a dingy cloth dotted with 'little piles of decayed biscuit'
and resembling 'a field of stubble scattered with mounds of manure'.
A grummet announced the meal with yet another lilt:

Table! Table! Captain, Sir, and Master and good company!
Table laid, dishes made!
Water as usual for Captain, Sir, and Master and good company!
Long live the King of Spain
By land and on the main!
He who offers him war,
May he have his head no more!
Who does not say, 'Amen,'
May he never drink again!
To table, with good speed!
Who comes not will not feed.[35]

The lower officers, including the gunnery officer – so often the
despised service – sat with the common seamen on the floor, paring
bones 'as if they had studied anatomy in Guadalupe or Valencia',
while the ship's notary and the captains of the armed guards stood

by, the notary and the captains at his portable desk, checking each other's accounts and countersigning them in their ledgers.

The diet was humdrum. Salazar's account of mealtime conversation – composed entirely of wistful exchanges about the fruits and vegetables one missed at home – becomes poignantly intelligible against the menu of dried and salted protein sources:

> One man says, 'Oh, is there no one who might have a bunch of white grapes from Guadalajara?' Another, 'Is there anyone here who has a plateful of cherries of Illescas?' Another, 'I could just do with a few turnips from Somo Sierra.' Another, 'A stick of chicory for me and an artichoke top from Medina del Campo.' And they all belch up their longings and disgruntlement over things they can't have in the place they're in. And if you want a drink in the midst of the sea, you can die of thirst, for they'll serve you your water by the ounce, as in an apothecary's shop, when you are full of dried beef and salt food. For my lady the sea will not suffer nor save meats nor fish that are not dressed in her salt. And everything else one eats is decayed and stinking like the blackamoor's boots.[36]

For most shipmates, prayer was probably a more welcome interlude on sea than on land. The sea in the age of sail was peculiarly God's medium, where life was precarious and contingent – so it seemed – on divine mercy. Mass could not be said aboard ship: regulations strictly forbade it, on the grounds that the rolling and pitching of the ship might cause the Sacrament to fall or even to pitch overboard. There was no regular provision for priests on board. As Salazar said, the ship's master was 'a priestling' and the grummet 'a little acolyte'. The Spanish Atlantic fleet held firmly to the belief that God preferred praise out of the mouths of babes and sucklings. So the ships' boys raised the voice of innocence aloft. The Salve and Ave Maria, sung at the foot of the mainmast, bracketed the day at dawn and nightfall. The Marian emphasis of all the services – especially on ordinary days, when no Credo was sung – is understandable. Stella Maris was, for sailors, the most heartfelt of our Lady's advocations, and Marian devotion was a meeting-place of the traditional, propitiatory religion of seamen with one of the great universal cults of the Church. Morning service followed the daybreak lilt and consisted of the Pater Noster and another Salve.

On Salazar's ship, a single boy rendered them without congregational participation. A lilt to bid good morning followed, before the company dispersed to the duties of the day. The evening office was more elaborate. On ordinary days the ritual began when a boy brought the newly lighted lantern on deck, singing his evening lilt: 'Amen and God give us good night. May the ship make a good passage and have a safe voyage, Captain, Sir, Master, and all the company.' Two grummets then chanted the Ave Maria, perhaps with reprises of the Pater Noster and the Salve.

On the eve of a feast day or of a Sunday, a table was set with candles and images – perhaps a triptych or travelling altarpiece – and the ship's master cried in a loud voice, 'Are all present?' The men responded, 'God be with us.' The master then chanted, 'A Salve let us say, to speed us on our way. A Salve let us sing: a good voyage may it bring.' After the Salve and the Litany of our Lady, the master might introduce the Credo by saying, 'Let us all profess our creed to the honour and worship of the Blessed Apostles, that they may pray for us to the Lord Jesus Christ to grant us a good voyage.' A boy would announce the Ave by chanting, 'Let us say our Ave – 'Hail!' – For the ship and all who in her sail,' with the other lads responding, 'Blessed may she be.' The service ended with the usual evening lilt. For the Slave and the Litany, all voices would unite in one thunderous cacophony, 'a tempest of hurricanes of music' and 'a babble of braying', as Salazar said of the crooning of the sailors.

Performance in unison occurred in a secular setting whenever a capstan needed turning, to raise the anchor, or some other activity might benefit from being set to the rhythm of a shanty. Salazar heard shanties that assumed that every enemy, of whatever provenance, was a Moor. On the haul of the rope, the men were exhorted to 'maintain the faith' and to 'confound and kill . . . Muslims, pagans, and Saracens.' On the slack they would shout a cry of assent:

Oh they deny – the Holy Faith,
Oh Holy Faith – the Roman faith!
Oh from Rome – does mercy flood,
Oh from Peter – great and good.

If the anchor cable was long, or a sail took too long to hoist, these exchanges could be considerably protracted, growing more secular in tone and content as time wore on and improvisation grew more desperate. By the end of the shanty, thoughts of faith and war might yield to the seamen's more worldly concerns, like wind and sun, love and youth:

> From the east – the sun arose.
> In the west – the sunset glows.
> Hey, my girl – may love last long!
> Rejoice, my lad, while you are young.[37]

And so the shanties proceeded, with increasingly ribald, wild paganism, set to the quasi-liturgical alternation of versicle and response.[38]

Retrospect and Prospect

The fragility of the maritime communications system of Spain's global monarchy seems astonishing. In some ways, the empire survived by adjusting to the imperfections of sea lanes confined by winds and currents, battered by storms, and ravaged by rivals and pirates. Control of remote peripheries could never be achieved by sending messages across thousands of miles of sea: the monarchy relied rather on frequent changes of administrative personnel and on retrospective punishment of abuses. Yet messages, however ineffective at their points of destination, continued to be exchanged. Though the gold and silver of the Indies could not sustain empire unaided, or even pay for most of its costs, except by bolstering the monarchy's credit,[39] shipments continued to reach Spain. Until the end of the colonial period in mainland America, improvements in shipping were slowly, almost painfully incremental; frail wooden vessels continued to flow like corpuscles in the bloodstream of the empire. Only in the last two generations did navigation make a leap forward, thanks to the perfection of longitude-finding and the consequent multiplication of reliable charts. Meanwhile, nonetheless, ships managed to elude reefs and rocks. Security at sea did not improve significantly until the establishment of the European diplomatic system at the Congress of Vienna, which kept peace – with few breakdowns – among the powers and facilitated co-operation against pirates. Yet danger and disaster never interrupted commerce for long. The trade of the Indies failed, in the early modern period, to generate economic benefits in line with Marxist theory or mercantilist expectations, but the trade did not stop. By the time industrialization revolutionized the exploitation of seaways with steam power and iron cladding, the Spanish Empire was a vestige of its former self. Sea lanes, of course, still held together what remained. Against the background of the industrialized empires that succeeded Spain's, the durability of the maritime scaffolding that Spain stretched across the oceans and erected around distant coasts seems more remarkable than its ultimate collapse.

3

MAKING WAYS
Landward Communications

Prepare ye the ways of the Lord. Make His paths straight.
(MATTHEW 3:3, MARK 1:3)

Highways, waterways and bridges turn disconnected areas into a
stable, renewable whole. In the European successor-states of the
Roman Empire, roads and bridges still evoke the Romans who trod
and crossed them. The landscapes of formerly Spanish America, too,
exhibit a common legacy and traces of similar ways of organizing space,
with towns and cities linked by major and minor roads and water-routes.
Even place names recur over and again. The urban grid is almost ubiquitous, from California to Patagonia. 'Spanish roads' are so called all
over the Americas. Colonial-era bridges are still widely in use.

Spaniards were not, of course, the only people involved in
conceiving and building the infrastructure of travel over land. Links
were products of diverse experience, knowledge and techniques, and
of European, Indigenous and African know-how and labour. They
joined places and cultures once inaccessibly remote from each other.
Surviving imperial public works constitute a vast collective monument
to cultural hybridity and interchange – sometimes forced, sometimes
free. They are evidence of the remarkable social cohesion that made
their construction possible and worthwhile. They represent an enduring
return on the human capital invested in creating them.

In December 1700, Philip V, the new Bourbon pretender to the
global monarchy, arrived in Irún, just across the border from his
French homeland, on his way to the Spanish capital. It took him 25
days to get to Madrid, albeit with pauses to enjoy bullfights (which
fascinated him), and endure Masses, Te Deums and frequent festivities

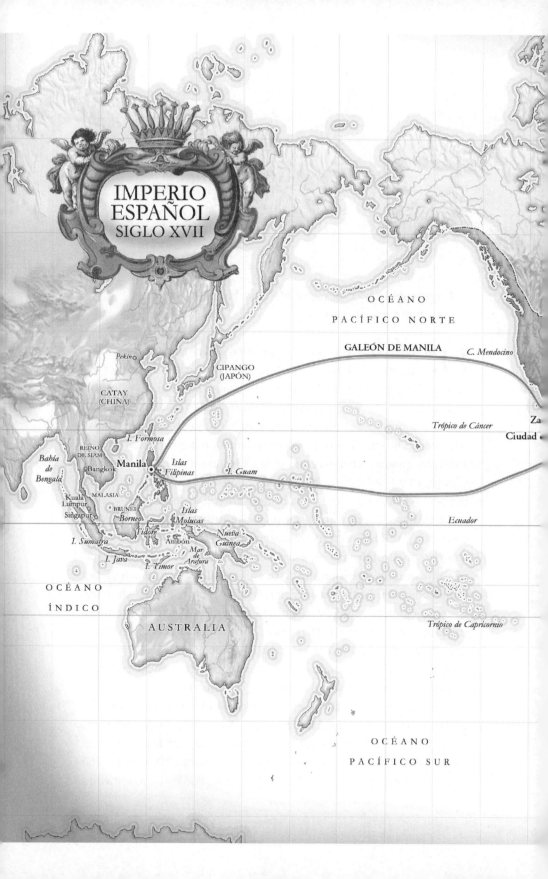

IMPERIO ESPAÑOL
SIGLO XVII

OCÉANO

PACÍFICO NORTE

GALEÓN DE MANILA

C. Mendocino

Pekín

CIPANGO
(JAPÓN)

CATAY
(CHINA)

I. Formosa

Trópico de Cáncer

Za

Ciudad

REINO
DE SIAM

Manila

Islas
Filipinas

I. Guam

Bahía
de
Bengala

Bangkok

Kuala
Lumpur

MALASIA

Singapur

BRUNEI

Borneo

Islas
Molucas

Tidore

Nueva
Guinea

Ecuador

I. Sumatra

Ambón

I. Java

Mar
de
Arafura

I. Timor

OCÉANO

ÍNDICO

AUSTRALIA

Trópico de Capricornio

OCÉANO

PACÍFICO SUR

Typical course of the Manila galleon, 18th century.

of thanksgiving and welcome. The following year, in September, a journey to Barcelona absorbed 23 days. On the way, he collected his thirteen-year-old cousin, Marie-Louise of Savoy – the intended bride with whom, three days later, he managed to consummate an unutterably painful marriage. The expedition included three hundred horses, with fourteen coaches and two litters to accommodate the king and, for his spouse, another twelve coaches, plus a state coach ornately carved and gilded, another litter, a sedan chair, and two four-horse coaches with velvet trim.[1]

Speeds improved a little, but only a little, over the following century or so. In about 1775, ten and a half days was the normal projected duration of a coach journey between Madrid and Seville. But in a sudden spurt of progress, by about 1850, a little over two days sufficed in a stagecoach – at the very moment when mechanical traction was beginning to replace animal muscle-power, with revolutionary effect on the way people understood distance. [2] The reduction over a relatively short span – only three generations – seems extraordinary. Changes in the way traffic was organized was in part responsible, together with improvements in road building. As we review the internal communications systems of Spanish America – first the environmental background, then the Indigenous legacy and legal framework, then, one by one, the various regional networks, before turning to particular routes – the accelerating chronology of road travel is worth bearing in mind. The eighteenth-century New World experienced even more rapid change, even more investment, with even greater results, than metropolitan Spain.

Nature and Distance in Theory and Practice

Nature has many ways of impeding humans: earthquakes, hurricanes, volcanic eruptions, landslides, floods, catastrophic weather, blights, plagues. But the tyranny of distance was one of the most effective and obstructive afflictions she wielded in pre-industrial times. Humans have expended more ingenuity on overcoming it than on any other challenge, save that of devising means of killing each other.

In the Western world, from classical antiquity onwards, philosophers have debated the subject of human stewardship or lordship over the natural world; today anthropogenically induced harm to the environment is a major topic. But the more conspicuous reality has always been that of how limited and ill-planned human interventions are. Most of the effects visible in the environment resemble random scars, without any of the coherence for which we look to the laws of nature or the singularity of a divine mind.[3] Spanish America exhibited these truths to a marked degree.

From the late fifteenth century, discoveries beyond the oceans bewildered European minds, presenting a kind of monstrous mix that was half earthly Paradise, half mortal peril. It made sense for Spaniards, in their efforts to master it, to look back to ancient Rome. In the 1520s Alonso de Castrillo recalled that in 'winning all the world' the Romans took all comers under their protection. In his alluring formula, the protective wing was empire's essential organ, and linkage to Rome's influence and identity justified and magnified imperial power. The grant of citizenship to all, irrespective of culture or origin, was a guarantee of benignity. Whoever came in search of refuge and of a place to live, so Castrillo thought, was unhesitatingly welcome.[4]

In 1755 Tomás Manuel Fernández de Mesa y Moreno, a Valencian jurist, praised the Romans, 'whom we are going to imitate', as masters of materials and quantities.[5] Spanish conceptions of empire were crafted from the model of Romanization – just as the emphasis on infrastructure was imitated from the Roman example – and supplemented with those of the Christianization of sometime barbarians and of the Reconquest of Iberia from the Moors, of which the Spanish conquests in America seemed, to some observers, a sort of prolongation.

These models encouraged Spaniards to begin to think of the vast distances their empire spanned as relative and therefore perhaps manageable, rather than absolutely and defiantly indomitable. By opening or improving communications they bade for permanence in occupation and asserted the power of structuring space, disciplining distance. In 1589, in his 'Elegy for Famous Men of the Indies', the soldier-adventurer-turned-cleric Juan de Castellanos glossed in verse the deeds of conquistadores who crossed banks and beachheads, clove paths and puzzled over trails. In his work, Spaniards and natives wander 'peopling new settlements', sometimes without hitting a trail, sometimes 'marching along the road', sometimes crossing 'trackless mountains'.[6] For the historian of Venezuela José Oviedo y Baños, distance was 'delightful to contemplate'.[7]

Distance was an element in conflicts between conquistadores and the crown. Officials and bureaucrats consistently questioned the value of conquistadores' deeds, accusing them – not always justly – of exaggerating their merits, and arrogating unearned honours and rewards. Clerics were among the most hostile and impassioned critics – especially, of course, Bartolomé de las Casas, the royally appointed defender of Indigenous rights, whose fulminations blackened the 'Black Legend' of Spanish cruelty and avarice. Juan Ponce de León, conquistador and governor of Hispaniola, explained the relevance of distance: 'since the ways are so long', he claimed to be unable to 'send explanations' sufficient to rebut all the accusations he faced.[8] After returning home to present his defence and achieving exoneration, he set off for Florida, allegedly in search of the Fountain of Youth, ending up dead.

Communications, moreover, figured in the debate over the legitimacy of the Spanish presence in America, since rights of access to forums and markets were deemed 'natural' or what we might now call 'human rights': it was therefore valid to assert them, by force if necessary. Even radical friars agreed that much.

From what one might call a theo-political perspective, the construction of routes of communication and networks of exchange contributed to the legitimation of empire. In his account of how commerce originated in the remote past, Fray Tomás de Mercado explained that property, human needfulness and the obligation to distribute, share and circulate goods across 'this vale of tears' were all inevitable consequences of original sin: 'Necessity', he remarked, 'knows no law. Neither does it evince patience or restraint. When one man came to want what another had, they began to trade rather than resort to deprivation or despoliation.'[9]

When the world began, in the version of Fray Francisco de Vitoria, who was at once the Spanish monarch's most judicious critic and most subtle apologist in the sixteenth century, all property was held in common. Men's rights to visit each other and to be in touch were unaffected by the inequalities subsequently imposed. Spaniards therefore had a natural right, indisputable by Christian, pagan or infidel, to migrate, settle and trade in peace. Hugo Grotius endorsed these views in his *Mare liberum* of 1609.[10] Vitoria extended the right to be in touch, the *ius communicationis*, into a right of domicile for new arrivals in a community, with the same duties and privileges as prior residents. His argument anticipated future notions of universal citizenship, but it was hard to reconcile with the policy Spain adopted in the New World and embodied in its laws: to preserve Indigenous peoples from grievances inflicted at colonists' hands by keeping separate 'republics' of indios and Spaniards respectively in their proper spheres. Las Casas's followers feared that contact with European sinfulness would inevitably corrupt native innocence of soul and body. From the early sixteenth century, the plan to keep Spaniards and indios apart proved impossible: native elites were an inseparable part of the system of government; intermarriage was the ineradicable foundation of a governable multi-racial society; people of Indigenous, European and African origin rapidly coalesced in growing cities; and the formation of mixed-race communities transformed or displaced formerly existing social, ethnic and legal categories. Most Spaniards lived in the midst of servants and slaves of African or Indigenous origin.[11] There could be no separation among people who depended on each other for peace, patronage, work, love and sustainable life. Cities, in these circumstances, did more than impart civil and communal feelings to those who dwelt in them. By radiating roads and routes, they extended common sentiments of mutual belonging across hinterlands, helping to turn into realities the sketchy realms and provinces rulers marked on maps. If such were not the case, as Alonso de Castrillo remarked, and human contact generated misery or poverty, people would not seek each other's company and would recoil from cities.[12] Non-communication was literally barbarous.

The history of technology is full of Promethean tales that exalt heroic pioneers and inventors, while sidelining the force of circumstances and the roles of plagiarism, cheating, fortune and fair exchange. But engineers do tend to have a vital personal quality: curiosity. In Spanish America it served as a kind of adaptive mechanism, multiplying the value of human capital. Attempts simply to transfer European methods across the ocean did not survive the first few months of the Spanish presence. Unfamiliar environmental conditions placed new demands on Spaniards' experience. Military engineers, with backgrounds in battle, and veterans of Old World public works were more successful than theorists and academics who were unused to interaction with local conditions and traditions.

This was especially so in two respects. First, an open attitude was vital in selecting building materials and applying native techniques. Second, in planning, surveying, designing and mapping new projects, innovators had to adjust their visions to new surroundings: the result was creative synthesis.[13] Nature in the New World came to be known, understood and represented by virtue of the ways in which it was different from Europe. It defied prejudices and precedents formed in the Old World.[14] The Count of Floridablanca, who headed the Spanish government in the late eighteenth century, lost his temper when he read reports of commissioners' remapping of the Amazonian frontiers that he had laboriously negotiated with Portugal: it turned out that floods, erosion and landslides had changed the topography. In Colombia towards the end of the following century the engineer Aníbal Galindo sadly noted in *Recuerdos históricos*, with mingled resignation and fatalism, that 'the normal state of communications between Bogotá and the River Magdalena is normally abnormal. Vessels cannot reach Honda unless it rains. If it rains, communications by land become impassable and transport is delayed. To avoid delay, drought is necessary. And in case of drought, steamboats cannot get upriver.'[15] The land defied logic in paradoxes that frustrated Spaniards' expectations.

The saga of Spanish route-making started on water rather than land. In the first decades of the sixteenth century, conquistadores followed mixed itineraries that linked coastal landing places and would lead, in their fondest aspirations, towards Asia and the lands of spices. Soon, however, transit on horseback or by pack mule – animals alien to the design and nature of indigenous trails and roads, which were made for human load-bearers or, in the Andean region, temperamentally recalcitrant llamas – had a transforming effect on the volume, value, practices and concepts of trade.[16]

Wheeled vehicles were harder to integrate into the transport system: flatlands were rare; draught animals exotic and costly. Much of the story of this chapter is of laborious struggles to ease fearsome slopes, widen paths, skirt morasses and shore up dangerous roadways to extend vehicular access. New Spain's first builder of wagons was Fray Sebastián de Aparicio, who was born in Orense in Galicia in 1502 and died in Puebla de los Ángeles in 1600. Having settled in that city in 1533, he devoted his life to the tracing of a wagon-adapted roadway over 600 kilometres (375 mi.) towards Veracruz in the south and Zacatecas in the north. It became a *camino real*, vital for the transportation of silver from the mines to the sea. By the end of the eighteenth century extensions had elongated the road to some 3,000 kilometres (1,865 mi.), across Nueva Vizcaya, Sonora, Coahuila, Texas and New Mexico to Santa Fe. Two major arteries connected Monterrey and San

Luis Potosí. Aparicio joined the Franciscans at the advanced age of 73 years but continued his work as a wagoner, teaching indios how to make wheels and train oxen. In an image made to promote the cause of his sanctification, the amiable friar appears standing, unshod, beside a cart drawn by a yoke of oxen, with a goad in his hand, in a well-tilled, harmonious landscape, though Aparicio does not seem to have invented anything: the same cart – with two wheels of eight spokes aligned at angles of 45 degrees – appears in depictions as early as the eighth century BC. Another image features his miraculous intervention in favour of a threatened carter: 'Cart and oxen tumble from the bridge into the river. Blessed Aparicio invokes the apostle St James. Disaster is averted.'[17] As we shall see, it was only in the pampa that wagons ever really dominated long-range communications.

The Indigenous Legacy

When Spaniards began to forge a network of routes that put all their territories in mutual contact, they did so by enhancing, modifying and supplementing existing infrastructure. The Aztec and Inca empires were not alone in establishing long-range pre-colonial itineraries. Routes of war and exchange by land and water connected peoples in the Caribbean and in North America; even where economic surpluses were small and trade limited. Communities swapped manpower, captives, women, symbolic and ritual objects and proto-monetary items of mother of pearl, say, shells, and amulets of gold.[18]

In Indigenous land routes were designed for traffic on foot. Draught animals were unavailable. Only llamas – eccentric and obstinate – served as pack animals, and only in the Andean region, where the environment seemed hostile to wheels and to increased loads, owing to steep gradients, broken contours, precipitate stepways and abrupt changes of level. Roads were commonly between 1 and 3 metres (3 and 10 ft) wide. Slopes frequently featured thousands of stairs carved by native labourers which were impassable for horses or mules.[19]

In Mesoamerica the noteworthy roads that survived in Maya country were often in disrepair by the time the Spaniards arrived. Typically they were 4.5 metres (14½ ft) wide, raised above grade by between 60 and 250 centimetres (23½–98 in.), built of rubble to facilitate drainage, and levelled with heavy cylindrical rollers of stone; but the technology of rollers was never applied to vehicles. In their region, across the valley of Mexico, the Aztecs built a series of flat-topped barriers, which served as roads but were chiefly designed to block flooding.

In the arid coastal regions of the Andean South, the Mochica and Chimú protected the roads with which they connected cultivable riverbanks by building 'walls made of metre-high blocks of adobe, cemented with mud to keep windblown sand away'.[20] Inca roads, especially between the major centres of Quito and Cuzco, typically covered steep gradients with paved surfaces over long, straight ramps and supports of large, dry-stone masonry. The builders favoured high altitudes, avoiding deep valleys with unreliable rivers, which they crossed with rope bridges.

Being characteristically practical and sensible, Spanish observers admired Andean peoples' work. Chroniclers of the colonial era who recorded data from pre-colonial times, from Pedro Cieza de León onwards, were right to see the perfection of Inca roadworks as expressions of the power of the state: 'This Inca road is as impressive as Hannibal's conquest of the Alps and the sight of it inspires admiration.'[21] With construction in stone, and ample bulwarks for protection against precipices and ravines without cement, in places, the breadth would accommodate six horsemen abreast. Runners could get messages over the 470 leagues from Quito to Cuzco in only eight days. The coastal road, with a width of 7.3 metres (24 ft), against the 6-metre (20 ft) span of the breadth of the high road, seemed in places like 'a broad street'. The way stations and warehouses were still making a forceful impression on the chronicler Bernabé Cobo in 1563: 'They functioned like our inns or taverns, save that they were no one's property, but were communal works and the town or province had the responsibility of preserving them in perfect condition and cleanliness and supplying them with staff.'[22] He denounced instances of neglect that left surfaces worn, stones broken and storerooms abandoned or eroded.

Expeditionaries under the conquistador Gonzalo Jiménez de Quesada marvelled, as they marched into New Granada in 1537, at a 'bridge woven from the vines that dangle from the tall trees. Juan Rodríguez Gil was bold enough to climb up and examine the knots. They seemed well tied; so, with great caution, testing them as he went, he made his way, little by little across the ravine.'[23] From the mid-sixteenth century, storehouses appeared at fords and crossings, where tolls and taxes were collected and transport hired.

Although rope bridges of Indigenous construction fascinated observers, and remained in service for centuries, Spaniards only really felt at home with those made of stone. It was hard or impossible, moreover, to adapt such routes for mule trains, with loads heavier than llamas could manage, much less for heavy wagons.

Ruling the Road:
The *Camino Real*

The laws of the road in America broadly followed those in Spain. The main medieval code, the *Partidas* of Alfonso x 'the Wise', ordered town authorities to maintain roads and bridges at their own expense. 'It is the king's duty to order bridges and roads to be built, and to have bad terrain levelled . . . It is an adornment and ennoblement of the realm to maintain bridges and roads so that they neither decay nor deteriorate.'[24] In 1354 the protection of livestock and of the drovers' trails became a royal responsibility. In 1487 taxes on the transportation of such products as bread, wine and oil were assigned to bridge and road construction and for the widening and strengthening of cart tracks, as wagons were getting bigger, with iron-hooped wheels that required a firmer footing.[25] Carters' privileges kept potentially interfering nobles at bay. The policy of improving Spain's network of communication never wavered. A total of 240 new bridges appeared in Castile from 1580 to 1610, many of which had starlings – perforated pilings around the arched supports – to let water, as recorded in the published gazetteers of routes between cities and towns. Philip II was obsessed with road building in pursuit of an infrastructure worthy of his court, capital and crown. [26] In Madrid the growth in average occupancy of a dwelling from five persons in 1563 to twelve in 1597 suggests how the need for new infrastructure must have increased as a result of the king's adoption of that city as a courtly centre. America, as the monarch well knew, demanded even more effort.

Although the Spanish New World was officially an extension of the kingdom of Castile, and Castilian law applied there, in practice vast amounts of new rules and regulations were required, especially at local and municipal levels. Some features of the regime that governed road building remained constant: decentralized, for instance, and responsive to initiatives from privileged individuals or corporations, and to chance, chaos, passing circumstances. The monarch received proposals that varied from commonsensical to crazy. Some attracted royal rewards and privileges, as roads were thought of as axes of economic development and vertebrae of the political order. In the *Recopilación de leyes de los reinos de Indias* of 1681, the definitive compilation of Spanish laws for overseas territories, the heading 'Public Highways' (*caminos públicos*) covers dispositions concerning, inter alia, pasture, woodland, waterways, orchards and vineyards.[27] The key idea, as in the Roman Empire, was that roads forge realms.

The designation of a road as 'royal' expressed a commitment to permanent colonization, and signified stability. Ordinances of 1573, which defined the drive to urbanize, stressed the importance of highway construction, insisting that new settlements have 'good outlets by water and land to good highways and navigable routes, easy of access and adapted for commerce, government and defence', while conquistadores whose responsibilities on dangerous frontiers won them appointments as *adelantados* were enjoined to 'provide common spaces, watering places, highways and pathways for newly established townships'.[28] Nonetheless, after the initial frustrations associated with the ill-regulated governance of Columbus and his heirs, the crown followed a consistent if delicately balanced policy of devolving risk and cost, while maintaining control. The watchwords were *laissez-aller* and *laissez-faire*, as long as their authorized representatives 'continued to win kingdoms and provinces for them'.[29] A regulation decreed by the crown on 16 August 1563,[30] ordering 'bridges and highways to be built and maintained at the expense of those whom they benefit', remained in force in independent Mexico well into the nineteenth century.[31] Such regulations survived the Enlightenment because they expressed the philosophes' principle that public works served human happiness: thus the municipal ordinances of 1803, which are properly thought of as perfectly expressing Spanish policy and Enlightened principles, stress street cleaning, hygiene generally, well-ordered housing and aesthetically improved architecture for churches and public buildings as means of enhancing citizens' lives. Convenient, safe bridges and roads formed part of the same project.

The defining features of a *camino real*, as laid down two and a half centuries earlier, required that it be 12 yards (11 metres) wide, or at least 8 yards (7.3 metres) within the precincts of a town, mine or commercial establishment. In 1540 some hundred mule trains were on the road between Mexico City and Veracruz at any one time.[32] This was the road that Alexander von Humboldt, as sagacious as ever when he toured New Spain in 1801, called the 'road to Europe' as against the route from the capital to Acapulco, which was 'the road to Asia'. Arteries to north and south joined the transcontinental highway, as far as Santa Fe in New Mexico, and Guatemala via Chiapas.

The equivalent *camino real* in South America went 1,000 leagues from Lima to Caracas, across Nueva Granada. The creole soldier and naturalist from Panama Miguel de Santisteban travelled along it between 1740 and 1742, during the War of Jenkins' Ear – so-called after the incident that provoked it, when a Spanish coastguard allegedly sliced the organ from an intruding Englishman's head. After reaching Guayaquil by sea from Lima, Santisteban continued his journey by land via Bogotá and Mompós on the banks of the Magdalena and back, and thence again to La Guaira, the port of Caracas, arriving on 20 April 1742, after nearly three years of travel. Santisteban went on to other labours, studying quinine, supervising the mint and undertaking an official enquiry, such as every functionary in the Spanish monarchy had to endure at the completion of a term of office, into the conduct of Viceroy Solís; but the record of his adventures on the *camino real* constitutes a valuable achievement, as well as capturing his taste for travel.

The first stretches by sea to Guayaquil and a rafting expedition to Yaguachi comprised 280 leagues and took about a month. A further 365 leagues took Santisteban to Honda, a landing-stage along the Magdalena, via Riobamba, Quito, Pasto and Popayán. In Honda, he and his fellow travellers took an eighteen-paddle canoe to Mompós, not far from Cartagena, in nine days. The return route to Honda took twenty days against the current. The next phase, the ascent to Bogotá, lasted from 26 May to 7 June 1741. Santisteban did not make it to Caracas until 21 September owing to travails, intrusions and his own insatiable curiosity, which led him to undertake a detour of 283 leagues through Tunja, Pamplona, Mérida and El Tocuyo. The voyagers arose with the dawn and journeyed until noon, when they lunched, justifying the subsequent siesta on the grounds that the mules needed a rest.

The next stage lasted until sunset without ever knowing whether they would spend the night in an inn or in some nearby private house, such as accounted for 42 of the 175 dwellings they visited, or in the tents they carried in case of need. There were days when they longed for downpours to cease, others when the heat of noon was nearly intolerable. Opportunities to hear Mass and obligations to households where hospitality was provided caused interruptions and delays. Nights were spent in chatting, smoking, eating and playing cards. Menus might feature milk, fowl, beef or goat, rice and fish. They accounted it a banquet one night when they ate eggs, fruit, chilli stew, 'jellies from Quito, hams and hocks from Lacatunga, floury cakes from Ambato, preserved meats, quinoa, oil cakes and rice'.[33]

At each new departure, while one of the expeditionaries accompanied the mules and the baggage, others went ahead with guides and scouts. If the road seemed impassable, machete-wielders were called in to ease the path. Native guides saw the party across the rivers, while the muleteers took care that the animals, who bore fifty loads of two quintals – about 46 kilograms (over 100 lb) – suffered no mishap. Pasture and water had to be found for the mules, whether pack animals or mounts. News of their progress preceded the column. Passage from Barquisimeto to Caracas cost extra because travellers known to come from Peru were notoriously flush. The laws of supply and demand could be provided for, but hazards along the roads were often unforeseeable. To cross the rope bridge at Estanques, near Mérida in Yucatán, cost the travellers what, to Santisteban, seemed an unconscionable peso per mule load. Travellers were at the mercy of need and greed, diverted into the hands of corrupt storekeepers, or extorted for extemporized and fictitious tolls and charges.

Yet the law was explicit: guides were supposed to favour the most direct and commodious routes. As early as 1568 Philip II ordered viceroys and governors to prevent 'interested parties from unnecessarily detaining travellers overnight and for half the following day in their taverns and stores' because the king wished 'no impediment to the freedom of passage by any route of the traveller's choice'. Two centuries later, in 1796, muleteers on the Mexico–Veracruz road complained at an attempt to re-route the *camino* via Córdoba and Orizaba, instead of via Perote. According to their petition, it was a manoeuvre to impose in perpetuity 'the wickedness of exacting the tax we pay for the upkeep of boats in royal service, for we cannot believe that those who solicit the protection of Your Majesty, whom God preserve, will be dismissed without heed to their just requests'.[34]

Highways in New Spain

In contrast with Francisco Pizarro's decision to found a coastal capital at Lima in 1535, Hernán Cortés in Mexico opted to establish the capital on the site of the Aztec centre of Tenochtitlán. High in the central uplands, at 2,250 metres (7,380 ft), the city was the middle of the mesh of routes that covered the viceroyalty of New Spain. At the centre of the routes that bore commerce from Veracruz on the Atlantic and Acapulco on the Pacific, Mexico presided over two oceans. The eastward road went straight for 80 leagues through Puebla and Jalapa. Towards the west, the way led through Chilpancingo. The southern artery, bound for Guatemala, went through Oaxaca; northwards, the road headed for Santa Fe across Durango, with branches off to San Luis Potosí, Monterrey, Guadalajara and Valladolid. Unlike in the vast lands of South America, there were few big rivers and little need or opportunity for routes that combined road and river.

Veracruz was the mouth of the region, swallowing and disgorging the commerce of the Atlantic. From 1564, along with Nombre de Dios in Panama, Cartagena de Indias and Havana, it was a vital link in the great transatlantic axis of empire. On arrival, passengers would hasten to Jalapa to escape the insalubrious climate and take a road through the hinterland that the conquistadores condemned as steep and broken through narrow defiles. But the need to provide for mule trains impelled successive viceroys to pave the way and promote inns and stores at suitable intervals. In 1673 the Carmelite visitor Fray Isidoro de la Asunción took a month to complete the journey, making stops in Córdoba, Orizaba, Puebla and various indio villages. Inns provided some alleviation. The Capuchin friar Francisco de Ajofrín, who was in Mexico from 1763 to 1766, collecting alms for the mission in Tibet, copied into his diary a lavish recommendation that he found scrawled on a tavern wall. You got, it seems, what you paid for, if you paid enough:

> Bread and chicken, finest mutton,
> Wine, liquor, cheese fit for a glutton,
> All are here for him who comes
> Well equipped with ready sums.
> Well seasoned stews, good straw and hay
> For beasts and boys of masters who pay

And pulque, soup, tortillas, beer?
Yes sir, no trouble. We have them here.[35]

Improvements continued to be sought. Towards the end of the eighteenth century the viceroyalty had an impressive road network, encompassing 27,325 kilometres (16,980 mi.), of which 19,720 (12,255 mi.) were traversable only on foot or by equine traffic, while 7,605 (4,725 mi.) were suitable for wheeled vehicles.[36] In 1804, despite reservations at court, in Veracruz the Chamber of Commerce, the merchants' organization, began work on improving the road to Jalapa, adding, for travellers' reassurance and admiration, milestones with data on altitude and distance traversed. The road was 'broad and solid, with a very manageable gradient', according to Humboldt, who, with his usual enthusiasm, ventured comparisons with the roads through the Alps via Simplon and the Mont Cenis pass.

The details of the engineering were remarkable. The old road, narrow and paved with basalt, was replaced with a design by engineer Diego García Conde, who eliminated hostile slopes and widened the causeway, making it possible for carriages to carry passengers where only equines had served previously.[37] Patriotic fervour inspired José Donato de Austria, the treasurer of the merchants' exchange in Veracruz, to declare that 'our public roads present the intelligent traveller with the agreeable prospect of long highways as pleasurable as avenues, which advertise the beauties of the great cities to which they lead and adorn the majesty of the state.'[38] Journeys with mules were never less than fatiguing. Even at the beginning of the nineteenth century, mule trains from Veracruz to Mexico reckoned on 22 days, or 35 in the rainy season. The usual charge was 11 pesos per 138-kilogram (305 lb) load. By then, however, three-quarters of the journey could be made by coach or cart, leaving the rest to the mules and reducing the overall time required to only one week on average.

In the opposite direction, from Mexico City to Acapulco, there appears never to have been an indigenous road, though pre-colonial routes did lead south and west. Towards the end of the sixteenth century, Acapulco, with its good harbour and potentially good defensive location, was designated as the port of call for the Manila galleon or 'China ship', which crossed the Pacific once or twice a year. Because sailings were unreliable and the main markets seasonal, it was not worth paving the road, which had to negotiate rivers, ravines and dangerous slopes. The route led through Ejido, Mazatlán, Zumpango, Chimpancingo, Cuernavaca and other centres, on muleback and across rivers through fords or on rafts. At the end of the eighteenth century a traveller could do the whole journey in thirteen days, with luck. A stone bridge was flung across the Papagayo River, and a pulley-operated ferry across the Mezcala, replacing the former systems of flimsy pontoons, maintained by natives, which tended to break up when rains augmented the current. In the same period the roadway was elevated and protected with stone curbs, while gradients were modified and irregularities that impeded wheeled vehicles were cleared. The impression lingered, however, of a road that one Spanish migrant, despite his resolve to 'toil, suffer and have no time for vice', described as so cleft by 'endless ravines, deflected by rivers, and interrupted by mountains that one arrives more dead than alive'.[39]

From 1546, the discovery of silver in Zacatecas ('Mother-city of the North') demanded more roads and displaced the centre of gravity of agriculture and ranching northwards. Travellers sought silver along the *camino real*, at first from Mexico City through San Juan del Río to Aguascalientes, Fresnillo and Sombrerete. By 1555, the road was complete as far as Zacatecas, thanks to the lure of the mines. Later, after reaching Durango, it would continue via the mining settlements of El Parral, through Chihuahua and El Paso to Santa Fe. Branches that were often mere tracks led to scattered localities northeastwards in Texas: Saltillo, Monclova, Béjar. Over the 440 leagues from Mexico to Santa Fe, however, wheeled transport encountered few difficulties. Individuals in horse-drawn carriages vied for space with commercial mule trains that bore to the mining districts such essentials as iron, mercury for amalgamation, foodstuffs and textiles from factories in Querétaro and Puebla. They headed back south with silver, hides, tallow, wine from El Paso and flour. Mule trains of all sizes were run by indios or mestizos with the aid of dogs. In the early nineteenth century, some 60,000 mules made the journey annually, each with a load of about 130 kilograms (286 lb) – the potential booty of the foraging folk and bandits who prowled in the hope of picking off defenceless stragglers.

It was a long road; but in some ways the worst parts of it were nearest to the capital city, owing to the floods and the accompanying menace of losing animals, especially in winter. At the northern end of the route, the shortage of pasture was another potentially fatal threat. Constant demands for wheel-friendly roadways bore witness to the difficulties; everyone knew that with good highways 'the tiller will cast more seed, the breeder nourish more livestock, and the ʔrtisan augment his output so that consumers will have the best, cheapest and most abundant provision of all that is needful and useful to human lives.'[40] In Guadalajara, for instance, in the eighteenth century, the roads to Sinaloa, Aguascalientes and Colima were improved, the last in order to facilitate supplies of cotton. Metalling surfaces, bridging ravines, improving fords, organizing stagecoach lines and contracting expert engineers were constant expedients until independence came; eventually, the railway era made them superannuated. In 1804, just before his transfer to be viceroy of Peru, the local superintendent, José Fernando de Abascal, reported that almost 11,000 workers were employed on wagons and mule trains transporting cereals, wood and charcoal of Indigenous manufacture, together with salt and nuts from Colima on the Pacific coast to Zacatecas and Guadalajara, or ceramics from Tonalá and fish to Mexico City. Prospects of improving the roads especially favoured producers of flour, a vital product that internal transportation costs priced out of competitiveness with imports from the United States, New Orleans or Havana.

In, over and around the Isthmus

Towards the southern end of Mesoamerica, the Captaincy General of Guatemala served to consolidate the region and manage communications with Mexico, from where a road, mainly unfit for wheeled traffic, wound through Santiago Tlatelolco, Hueyotlipan, Zupango and Antequera in Oaxaca. From there, it led towards the Isthmus via the Quelenes mountains and the uplands of Chiapas to cross the Grijalva River and continue to Atitlán. There you had to cross the lake to reach Guatemala, from where various roads led to the Caribbean coast and the Gulf of Honduras to link up with the galleons of the Tierra Firme Fleet, or towards Granada, in Nicaragua, to meet seaborne traffic from the Pacific and the Peru fleet. These routes were so exposed to foreign and piratical attacks that the crown recommended recourse to Panama or Veracruz for the export of cacao, silver or indigo, however much it might cost in cash or trouble. Access to Nicaragua and Costa Rica was unserviceable through forests and swamps, by narrow and often unnegotiable tracks. There were always some merchants who favoured the route and despatched mule trains along it, but most preferred to embark their goods in Puerto de Caldera or Puerto Coronado for shipment to Panama.

Commercial decline on the eastern coast of the Isthmus inspired various road-building initiatives. One was a proposal to connect Guatemala City, newly relocated after a terrible earthquake in 1773 destroyed Antigua, or Santiago de los Caballeros, as it was then known, with the fortress of San Fernando de Omoa on the Caribbean coast of Honduras. When it was completed in 1779, the road reduced the distance for equine traffic, made Chaves accessible from Omoa on wheels, and linked Guatemala City to Puerto Caballos via Esquipulas, and Copán. A measure of the impact is that the post from Havana now took two months less than previously, when they went via Veracruz. In 1808 Guatemala's Chamber of Commerce was working on a scheme for a wheel-friendly road all the way to the Gulf, to carry cacao, indigo, coffee, sugar, tobacco and cotton. Doubts about the best destination on the coast, which oscillated between Izabal and Santo Tomás, remained unresolved, though recruitment of manpower was undeterred, with the promoters claiming that their project would be like a 'mobile penitentiary, in which all the idle, vagrant and delincuent elements in the kingdom can be enlisted for periods determined by the courts'.[41]

Panama was the great gateway where much long-range traffic in the region was bound. Vasco Núñez de Balboa's revelation of the Pacific in 1513 had inaugurated Panama's mythic status in geography: the 'focal point of the world', as the tourist pamphlets say. Six years later, Balboa's nemesis, Pedrarias Dávila, founded the capital city on the Pacific shore to be the terminus of transisthmian traffic from the Atlantic and, in due time, the launchpad for expeditions towards Peru, Chile and New Granada. From 1564 the city's strategic importance was crucial with the displacement of transatlantic traffic towards the ports of Cartagena, Nombre de Dios and, later, Portobelo. The tedium and dangers of the route through the Strait of Magellan (or via the fearsome Cape Horn from 1616 onwards) made improved ways of linking the commerce of the two oceans essential. Discovery of silver in Potosí in 1545 reinforced the need. Traders in Lima loaded their produce – silver above all – in the port of Callao; via Panama it crossed the Isthmus to the great fairs that lasted from ten to fifty days, where Spanish exports, including oil, wine, iron and gunpowder, could be acquired.

In those days the port of Nombre de Dios numbered about 150 straw hovels between forest and beach, with a shallow harbour and a defenceless roadstead. It was so unhealthy that pregnant women were sent to Venta de Cruces, about three days' journey away, not only to give birth but to raise their newborns there for six months.[42] Portobelo, to the west, was equally insalubrious, but its natural harbour was extraordinary, with a good bottom and defensible approach. Settlers and fairs moved there in 1598, requiring a new effort to improve the route to Panama and the Pacific. The direct route, 18 leagues long, was usable only in the dry season. During the rains – or, rather, the floods – from May to August, eight or nine hours were needed to the mouth of the River Chagres by sea before taking nineteen days to paddle flat-bottomed boats, each with 25 Black oarsmen, 18 leagues upriver to Venta de Cruces. There one resorted to portage for the final 5 leagues' journey to Panama.[43]

Travellers' accounts of the hardships include unforgettable evocations of the hostility of tropical extremes. In 1587, for instance, Celedón Favalis wrote to his father:

> I embarked at Nombre de Dios and a thousand times I was convinced that I was about to die. Once I was half drowned when more than twenty blacks combined to save me. My clothes rotted. God knows what bugs bit me. No human life is there – only monkeys of assorted sizes and innumerable caymans. Never in my life have I suffered so much tribulation.[44]

On the final stretch to Panama horses were useless: mules here were more serviceable and more expensive, coaxed through the mire, under loads of about a hundredweight, by Black hero-muleteers. In places, the road was so narrow that two beasts could not move abreast. A typical train comprised six hundred mules and four hundred drovers – measures of the exigencies of the route and the costs it might involve. Jesuit breeders kept up the supply of beasts. Fray Diego de Ocaña, who had the good fortune to make the crossing in the dry season, took only three days to get from Portobelo all the way to Panama, but the impression the floods, mountains, ravines, quagmires and river crossings made on him were of problems that lapped the limits of the possible. 'It is harder to get goods from Portobelo to Panama', opined a travelling complainant at the beginning of the seventeenth century, 'than over the rest of the route from Seville to Lima.'[45] Yet 65 per cent of the Spanish silver that flowed into the world economy between

1576 and 1660 crossed the Isthmus of Panama by one or other of the available routes.

Despite seventeenth-century fluctuations in silver production and transatlantic traffic, improvements continued in the eighteenth century: the transfer of the customs facilities, for instance, from Cruces to Gorgona, or the opening of alternative routes via Darién. In 1788 Antonio Caballero y Góngora, Archbishop and viceroy of New Granada, was still optimistic enough to believe that it would be possible to construct 'a short path for a man on foot' or 'a fair and free route for pack animals and cart traffic'.[46]

Venezuela and the East

In 1777 a number of scattered jurisdictions combined to form the Captaincy General of Venezuela. Two surprising features combined in the new entity: first the coast, where arrivals from Europe often made landfall, but where no secure or adequate port awaited them; hence the importance of Cartagena, across the border of New Granada. Second, owing to the absence of products that typically made transatlantic trade viable, such as gold and silver, cacao, hugely demanded in New Spain, became the main reason for keeping Venezuela going as a colony. Despite the dearth of population, the Spanish crown's policy of giving different colonies discrete economic roles favoured survival. Ships that left La Guaira for Veracruz with cacao returned with silver in the hold. The colony became viable in consequence.

But there was more to Venezuela than Caracas. Despite the linkage of rivers, with the Orinoco forming the frontier of a demographically barely discernible colony, it was hard to find ways to remedy the lack of exploitable routes across the territory, and into the Andean world. In the plains of Los Llanos, rains obliterated trails. Horsemen used compasses to find their way. In the dry season small loads could make their way along narrow corridors to the coast in search of markets and consumers.

The foundation of a chamber of commerce in Caracas in 1793 stimulated work on the routes. Inspired by optimistic, physiocratic doctrines, the entrepreneurs who formed the new organization focused on roadworks, especially in the first place the *camino* from La Guaira, known as the Spanish *camino*. Francisco Jacott, an army engineer, advocated limited but efficient action towards what he hoped would be smooth, if shallow, surfaces, uniform breadth of 7 metres (23 ft) between banks, good drainage and adequate resting places.[47] Landowners and traders wanted roads to Capaya, Caucagua, Barlovento or La Victoria but improvements were stymied by conflicts over jurisdiction. Where the proposed roads would touch haciendas, sugar mills and grazing, proprietors refused to yield land for the purpose. Similar influences frustrated plans for roads towards the Aragua and Caucagua valleys, even though their rich produce had no existing means of getting to market.

Between Puerto Cabello and Valencia, on the other hand, new road plans were effective. There were 9 leagues to traverse. Useful metalling and levelling jobs were accomplished, and a bridge laid at Paso Hondo. Widening of the road through Aguas Calientes enabled carts and coaches to pass through, and the San Felipe route was modified so that inland haciendas had access to the sea.[48] In the west of the Captaincy, the old road to Coro was in the hands of native muleteers, who had no fear of deserted spaces. In eastern Venezuela, the road from Cumaná to Barcelona was available for the transport of foodstuffs, the flow of goods, the transfer of troops and the posting of mail. In 1803 new work began, albeit without being close to achieving the objective of replacing equine tracks and waterborne transport with roads for wheeled vehicles.

Between Oceans:
New Granada

Political tract-writers referred to roads as the veins and arteries of empires. Traffic was their blood. The geography of the New World had been designed by God.[49] So in principle there should be no insuperable obstacles to the life-giving flow – only challenges that were temptations to faith. In what is now Colombia, however, the evidence seemed to be to the contrary. Three gigantic Andean ranges and two monstrous rivers – the Magdalena and the Cauca – split the territory. Unlike in the Aztec and Inca cultures' lands, there was no centre of power – only chieftaincies and lordships, which, in the central valley, functioned rather like a confederation. Spanish settlement of the interior began with the foundation of Santa Fe de Bogotá in 1538. Five years before, Pedro de Heredia had set up Cartagena de Indias, intended as a metropolis of empire and a key stage on the route of the

Tierra Firme Fleet. From the Caribbean coast, Spaniards and their native allies headed inland with the rivers, especially the Magdalena, to the high plateau of Cundiboyaca. Other rivers led towards Los Llanos, the Orinoco and the Amazon, on the putative track of the ever-receding goal they called El Dorado.

The early history of New Granada was therefore of the transformation of a maritime into a fluvial frontier. But it is also helpful to see it as a struggle between men and nature: on the one hand, a design that began in the minds of Jesuits and of the administrators who ran the Council of the Indies in Spain and who envisaged a kingdom that would unite two oceans from east to west; on the other, the geography of a region divided along lines of longitude from north to south. At the start of the seventeenth century it looked as if the Orinoco, which flows westward for much of its course, would be the axis along which the kingdom would take shape. But geography soon asserted its influence: the densely populated and productive central highlands would house the institutions of government in Bogotá, and the Magdalena would link them with Cartagena.

In western New Granada the course of the Cauca, a tributary of the Magdalena, helped shape the north–south direction of colonization. Land routes could not rival the rivers for importance, but they served as links to Venezuela and Caracas and over the Peruvian highlands, via Cali, Pasto and Popayán and from Quito to Lima. Portage routes were needed, too, to get from one river route to the next. A complete journey from Cartagena to Bogotá might take 38 days. From Cartagena to Barranca on the Magdalena, four days on the road were needed, unless the Canal del Dique, open intermittently from 1650, was operable. At Barranca the loads were shifted from muleback to the depths of *bongos* (canoes hollowed from tree-trunks) or the larger vessels known as *champanes*, constructed by the same method but equipped with aedicules (shelters raised on deck) made of sticks and palm leaves. They could reach Mompos in 4 days and Honda in 26, always against the current, straining and taxing the oarsmen. For the next stage, of about a further 8 days, the cargo reverted to mule trains that picked their way across the eastern range of the Andes along a heavily forested route that reached Bogotá via Villeta.

A series of initiatives sought to ease the way. From around the middle course of the Magdalena, cereals grown in the interior could do part of the journey to Cartagena by road, avoiding the worst stretch of river. From time to time, plans were broached to link Bogotá with Ocaña, or with eastern Venezuela and Maracaibo via de Tunja, Pamplona and Mérida, using a lake for part of the way. In 1543 the optimistic official Tomás López suggested that 'by that means without prejudice to Christians or natives all things needful can be supplied to this colony, including horses, cattle, goats and sheep, clothing, slaves and mining equipment at moderate cost and without risk.'[50] Indian paddlers were increasingly hard to recruit as the Indigenous population declined, and teams of Black people and those called 'mulattos' increasingly took over.[51] But despite these difficulties, the Magdalena route remained the first choice of the monarch's representatives because of the overwhelming commercial and strategic importance of Cartagena. In 1601 the citizens of Maracaibo and San Cristóbal bade to challenge Cartagena's interests by calling for construction of a route via their lake. But the existing order proved inviolable.

Even as late as 1762, the projector Bernardo Ward wrote in his 'Proyecto económico' of the impossibility of 'making such paved and permanent roads as the Romans built, or establishing a fast mail service, but I do ask', he continued, 'whether it might be possible to force cuts through forest to link towns or provinces, or provide boats on rivers, or, in scantily populated regions thirty or forty leagues wide, to set up way stations, if only in the form of huts to shelter travellers and serve commerce'.[52] Ward's lament seemed to address the problems of New Granada in particular. Towards the Pacific, a range of routes competed for unsatisfactory supremacy. From Panama, for instance, a vessel might land at Buenaventura, whence a foot trail led via Cali, Cartago, Ibagué and Tocaima, crossing three mountain ranges up to 3,000 metres (9,840 ft) high, and the Cauca and the Magdalena. Critics pointed out that the only way to avoid the problems of recruiting paddlers was to hire porters to carry cargo and even passengers on their backs. What was the best plan for arrivals from the Pacific? In theory it would be ideal to link up with the *camino real* from Quito and Pasto to Bogotá; in practice the obstacles were too daunting. No wonder that after the foundation of Cartagena's Chamber of Commerce in 1795, anxiety over improved communications increased to obsessive levels.

In 1805 the chamber commissioned a report on the subject from José Ignacio de Pombo, a free-trader, physiocrat and abolitionist. In effect, Pombo nominated himself for the role, for he was the leading light of the organization. His analysis was both visionary and stunning. His remedy was to return with new vigour to the amelioration of the Canal del Dique between Cartagena and the Magdalena and to extend it exponentially – joining the Atlantic and Pacific Oceans by a navigable route via the Aratro and other rivers. The effect would be to bring the western settlements of Chocó, Popayán and even Quito and Guayaquil into the orbit of Cartagena, and displace power from Bogotá.

The vision was unrealizable, but a useful new conception of the geography of the kingdom underpinned it. For Pombo, New Granada was made up of two discrete systems: a mountain country centred on Bogotá and a maritime New Granada encompassing the Atlantic and Pacific shores, with its natural capital at Cartagena. 'Our land routes', he wrote, 'are diffuse and decrepit. We hardly know how the rivers run; we under-use them. We are ill-informed about the exact locations of settlements and the distances between them.'[53] He thought he had a solution. A group of commissioners would set off from Cartagena to explore possible aquatic routes, such as that previously postulated via the Aratro to conquer the isolation of the interior. Pombo's hope was that Francisco José de Caldas would be one of the party, but the naturalist and cartographer turned down the invitation and the results of the inquiry were indecisive. In 1806, reverting to a more modest scheme, Pombo came up with six possible new road plans for evaluation, listing them in order of presumed economic value. The first, from Vélez to Opón, would facilitate the export of flour, sugar, quinine and copper. The second, from Girón to Sogamoso, would provide an outlet for cacao, cotton, indigo and canvas; the third, from Zapatoca to La Colorada, would complement both. The fourth route would link Zipaquirá with Carare. Two more remained: one would extend to Puente Real, while the other would join Guaduas and Villeta with Río Negro. Thanks to Pombo's influence, work was in hand by 1810: a better network than New Granada had ever had was in prospect.

Quito:
Juggling Mountains and Coast

The conquistadores who reached Quito in 1532 knew that they would find an accomplished network of roads already in place. In Spanish perceptions, the Inca, 'Romans of the New World', as one analogist – the humanist El Inca Garcilaso de la Vega, whose mother was a native princess – called them, were efficient technocrats, whose vision of the cosmos seemed compounded of arithmetic and engineering. Power was transmitted along lines that radiated from Cuzco – the presumed centre, politically and symbolically, of the world. For the geopolitics of the Andes, and therefore for Spanish imperial strategy, communications with Cuzco were the highest priority.

Cuzco and Bogotá were linked by the ancient Chinchaysuyo road that formed part of the system that fused the northern and southern moieties of Tawantinsuyu (the Inca Empire). Between Quito and Lima, Spaniards called it the *Camino Real de la Sierra*, or the Lima Post Road (*correo de Lima*). Spanish conquest opened the region to the sea. In the interior governed by Quito's *audiencia* – an institution combining administrative and jurisdictional roles – the big problem was, as usual, how to connect the existing north–south roads to the coast.

Guayaquil, for instance, was an important port with problematic links to Quito. The best of them, which led through Babahoyo, Guaranda and Riobamba, required seven hours of suffering for men and beasts to ascend the notorious Cuesta de San Antonio Tarigagua. At Alausí a trail to Guayaquil intersected with the high road atop the Andes from Peru via Riobamba to Quito and Pasto. Similar routes often provided opportunities for portage between navigable river courses. Spanish muleteers began operations soon after the conquest, managing overladen trains that struggled with foodstuffs from Quito. At Guayaquil, salt and fish products would be added to the loads that were then hauled aboard ships for transportation to Lima, where silver, wine, spirits and oil from Chile paid for them.

Typically, the road was passable for six months a year, until the rains set in. Three dry days sufficed to reach Guaranda from Babahoyo. In winter, between 12 and 25 days were needed. In 1736 the great scientific explorers and naval officers Jorge Juan and Antonio de Ulloa left Guayaquil on 3 May and arrived in Quito on 29 May, expressing horror over the crossing of the Cuesta de San Antonio Tarigagua: 'The gradient is so steep that the mules can barely manage it. In places the passage is so narrow that a normal load is too wide to get through it and in others precipices loom at almost every turn.'[54] Although schemes were floated for improved communications inland to Quito and Cuenca, Guayaquil became a port largely devoted to coastal cabotage, especially towards Panama, Peru and Chile. In the north of what is now Ecuador, the province of Esmeraldas was virtually cut off, save by sea or by the coast road from Guayaquil. Construction of a trail accessible on horseback had been proposed as early as 1615, but, as the Carmelite geographer Antonio Vázquez de Espinosa observed, 'The rain there hardly ever stops.'[55]

A more promising scheme envisaged a road from San Miguel de Ibarra to the ports of Limones or Tumaco, and thence by sea to Panama. In 1656 the crown issued a contract for a Tumaco road to an Italian engineer, known in Spanish as Juan Vicencio Justiniani. It was to be at least 4.5 metres (5 yd) wide, 9 metres (10 yd) where possible, with way stations or storehouses every 3 or 4 leagues, bridges of wood and, at the crossing over the River Mira, a customs post. The plan seemed attractive but the Italian demanded scandalously excessive compensation.

No further scheme was broached until 1734, when a brilliant creole native of Riobamba was governor of Esmeraldas: Pedro Vicente Maldonado, who was also a cartographer of scientific inclinations, sought to replace the 'devious and circuitous route that condemns the region'.[56] The following year, with support from Dionisio de Alcedo y Herrera, who headed the *audiencia*, Maldonado began construction of his proposed route. Extending for 46 leagues, of which 24 were by land, it joined the confluence of the rivers Caoni and Blanco, before continuing to the sea. Contending with Andean topography and dense tropical forest, construction took seven years. Maldonado went on to promote the creation of a further road from Ibarra to a landing stage on the Santiago River. Few traders used the extension, however, despite the opportunity to send textiles from Quito or panned gold from Barbacoas to Panama and the Pacific. The projector left for Europe, where fellow scientists acclaimed him, and died in London in 1745. To the unavailing indignation of the king, who issued a reprimand in 1756, successors in office failed to continue or maintain Maldonado's work.[57]

To Peru from Tawantinsuyu

In the words of the great Italian historian Antonello Gerbi, countries 'can be summed up in geographical figures of speech. Egypt is a valley, Brazil a forest, Argentina a plain, Siberia a steppeland, Great Britain an island, Panama a severed isthmus, and Switzerland a fistful of mountains scattered with hotels.' Peru, by the same token, he opined, 'is a valley'.[58] For other historians it was too diverse for glib summation: the New World's equivalent of the Austro-Hungarian empire.[59]

It was a viceroyalty from 1569, with authority not only over adjacent territory from Panama to Patagonia but also even the distant Solomon Islands. In its heartland the Inca left an engineering legacy unsurpassed elsewhere in the hemisphere (albeit on the basis of techniques already traditional in Inca times), with settlements adjusted everywhere to their environments, and an infrastructure of administrative posts at various altitudes, ceremonial gathering-places, way stations, warehouses, fortresses and post-houses for messengers. Stores deposited at strategic intervals facilitated, for instance, transfers across country between paved roads for the Inca and his armies, and the people and their products. In 1532 the Inca Empire may have attained nearly 1 million square kilometres (386,100 square mi.) of territory, stretching over 4,600 kilometres (2,860 mi.) from north to south, linked by some 40,000 kilometres (24,855 mi.) of roads, some of which were legacies of earlier empires or subject peoples.[60]

Two routes were fundamental. The so-called *Camino Real de la Sierra*, 5,200 kilometres (3,230 mi.) long, ran from Quito to Cuzco through Cuenca, Cajamarca and Jauja, before deviating towards Lake Titicaca, Cochabamba and Salta in what is now Argentina. The main coast road, of 4,000 kilometres (2,485 mi.), began in the north at Túmbez and descended to the Maule River in Chile, always hugging the Pacific. Every significant coastal valley was traversed by a route of its own, facilitating the exchange of products from different environments and the passage of migrant labour. In the Cañete valley, for instance, the road was stone-built for much of the way and climbed from sea level to an altitude of 4,700 metres (15,420 ft).

The Inca legacy underlay these routes. Under the viceroys, however, Peru so outgrew the reach of the Inca system that it relied mainly on seaborne communications with Pacific and Atlantic worlds alike. 'The real *Camino Real*', it has justly been said, 'was the route of the galleons.'[61] For a long time, Panama and Buenos Aires represented the extremities of Peru's transport network. Coastal Lima replaced inland Cuzco as the capital. Some trunk roads decayed, while others emerged to supply Chilean grain or mules from Tucumán to the new highland mining megalopolis of Potosí, where the 100,000 inhabitants, many of whom were indios performing tributary service, created a focus of consumer demand. Bridges and way stations might come and go, but, alongside newly introduced mules, old-style llamas (which the Spaniards called sheep and which required neither shoes nor bridles) defied the highest defiles in trains of between 500 and 2,000. Eight native drovers were needed to look after 100 animals.

Towards the end of the sixteenth century the road network of the viceroyalty included the coast road from Lima to Túmbez; the high road north through Jauja and Cajamarca towards Quito, Pasto, Popayán, the River Magdalena and thence to Cartagena or else to Bogotá or Caracas; the southern coastal road from Lima to Santiago and Valparaíso; the southern mountain road to Cuzco and across what is now Bolivia to Tucumán and Buenos Aires; and finally the transmontane roads that joined Valparaíso to Buenos Aires and the latter to Asunción, by mule to Santafe and thence along the Paraná River.

Potosí restored some of Cuzco's importance because of the direction the road had to take. From the port of Callao, the mercury produced in Almadén in Spain made its way to Potosí by mule train, packed in leather, to provide the mines with the means of amalgamation to refine silver ores. There were 1,200 kilometres (745 mi.) to cover, rising from sea level to a height of almost 5,000 metres (16,400 ft). There was also a source of mercury in Huancavelica, north of Cuzco, from where, from 1580 onwards, the route went through Oruro and La Plata, on muleback as far as the landing stage at Chincha, then by river, before being re-laden onto mules at Arica. Having made the return journey to Callao, the silver sailed to Panama under the protection of the Armada del Sur. Typical timetables for travel added up to between 38 and 43 days – 15 from Potosí to Arica, 8 from there to Callao, and between 15 and 20 more as far as Panama. At the moment of maximum productivity in 1640, half of American silver exports originated in Potosí.

Traffic in livestock multiplied for the insatiable market of Potosí. From 1610 to 1630, between 3,000 and 10,000 mules annually were sold in Upper Peru, about 70 per cent of which were destined for local use. Salta was the emporium for this remarkable trade: herds arrived there from Santiago, Tucumán, Buenos Aires and Entre Ríos, and every February 'the world's biggest line-up of mules' took place.[62] In 1778 Salta was still sending mules to Upper Peru – 40,000 in that same year, with similar totals recorded for 1805, though there were considerable fluctuations from time to time. The *camino real* now led all the way from Buenos Aires to Lima, through Saladillo, Córdoba, Tucumán,

Salta, Jujuy, Tupiza, Potosí, Oruro, La Paz, Puno, Huamanga and Huancavelica. The ninety days on the road uphill and down dale as far as Salta could be travelled in carts such as were ubiquitous in the flatlands. In the Andes, however, muleback was still the exclusive means of commerce. Alonso Carrió de la Vandera, from Gijón, was probably the anonymous author of the famous *Lazarillo de ciegos caminantes*, a novelized version of his journey across the South American continent. The protagonist departs Buenos Aires on 5 November 1771, with three wagons, two secretaries and five other servants. After 158 days the group reach Salta. There they switch to eight saddle mules and seven pack animals, as there is no longer a road suitable for vehicles. It takes them 47 days to get from Jujuy to Potosí and 144 more from there to Cuzco. Another 54 days on the road gets them to Lima. The entire journey, including stopovers, consumes almost a year and a half.[63]

The Outliers

At first, because rates of loss to contraband and peculation were always relatively high in Buenos Aires, most of the silver headed west across the continent, and Potosí's output declined in the second half of the seventeenth century. Nonetheless, Atlantic-side demand for products of the interior, such as dried meat, cacao, quinine, tobacco and dyestuffs, kept the eastward route busy. New roads from such centres as Charcas and Santa Cruz de la Sierra led to frontier missions in Mojos and Chiquitos. In 1767 a mixed road and river route opened between Cochabamba and the Loreto mission. By 1776, when the viceroyalty of Río de la Plata was established, Buenos Aires had established a role as an economically indispensable outpost of the global monarchy. Incorporation of much of Upper Peru into the new viceroyalty was a sign of how the relative importance of Atlantic-side and Pacific-side communications had shifted, and of how commerce, formerly dominated by silver, had diversified. Now there were lords of sugar and cacao as well as of silver. The magnetism of Buenos Aires reshaped the region.

In South America, the River Plate region was destined to be the land of the wagon par excellence. Refounded successfully in 1580, Buenos Aires, a port equally serviceable for legitimate commerce and for contraband, supplied vehicles for an enormous and growing demand from the hinterland. As early as 1611 the town council introduced a tax on carpenters' manufactures. For a single-axle vehicle the rate was 1 peso, or 2 pesos for a bed, or – for unspecified reasons – 4 pesos for a chair or window frame. In the mid-eighteenth century most production was of two- or four-wheeled vehicles, with two yokes of oxen, 'on the pattern of the wagons of La Mancha', with storage 4.18 metres (13½ ft) long by 1.25 wide (4 ft), lined with leather and with openings fore and aft.[64]

With no way stations or inns along the roads – only a few cabin-dwellers and widely scattered ranchers – the way inland beyond the river was notoriously hard. A journey of 100 leagues – a little less than 500 kilometres (310 mi.) – typically took twenty days, or twice as long as in Spain. Even in the eighteenth century, when taverns began to appear, travellers' complaints about uncivil treatment, filthy accommodation and abominable food were invariable.

The allure of Asia and the lands of spices explains the early exploration and colonization of much of the Pacific face of America. But Chile, with its reputation as the 'Flanders of the Indies', was hard to incorporate and the immensity and intractability of remoter spaces delayed the inclusion of the South American cone.

In 1602, in order to promote development ('sustentar la tierra'), the Spanish authorities authorized a Portuguese slaver, Pedro Gómez, who had imported six hundred slaves to Tucumán and Charcas, to exchange Brazilian products for local flour, tallow, dried meats, sugar and dyewoods.[65] Silver was excluded, but the terms of the deal marked the beginnings of a new, if fitful, direction of trade. The crown ordered an inland customs post to be opened on the road to Córdoba, where the track from Buenos Aires to the foothills of the Andes deviated to include San Luis y Mendoza, before penetrating Chile over the fearsome Aconcagua range, where the tallest peak was almost 7,000 metres (22,965 ft) high.

Until 1776 the province of Mendoza, in what is now Argentina, belonged to the Captaincy General of Chile. When the Marqués of Cañete founded its principal city in 1559, approaching from the Chilean side of the mountains, Buenos Aires did not exist, and there was no prospect of a commercially useful transmontane road. Over the next hundred years or so developments in the La Plata region changed the game. In an account published in 1698, a mid-century traveller who called himself Acarrete du Biscay claimed to cover the

266 leagues from Buenos Aires to Mendoza in 47 days, in a wagon train drawn by 370 oxen, 4 to a vehicle, with 200 mules to carry the staff and armed escort.[66]

The Neapolitan Jesuit Antonio María Fanelli called the wagons 'ambulant prisons', because of the tedium of the interminable pampa, which, conventionally, he likened to oceans – treeless, with nowhere to lodge.[67] Heat, dust and bugs afflicted the traveller and banished sleep. The distinguished naturalist Félix de Azara told of how on one occasion he had eluded the mosquitos only by almost total submersion in a nearby pool. The only relief from boredom came from occasional encounters with dangerous wild cattle, unforeseen fords and the infrequent but terrible storms. Travellers entering the jurisdiction of Buenos Aires still had 90 leagues to go but could count on nine posts or way stations for the relief of the animals and the repose of the men. In the opposite direction, in the 98 leagues over which Mendoza extended jurisdiction there were seven stations. Córdoba presided over 78 leagues and eight posts.

From Mendoza, if you were bound for Chile, the truly perilous stretch of 105 leagues via La Cumbre to Santiago had to be faced. The relative comfort of a wagon had to be abandoned for a crude trail exposed to attack from errant natives. Comparison with seaborne corsairs was irresistible to most narrators. A mare or mule would be selected to lead the train, dangling a bell to give direction to the rest. Abrupt slopes, sharp ridges and sudden precipices were hazards of the snowbound heights, passable only from November to April. Men and animals tumbled into treacherous crevasses. Fanelli described his revulsion:

> The road, barely a palm in width, skirted a horrifying abyss. A river ran by, so impetuous as to strike fear into the heart at the merest glance. On seeing the snows, we nearly wept in dismay. I said to my companions that if the devil offered me a thousand souls if I agreed to attempt the crossing on a horse, the dangers would make me turn his offer down. The cold is so intense that your lips crack and your cheeks stand out from your bones. Your hands and feet seem dead with cold and your teeth rattle so much that it takes all the care you can muster to keep them from severing your tongue.[68]

After fourteen days of suffering, the Jesuit reached Santiago, which seemed like 'the promised land or the terrestrial Paradise'. Carrió de la Vandera's advice was to hire an experienced Chilean muleteer or countryman as a guide for the trip from Mendoza to Santiago, and to take lightly laden mules to shorten the time. Mountain men were required, because Black or mulatto muleteers, he claimed, would be unable to endure the cold. Drovers from Mendoza were renowned for their efficiency, like the Maragatos – supposed descendants of Moriscos who eluded expulsion from Spain in the seventeenth century – who guided travellers over the mountains between Galicia and Castile. But clients frequently complained of being abandoned in bad weather to the mercies of bandits and rustlers.

The route was known as the terror of travellers ('terror de los viajantes'). In 1790 Captain General Ambrosio O'Higgins launched a programme of improvements to widen the path and make crossings of gorges and waterways safer. For the 'consolation of travellers' he scattered huts along the way, provided with coal, hard tack and dried meat. The names the huts bore evoked the hardships of the route: the House at Cow Point, the House at the Foot of the Waste of the Cave, the House Between the Inca's Pond and the Skulls, the Peak, the Water's Eyes and the Aconagua. On the route towards Valparaíso, O'Higgins won deserved acclaim by laying a surface suitable for wagons over the 22 leagues that separated the capital from the port. The northward route was more intractable. The Camino de los Patos, which led to San Juan, on the eastern flank of the mountains, was usable for only two months a year.

Towards the south, beyond Concepción, maritime routes took overall responsibility for imperial communications, as they did in the northern extremities of Spanish America, beyond New Mexico. Apart from the 'Santa Fe Trail', which clambered and slithered its way over the mountains and deserts, California relied on sail to stay in touch with the rest of the empire. So did Florida, where most Spanish settlement clung to the coast. In the interior of the coastal provinces, communities – scattered forts and missions, mining clusters, precarious settlements, ranchers' homes and indio towns – made and maintained their own trails. The same was true in the offshore world of islands in the Caribbean and Pacific, where commerce needed inland routes only to get the produce of remote estates to the towns and cities of the coasts.

Cuba was the exception, owing to its outstanding roles in commerce, cash-crop production, grand strategy and imperial communications. As Cuban historian Manuel Moreno Fraginals has pointed out, sugar determined the disposition of routes. Isolation and fear of pirates, who tended to exploit abandoned or little-used roads to attack the interior, restrained road building. Footpaths preceded equine trails along which muleteers transported sugar and molasses. Havana kept its merchants supplied in the mid-eighteenth century by means of carts within a radius of 7 leagues, or by mules or horses laden with baskets. By 1780 there were wagon roads capable of bearing loads of ten arrobas (perhaps around 100 kg) from mills – which, though small at first, grew in some cases to gigantic dimensions – sited on riverbanks. A travellers' guide of 1821 informed curious members of the public that a total of 10,132 beasts of burden serviced the capital. From there the *camino real* went clockwise to reach Bejucal and San Antonio in the west, while another crossed the island to Baracoa, some 1,000 kilometres (621 mi.) to the east. A road 'unbearably troublesome' ('penoso e insoportable') reached Santiago and Guantánamo.[69] In 1786, anxious about the flooding that made roads unusable for half the year, the governor ordered citizenry and soldiers to keep the routes open at a cost shared between military and civilian authorities. No one took any notice. Without civic goodwill, nothing could be done, even though non-collaborators were threatened with imprisonment. The sugar barons – the saccharocracy – preferred coastal cabotage and, as usual, their will prevailed. In 1865 the island had 659 roads, of which 637 were merely local.[70]

4

TROUBLED WATERS
Along and Across
Internal Waterways

My river is mine own, and I have made it for myself. (EZEKIEL 29:3)

At noon on Friday 20 July 1714, the finest bridge in all Peru broke and hurled five travellers into the gulf below. This bridge was on the high road between Lima and Cuzco and hundreds of people passed over it every day. Incas had woven it of osier more than a century before. Visitors to the city were always led out to see it.[1] The 'accident, perhaps' or presumed 'act of God' that launches Thornton Wilder's tale of *The Bridge of San Luis Rey* induces Fray Junípero, the author's quasi-detective, to investigate colourful fellow travellers for suspected murder. The novel captures something of what colonial bridges were like. An old Inca bridge was, indeed, the only way over the Apurimac River. Mounts, litters and wheeled vehicles had to pick their way down, hundreds of metres below the high road, to cross the narrow, torrential defile before resuming the journey, and Wilder was right to emphasize the socially levelling effect of the bridge: everyone, from the viceroy and archbishop down, had to dismount and cross it on foot.

Material World:
Fibrous River-Crossings

The yarns Wilder wove and the workmanship he described recalled the way Andean bridges were really made. When the Spaniards arrived in the Americas, ropework suspension bridges amazed and fascinated them, as did the frequently encountered simpler rope contraptions strung across rivers and ravines to assist travellers. The amazement was surely reciprocated. We can only imagine how Spaniards' first

RUTAS DEL
IMPERIO
ESPAÑOL
1790

Paralelo 61

Territorio
de
Nutka

**Camino Real
de California**
San Francisco-Los Cabos

Luisiana

Tratado de París

Provincias
Internas de
Occidente

VIRREINATO DE
NUEVA ESPAÑA

Vieja ruta española
Los Ángeles-San Agustín

Camino Real de los Tejas
Texas-Luisiana

Provincias
Internas de
Oriente

Golfo
de
México

Florida

Camino Real de Cuba
La Habana-Santiago de Cuba

Nueva
Galicia

México

Yucatán

CAPITANÍA GENERAL
DE CUBA

Puerto Rico

Santo Domingo

**Camino Real
de Tierra Adentro**
México-Santa Fe

Red de caminos reales de Chulpas
Mexico-Guatemala-Panamá

CAPITANÍA GENERAL
DE GUATEMALA

Margarita Trinidad

Carácas

CAPITANÍA GENERAL
DE VENEZUELA

A M É R I C A

E S P A Ñ O L A

VIRREINATO
DE NUEVA
GRANADA

Audiencia
de Santa Fe

Azores

Madeira

Islas Canarias

Cabo Verde

Islas Galápagos

Camino Real
Lima-Santa Fe de Bogotá

Audiencia
de Quito

Audiencia
de Lima

VIRREINATO
DEL PERÚ

Audiencia
de Cuzco

Grão Pará

Tratado de San Ildefonso

Mato Grosso

Audiencia
de Charcas

Camino Real de Sudamérica
Lima-Buenos Aires

Río Grande do Norte
Ceará
Paraíba
Pernambuco
Alagoas
Sergipe

Maranhão

Piauí

Goiás

Bahia

Minas
Gerais

Espírito Santo

São Paulo

Río de Janeiro

ESTADO DE BRASIL

Santa Catarina

Río Grande

*Islas de
Juan Fernández*

Camino Real de Oeste
Santiago de Chile-Buenos Aires

Audiencia
de Buenos Aires

CAPITANÍA GENERAL
DE CHILE

VIRREINATO
DEL RÍO
DE LA PLATA

Roads in continental Spanish America, 1790.

*Estrecho
de Magallanes*

Islas Malvinas

Cabo de Hornos

efforts to explain bridges of stone must have puzzled people unac-
quainted with the technology in question. Even in the inventive civilizations of the Maya, the use of the arch as a means of distributing stress
was unknown: engineers covered spaces and constructed openings in
a way directly imitated from nature, by erecting two walls or pillars
and joining them with a lintel.[2] Lightly laden foot traffic imposed little
strain on their powers of innovation in bridge-building. As with so
many other features of colonial culture – from the Roman alphabet
to the Catholic faith – Indigenous minds rapidly grasped new opportunities, but, for want of means to replace them, their bridge-building
techniques endured.

The Apurimac, at the crossing that linked Lima to Cuzco, was the
river that most persistently defied Spanish ambitions to outdo the Inca
engineers. The gap was only 44 metres (144 ft): in theory, a single stone
arch would span it, but the practical difficulties seemed insuperable.
The Inca solution was, in any case, admirable. As a description written
in 1600 put it:

> The bridge has been made with much artifice and effort. On one
> side, the ropes have been hung from some boulders, and on the
> other from a pillar on a tower of stone and mortar. The way to
> the far bank seems suspended in air, for the ravine is so deep
> that it would be impossible to secure a footing in the river for
> a stone bridge. And the current is intractable. For the causeway,
> the builders assembled hardwood planks of two-year-old timber,
> about a foot wide. You cannot cross without getting all a-tremble.
> Owing to the risk of excessive loads, laden mules are not allowed,
> and only one can be on the bridge at any one time. So they go,
> one by one. Trains of big, strong mules use the bridge, each of
> seventy or eighty beasts, in groups of ten under the control of an
> indio or black. They leave Lima for Cuzco with great cargoes
> of goods. Under orders from their paymasters in Lima, when the
> trains reach the Apurimac crossing, or come to other suspension
> bridges over rivers along the way, the captains arrange for the
> loads to be transferred to the backs of indio or black porters, who
> have to pay for any wares they let fall.[3]

It took two hundred paces to reach the safety of the bank. In 1618,
faced with the job of finding a crossing-place where a stone alternative

might be possible, the engineer Bernabé Florines renounced the task, telling the viceroy that, 'If there were a better place in this kingdom, the Incas would have used it and we would know about it.'[4] The similar suspension bridge slung over the River Santa in 1599 benefited from enhancements of Spanish design, but produced similar sensations in beholders. 'It looks as if it were floating in the air,' said a Jesuit reporter, 'because of the way the wooden planking, held together with iron stanchions, dangles between the banks.'[5] Ropes had to be thigh-thick, but the materials from which they were woven drew on local ecologies: agave in many places, maguey in New Spain and Ecuadorean *piquigua* (*Heperopsis ecuadorensis*, Araceae).

For river crossings, the real-estate agent's rule always applied. Location, location, location were the top three requirements. Fords in season never ceased to be important in the colonial era, and knowing where to find them was part of every guide's professional wisdom. Peru had a special class of horses dedicated to swimming, where suitable crossings existed, with riders on their backs – an experience Humboldt reported, known as *pasar a volapié* or 'half-flying across'. In the Lake Titicaca region, there were flat bridges made of reeds, laid over the surface of the water and renewed twice yearly: in suitable places, they might be good for crossings of up to 90 metres (295 ft). In some places, all over the empire, ferries operated by means of rafts, tied to the shore on long leads, that the crew would guide across with punts or poles, tacking with the current. In examples reported from Quito, the rafts were made of five or six big planks, trussed together and tapering fore and aft; in some cases, where there was no strong current, passengers could operate them by tugging hand over hand at guy-ropes slung from shore to shore. Balsa wood was used in Guayaquil, buoyant species of local rushes in Upper Peru. Boat bridges were common, including fragile, temporary affairs made of traditional rafts as well as major engineering accomplishments, with heavy boats and floats supporting substantial causeways, such as the formidable example planned at Matanzas over the San Juan River in 1774.

A similar method, familiar from Indigenous tradition, employed woven baskets, suspended from the ropes, to hold up to four individuals and send them dangling over gulches. Garcilaso de la Vega described how shoremen on one side of the river would play out the rope as far as mid-stream, whereupon a second crew on the far bank would haul the basket home. One might see turkeys clucking or pigs snorting, or other small livestock, in these contraptions; for cattle, horses and mules, however, Spaniards contrived something more elaborate: a kind of cable-car, suspended on leather ropes: the terrified animals might have to endure this traumatic accommodation for trips of up to 75 metres (246 ft) over precipices 50 metres (164 ft) deep. Managing the beasts was one of the hardest parts of the herders' jobs as the cars bucked and swayed perilously above the defiles. Every region had a particular name for these contraptions: *tramoya* or *zurrón* in Guatemala, *oroya* or *huaro* in Peru, *tarabita* (or *cabuya*, *garucha* or *cuerda*) in New Granada. For one of the main routes across the last kingdom to Venezuela, the *cabuya* that spanned the Chicamocha River was vital: indio haulers could be supplemented there by horses who pulled the cars across with a cord tied to their tails. Travellers – indios and runaways, overwhelmingly – sometimes dodged the tolls by swinging from the undercarriage, 'like spiders'. In 1785 the mayor of Chima, near Tunja, ordered the managers of *cabuyas* to arrest clandestine passengers: undocumented slaves and presumable runaways, absconding servants and children, eloping couples, and women whose marital status was in doubt.[6]

El Inca Garcilaso de la Vega, writing about his homeland with vision distorted by his life in Spain as a local celebrity in the town of Montilla, fancied that his native countrymen marvelled at 'stone bridges where all the weight seemed to them to be up in the air'.[7] The Jesuit polymath José de Acosta described Indigenous people's reactions at the genesis of a bridge over the River Jauja in Peru in around 1560:

> They had no knowledge of how to build arches. When they saw the wooden framework of the bridge removed on completion, they fled in terror, supposing that the apparently unsupported stonework was about to collapse. When they saw how it stayed in place, and how Spaniards crossed it, the chief said to his companions, 'This is why we should serve these people.'[8]

From Rope to Stone

One of the most spectacular travelogues of the colonial era was the *Compendio y descripción de las Indias occidentales* (Compendium and Description of the Indies of the West) by the Carmelite from Jeréz, Antonio Vázquez de Espinosa, who returned from America to Spain in 1622. His account of his journey reads like a picaresque novel or a Munchausian caprice. One cayman devours an Indian woman. A chieftainess strangles another with her bare hands. The friar observes a whale fishery, the baptism of a young Gauicurú chief, the splendours of Lima's hospitals and Spaniards' disillusionment with the infertility of the Atacama Desert. He wends to Tucumán amid orange groves. In Guayaquil he fends off mosquitoes. But the bridges – and the tolls they demand – are the connecting threads. In Patate (now part of Quito) and Cajamarca, he admires bridges woven from vegetation – 'lianas twisted like wickerwork'; in Lima and Arequipa, by contrast, stone bridges 'span the river with a single arc'.[9] In Mexico City, he praises the bridges that carry, daily, more than 3,000 mules over canals crowded with some 10,000 laden canoes, between 'straight, wide, well-cleared roadways'. In Bogotá he notes the two fine bridges that cross the rivers San Francisco and San Agustín.

It was a case of necessity that hath no law. The Spanish navy's outstanding scientists, Jorge Juan and Antonio de Ulloa, experienced the demands of the environment and the decisive measures they imposed, in what is now Ecuador, and described the 'mighty crags, with only four big staves levelled across them to make a bridge, to the great peril of lives and property' in their *Relación histórica del viaje a la América* (Historical Account of the Journey to America) in 1748.[10] They argued, somewhat unrealistically in view of technical limitations and problems of supply, for the superiority of wood over fibre and stone over wood. In a further instance of cultural hybridity, materials and techniques were blended and deployed according to circumstances. Over narrow waterways, planks might serve, or tree trunks supported on wooden or stone pillars. Where the width of the gap to be traversed and the ferocity of the flow demanded, long, wavering strands of twisted rope took their place. Economy and convenience were served. In less precipitate terrain, the best option was the pontoon bridge of military tradition, well represented on the 'Spanish Road' from Flanders to Milan.[11] Earthquake zones required light wooden superstructures on unshakeably vast stone supports. In 1766 the reforming governor Pedro de Urrutía flung a wooden bridge, resting on pillars of cemented stone blocks, across the Manzanares at Cumaná in eastern Venezuela to spare residents from swimming or wading or resorting to the good offices of a notoriously disobliging Black ferryman who overcharged for the use of his little canoe. An earthquake brought the bridge down, but not, as an official reported, 'because of defective construction, for other constructions suffered damage or collapse despite their solidity and strength'.[12] In 1772 Urrutía secured royal permission to use the proceeds of cockfights to pay for repairs. He did not hesitate to divert soldiers to work on the job or to appropriate stone earmarked for the cathedral's sedilia, and reacted angrily when the clergy complained.

In default of adequate hoisting equipment and piledrivers to secure supports, the images – often based on Roman models – that engineers brought from Europe were undeliverable. Among the difficulties that impeded bridge-building in stone, fixing the footings was among the toughest. It was sometimes hard to find materials or expertise to erect the temporary supports and scaffolding of wood that kept the wedges in place while an arch was under construction. On small jobs, sticks and canes were used for the framework, wood on larger works, and cranes of ancient Roman style – usually hefty poles pivoted on big stones – fitted with iron hooks or jaws. In 1795, in the century Wilder depicted, the Conde de Cabarrús – that voice of the Spanish Enlightenment – railed against 'chimerical perfectionism' and imaginative paralysis that got in the way of the rapid execution of vital public works. 'Make every town', he wrote, 'function as it ought – as a society for mutual protection and the provision of services.'[13] Bridges were part of a moral economy, constitutive of the happiness of the people; delays were unacceptable. From a more practical perspective, repairs were like reforms: a preferred alternative to revolution.

Understandably, stone bridges were matters of regional pride and inter-regional competition: works that 'ennobled' the places where they appeared. The intensity, the investment of emotion involved, is apparent in engineers' submissions – documents nowadays that are typically dispassionate, but were charged with passion in colonial Spanish America, especially, perhaps, in New Granada, where the quality of the work (for instance, on the magnificent fortifications of Cartagena) belied petitioners' standard complaints about the poverty of the creole world. Stone bridges spread as cities multiplied. La Paz, founded in 1548, got its bridge as soon as the Franciscan friary appeared on the far side of the river. Puebla, in New Spain, had a similar set-up: main settlement linked to a friary beyond the River Xonaca, now dry and tarmacadamed, in the upper quarter. The bridge, begun in 1555, was the work of Luis de León, who was also responsible for the fountain in the main square. It was 25 metres (82 ft) long and 8.4 metres (27½ ft) wide, 'so that two coaches can pass abreast with ease'.[14] Three arches sustained it, of which the middle one was 4.15 metres (13½ ft) above the level of the river, with a low, flat cusp to make the roadway above easily negotiable. The surface was paved, with stone balusters to minimize the danger of accidents, and an ostentatious scutcheon at its centre. The bridge was serviceable enough to survive floods in 1697 and 1743, and was widened in 1878. Among embellishments added, meanwhile, were a pipe to supply water to the friary, a drainage channel, a chain for pedestrians to cling to and a chapel – all needful in view of the periodic floods and the recklessness of the locals, who, as in the surroundings of most bridges, neglected to clear the rubbish that accumulated around the supports.

The approach to colonial Puebla from the direction of Veracruz must have been quite a spectacle, as the traveller followed an avenue of palms, through the upper gate, across a small walled square, and passed through the arch that led to the forecourt of the friary of San Francisco. There he or she would find the stone balustrade that continued over the bridge, so that arrivals had to cross the forecourt and pass through a second archway to reach the city. The chapel dedicated to the Virgin of Sorrows – endowed by the occupier of the neighbouring house with its own adjoining oratory – was close at hand, as if to call to mind the travails of the road. In the same year, 1555, a second bridge was added, known as 'the Pox', because it was near a hospital that specialized in that characteristically, and perhaps originally, American disease, syphilis. From 1726 there was also an aqueduct that Jesuits had built to supply their College of the Holy Spirit from their estate at Amalucan. Less imposing was the third bridge, inaugurated in 1626: it had only 'two stout beams slung over some stones'. Intended at first only for foot traffic, it was reinforced in 1699 with stone supports and surface. In a state of collapse, however, in 1770 it was replaced by the Puente de Ovando, funded by the proceeds of a bullfight. In all, Puebla ended the colonial era with five bridges – an exceptional endowment, indicative of the commercial importance of the place.

Elsewhere in New Spain, the proliferation of bridges marked the expansion of the frontier, first by friars and later by trailblazers, surveyors and engineers. No one should evince surprise at the fact that when Agustín de Betancourt founded the civil engineering school of Madrid in 1802, his chief assistant was a native of Campeche in

Mexico.[15] Among his illustrious predecessors was Fray Andrés de San Miguel, architect and master of hydraulic engineering and landscaping, who was born in Medina Sidonia in Cádiz in 1577 and died in Mexico in 1652. He arrived in 1644 with orders to build a house of religion in Lerma and a bridge in Salvatierra to ease communications between Mexico City and Zacatecas. He completed the latter just before his death. Philip IV issued a moving tribute three years later, giving thanks for the lives the bridge had saved from drowning, and the commerce that would otherwise have been lost. 'There were', the king added, 'many who could not get to Mass on feast days, or to hear Lenten sermons, and many others who died without receiving the sacraments owing to the impossibility of crossing the river.'[16] The bridge was 180 metres (590½ ft) wide, all of stone, with security walls a yard wide, drains, embrasures, with foundations of natural rock. The cost was only 10,000 pesos – making it about the cheapest undertaking of its size at the time; it took only six months to build. It was hailed as miraculous. With a touch of practicality, King Philip IV noted that, owing to the bridge, the yield of the local toll rose from some 60 or 70 pesos to 500 pesos.[17]

The vital section of *camino real* that linked the oceans from Veracruz to Acapulco made huge demands on bridge-builders: a clear case of engineering called in to remedy the deficiencies of nature. Until 1812, the crossing of the Antigua River – the first obstacle as you head inland from Veracruz – exposed ferry-bound travellers to a hazardous passage among voracious caimans, but in that year the Gran Puente del Rey opened. The creation of an exemplary Valencian architect, Manuel Tolsá, who designed the bridge, and an outstanding military engineer from Barcelona, Diego García Conde, who was in charge of the work, its seven arches spanned 218 metres (715 ft), supporting a causeway 10 metres (33 ft) wide.[18] Nearer the capital, various obstacles were overcome by the so-called Puente Grande, which had a single arch, and the eighteenth-century bridges at Nogales, La Angostura, El Gallardo and Santa Gertrudis, among others. On the westward road, towards Acapulco, the big problems were the passages of the Papagayo and Mezcala Rivers. A military engineer, Miguel Constanzo (1741–1814), confronted the former in an effort to meet the demand, by now intense, for stone bridges to replace those of wood; but the twelve-arch bridge he planned succumbed to flooding. To cross the Mezcala, the only recourse was to a system of pontoons fixed in place by ropes from on shore. The improvement on the former, indigenous system – reed or gourd rafts guided by swimmers – was marked but still imperfect.[19] But engineers' optimism was boundless. In 1807 Francisco Antonio Ramírez proposed a fairly simple bridge at San Salvador Atoyactempán, outside Puebla: his sketch shows benign waters flowing gently through a leafy, idyillic landscape. Sometimes, utopianism triumphed. Near Guadalajara, there was the great bridge at Zapotlanejo, privately financed, 9 yards wide and spanning some 17 metres with 26 arches.

South of New Spain

In Central America and the Caribbean, the range of solutions resembled those in Mexico. In Santo Domingo, for instance, in 1610, there were two bridges, one of wood and one of stone. In the original plan for Panama, the army engineer Cristóbal de Roda proposed a single-arch stone bridge over the Algarroba, and a pontoon affair, to be called Puente del Rey, across the same river. In Guatemala, at Cuilapa, south of the capital, the impressive Puente de los Esclavos had to be made of stone to resist the impact of the logs and flotsam that cascaded down the river. Tegucigalpa, now the capital of Honduras, had the benefit of a huge span of stone across the Choluteca River. In Puerto Rico in 1519, when the inhabitants of Caparra were obliged to remove to San Juan, two wooden bridges were ordained among the preparations. They were rebuilt in stone in 1786, when the problems of fixing piles in the swampy, mangrove-ridden riverbed were solved. In the Philippines the Pasig River posed a similar problem in Manila; stone pillars were sunk in 1630 to support a wooden superstructure of ten arches, 11 yards wide. In modifications in 1814, the gradient was smoothed and lamp-posts were added.

In parts of South America, demand for stone to replace woven materials was insistent, from the sixteenth century onwards, but not always realizable. Every outgoing viceroy of New Granada enjoined his successor to prioritize improved communications. Successes in relatively tractable environments included the stone bridge over the Magdalena at Honda, and another at Cali on the road to Quito. The example over the Funza at Bogotá, built in the mid-seventeenth century, sprang from pillars on the shore, not raised from the riverbed. A notable achievement was that of the Neapolitan engineer Domingo de Esquiaqui, who arrived in 1770 under threat of dismissal from the army because his devotion to music – he was an accomplished flautist – was said to detract from his service. He built the Puente de los Micos over the Serrezuela River and, with the support of the viceroy, José de Ezpeleta, the Puente del Común, so-called because the city council paid for it, over the Funza, 6 leagues from Bogotá. Inaugurated in 1792, it was quite a gem, with three arches supporting a causeway more than 18 metres (60 ft) wide, adorned with little garden squares and pedestrian paths that evinced civic pride and regal airs. Still visible on the cutwaters of the arches are devices that recall others at the Escorial – a conspicuous instance of the engineer's artistry.[20]

Repair and maintenance demanded a lot of energy, attention and provision against disaster. At Santa Fe de Bogotá the bridge now known as San Miguel's seemed typically accident-prone. A brick structure succeeded the first, wooden version, only to collapse in a flood. Reconstruction in 1664, under the supervision of the Dominican savant Fray Antonio Zambrano, proved more durable, surviving to be enlarged in 1883. In 1796 the bridge at Topo, in Tunja, needed urgent restoration; Medellín's, where a stonework causeway rested on a structure of tropical hardwood over the Santa Ana ravine, needed a total overhaul. In 1806 the army engineer Vicente Talledo issued a memorandum to authorities in Tunja demanding lists of fords passable in times of flood, bridges in need of repair with details of the extent of the work required, and notes on the location of bridges, boats and serviceable fibre coracles for river crossings.[21]

Outlying regions of New Granada bore similar afflictions. In Caracas, at the eastern extension of the kingdom, where the valley location had some similarities with Santa Fe's, the environment of precipitous slopes and gullies was constantly troublesome to the city council that had to keep the traffic running and the bridges operating. There were five bridges along the approaches, at La Pastora, Trinidad, San Pablo, Punceres and La Candelaria. The city's chief engineer, however, thought at least 25 were needed. In the 1780s La Pastora was rebuilt with a single arch of narrow bricks, crammed like the flaps of an open fan. In the same year, the mulatto engineer Juan Domingo del Sacramento Infante, who was proud of his status as a free man in royal service, rebuilt the bridge at Trinidad. On the far, western side of New Granada, Quito's communications depended on a bridge 6 leagues away, where a stonemason, Juan Corrales, flung three arches across the River Pisque in 1607.

To the south, in Upper Peru, the stone bridge over the Pilcomayo River, on the vital road from Lima to Potosí, had to be rebuilt over and again whenever the swollen river broke it. The restoration of 1786 gave it seven arches, each about 10 metres (33 ft) long. In Potosí itself, the mines required a canal, dividing the city in two; of the bridges that spanned the gap no fewer than eleven served 'the indios who thereby made their way to their allotments', while another five kept communications within the city viable during the rains. The celebrated Puente del Diablo, which overlapped nearly 20 metres (65½ ft) of space with a single arch, served trains of llamas that brought precious salt to the city in exchange for silver. Despite these and other cases of building in stone, rope bridges remained important in Upper Peru throughout the colonial period. In 1804 the royal representative in Huamanga, Demetrio O'Higgins, imposed a tax of 2 pesos on every bushel of coca, and 4 pesos on every load of spirituous liquor 'to provide for a strong bridge of stone and so prevent the recurrence of the sad events that have occurred so often on rope bridges'.[22]

Lima, where the viceroys held court, was the cynosure of coastal Peru from its foundation in 1535. Expansion across the Rímac created an almost immediate demand for bridges. In 1554 there were two – one of wood, the other of rope; ten years later, however, a stone bridge of eight arches joined them. Floods swept it away in 1607, but its successor, built in the same year and completed in 1610, still stands: six brick arches, footed in stone, with triangular sluices at water level and underground drainage available at need. Tolls on wine, sheep, soap and sails met the huge cost of 200,000 pesos. Juan del Corral, summoned from Quito to undertake the work, designed it, it seems, with the Puente de San Marcos in León in mind: with access through a lofty archway, adorned with scutcheons (to which a clock was added in 1752) and twin towers on the far side. It became (and remains) a focus of social life, where *limeños* gathered and strolled to parade their glamorous attire and exchange amorous looks.

Arequipa, founded in 1540, mirrored Lima's layout, placing the town bridge close to the main plaza, with access via a smaller square. In 1549 the Chili River rose to ruin the rope bridge inherited from the indigenous past but a replacement took a long time to negotiate, partly because of the opposition of Indigenous chiefs, who were unwilling to sacrifice any part of adjoining lands to meet the project's engineering problem: that is, an abrupt approach from the city, requiring enormous amounts of earth to raise the causeway to the much higher level of the far bank. At last in 1558 the town council arranged for a stonemason, Bernardino de Ávila, who served as the equivalent of the local clerk of works, to oversee the project with the help of a workman called Juan Blanco. The job passed into the hands of the Jesuits when they arrived in the city from Lima, bringing with them a construction surveyor of great renown, Gaspar Báez. Earthquakes and inundations held the work up. In 1608 there was still no protective rampart – or so it seems from the story of an indio who slipped to his death.

In Santiago de Chile, the normal history of bridges seemed to go into reverse, as the stone bridges, erected only to collapse in the abnormal floods of 1748 and 1763, were replaced with wooden crossings on the grounds that costs of repair would be lower. But hopes abided. In the 1770s an army engineer, José Antonio Birt, who had served in New Granada and Peru, was at work on a serviceable new plan for a durable stone structure. As the artillery engineer Diego García Panes avowed in 1783, in the environment of the South American cone, where landscapes were dramatic, rivers tumultuous and materials hard to come by, 'strong and commodious construction' was needed: 'bridges of stone, with inclines gentle enough to be manageable, but broad and secure, without wasting funds on frills and furbelows [*filetes y primores*]'.[23] A fall from a horse despatched Birt before the project was complete, but his successor, José del Pino, with the viceroy's help, added two arches to Birt's nine-arch design with suitable cutwaters and outlets for drainage. To reach Santiago from Buenos Aires remained a hazardous adventure, especially at the crossing of the River Desaguadero between San Luis and Mendoza. In 1778 a resident of the latter city, Manuel Viuda, commissioned a bridge at the spot, but his choice of engineer, Gregorio Ramos, failed to start work, 'finding it too difficult'. A temporary wooden affair filled the gap, but in 1785 a petition to the authorities from an engineer with a record of accomplishment in mining, Francisco Serra Canals of Barcelona, proposed a three-arch stone replacement, which he promised would rise gently from the road 'with scarcely more of a hump than an ass's back'. His death in 1803 left the work unfinished and the viceroy, Joaquín del Pino, fulminating at the failure. The necessary funds were levied from carters and carriers approaching from Mendoza.

Beyond Rivers, Between Oceans:
Canals in Aspiration and Reality

He already had seven parrots, two kinkajous, a motmot, two guans and eight monkeys aboard his canoe. They were arrayed in wicker baskets, or, in the case of the smaller monkeys, allowed to run about on board and nestle naughtily – to the hilarity of the crew – in the folds of the habit of Fr Zea, the expedition's Franciscan guide. But Alexander von Humboldt was always willing to add to the specimen collection he accumulated on his journey through Spanish America in 1800–1804. So, while navigating the Orinoco, the great systematizer of the scientific knowledge of his day eagerly accepted the opportunity to buy from native vendors a noisily squawking purple macaw and a mischievous toucan, who turned out to be quite a character, with a taste for teasing the monkeys. It was mid-May 1800. With Humboldt's redoubtable scientific assistant, Aimé Bonpland, and their native helpers, the whole menagerie, including twelve or thirteen humans, set off to explore the Casiquiare – the natural 'canal', 365 metres (1,200 ft) in breadth at its mouth and over 322 kilometres (200 mi.) long – which links the Orinoco to the Amazon river-system via the Río Negro.

The freak of nature – the world's longest breakwater-traversing natural waterway – flowed between abrupt banks, high and so densely smothered with vegetation that for the first few days the explorers could find no landing-place. The mosquitoes were so relentless that it was impossible to sleep on board, with hands and feet swollen and painful from the stings. The canoe could carry little food and those aboard had no means of replenishing their supplies. On the night of 20 May, when they were closing in on the juncture with the Río Negro, a meteor shower absorbed their attention – the urine of the stars, as the indio helpers called it. They had become used to the nightly howls of the jaguars but in the morning they discovered that their dog – who had eluded every danger and had even dared to swim among caimans – had disappeared: they were in no doubt of his fate. The sufferings and sacrifices seemed worthwhile. They had made the first detailed record and map of the course of the astonishing fluvial bifurcation that had been a major highway of travel for the inhabitants of the two great river valleys for centuries.[24]

The expedition illustrates a paradox: although the Americas are well served by navigable natural waterways, the Spanish Empire was seriously deficient in riverine communication. Of the rivers that had borne long-range indigenous commerce before the Spaniards arrived, most were inaccessible or unusable to the newcomers for most of the time. The Mississippi is exceptionally well suited to navigation, but was only in Spanish hands relatively briefly, from 1763 to 1802, although it was well frequented in that time, quadrupling the value of the trade it had carried under French rule. The Missouri, though envisaged as a further highway towards the remote northwest, was not serviceable: in the episode recounted above when John Evans undertook to navigate the river in 1796, it took him over a hundred days to return, with the stream, from his furthest destination in the Mandan country to the headquarters of the Missouri Company in St Louis. The Río Grande seems hardly to have been used for commerce before the nineteenth century. The other main long-range riverine and lacustrine arteries of the northern moiety of the hemisphere – the Mackenzie, the St Lawrence, the Ohio, the Great Lakes, the Amazon – were wholly or largely beyond Spanish frontiers. In the southern moiety, the Orinoco system was imperfectly serviceable, as Miguel de Ochogavia, 'the Columbus of the Apure', showed when he conquered the last of the river's Andean tributaries in 1647, celebrating his achievement in doggerel that proved delusive:

> I came, I saw, I conquered, and returned in glory
> From Orinoco – crystals cleft and fear allayed.
> To God I dedicate, in thanks, my wondrous story;
> To you, my readers, all the benefits to trade.[25]

In some cases, navigable rivers were rendered useless by their own inaccessibility, as was the Esmeraldas, unapproachable for commercial purposes from Quito until Pedro Vicente Maldonado built a road across the 46-league gap. The job was finished in 1741, to the satisfaction of the Council of the Indies, whose report praised

> Maldonado's conduct and perseverance, and his improvements to the proposed route, whereby he has solved the problems of the heavily forested Pichincha range, the impenetrability of the uplands, and the difficulties posed by the swift-flowing rivers that rise and race through that region. He has, it seems, at his own expense, opened a broad, clear, direct, and capacious road

for mule trains to traverse at any season of the year without crossing any ford or bridge between Quito and the trading quays on the Esmeraldas River, where the landward road terminates.[26]

The only systems extensively exploited throughout the colonial period were the Magdalena, joining the Ecuadorian highlands to the Caribbean port of Cartagena, and the complex river-system that debouches in the Río de la Plata linking the Andean Altiplano to the Atlantic. Even here, the limitations of the use Spaniards made of the rivers were obvious. Although, as the name implies, the Río de la Plata was, at least in conception, a terminus for the silver trade of the Andean tablelands, Potosí was never effectively connected with Buenos Aires: the Pilcomayo was too unstable, the Indigenous people of Chaco too indomitable.[27] When Spain and Portugal set the frontiers of Brazil in a treaty of 1777, the Río de la Plata system was so little known that rivers referred to in the treaty were inaccurately placed and in one case non-existent.[28] In imperial rivalry Portuguese establishments on the east banks of some of the main rivers impeded Spanish commerce.

Because the exploitation of rivers was limited, the amount of investment in improving riverine navigation was modest in the colonial period: building quays at settlements and junctions with other routes, and dredging some riverside anchorages. The main internal routes of communication between Spanish colonies lay, as we have seen, overland, via the spines of sierras or through mountains, across deserts or by laborious mule tracks between outlets to the sea. It was therefore desirable, in principle, though hard in practice, to supplement the deficiencies of nature by creating new canals.

In pre-industrial economies, where no means existed of hauling goods in bulk over long distances over land, save by muscle power and the use of wheeled vehicles, waterborne communications always attracted a great deal of attention and investment. The seventeenth and eighteenth centuries were therefore the golden age of canal construction in Europe. Peter the Great's Volga navigation project linked the river to the Don and the Kabona as part of an unfulfilled plan to join the Caspian to the Black Sea. Louis XIV patronized the construction of the Canal du Midi, complete before the seventeenth century was over, in order to join the Atlantic with the Mediterranean Sea, and began a series of canals to back up the frontier he established on France's continental side. Frederick the Great joined the Havel to the Elbe. The history of Britain's Industrial Revolution usually begins with a narrative of the formidable network of eighteenth-century canals that preceded the coming of the railways.

Echoes of such enterprises in Spanish America included only one substantial complete canal and a series of plans for another – respectively, the Canal del Dique, which filled the gap between the navigable stretch of the Magdalena and the port of Cartagena, and what we now call the Panama Canal. The former is best understood in the context of the gradual focusing of the trade of the colony of New Granada – roughly corresponding to modern Colombia, Panama and Ecuador – towards the Atlantic. By the mid-seventeenth century it was obvious that the Orinoco would not serve as the outlet from the highlands to the ocean. It became necessary to find ways of exploiting the Magdalena instead.[29] Pedro Zapata de Mendoza, the indefatigable governor of Cartagena, launched a multi-pronged strategy, including new fortifications for the port, the expulsion of foreigners from Darién, and the construction of the canal.[30] When he inaugurated construction in March 1650, the 2,000 navvies and supervisors found themselves engaged in a race against time, as the digging had to be complete by the time the winter rains arrived.[31] All available indio and Black labour was pressed into service. Five hundred prisoners and captured pirates joined the chain gang. Local *hacenderos* had to hand over their peons on pain of heavy fines. Chaplains and a field hospital cared for the workers' spiritual and bodily infirmities – with some success in the latter case if we can believe Mendoza's assertion that only two workers died despite the ferocity of the torrid climate.[32] The first stretch from the sea to Mahates comprised 39 kilometres (24 mi.) of linked lagoons; a further 67.5 kilometres (42 mi.) reached as far as the Magdalena, with little use of natural waterways.

At first the results seemed eminently satisfactory. The canal was completed with amazing speed. The scribe of Cartagena's town council captured the moment on 20 August 1650:

[B]etween four and five o'clock in the afternoon, to judge by the position of the sun, I saw the men who were at work on the canal break through the earth wall at the mouth of the canal along the bank of the Magdalena, and as soon as they had done so a great volume of water spurted through and plunged very violently with the current down the new waterway.[33]

Mendoza was proud of having kept the cost down to 50,000 pesos, of which the municipality of Cartagena contributed 10,000, with most of the balance subscribed by other townships: 'a price so cheap as to detract from the grandeur of the work', which its beneficiaries hailed as 'a work equal to that of the Romans'.[34] It took only three or four days to navigate the length of the canal. In its first month of operation, the new waterway bore more than thirty small vessels, carrying wines and spirits, soap and candlewax, iron and pitch and pots, demonstrating the superiority of waterborne transport, at roughly half the cost per unit of bulk on average, over the laborious mule trains it replaced. Over the period as a whole, flour and sugar were the main products shipped to Cartagena, while the inland trade featured mainly wines and oil, along with soap, wax, tallow, ploughshares, spirits, salt meat and cheese, textiles, pitch and ironware.[35]

Maintenance, however, proved beyond the means of the investing communities, while the muleteers and the political factions opposed to Mendoza's government did their best to clog the canal, arraigning him, in complaints of anonymous or suppositious authorship, for every kind of excess, from provocation of dissidence to subornation of women. The canal decayed rapidly, owing to silting of the river mouth and vandalism by muleteers and profiteers, until by 1679 only a stretch between Matumilla and Mahates, amounting to about half the total length, remained permanently navigable. The rest could be used only for three months a year, when the floods of the Magdalena forced it open.

In 1724 the commander of the Tierra Firme fleet, Francisco Cornejo, took Cartagena's governor and Juan de Herrera y Sotomayor, the chief engineer, on an inspection of the canal to back up his shocking report on its state of deterioration. Herrera believed the entire route could be made navigable with a few years' work with equipment to be imported from the Netherlands and France. That was an illusion, evoking the habitual optimism we have so often encountered with the empire's engineers. But the result included a renewed assault on the technical problems during repairs that took five months to complete in 1726 and reduced the prices of some goods by 300 per cent.[36] The *cabildo* – the town council – of Cartagena was obliged to renounce its right to tolls for ten years to the private investors who paid for the work. Under private management the canal prospered but when the *cabildo* resumed control, deterioration set in again. In 1748, when the canal was back to its former sad condition, Ignacio Sala – an engineer of repute who had worked on improvements to the course of the Guadalete in Andalusia and whom the crown appointed to the governorship of Cartagena – adumbrated a new project, involving dredging the river mouth and speeding the flow of water through the canal by redesigning its banks. Political distractions and recurrent wars stranded the work, unattempted until the last decade of the century. By then, the viceroy and archbishop, Antonio Caballero y Góngora, had put together a powerful coalition – including José Celestino Mutis, celebrated for his adventurous innovations in botany and widely acclaimed as the most eminent savant in Enlightenment America, and Pedro Fermín de Vargas, a creole enthusiast for reforms of all kinds – in favour of an ambitious approach. Sectors formerly obstructive to the work became permissive, if not supportive. The city council of Cartagena renounced its rights to the canal to the crown in 1791. The viceroy hired a new chief engineer, Antonio de Arévalo, with an assistant who churned out maps and surveys. Yet in 1794 only 47 kilometres (29 mi.) were open all year round, with a further stretch of 21 kilometres (13 mi.) (to the mouth of the Sanaguare) interrupted by the periodically impracticable, narrow reach known as Caño de las Flechas. The rest of the canal could be used only when the Magdalena was in flood. The leading creole merchant José Ignacio de Pombo deplored the state of the canal:

Far from appearing to be an estimable work of human ingenuity, reflecting the application of industry and care to the duty of conservation, it looks rather more like a ruin or a work of nature. Brush covers the unlevelled banks. A thousand obstacles obstruct the flow. The pools of standing water that the canal links are filthy and full of vegetation. Most of the course is neglected and in disrepair. Navigability is diminished in consequence and lasts for barely three months a year. Such is the lamentable condition and the main current focus of interest. The defects arise partly from neglect, partly from deficiencies in construction, and partly from the environment of the canal.[37]

Pombo lost little time in seeking remedies. In mid-1794 Arévalo came up with a promising and comprehensive plan: a new, gateless approach, lined with stone; reconfiguration of the entry to the canal so that it would be fully 1.5 metres (5 ft) below the lowest level to which the River Magdalena could be expected to fall, so that sufficient draft would never be wanting; and improved guttering and drainage. The work began in 1806.

The Prehistory of the Panama Canal

According to Ignacio González Tascón, the authority par excellence on Spanish engineering in the Enlightenment, the Canal del Dique, as it emerged from the reforms that Arévalo planned, was 'the greatest achievement' in canal-building in Spanish America.[38] That is not, perhaps, to say very much, as the other big canal project of the era remained unaccomplished until nearly a century after the collapse of Spain's mainland American empire. The first surveys of a potential canal route across the Isthmus of Panama were conducted in the reigns of Charles v and Philip II, but in 1534 and 1567 reports on the potential for canals through Panama or Nicaragua were dispiriting.[39] On the first of these occasions the conquistador-turned-administrator Gaspar de Espinosa insisted that it must be possible to cut a canal through the mere 4 leagues of land that lay beyond Lake Nicaragua to the sea, but a canal would be almost as accessible – or, at least, as tempting – to interlopers and pirates as to Spanish ships. For the same reason, it seemed ill-advised even to extend the size of the port at the Atlantic end of the transisthmian route: the wider the harbour, the harder it would be to defend.[40]

Daunting practicalities and enormous costs postponed every recurrence of the notion, while the amount of traffic remained insufficient as an incentive. The idea was re-mooted in earnest in the 1730s, when Charles de La Condamine and his companions crossed the Isthmus on their way to Quito to measure the circumference of the Earth at the equator, and suggested that Lake Chagres could be the central axis of an interoceanic canal. When, however, a survey arrived to follow up on the initiative in 1744, the report was unfavourable, noting the difference in sea level on the two shores and the torturous terrain that lay between them. A canal would be 'hazardous to enter and hard to leave'.[41]

For a while, dreams of a canal switched focus to the north, to Mexico, where, in the central valley around Lake Texcoco, the pre-conquest system of waterways was still in use. In 1774 the viceroy Antonio María de Bucareli, who had swept into New Spain like a reforming wind, ordered an inquiry into the prospects of linking internal waterways so as to create a route from ocean to ocean. The outcome was negative: the scheme was 'not found to be an impossibility', but it was 'believe[d] the cost would be great and the usefulness little'.[42] The shortest distance from the Gulf of Mexico to the Pacific, across the neck of land from Santo Domingo Tehauntepec, was the future site of a transisthmian railway, but, at over 193 kilometres (120 mi.) even at the narrowest point, was judged to be long for a canal, too.

As attention shifted back towards Nicaragua and Panama, security considerations were more significant than ever – paramount, indeed, in the increasingly competitive world of rival empires. The Pacific was no longer a 'Spanish lake'.[43] Scientific expeditions, whaling, the allure of the products of the South Seas, colonial prospects and geopolitical strategy all brought French, British and Russian fleets to the ocean. Rebellion in most of Britain's mainland American colonies plunged the Spanish monarchy into war on the rebels' behalf.[44] The danger that France would seek to recover or replace the empire she had handed to Spain in Louisiana was ever present. In such circumstances, if a canal were built, would Spain be able to retain control of it or enforce a monopoly? If England or France were to deem a project feasible, would either go to war to put it into practice or to reap the benefits?

In 1778–9 José de Inzaurrandiaga surveyed the terrain from Cartago to Panama and the route via Lake Nicaragua in 23 days – a little less time than normal. His reports – in common with the heroic self-image of most great-journey narratives – focused on hardships and obstacles: abominable climate, indomitable terrain, sparse opportunities for resupply, unreliable indios.[45] In 1781 the Captain General of Guatemala, the energetic Matías Gálvez, who later supervised extensive public works in Mexico, commissioned a new study of the feasibility of a canal from Lake Nicaragua to the Pacific. His surveyor, Manuel Galisteo, undertook a meticulous study of the problems posed by the variations in altitude along and across the route. He showed that a canal would have to overcome the 39-metre (128 ft) surface elevation that separated Lake Nicaragua from the Atlantic, before coping with a further 132-metre (433 ft) ascent to the highest potential point along the route, and adjusting from there to sea level on the Pacific, 170 metres (558 ft) further down. His findings were technically encouraging but politically negative. Spanish officials were left assured that even if foreigners seized the region or enforced its sale, they would be unable to bring the project to fruition.

The inescapable background to all these developments and to the corresponding hopes and fears was the growth of international trade, which attracted private investors to the idea of a canal. The first project emerged in France in 1785, when a former army engineer, Nicolas de Fer, read a paper on the prospects of an interoceanic canal at the Académie des sciences. His scheme approached fantasy: he proposed a single giant lock to equalize the difference in sea level between the Atlantic and the Pacific. He lobbied the Spanish government relentlessly through the Conde de Aranda, who at the time was Spain's minister plenipotentiary in Paris. From the Spanish point of view, Fer's paper signalled a danger: he stressed the advantages to France. Nevertheless, perhaps, under the influence of the general enthusiasm in pre-revolutionary Paris for mega-canals – a Suez Project was widely mooted as well as a Panamanian one – Aranda decided to recommend Fer's plan.[46] The Spanish government's official consultant on cosmography, Juan Bautista Muñoz, responded enthusiastically. A canal, he opined, would justify its cost 'beyond comparison' and excite 'the emulation and envy of all the powers' for 'the greatest, most glorious, and most useful undertaking in the world of today'.[47] His view, however, suffered from two defects. Although it was the product of impressive scholarly labour, it was based entirely on research into existing surveys, many of which were centuries old, by an investigator who did not know the terrain at first hand. And Muñoz's report included a fatal admonition: a successful canal would become the object of the cupidity of rival powers.[48]

On that point, the author was evidently correct. In 1780, during the hostilities with Spain unleashed by the American War of Independence, Britain sent a fleet to seize Nicaragua. The expedition failed owing to the intervention of the torrid climate and the malaria-bearing mosquito – those unsurpassed defenders of tropical colonies – but Nelson, who was a captain at the time, emerged with the conviction that the Isthmus was 'the Gibraltar of Spanish America', controlling communications between the Atlantic and Pacific as Gibraltar did those between the Atlantic and the Mediterranean. 'If we capture it,' he concluded, 'we shall cut Spanish America in two.' Meanwhile projectors in England revived a scheme previously mooted during Scotland's abortive attempt to colonize Darién in the late seventeenth century: a canal to debouch in the Gulf of San Miguel.

In 1787 Thomas Jefferson, who at the time represented the United States in Paris, wrote to his counterpart in Madrid requesting data on the documentation Muñoz had deployed. He adjudged a canal to be perfectly practicable.[49] Three years later, Francisco de Miranda, ever watchful for ways of involving foreign powers in his ambitions for Spanish American independence, offered to grant the British government rights to open a canal in exchange for help in his struggle. Rebuffed, he made the same offer to the United States.

In a memoir addressed to the crown in response to Gálvez's project, the Conde de Fernán Núñez acknowledged that a canal would 'be of general advantage to the commerce of Europe and the world' but for that very reason advised against opening it: it would not make sense for Spain to bear the cost of a universal benefit. He feared not only the avarice of Spain's rivals but the self-interest of her colonies: in an image that seems to have been borrowed from the *commedia dell'arte*, Spanish America resembled 'a lovely woman, who has become the possession of an elderly man who takes care of her, watches over her and keeps her as well as he is able' and who, 'though her needs and desires are beyond protector's power to satisfy, she keeps her counsel in order to avoid displeasing him, while he locks the doors closed and sees to it that admirers from outside are kept at bay.' Fernán Núñez drew, nonetheless, a comforting conclusion: a canal would be more difficult to defend than the existing trail across Panama. The considerations of geopolitical rivalry that deterred Spain from investing in a canal would have similarly repressive effects on the ambitions of other powers. The count used the case to argue for the reformation of international law, proposing – albeit with avowed diffidence about the practicability of the notion – that the powers should collectively guarantee an agreed distribution of territory and free rights of navigation around the world. 'Nowadays,' he wrote, 'the spirit of commerce is what counts for most, and attempts by governments to extend the reach of their own subjects is incompatible with the principles of free trade.'[50]

Commercial appetites, however, had been aroused and two proposals of increasing elaboration followed. In 1788 a consortium applied for permission to build an ocean-to-ocean canal via Nicaragua, trading investment in the project for profits from expected outcomes.[51] The author of the proposal, the mining engineer Joaquín Antonio Escartín, appealed to Enlightenment ideas of progress: though earlier surveys had dismissed a canal as unfeasible, the difficulties, however admittedly arduous, could now be overcome by techniques already in use in France and Spain. For Escartín, canal-building was about more than profit and loss or practicality and utility: it was a source of majesty, like the feats of ancient Roman engineers, and a means for Spaniards to perfect 'the glory of an empire they have inherited from their ancestors'. In a sense, he was surely right: the message of the present book is that engineering serves empires as well as economies. Escartín realized, of course, that he had to look to the bottom line. He reckoned – or rather guessed – the costs at between 30 and 40 million *livres tournois* (perhaps U.S.$6 to 8 million today) for 'considerable' benefits to Spain and to commerce and 'inestimable advantage . . . to the prospects and power of the monarchy'. The outcome would be a magnet for trade. 'The trade of China, Japan, and even India would fall entirely' into the hands of the Spanish crown. The viability of the Philippines would be transformed by new industrial and agrarian opportunities that would make the colony as rich as China. Like successive colonial projectors depicting utopias refracted through rose-tinted lenses, Escartín commended the region of Lake Nicaragua – his proposed route – as exceptionally healthful and productive and altogether superior to the 'swampy, irregular and insanitary' region at the neck of the Isthmus.[52]

The second project, presented by a mixed French and Spanish group of financiers led by Martín de la Bastide in 1790, was similar but even more elaborate and convincing in its vision of a new era for the Spanish Empire.[53] Bastide was as besotted as Escartín with the 'grandeur and importance' of an objective which, he claimed, previous surveyors had insufficiently appreciated. 'They did not give enough thought either to how best to bring the work to a speedy and successful conclusion or how to choose the best location for so great an undertaking.'[54] His preferred route, straight across the shortest cut through the Isthmus, would, he averred, facilitate existing commerce and augment its range, drawing trade between Europe and Asia away from the Cape of Good Hope, and unify the commerce of China and the East Indies in Spanish hands.

In 1811 Humboldt announced his own views on the canal question. He reverted to favouring the route through Lake Nicaragua, but in other respects his confidence in the desirability and viability of the project was decisive in clinching approval. But his intervention came just too late. The Spanish American independence movements were breaking out in uncontainable violence. The interoceanic canal had become an irresistible prospect, but its realization seemed as far distant as ever.[55]

5

THE RINGS OF STONE
Fortifying the Frontiers

Be thou my strong habitation, whereunto I may continually resort:
thou hast given commandment to save me; for thou art my rock
and my fortress. (PSALM 71:3)

'I will not say I ever saw a better king,' wrote Philippe de Commynes
of Louis XI of France, 'Because, although he oppressed his subjects
himself, he would never allow anyone else to do so.'[1] Protection against
external enemies is the only inescapable obligation of the state. Political legitimacy is measurable by the difference between tribute – the
purchase price of a tyrant's forbearance – and taxation, the means by
which subjects and citizens pay for defence. Frontier security is
therefore an objective of every state.

The Spanish global monarchy's record in border control was equivocal: it was impressive, inasmuch as the monarchy endured for a long
time, maintaining and expanding its borders, except in peripheral
plases of little importance, such as the Antillean islands occupied by
France in 1635, or Jamaica, lost to English invaders in 1654. What proved
to be untenable toeholds were relinquished on the Chesapeake in the
seventeenth century or, in the eighteenth, in Honduras, where British
interlopers got a permanent foothold in what is now Belize, and the
Brazilian frontier with Portugal, where some Jesuit reductions – as
their settlements were called, where natives were 'reduced' or, literally,
'led back' to salvation – were sacrificed in the interest of wider peace
and for gains in what is now Uruguay. There were, of course, temporary
failures – in keeping interlopers out of northern Hispaniola, for
instance, in the 1660s, or from parts of the Portuguese dominions at
moments during the union of the Spanish and Portuguese crowns from

the 1580s to the 1640s; and in excluding the Dutch from unoccupied islands and shores of the Caribbean. Withdrawals elsewhere were from ungovernably intractable places or in the interests of wider security or countervailing gains. The northern Netherlands and Portugal in the mid-seventeenth century, and the southern Netherlands and the Italian dominions in the eighteenth, were cases in point. The overall balance favoured Spain to a surprising degree, especially in view of the remarkable longevity of its empire in mainland America, compared with European and Indigenous rivals.

On the other hand, the American frontiers were always permeable by raiders and looters. Like that of the Romans, whose empire was always the Spaniards' model, the landward *limes*, or frontier, was indefensibly long and irrationally angular, while the vast seaward outlook could never be adequately patrolled. The shape of the empire was too sprawling for defence on interior lines. Fortifications therefore constituted the essential infrastructure of imperial peace, to deter invaders and intimidate insurgents. Eventually Spain's empire became probably the most heavily fortified in history.[2]

Battlements and bastions absorbed a lot of attention and resources. They remain, sometimes in the form of ruins but often still in daunting order, prodding vertices into the ocean, raising ramparts over suburbs and countryside or staring over imaginary enemies through the embrasures of batteries: evidence of the power and prosperity of the colonial era. Humboldt, for instance, on his famous tour of Spanish America in 1800, contemplated, with the kind of jaw-dropping awe that any modern tourist will recognize, the ruins of the defences of Santiago de Araya in Venezuela: dynamited to keep the fortress from English hands, the remains in his day already had a half-natural air, combining evidence of the genius of man and the power of the elements. They appealed to both sides of Humboldt's character: the hard-headed, scientific engineer and the irrepressible romantic. Like a traveller in an antique land, he beheld 'apparently superhuman works, comparable to the masses of shattered rocks that appeared when the planet first took shape'.[3] Today no visitor to Cartagena de Indias – the reputed 'key' to eighteenth-century South America'[4] – can feel unmoved by the evidence of indomitable effort that went into the construction of the great seaward walls: they are 7.6 metres (25 ft) thick with a 1.8-metre-deep (6 ft) skin of stone over a timber core, and upwards of 6.7 metres (22 ft) high.

Whether the rings of stone that circled the empire were cost-effective, however, or even very useful, is open to debate. The maintenance of the monarchy depended most, as we see repeatedly throughout the present book, on the loyalty or at least the resignation of its subjects. But like every part of the infrastructure of the empire, the fortifications served for psychological effect, even when they functioned poorly as physical protection. The inhabitants of Spanish America, as this chapter helps to show, invested materially and probably emotionally in the defensive system; and although, as we shall see, the decision-makers in Spain and, to a lesser extent, in the American and Filipino dominions prioritized the guardianship of commerce above the safety of settlements, the best reason for adhering to the monarchy, from the point of view of Indigenous and creole elites, was access to a vast network of trade, secured against pirates and rivals. In that respect, fortification helped.

Shouldering the Burden:
The Slow and Reluctant Beginnings of Fortification

The difficulties of constructing workable defences were formidable. Two huge disparities got in the way: first, between the enormity of the task and the extent of the work; and second, between the constructors' vast ambitions and their limited practical attainments. A woodcut in one of the earliest editions of Columbus's first report of his discoveries illustrates the latter contrast and shows how the Spanish Empire was born – as it were – with unrealistically great expectations. In the engraver's imagination, which was a reflection of Columbus's own fantasies, gantries raised huge blocks of perfect masonry, as the battlements and towers of an accomplished town took shape. The image was grand; the reality was scrappy. The first fort Columbus built on Hispaniola was a stockade (in which the entire garrison perished in a massacre) hurriedly cobbled together from the timbers of his grounded flagship. The second was an earthwork modelled on traditional native designs by Taino craftsmen. Columbus's headquarters, his *casa fuerte* in the short-lived, unhealthy, uninhabitable capital with which he endowed the island at Isabela, was just a squat building of less than 100 square metres (1,076 sq. ft), with a small tower at one corner.[5] The fort that Columbus's successor as governor of Hispaniola built in the interior, at Concepción, to oversee gold production, was more substantial at 47 × 24 metres (154 × 79 ft), with a brick wall 2 metres (6½ ft) thick and twin towers, but the garrison never exceeded thirty men.

It remained easier, of course, to put defences on a map than on the ground. Plans adumbrated in 1526 anticipated a well-fortified Spanish Main – better fortified, in some respects, than it ever became. Forts authorized by the crown and erected without harm or loss to the Indigenous population – a condition which alone consigned the scheme to the realms of fancy, even though the intractable Caribs were exempted from the benign injunctions – would fringe the seaboard and tower over major inland cities: three in Hispaniola, where Santo Domingo would be protected by a chain slung across the harbour between protective towers, two each in Cuba and Puerto Rico, and one on Guadalupe. In New Spain, Mexico City, Puebla and Antequera in Oaxaca would all have forts to protect them, as would Veracruz, where the island of San Juan de Ulúa guarded the bay. A manuscript dialogue of a little later in the sixteenth century sustains the fantasy, describing San Juan de Ulúa as 'impregnable' at a time when its defence consisted only of a square tower, one-quarter complete.[6] Further south, there would be a tower to rival the volcano at Santiago de Guatemala, three forts in Nicaragua and two in Tierra Firme. The south coast of the Caribbean would be defended at Santa Marta and Cartagena, with another stronghold in between, and five more at inland locations as far east as Venezuela. There would be four forts in New Toledo and five to guard the Río de la Plata, which had barely been explored at the time.[7]

The scheme was visionary not only in its extent, which exceeded the limits of effective Spanish occupation at the time, but in its potentially transmutative power: except in parts of the Andes, Indigenous societies were not greatly interested in fortified warfare. In recent years, aerial photography, supplemented by digs, has revealed unsuspected extents of city fortification in pre-colonial Mesoamerica, including series of palisades that date back to Olmec times and the 3.2 kilometres (2 mi.) of walls that made a sort of citadel at Monte Albán and the network barriers that 'sealed' its environs.[8] El Mirador, one of the earliest and most formidable of Maya cities, had ramparts perhaps 4 metres (13 ft) high; those from the same late pre-classic era at Becán rose to 5 metres (16½ ft).[9] Earthworks surrounded Tikal, and those that protected Los Naranjos extended over 1,300 metres (4,265 ft).

Pre-conquest cities commonly had walls of some sort, albeit, by the fifteenth century, modest structures like those that can be seen at Tulúm today – apparently serving more for demarcation than defence.[10] Andean centres also had formidable walls: Chan Chan needed towering defences because of its lowland position, Kuélap less so because it stood on a mountain top; yet its engineers heaped dressed stones in the mid-sixth century, perhaps to define a sacred zone.[11] Some of the most impressive structures, apparently built to screen entire valleys from pillage, were, of course, in ruins – and often barely visible – by the time the Spaniards arrived, but 145 kilometres (90 mi.) of ancient wall, of still unelucidated provenance, snake along the course of the Santa River in northern Peru. Inca engineers built walls in the same tradition and to demarcate consecrated ground; though they seem to have preferred to rely on terrain for natural defence, they erected at least twenty forts to guard their northern border, and Cuzco was protected by the great fortress of Sacsahuamán, with masonry blocks sometimes of up to forty tons in weight piled to daunting heights.[12]

There were, however, strictly no precedents for Spanish methods of fortification. It is therefore perhaps unsurprising that so ambitious and novel a future as Spaniards envisaged for the protection of their colonies took centuries to put into effect, and was never perfected.

Moreover, Spanish authorities tended to await disaster before investing in fortification – responding to raids or defeats rather than preventing them in the first place. Pedro Menéndez de Áviles proposed the fortification of all major harbours in his comprehensive advice for imperial defence in the 1550s.[13] Such counsels of perfection were hardly likely to transform into real achievements. Until the 1580s, all Spanish fortification in the Americas was rudimentary, where it existed at all, and was generally unfit for purpose. The depredations and effrontery of pirates made it increasingly evident that something would have to be done.

The outbreak of war with England in the 1570s provided some stimulus: in 1573 Francisco de Toledo, viceroy of Peru, proposed fortifying the ports of Guayaquil, Paita, Santa, Callao and Arica in anticipation of English incursions into the Pacific, but the Council of the Indies voted him down.[14] From 1576 the compilation of the royally ordained great survey of the colonies, the *Relaciones geográficas*, supplied preliminary data – essential for a comprehensive scheme of defence

– about distribution of population and wealth, with basic information about the terrain and the location of pre-conquest fortifications. By the 1580s 'a mammoth pile' of petitions had built up in demand for fortifications.[15]

In 1586, after Francis Drake had shocked the world with a piratical cruise around the Pacific and a series of daring and successful raids from Vigo to Nombre de Dios, Santo Domingo and Cartagena, the crown took the first step towards a plan for the entire seaboard monarchy by commissioning the best Italian engineers to survey all its vulnerable points. Bautista Antonelli, the leading expert at the time, was entrusted with the planning in the Indies. He recommended barring the harbour of Cartagena and moving the terminus of Isthmus trade from Nombre de Dios to Portobelo, with a fort at the mouth of the Chagres River, where the sentinel station of San Lorenzo now adorns the peninsula that juts into the approach to the river mouth. Antonelli's scheme for Puerto Rico demonstrated his thoroughness: blocking a channel, even though the locals considered it too narrow for assailants, rebuilding the fort on modern principles and forming three lines of fortified defence. His plan for Havana, which by then was the most important rendezvous point for transatlantic shipping, included replacing the existing earthworks in stone, and covering the harbour with cross-fire from strong embrasures.

The crown authorized a start on the plans, but also essayed a cheaper and more direct option: invading or intimidating England into submission. In 1588 the 'Invincible' Armada was launched. In some ways, it justified the ambitious strategy of which it was the key ingredient by exposing the weakness of English defences; but a freak storm dispersed it with heavy losses. Ships and equipment were easily replaced, but the failure of the Armada proved to be a sort of Spanish Flodden, in which many of the *jeunesse dorée* of the realm were lost in the wreck of *La Girona*, a galleass that bore the most promising youth of the kingdom and the natural future leaders of Spanish war efforts. The disaster convinced the king to invest whatever the engineering experts deemed necessary to protect the empire.[16]

Antonelli's plan was undertaken in earnest despite the enormous budget of 150,000 ducats, and the failure of England's 'counterarmada' at Corunna and Lisbon in 1589.[17] Storms destroyed Antonelli's first, emergency measures at Cartagena in 1588. But in November of that year he was ordered back from Spain to build defences for Puerto

Rico, Cuba, Veracruz and Panama, taking a team of engineers and stonecutters with him. Sickness, routine obstruction by local interests and officials, the vagaries of shipping, and above all the torpor of construction delayed him. Nonetheless, between 1588 and 1599, when he retired to Spain, Antonelli built fourteen forts, covering all the major occupied New World harbours, including those of San Juan, Cartagena, Veracruz and Panama, with the strongholds of Santiago and San Felipe to guard the approach to Portobelo. He also found time to supervise the defence of Nombre de Dios against Drake in 1596 – this time successfully, with an outcome in which Drake died and the English retreated. In 1598 one of the guardian forts of Puerto Rico fell to an English attack; the improvements that followed were proof against the next attempt, by Dutch assailants in 1625. Similar programmes of fortification in Spain and the Canaries complemented Antonelli's, while the ships lost to the storm of 1588 were replaced by tougher, trimmer, better-armed and more efficient vessels. The overall results made the Spanish Empire more formidable than ever, and helped to make transatlantic trade surprisingly secure, but still could not provide guarantees against enemies who remained free to concentrate forces at any point along the vast reaches of the empire's coastline and to raid settlements by bypassing harbour defences.

The Paucity of Resources

Even when the monarchy bent to the task of defence-building, from the 1580s onward, when the insolence of pirates and the perils of war made a response inevitable, resources were always hard to come by. In 1649 Antonelli's son, Juan Bautista, current representative of perhaps the greatest engineering dynasty in the history of Spain, died in Cartagena, amid the still inchoate defences, lamenting the way delayed wages for the workers held the job up.[18] Construction usually demanded more labour than was freely available or than slaves and convicts could supply. In Cartagena in 1795 Antonio de Arévalo, the engineer in charge of maintaining the walls, painfully listed the workers incapacitated by age and infirmity: one was over eighty years old and blind; another was a septuagenarian who suffered from impaired vision and was 'full of agues'. The workforce included idiots, paralytics and others enfeebled by poor nourishment, injuries or nameless illness, or simply buckled or blinded by senectitude.[19] It is hard to believe that even healthy slaves, convicts and conscripts worked with maximum efficiency. Other manpower constraints limited most forts to the most compact dimensions imaginable, with as few outworks as possible.[20] Numbers of men available for garrison duty increased relentlessly over the entire colonial period, but fluctuations were inevitable and it never made sense to keep numbers up to strength in times of peace. At Atalaya, Río Lagartos, for instance, a stone structure capable of holding 250 men and dated from a time of former prosperity, had to be reduced during reforms to hold only 50 or 60 in the mid-eighteenth century.[21] Many more examples can be traced among the stories of inland frontier forts, summarized below.

Designers were even rarer than defenders. The number of serving engineers in the whole of Spanish America in the seventeenth century amounted to less than one-tenth of those in Spain.[22] Some remote places never had the services of a professional: locals extemporized, drawing for their designs on childhood memories of woodcuts from chapbooks or memories frozen in time: that is probably why the Castillo de San Felipe del Golfo Dulce in Guatemala looks like a medieval tower. Because Santo Domingo receded in importance, the Torre del Homenaje on the banks of the River Ozama was never rebuilt. So it retains to this day its old-fashioned outline, with square plan and crenellated elevation.

Contemplating the empire from Barcelona in 1771 the engineer Juan Martín Cermeño blamed creole complacency for putting 'less solidity and care' into American fortifications than was normal in Europe,[23] but he probably failed to appreciate the paucity of resources and the problems of scale. Still, he may have had a point: between wars and raids, it was hard to maintain the effort of building walls and forts.[24] When Henry Morgan sacked Portobelo in 1668, officials' first reaction was to move the town; when the decision was made to stay and improve the defences, work proceeded in fits and starts before being abandoned in 1686. Six years later the Marqués de la Mina demanded that the work either be finished to keep the place in Spanish hands or demolished to deny its benefits to the British, who would surely take over.[25]

Effective defence demanded costly materials and it took generations, or centuries in some cases, for sufficient resources to accumulate or sufficient urgency to arise, even in defensively sensitive locations. San Agustín, for instance, founded in Florida in 1565 to counteract

French interest and to secure access to the Gulf Stream for fleets returning from the Caribbean to Spain, was a strategically vital point, but eight successive stockades of wood occupied the site until 1670, when the foundation of an English colony at Charleston obliged the Spaniards to rebuild it in stone.[26] The cost of stone for the bastion of San Marcos at San Augustín was not approved until 1669. In Yucatán, despite exposure to foreigners' incursions, much of the coast was defended by cheapskate, gimcrack measures, as the engineer Juan de Dios González complained in a report of February 1766: at the time, the fort of Omoa, intended to control the Mosquito indios' contraband business, was made only of wood and guano and Mérida was protected by only nine wooden watchtowers.[27] There, a further impediment had frustrated engineers' efforts: as in many other places, the Franciscan missionaries opposed military measures that might undermine indio confidence in Spanish benevolence, multiply the numbers of licentious soldiery and impede attempts at evangelization. In some places, such as Vera Cruz in Guatemala, indio menace rapidly dispelled such missionary idealism. At Mérida, the Franciscans held out against fortification until 1669.[28]

Acapulco presents a further instance of a place of incalculable importance where effective defence seemed strangely delayed. Bernardo de Balbuena's oft-quoted *Grandeza mexicana* of 1604 leaves no doubt of the esteem the place commanded as the New Spain terminus of transpacific trade:

En tí se junta España con la China,
Italia con Japón y finalmente
Un mundo entero en trato y disciplina.

Here Spain meets China; Italy Japan,
Encompassing in trade the whole world's span.[29]

Yet defences were sketchy until the Flemish engineer Adriaan Boot arrived in November 1615, on secondment from Mexico City, where he had gone to inspect the drainage. His new commission was to build a redoubt to defend Acapulco, but he rejected the scheme as insufficient and recommended a fortress for a garrison of seventy. The authorities accepted the proposal – reluctantly in view of the cost, but urgently because of fear of Dutch interlopers. Acapulco had only

Boot's fort to guard it until an earthquake in 1776, which prompted works and the addition of forts. Boot's now sleeps peaceably inside the town. Within a couple of years, free-trade principles were adopted, which diverted Filipino traffic via the Indian Ocean; earthquakes and increasing Pacific competition from other powers diminished trade and deterred further outlay.

If Acapulco was a vital Pacific hub, so in the Atlantic was eighteenth-century Puerto Rico, important for access to the Antilles and Central America. There too fortification proceeded slowly. The Conde O'Reilly – the Jacobite exile whom rebels in New Orleans would later denounce as 'Bloody O'Reilly' when he served there as a repressive governor – proposed a scheme in 1765, as a result of which the Castillo de San Cristóbal was added to the defences in 1771. It was only in the 1790s, however, that the engineer Tomás O'Daly executed the rest of the plan, rebuilding the main fort of San Jerónimo on modern lines and closing the Boquerón.[30] If such places as Puerto Rico and Acapulco took so long to fortify it is not surprising that remoter reaches of the empire were poorly served. Nowhere in Chile had much protection from seaborne attack, even in the Strait of Magellan, until the second half of the eighteenth century, despite efforts in Philip II's time to protect the strait with a cordon of forts – Carelmapu, Chacao (with an extensive system of outworks), Castro and San Carlos de Ancud y de Agüi with its outlying batteries.[31] In mid-eighteenth-century Paraguay the extension of Portuguese occupation towards the Paraná valley and the suppression of the Jesuit reductions that formerly guarded the frontier made it obvious that new defences were required. But the Fort of San Carlos del Río Apa y Borbón was not begun until 1792 nor finished until 1806.[32] Montevideo was always a serious garrison town and potentially 'another Gibraltar', guarding the River Plate as the Rock guarded the Mediterranean. Yet Domingo Petrarca's designs for the citadel were frustrated by professional disputes over location, problems of water supply, lack of funds, the death of the designer and delay in replacing him. The project was begun in 1741, following the cheapest option, which left water sources outside the fortified area. One gimcrack bastion collapsed after a few years, another in 1770. The circuit of the walls was not complete until 1800. Visitors throughout the eighteenth century echoed each other's convictions about the deficiencies of the design and repair of the defences. John Constantine Davie was one of the minority who approved; but he regarded the outpost as defensible only against indios and Portuguese, not British assailants, perhaps because in contrast to most of the more northerly ports, Montevideo's landward defences were more mature than those to seaward.[33]

As Francisco de Castejon, commander of the fort of San Juan de Ulúa, remarked in the course of his efforts in 1658 to obtain subventions for work he deemed vital, 'to maintain defences without resources is a job not for men but for God.'[34] He was embroiled in another of the circumstances that frequently impeded engineering work: a dispute, part professional and part personal, between rival officials. Castejón worried that his fort was exposed to attack. The engineer in charge, Marcos de Lucio, countered that Castejon's demands were unnecessarily expensive, and that the purpose of the fort was to defend the port, not the land: it was, he thought, vital to keep the ground area compact and defensible by a small garrison. The dispute, exacerbated by the effects of a destructive hurricane in 1661, ended with Castejón's death in prison, shortly before an order for his release arrived.[35] Thereafter the German engineer Jaime Franck completed the reform of the defences at San Juan in 1692, on a new, rectangular plan, which echoed some of his dead predecessor's ideas.

Towns versus Trade

Lucio's dispute with Castejón revealed a common dilemma: how to balance the demands of seaward and landward defence. Almost everywhere, the protection of commerce took priority over that of settlements. Santo Domingo was encircled relatively early, in works that lasted from 1543 to 1567.[36] But it proved exceptional. From Antonelli's first forays, locals generally wanted urban rather than harbour defences – an objective inconsistent with the engineer's brief and with the primary interests of the monarchy. The citizens of Cartagena asked Antonelli for heavy walls and cannon rather than bulwarks to guard the harbour mouth.[37] They never came to regard the harbour defences as theirs, but rather as a royal enterprise in which they were little concerned.[38] The policy of prioritizing harbour defence left the adjoining towns vulnerable to raiders who simply bypassed the forts, advancing on the settlements from the landward side. When Lima was circled with walls in the 1690s the initiative came from the awareness – expressed by the Jesuit engineer Juan Ramón Coninck, a professor at the Universidad de San Marcos and a cosmographer-royal – that pirate-attackers could evade the fort of Callao. In 1687, with danger approaching from the sea, he answered the summons to the city's defence. Around 920 hectares (2,275 ac.) he threw an adobe wall, 11,700 metres (38,385 ft) long and up to 11 metres (36 ft) high, fitted with firing platforms and 25 redoubts. It was ready the same year but no assault ever put it to the test, luckily.[39] His plans included the enclosure of wheat fields to help withstand a long siege.

In some ways, merchant-citizens and their rulers were at odds over how to receive interlopers. When the English privateer and slaver John Hawkins made his first illegal overtures in the 1560s he found opportunities to trade at Santo Domingo and Veracruz, after threatening the denizens with fire and sword and thereby providing them with an excuse to break the laws against fraternization with foreign merchants.[40] No subsequent intruder found it easy to bypass imperial restraints on trade, but control remained a priority for the rulers rather than the ruled. In any case the control of commerce and the defence of settlement were irremediably incompatible: every effective harbour fort deflected attackers, who always sought relatively easy pickings, in the direction of some ill-defended town.

One solution was to make a virtue of necessity and leave settlements undefended, in order to prevent them from becoming enemy strongholds. Antonelli complained that Veracruz was open, defenceless and disarmed.[41] In 1590 he left it equipped with only two squat towers linking a curtain wall, which he extended inside the harbour, while switching the landing site to a better-protected spot. There were no landward defences. As time went on and vulnerability remained unremedied, it came to be seen as counter-intuitively advantageous. The most eloquent and impactful spokesman for 'open cities' or 'defensa por indefensión' was the outstanding statesman of the Enlightenment, the Conde de Aranda. He favoured the policy, partly on the grounds that well-fortified towns fallen into enemy hands would be hard to recover, and partly in order to maximize the advantages of defence on interior lines.[42] In consequence, for instance, the stronghold of San Carlos de Perote, three days' march inland, on the edge of the central sierra of Mexico, was built under Viceroy Bucareli to defend the coast, as it were, from a distance, with forces despatched from a base inaccessible to attack from the sea. On the Orinoco delta, similar thinking inspired what became ecological conservation: the absolute prohibition of logging, in order to screen the coast with what was supposedly the best possible defence – a forest rampart.

Havana was the scene of similar controversy over the usefulness of fortified towns. It was already the most important port in the New World before getting its first angle-bastioned fort in reaction to a French raid in 1555.[43] Its defences were improved at intervals thereafter but without conforming to the importance of the place. In 1601 Cristóbal de Roda, heir of the greatest military engineering dynasty of the day, advised against spending heavily to protect so small a settlement; a wall around the town was begun half-heartedly at intervals with locally raised funds but remained incomplete until 1740. The need to make Havana fully secure remained unfelt until 1762–3, when a British force captured and occupied the town. Even so, it required a force of 38,000 men in a fleet of 28 ships of the line and 148 transports to accomplish the feat, perhaps because, though weakened by a yellow fever epidemic in 1761, the defenders were in a high state of vigilance at the time. The king had personally attested to the need to 'get ready for the English with increased urgency'. Since the outbreak of hostilities in 1761, the city had been reinforced with 153 heavy guns, more than 78,000 rounds of shot, 5,000 small arms, 400 quintals of powder and over 1,000 men. The shipyards had built 12 warships and 6 frigates. The fort that Bautista Antonelli had designed in the 1590s to control the approach by sea was in a good state of repair. But like Singapore in 1940, Havana was what Churchill would have called 'a battleship without a bottom'. The guns all faced outward, and the English effected a relatively easy route of assault by landing nearby and outflanking the harbour defences.[44] As Antonelli had predicted, possession of the city would depend on control of the heights of La Cabaña, still inadequately protected. The British seized them and the fort of El Morro was obliged to capitulate.[45]

Once Spain retook the city, Havana was at last properly secured by the erection of defences based on the theories of Sébastien de Vauban, the celebrated genius whose designs revolutionized the art of fortification in the later sevententh century. Complementary cross-fire now safeguarded harbour and town alike. San Diego de Atarés was completed in 1767, in hexagonal form high above the town. San Carlos de la Cabaña, 700 metres (nearly 2,300 ft) wide and covering 10 square hectares, was finished in 1774; a tunnel linked it to El Morro, making it possible for reinforcements to go back and forth securely. The builders did not neglect aesthetic embellishments, carved in sandstone, while a fancy entablature lined the inner sufaces of the walls and the chapel facade. The last fort, El Príncipe, perfected by the addition of two half-bastions projecting outward, followed in 1779.[46]

Campeche, today impressive for the magnificence of its surviving defences, demonstrates the same complications, where Spanish engineers turned what had been a Maya trading beach into a serviceable port, but without at first protecting the settlers from raids. Assessors of the need to fortify the Spanish Main long underrated the city and the coast of which it was the heart, perhaps because, bereft of deep harbours, it was more important for regional cabotage than transatlantic trade. The settlements were in any case neglected in favour of the safeguarding of shipping. In 1663 an English assault on Campeche led to the demolition of much of the ramshackle existing defensive system and its replacement with a long trench, but further plans for an encircling wall were postponed owing to experts' differences over the shape they should take. A new and devastating raid in 1678 exposed the city as 'indefensible', according to Governor Antonio de Layseca, in a report of May 1680, even with a notional garrison of three hundred men. The inhabitants, Lyseca reported, were so terrified by former invasion that they needed only to see a distant sail to snatch their flocks and families and head for the hills. Assailants returned in 1683 and 1685, when the town self-financed a hexagonal outwork of walls, with redoubts to control the harbour, to a design by Jaime Frank.[47] Improved after his death by Luis Bouchard de Bécour, the work was finished in 1709 and brought up to date in the 1770s and '80s with a new suite of fortified batteries placed to cover all approaches with cross-fire. Meanwhile, the crown remained unwilling to undertake the wholehearted defence of the surrounding region before 1717, when the menace of English logwood-cutters and poachers of mahogany forced official hands. Laguna de Términos – potentially a highly strategic refuge for low-draft craft – was neglected until then because no threat aroused any Spanish interest in defending it.[48]

At the eastern extremity of Yucatán, a fort at San Felipe de Bacalar was built in 1727 to house a garrison of 45 men in response to English incursions three years previously. Demolition, contemplated in 1746, was waived after an inspection by governor Antonio de Benavides, who predicted that without a permanent Spanish presence, an enemy would take over in the region with help from the monarchy's unreliable

Indigenous subjects, the Zambos, of mixed ancestry, and Mosquitos. As in so many peripheral zones, territory useless for direct exploitation was valuable to interlopers who could use it as a base for raids. Nonetheless, in the stretch of Yucatán coast of which Campeche is the centre, the population was left with little protection against raiders.

Veracruz long remained the model of an 'open' city, unwalled until after French pirates had massacred inhabitants in 1683. Even then, the work would probably have been considered prohibitively expensive but for the discovery of local quarries. No assault recurred until the Seven Years' War, but at that time, according to a report by the engineer Pedro Ponce in 1764, the wall was only 3 metres (10 ft) high, less than half that in thickness, wave-ravaged and incapable of withstanding artillery. Aranda, however, blocked any idea of replacing it, save with his plan to place a garrison at a safe distance inland.[49] While the city remained exposed, the harbour of Veracruz enjoyed the most redoubtable protection in the entire Indies: the fort of San Juan de Ulúa on an island that blocked the bay, where Castejón and Lucio had bickered so unproductively more than a century before. Reputedly, according to a decree of 1765, San Juan was 'the bulwark of the Antilles, the protectress of the Gulf of Mexico, and the guardian of our fleets'.[50] In 1800 the new viceroy, Félix Berenguer de Marquina, took a gloomy view of the general state of imperial defence, but still rated San Juan de Ulúa as impregnable, whereas Veracruz was more effectively defended by yellow fever, against which armies from Europe had no immunity other than expensive bomb-proof buildings.[51] He had a point. When Spanish forces arrived to suppress rebellion in the colonies a few years later, they succumbed more often to fever than to 'patriot' arms.[52] At the fort at San Juan, however, the loyalist garrison outlasted every other stronghold in New Spain, resisting until 1825.[53]

Despite the intractability of the problems, the outcomes remain admirable to beholders of the surviving fortifications, as they did to the assailants whom they so often thwarted. To ring the Spanish Main with stone was like the impossible tasks that induced a frustrating vision in St Augustine's mind: trying to comprehend the Trinity or channel the sea. Yet the extent to which the monarchy succeeded is more worthy of remark than the fact that it ultimately failed. In 1776, at royal behest, Agustín Crame, an engineer of wide experience who commanded the fort of San Juan de Ulúa, set out on a comprehensive tour of inspection of the seaward defences of the mainland

Caribbean shore. It took him three years to develop detailed schemes for the fortification or re-fortification, manning, arming and supply of every major port. The most remarkable feature of his work is how seriously the top brass of the empire took it and how much of it was implemented – working in stages, as Crame's recommendations arrived piecemeal, even before the inspection was complete, in time for Spain's intervention in the American War of Independence.

The Barbarian *Limes*: Sentry-Duty on Landward Lines

Seaward defences, however slowly, followed changes in engineering theory, from those introduced by Antonelli to take into account the geometry of lines of fire and enshrined in *Teoría y práctica de la fortificación* (Theory and Practice of Fortification) by his nephew, Cristóbal de Roda, to the sophisticated designs advocated at engineering academies in the Low Countries and in Barcelona in the late seventeenth and eighteenth centuries, and perfected by Vauban. The inland frontiers never received comparable attention. The vastness of the land frontiers made security unimaginable: fortifications had to minimize damage, not maintain defence. Of the enemies Spain faced, even the most powerful Indigenous units, such as the Comanche and Mapuche empires in the eighteenth century, had no interest in the extinction of Spanish enterprise, on which they relied for ransom and raids. The rival European empires were themselves overstretched and undermanned. On the frontier with Portugal, for most of the time it was possible to make mutual accommodations. In Patagonia, until peace arrived with the great *parlamento* of Negrete in 1793, when Ambrosio O'Higgins prevailed on the Mapuche chiefs to join the monarchy on favourable terms, the *bárbaros* – indios who resisted sedentary life – could only be placated or endured. Fortifications in the Philippines were almost entirely oriented towards the sea.[54] The key frontier was along the northern edge of Spanish North America, where the empire spread over the broadest portion of the hemisphere, across great stretches of plain and desert, without natural defences, in regions where nomadic and pastoral ways of life made a fixed border impossible.

Fortification started, indeed, not along the frontier but along the road northward from San Felipe de los Reyes to the silver mine of

Zacatecas, where five stockades, less than a day's march apart, arose in the 1570s to be manned by half a dozen soldiers each. In the early days of New Spain, Fray Toribio de Motolinía had marvelled at how silver could be carried around the country by one man on a mule with 'as much security as on the road to Benavente', his home town in Spain.[55] The northward extension of the frontier, however, beyond any region ever dominated by the Aztecs, into the 'barbarian' world of the nomadic Chichimecas – literally, 'dog-eaters', the name Spaniards adopted from Nahuatl – inaugurated an era of raiding and revenge, tit for tat, with indomitable 'hostiles'. During the Chichimeca War of the second half of the sixteenth century, the number of garrisons grew to thirty: one chain of presidios, that is, a fortified frontier settlement as they came to be called, led to Durango, where the *camino* terminated; beyond, others were spread like the points of a fan across the Sierra Madre Occidental, usually housing at most about fourteen defenders.[56] The forts proved marginally effective at best, compared with the conciliatory policy that the Marqués de Villamanrique introduced when he became viceroy in 1585. The Chichimeca would rather receive payola in peace than risk rewards in warfare.

Meanwhile, further afield in Sinaloa, the presidio of San Felipe was established in 1595 on what, until the founding of the presidio of Fronteras in 1689, remained the remotest defended point on the northwestern corner of the empire. By 1671, the garrison, originally of fifteen, had grown to 43 in number, but still seemed inadequate for its onerous responsibilities, which included the pacification of all indios within reach, the policing of the north coast of the Gulf of California, and keeping order amid the missions and ranchlands of Sonora and Pimería Alta. 'The task was formidable,' as the historians Thomas Naylor and Charles Polzer have averred, 'even by the standards of the time.'[57]

A precious document of 1646 from the presidio of Cerro Gordo, founded the previous year, helps explain how the costs of frontier defence were met. The treasury would pay the soldiers' wages, but not the costs of construction or of the food for the gangs of workers, all of which came out of contributions levied from merchants who used the Durango road. The standard levy was 12 pesos, though some who pleaded poverty paid as little as 4 pesos and many others substituted goods, usually of silk or other cloth. One contributor, who claimed to have nothing to pay with, suffered distraint of his silver plate. The

Juan Martínez Zermeño, widely hailed as 'the Vauban of Spain', submitted this design for a proposed uniform for members of the Corps of Engineers to the king's 'universal minister', the Marqués de la Ensenada, who prioritized engineering projects among his all-encompassing responsibilities, in 1751.

A screen of *c.* 1675–92 depicting 'the Conquest of Mexico and the Very Noble and Loyal City of Mexico', imitating – as was common in New Spain at the time – the Japanese style in oil and gold leaf on canvas, mounted on a wooden frame.

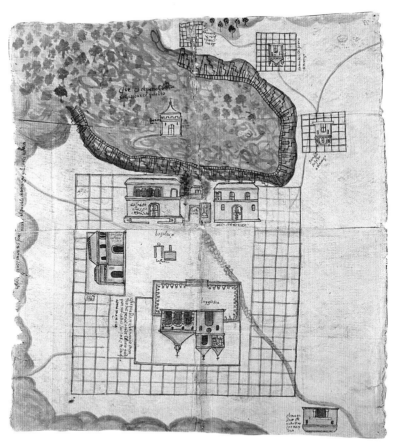

Teotenango in the Toluca Valley, as it appeared in 1589 to an Indigenous mapmaker who incorporated aspects of European technique. Prior to incorporation in the Spanish monarchy, the town was a stronghold of the Matlatzinca, whom the Aztecs conquered late in the fifteenth century.

The coat of arms granted to the city of Nuestra Señora de Zacatecas, the location of New Spain's most productive silver mines, in 1586. 'Ennoblement' was a quality much sought-after for towns, both literally and metaphorically.

Alejo Fernández, *The Virgin of the Navigators*, 1531, oil on board. Alejo Fernández painted this, along with portraits of early pioneers of transatlantic exploration, for the chapel of the Casa de Contratación – the headquarters of the organization that supervised Spain's ocean-going trade.

The survivors are shown escaping in boats from the *Nuestra Señora de la Mar, San José y San Francisco de Paula,* which foundered off Bermuda in 1691. The drawing was made for the investigation that followed into the conduct of the captain, Francisco de Pineda.

Francisco Antonio de Horcasitas's machine for milling flour and making dough, 1786. The inventor was granted a patent to last for twenty years.

Model of the water-powered saw designed but never executed by Francisco Suárez Calderín for the Arsenal of Havana, Cuba, in 1757, to replace the existing machine, probably installed in 1748, and double its output.

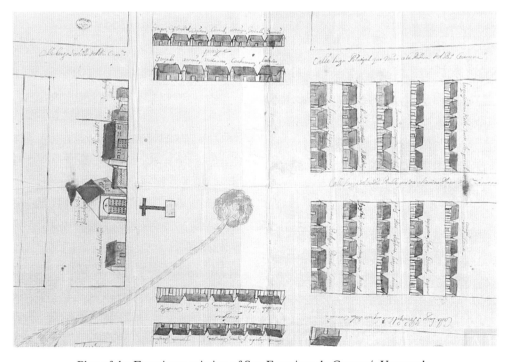

Plan of the Franciscan mission of San Francisco de Cumaná, Venezuela, 1690. The first friars arrived in 1501, so the settlement has some claim to be the oldest mission on the American mainland. The well-ordered plan reflects Franciscan notions of celestial order.

Drawing of a fulling mill from the manuscript work compiled in the early 1780s by Baltasar Martínez Compañon, Bishop of Trujillo, Peru, *Códice Trujillo del Perú*, II, plate 94.

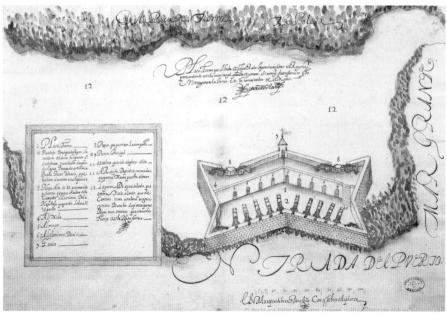

Drawing made in 1617 by the engineer Cristóbal de Roda Antonelli during his work on the fortifications of Cartagena, showing the bastion of Santángel, reportedly in a state of collapse and demolished nine years later.

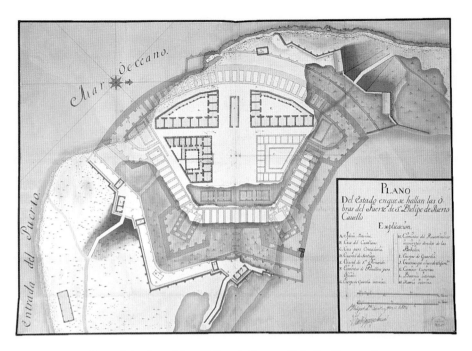

Plan of the fort of San Felipe de Puerto Cabello, Venezuela,
around the time of its construction, 1736.

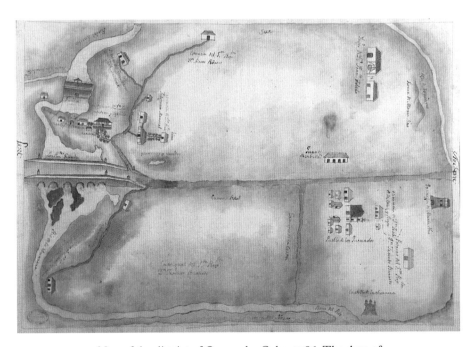

Map of the district of Quemado, Cuba, 1786. The dam of
El Husillo appears on the viewer's left. From there, the canalized
section of river led to Havana.

Railway installed in a sugar manufactory in Cuba in 1857.

Domingo de Roxas's paper-making mill in the Philippines, 1822.
Roxas (1782–1843) was an innovative entrepreneur and a major figure
in the islands' constitutionalist movement.

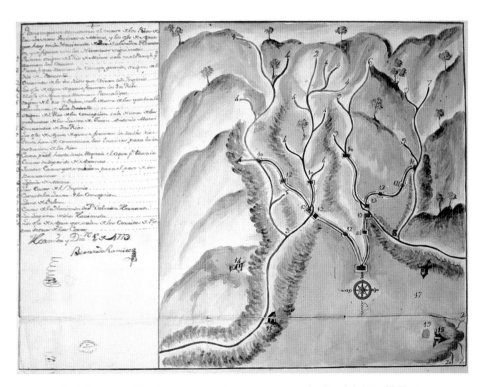

José Bernardo Ramírez's map of the watercourses in the vicinity of Mixco,
roughly adjacent to Guatemala City, in 1773, showing the aqueducts that
supplied the township of Mixco and San José Pinula. The hacienda of the local
landowner, Salvador Herrarte, appears towards the viewer's lower right.

The Aqueduct of Chapultepec, which carried the main water supply
to Mexico City, depicted by Lorenzo Rodríguez and others, 1754.
It was demolished and rebuilt in 1757.

Map of 1590 showing the
Camino de Virreyes, so-called
because newly arriving viceroys
followed it to Mexico City
from Veracruz.

Lighthouse of El Morro, Havana, Cuba, 1796. Construction began in 1763, after the withdrawal of British occupying forces, as part of the remodelling of the fortifications under Silvestre Abarca and Agustín Cramer, when the embellishment of the city kept pace with the growth of trade.

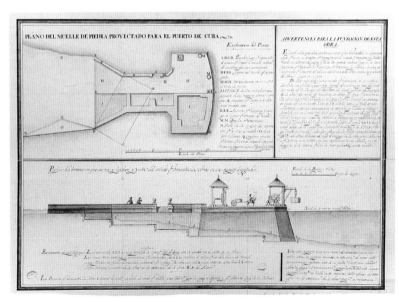

Plan and elevation of a projected new pier for the port of Santiago de Cuba, designed by Juan Pío de la Cruz, commander of the city's corps of engineers, in 1810, as part of a major project for clearing slums, rationalizing the townscape and extending the city and port. Construction was completed in 1815.

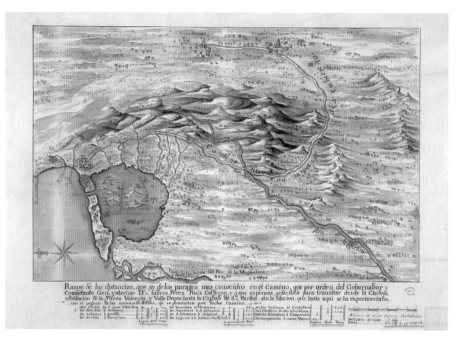

Plan of the proposed road from Nueva Valencia and Valledupar to Santa Marta to connect the coast to the interior in what is now Colombia, 1767.

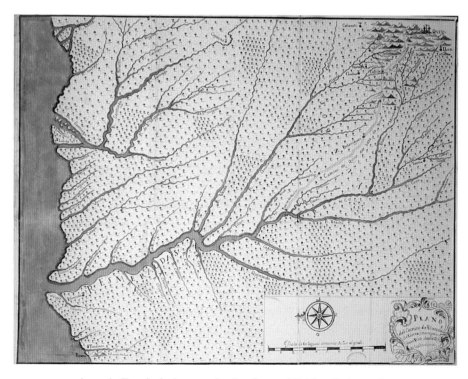

Antonio Fernández's map of 1785 of a road linking Quito to the navigable section of the Esmeraldas River.

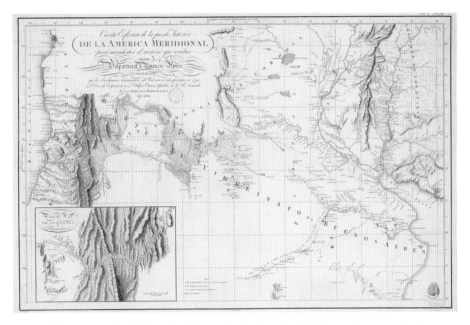

Map on a cylindrical projection, made in 1810 'on the basis of astronomical observations' of 1794 by the naval officers José de Espinosa and Felipe Bauzá, who had sailed with the Malaspina expedition, 'to show the road that leads from Valparaíso to Buenos Aires'.

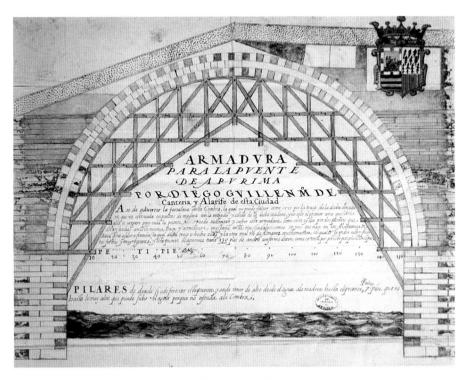

Plan of work on the Apurimac River Bridge, Peru, 1619, by the stonemason Bernardo Florines and Diego Guillén, master of works.

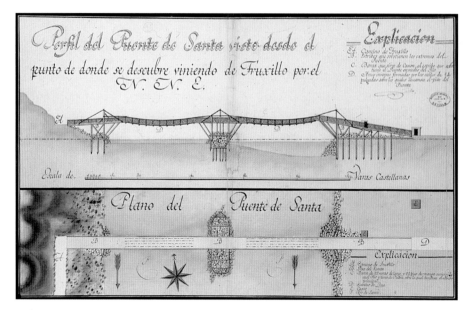

Plan and elevation of the Santa Bridge, as seen from the approach
via Trujillo, 1811.

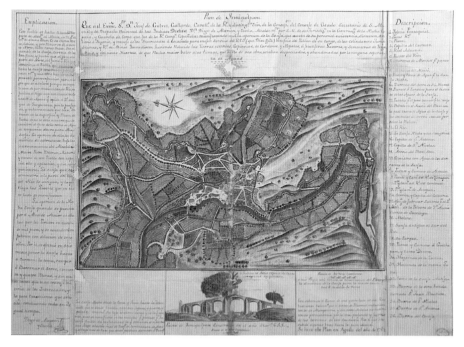

Diego de Alarcón y Ocaña's plan of the irrigation system of Ixmiquilpan,
in Hidalgo's Mezquital Valley, Mexico, as constructed in 1655. As mayor of
Ixmiquilpan from 1779, Alarcón introduced a water supply system both for
drinking water and, shown here in the plans he proposed, for irrigation.

Sebastián de Aracibia's plan of the drainage area of Lake Nicaragua, 1716. The draughtsman shows the settlements of the rebellious Zambo and the English allies in Puntagorda and Mosquitos 'and the coasts and hideouts where they carry out their raids and depredations'.

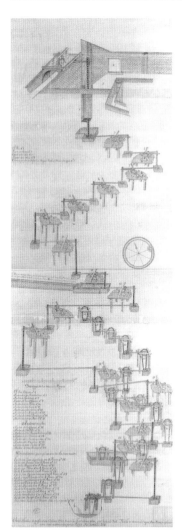

The interior and pumping system of the Rayas mine in Guanajuato [Mexico] – notable for its complex system of tunnels and stairwells – 'presented by Juan de Ledesma on behalf of the owner, Juan Díaz de Bracamonte, to Miguel Calderón de la Barca, Judge of the Regonal Court of Mexico City', who inspected the mine in 1704.

Made in 1787 by Manuel Antonio Jijón, a 'Plan Which Shows and Depicts the Location and Surroundings in Which are Placed the Mines of . . . Don Juan Francisco Echarri in the Province of Villalta in the New Enclosure which He Has Made at His Own Expense with a House and Pumping Station for the Enhancement of the Yield of the Mines in Lands Belonging to the Villages of San Miguel de Talea and San Bartolomé Yatoni', Oaxaca. Echarri began work here in 1753.

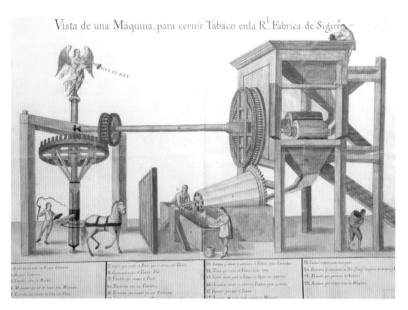

Machine for separating strands of tobacco, invented by Alonso González, and in production in the Royal Cigar Factory, Orizaba, Mexico, c. 1785.

wealthier inhabitants of San Bartolomé gave provisions in the form of maize or wheat in grain or flour. Each contributor in turn signed over his share, though one declined to sign 'as he did not know how'. Under the captain in command, the 24 soldiers, who included vagabonds pressed into service, were armed with bows and arrows.[58]

The northward scattering of presidios continued through the seventeenth century in an attempt to deter or monitor hostile incursions, to support the extension of the frontier from Santa Fe in 1598, and to cope with and reverse the revolt of the Pueblo that sent Spanish settlers scurrying out of New Mexico in the 1680s. As with the empire's seaward defences, the interior frontier was fortified bit by bit in response to external threats. In 1680 the presidio of Nuestra Señora de la Limpia Concepción del Pasaje and two other new presidios were built in response to the Pueblo revolt. The chaos of command – with some forts dependent directly on the viceroy, with others under regional governors – ended with integration under the command of the governor of New Mexico in 1682. In 1685 three new presidios appeared at Cuencamé and Gallo with 25 men in each (later raised to 50), and San Francisco de los Conchos, with at least 50 men in the garrison, to protect newly developed mining enterprises from insurgent indios. As time went on the garrisons became more widely spaced and larger, typically with up to 30 men in each. Average manpower per garrison rose to about 50 in the new century, though nominal strengths were rarely effective, owing to the opportunities that captains exploited to pocket the wages of dead and unreplaced soldiers.[59]

For the conduct of presidios, regulations of 1680 laid down ground rules, which are evidence of what was commonly overlooked in practice. Forts had to be surrounded by cleared land. If slave labour was used, labourers had to be lawfully enslaved and supplied through the officially sanctioned trade system of *asientos* or contracts for supply with merchants of authorized countries, such as Portugal and Britain. Every fort was supposed to have a resident priest and a place set aside for Mass. Officers and officials were not to make private contracts for any government business, nor were any of the garrison permitted to keep animals on their own account, other than their own mounts. Gaming was too pervasive to be banned, and so it was regulated by providing for sergeants major to 'enjoy the proceeds of gambling'.[60] At El Paso in 1684 the 27 defenders had each to have at muster at least fifteen musket balls, according to regulations, with one pound of gunpowder, an arquebus, a sword, a shield, a leather jacket and at least two mounts: these standard requirements were commonly met, according to the muster rolls, but the complaints of independent observers and official inspectors, who united in condemning failures to keep up standards, justify scepticism. Construction was usually of adobe, square with towers at each corner, enclosures set aside for barracks, chapel, infirmary and the commander's residence. Some forts had outer walls of wattle and daub. Nayarit had stone towers. San Sabá, on the Comanche frontier in Texas, was rebuilt in stone and rubble after a notorious massacre of the nearby Franciscan mission and the burning of the original fort in 1758.[61] Later presidios, established against French pressure on the Texas border with Louisiana or near the Gulf coast, commonly had angled bastions, often with stone foundations. They varied in size, as much because of the terrain as from any calculation of need: San Carlos had a perimeter of 508 metres (1,667 ft), whereas El Príncipe's was only 328 metres (1,076 ft) long.

The vigilance of critics helped to call the presidios to order from time to time. Missionaries were persistent complainants. In early eighteenth-century Sinaloa, Franciscans levied typical accusations against the garrison: neglecting defence for profit, dealing in provisions for the mines 'and confiscating hens for the captains', while playing cards, avoiding muster, coercing indio labour and lining the captain's pockets with dead men's wages.[62] An agenda of their own shaped missionary animadversions: presidio garrisons, typically drawn from the ranks of desperadoes and ne'er-do-wells, could not be relied on as models of Christian probity who might favourably impress potential converts. The reports of official inquiries, however, frequently echo the friars' dissatisfaction. In 1724, for instance, the report of Fernando Pérez de Almazán on the presidio of La Bahía, after the Karankawa revolt of the previous year, indicted the authorities for inadeqate appropriations for uniforms and arms; the troops, the report revealed, gambled away such horses, weapons and clothes as they had. They left their arms uncleaned. They tore the stakes out of their fences for firewood. 'I think', Pérez concluded, 'we could only make lasting walls out of brick, since there is no stone available and the wood does not last.'[63]

The year 1724 also involved the first of two comprehensive inspections of the frontier. Pedro de Rivera, governor of Tlaxcala, spent four years inspecting all 23 interior presidios at the command of the Marqués de Casa Fuerte, in response to the inspector's own suggestion. Economy was his unremitting priority. Peace, in his opinion, rendered some presidios pointless. Corruption – especially captains' practice of paying men with inflated doles of goods rather than real wages – made others ineffective. Even at full pay of typically 450 pesos, soldiers could not reliably afford the equipment with which they were supposed to supply themselves. It is hard, if Rivera was right, to see how recruitment levels were maintained. His recommendations, in any event, led to reductions in pay (on a scale varying according to the remoteness of particular garrisons, but to totals never exceeding 420 pesos). He also called for the suppression of some presidios and the reduction of many garrisons. His report is a litany of shortcomings. Nayarit 'lacked everything needful, both for equipment and sustenance, as well as for what was necessary to defend the place, the soldiers being far fewer than the King paid for, and utterly unworthy of the designation of soldiers'.[64] In Durango, Rivera reported garrisons unwilling to engage the enemy because they were too busy holidaying with their families. At El Paje, where he found the defenders 'devoted to leisure', he reduced the garrison to 33 men and 2 officers. He lambasted the commander of the fort at Santiago de Mapimi for dwelling 70 leagues away in Durango, and the men of Cerro Gordo for doing 'nothing except what suits them'. In Conchos, according to Rivera, the ill health of the garrison rendered it utterly ineffective.[65] In Fronteras, the fifty men there had no commander. At Santa Fe in New Mexico, one of the biggest contingents, one-hundred-men strong, was given to 'pernicious abuses', with an exorbitant number of so-called officers corruptly promoted. At Los Dolores in Texas the garrison was fully occupied in cultivating land; there were no indios in the adjoining mission. The fort, Rivera found, was 'of so little value . . . that it is not even worthy of the name of a presidio'.[66] It was suppressed in 1729. On the easternmost frontier with Louisiana, at Nuestra Señora de los Adaes, the nominal register of one hundred men was excessive, with officers disproportionately represented: sixty soldiers would be ample, the inspector opined, as the French were only concerned to keep hold of their own fort, with a garrison of only 25, while all nearby indios were friendly to Spain. Bahía del Espíritu Santo, with ninety names on the payroll, was another over-manned garrison of marginal utility. The garrisons for which Rivera had approving words were few: El Gallo was well conducted with 39 men under a conscientious captain; Janos was abuse-free, as were Sinaloa and Bejar on the Río Grande.

People on the frontier, unsurprisingly, were happy at the prospect of Rivera's proposed economies. Fray Juan Agustín Morfi – a corruption, no doubt, imperfectly concealing the provenance of a friar whose original name was probably Murphy – countered that reduced garrisons would leave the frontier prey to French invasion in case of renewed war and would leave remaining garrisons no leisure, whereas days off duty ('días francos') were essential for maintaining morale.[67] Events seemed to confirm that savings were easier to propose than execute. In the 1740s Yaqui rebelliousness required new presidios to be built at Piti, near the junction of the San Miguel and Sonora rivers, and Ternate at the headwaters of the Río San Pedro. Reforming measures in 1741 focused rather on the kinds of excesses of which the friars complained than on the campaign to save money. The authorities targeted garrison-members' attacks on women and children during raids on pagan indios, 'as such behaviour is quite alien from the Catholic faith and against the intentions of His Majesty' according to the governor of New Mexico.[68] Meanwhile at El Pasaje, the government solved the problem of how to maintain the presidio by what would now be called outsourcing. They shifted responsibility onto the shoulders of the Conde de San Pedro del Álamo, whose fortune included 213,000 head of livestock on 485,625 hectares (1.2 million ac.) of grazing within a domain extending over 6 million hectares (15 million ac.).

On other fronts the empire saved money by exceeding even Rivera's programme for suppressing presidios and replacing them with 'flying squads' (compañias volantes). Controversy over whether fixed stations worked better for peacemaking than mobile columns, which could defy enemy plans and home in on trouble spots as needed, was already prominent in the 1690s, while New Mexico was undergoing resettlement and the frontier was creeping northwards. The dilemma was false: presidios were needed to define the frontier zone against the neighbouring Comanche and French empires; columns were better at deflecting or catching marauders. In any case soldiers needed the respite of garrison life and most attempts to shut presidios permanently were short-lived. In 1751 those of El Gallo, Cerro Gordo, the Valle de San Bartolomé and Conchos were all replaced by a flying column, which 'was to be in constant motion throughout that area'.[69] At the same time on the New Mexico frontier, however, the growing pressure led to a new foundation at Tubac on the Santa Cruz River, in response to the revolt Onepicagua led among the Upper Pima in 1752.

If garrisons proved ineradicable, so did their shortcomings. In 1761 Manuel Portillo y Urrisola – a tough guy who took on the Comanche empire and replaced the policy of yielding to ransom with one of bloody reprisals – took over the garrison of Santa Fe. He found that apart from individuals' personal weapons there were only 5 French rifles and 21 muskets, of which only 10 were serviceable and all were in poor condition.[70] From March 1766, in the wake of the Seven Years' War, when the Spanish monarchy had ended by gaining territory despite generally disappointing performances in battle, the Marqués de Rubí undertook an inspection even more ambitious in scope than Rivera's. He covered 12,230 kilometres (7,600 mi.) in the space of 23 months, with the aim, according to his sidekick, Nicolás de Lafora, of 'making our arms respected in those remote countries'.[71] It was part of a new strategy to re-organize border defence after the acquisition of all former French claims west of the Mississippi, and, less auspiciously, of a new border, along that river, with the British Empire. Rubí's theory was clear: presidios should not and could not serve to withstand sieges, so they were there to deny passage to the enemy troops and facilitate the rapid concentration of defence forces whenever necessary. His plan of frontier defence, close to the strategy that eventually prevailed, was to string a cordon of presidios along the thirtieth parallel north, with outposts in New Mexico and Texas. Peace with a stable Comanche empire and its Caddo vassals, would guarantee stability and free the monarchy to deal with intractable and unreliable Apache opportunists.

As with Rivera's report, the inspectors' findings were again condemnatory. The presidio of San Buenaventura, they found, was 'newly erected with little foresight by the governor of Nueva Vizcaya . . . in a position so advantageous to the enemy that the latter themselves could not have suggested anything better for the total destruction and extermination of this presidio' by recalcitrant Apache.[72] In Janos, San Felipe and Santiago were forts well located for control of the passes into the province of Gila, but the garrisons were impoverished and the buildings decayed. From there the distance was too far – 60 leagues or five days' journey – to Corodeguachi or Fronteras in Sonora. The inspectors' next stop was in Terrenate at the presidio of San Felipe de Jesús, Guebabi, amid deserted pueblos. The garrison had to feed itself by planting grain 5 leagues away, in a place exposed to raids. Santa Gertrudis del Altar, the westernmost presidio, had to move: the existing site had too little water and pasture. Buenavista, the southern-most of the Sonora presidios, was too remote to be useful. The litany went on, of devastation, desertion and presidios too far apart for the mutual support which, in Rubí's view, alone could justify them. San Sabá should be abandoned as indefensible in the shadow of the Comanche empire. Los Adaes was in poor repair and there were no converts in the nearby missions: it too was not worth keeping. Nor were San Luis de Ahumada or Orcoquizac, badly sited on swampland near the coast. San Francisco Xavier in the Mesa de Tonatli was surplus to requirements because the region was secure and the indios loyal. The presidio of El Pasaje, which Rubí visited on his outward journey, might as well be wound up, as the garrison had nothing to do except escort occasional travellers and and act as a post office. At San Ignacio de Tabac, where the most accomplished Spanish commander of the day, Juan de Anza, was in command, Rubí found one of the few forts he could approve: well run, attractive to a large population, and large enough for self-defence; but it lacked adequate fortifications and funds.[73]

In the long run the policy usually called 'pacification' probably did more to stabilize the frontier than all the arts of war combined. Rather like Chinese debates about how to deal with nomads – teetering between trying to civilize the 'barbarians' according to Confucian principles and trying to force them into submission – Spanish decision-makers wavered between contradictory points of view. Rubí and the governors he influenced favoured ending the indio 'problem' with war. Others preferred a strategy of attraction. In 1778 Bernardo de Gálvez argued that through trade 'the king would keep them very contented for ten years with what he now spends in one year making war upon them.'[74] In the long run, many native peoples accepted resettlement in missions or new towns or agricultural settlements. Some positive results can be admired, for instance in a decorative plan of the settlement of San Juan Bautista on the Río Grande in 1754, where through the neat files of colonnaded streets processions of Spaniards and indios thread, with their traditional arms and music, to meet the mission folk in the main square and erect celebratory crosses at each corner. A party of religious sisters and children from the mission schools join the party.[75] Payola in the form of food, liquor, clothes, copper kettles and axes bought peace from others.[76] The Comanche had to be coerced into abstention from hostility: when Juan de Anza killed the famous paramount Cuerno Verde in battle in 1779 and captured his horde of loot, the rulers of the Indigenous empire realized that co-operation with Spain at the expense of common Apache foes was the best policy.

Many Apache responded in the spirit of the old adage, 'If you can't beat 'em, join 'em.' As an outstanding historian of the frontier put it, 'Internment camps and protected villages at the presidios . . . introduced tribesmen to the new way of life they would ultimately have to follow.'[77] The effects were slow to accumulate and imperfect in outcome. In July 1779 Teodoro de Croix, who had overall command of the indio frontier in the Revolutionary War, received Mescalero allies who had asked to form villages under presidio protection. They founded Nuestra Señora de la Buena Esperanza almost in the shadow of the presidio of El Norte (present-day Ojinaga, Mexico), though they abandoned it during a smallpox epidemic of 1780. An uneasy relationship persisted until 1788, when efforts at settlement were abandoned for a while. From 1790 to 1795, however, a substantial number of Mescaleros – perhaps up to a thousand – did congregate at El Norte, though without adopting farming, and in many cases without staying for long. A rather unstable Chiricahua settlement took shape at Bacoachi from 1786. By 1793 there were six reservations attached to presidios, embracing a total of perhaps 2,000 souls.

Meanwhile the presidio concept found a new role in newly colonized Upper California. Here, however, the term meant something different from on the more fiercely contested frontier further east: not so much a defensive position, except at the key station of Monterey, as one dedicated to the promotion of settlement. California was, in many ways, a western mirror-image of Florida: Spain occupied neither region in expectation of profitable exploitation, but only to deny coastal refuge to pirates and hostile navies. Just as the Gulf Stream skirted Florida, making control of the harbours essential for traffic from the Caribbean to Spain, so California guarded the Acapulco current, which carried the Manila galleons home. Like Florida, therefore, Upper California was safeguarded more by missions than by fortresses. There were only four presidios in the province, of which three – at San Diego, San Francisco and Santa Barbara – were not expected to face European foes and were neither designed nor equipped for major conflicts. Rather, they were there to 'show the flag', stake the Spanish claim, establish the Spanish presence, awe the natives, assist the missionaries and provide a focal point for settlers to gather around. San Diego, for instance, remained sketchily fortified throughout the colonial era, from its foundation in 1769. After trouble with the local Kumeyaay indios in 1775–6 a roughly square wood stockade began to surround the settlement, reinforced with adobe, and with bastions projecting from the corners, but it was still incomplete in 1779.[78] The garrison seems to have been dispersed among nearby missions until the 1790s, when a large force of regular troops supplemented or superseded the local recruits.

Monterey, to judge from the description the commander, Pedro de Fages, sent to the viceroy in 1773, was a more serious stronghold, with regular troops already permanently quartered alongside the local 'leather jackets', each group with its own dormitory. One facade already had stone walls and stone was being cut to replace the other temporary walls and foundations of adobe and pine, 'because the humidity of the place tends to rot and destroy the wood'. Bronze cannon loomed from the ravelins at the corners of the rectangular structure. Fages described the cesspool, the hog sties, the carts he built to transport salt from the marshes, and the rather inconveniently arrayed dependencies: the vegetable garden half a league distant, the latrine 'a musket shot away' and the powder magazine located 'fifteen minutes' walk away on the other side of the estuary'. The only deficiencies to which he drew urgent attention were of bells for the chapel and 'everything necessary to celebrate the holy sacrifice of the Mass'.[79]

The presidios are tourist traps today. A lingering echo of presidio life, however, can be experienced at Santa Barbara – an extraordinary town so devoted to its sense of Spanish heritage that even the Unitarian church is in the Hispanic revival style, and where the visionary architect Charles Loomis in 1923 claimed that Spanish-inflected romance was 'of greater economic benefit than oil, oranges, or even the climate'.[80] From its foundation in the 1780s, when Santa Barbara was on the remotest edge of the Spanish monarchy and on or perhaps beyond the outermost rim of what most people in Europe and America would acknowledge as the civilized world, no one able to make the grade elsewhere would have ventured to join the garrison. Now, however, when the city celebrates its foundation annually in a spectacular fiesta known as the 'Old Spanish Days', the descendants of the inhabitants of the presidio are honoured as the nearest thing the United States has to an aristocracy. Glory, proverbially, fades, but there are kinds of effulgence that seem to grow with time.

6

ON THE WATERFRONT
Ports and Shipyards

Or who shut up the sea with doors, when it brake forth, as if it
had issued out of the womb? . . . And said, Hitherto shalt thou
come, but no further: and here shall thy proud waves be stayed?
(JOB 38:8–11)

A global empire is unsustainable without sea power. As José de
Mazarredo, generally hailed as the most talented Spanish naval
commander of his time, told King Carlos IV in 1801, 'The navy should
be the most perfectly finished machine in the monarchy: the machine
to end all machines.'[1] The Bourbon monarchs shared the sentiment.
In that respect, they maintained the nautical outlook of the Habsburgs,
whom they replaced on the throne, despite rhetoric designed to flatter
the new dynasty by comparison with their supposedly inferior, decadent and opprobrious predecessors. The myth – exaggerated and
unfair though it was – of the senescence of the previous dynasty stimulated attention to everything that seemed up-to-date and fixated on
the future. As Christopher Storrs has pointed out, the Bourbons
inherited a monarchy – paradoxically divided and united by the oceans
it embraced – that demonstrated extraordinary resilience.[2] But the
resilience was demonstrated in defeat more often than in victory. So
profound were convictions among the elite that Spain's maritime
defences were antiquated, and her ships deficient in design, size, capacity
and equipment, that an entire lexicon came into being, or was developed to a novel extent, deploying nautical metaphors for the tribulations
of life, especially of political life. Fray Juan de los Ángeles, like so
many moralists of the time, expressed revulsion:

[A] very substantial fleet setting sail with its painted prows and mainsails, its gilded lanterns, its unfurled banners, its galleons in escort, with all the vast company of boys and men, marines and merchants, while trumpets sound and hautbois pipe. And where is that great city of wood headed? Whither those separate edifices, striving for unison, whither those floating islands, lurching alarmingly, and all those people within them, whom two fingers' breadth part from death and yet who seem so content, heedless of the fury of the waves and winds? What are they seeking? Riches.[3]

The Maritime Outlook

Maritime figures of speech expressed every hazard and every hope. A vessel aflame in the midst of the ocean represented the conflagrations of Christendom. From a 'safe haven' writers contemplated estuaries as thresholds and oceans as the menacing future that lay beyond them. Taking soundings, testing draught, reckoning leeway, weighing anchor – such were the operations that individuals at peril on the voyage of life must undertake. To make moral progress, as to make way under sail, one spoke of scraping away the barnacles. Harbours became metaphors for escape from ambition or pride. 'To find shelter from the stormy blast' was a common euphemism for death. For the just, as for ships, 'the storm shall not for ever trouble them.'[4] A ship's carved figurehead stood for the political profile of a maritime state. Extravagant altarpieces dedicated to the Virgen del Carmen – Our Lady of the Vine – were likened to the heavily carved adornments of ships' poops.

Such language was stimulated by visits to Cádiz, in 1694 and 1695, by depressingly impressive fleets of heretical foreigners – Dutch and English – whom the fortunes of war brought together for a while in the cause of Spain's Habsburg pretender. Objective comparisons with their own navy might not have alarmed Spaniards. The Spanish armada in Italy, for instance, had 21 ships of a total of nearly 14,000 tons and a complement of 8,197 men in all: by no means despicable. *Nuestra Señora de la Concepción y de las Ánimas*, the vice-flagship, displaced 1,500 tons and bore 92 guns, with a crew 1,110 strong. The flagship had the insuperably optimistic name of *Nuestra Señora de la Esperanza* – Our Lady of Hope. Was imperial defence irremediably decadent? The mixture of curiosity, resentment and fear with which Spaniards beheld their competitors made it seem so.[5]

In the opening decades of the eighteenth century the monarchy, formerly an empire with engineers, became an empire of engineers. After a stuttering start to their rule, the Bourbons could usually be relied on for a rational or at least reasonable approach to policy-making. In 1747 Felipe V created a regime of uniform jurisdiction and consistent law throughout the monarchy's disparate peninsular dominions. A group of what we would now call technocrats shaped his reign by defining his policies for trade and his strategies for war.

After half a century of Bourbon rule, in 1759, Abbot Miguel Antonio de la Gándara took a position roughly opposite to that of Fray Juan de los Ángeles. In *Notes on What Is Good and Bad in Spain* (*Apuntes sobre el mal y el bien de España*) – a purported programme of government for the future Carlos III of Spain, written while he was still merely king of Naples – the author contended that industriousness and what we should now call productivity were evidence of orthodoxy. As far as empires were concerned, however, he agreed that decline was inevitable – but not necessarily definitive. Fall succeeds climb, he opined, and 'no sooner does one ascend to the pinnacle than one falls, and on reaching rock bottom one ascends. Nothing is closer to night than day and light is the immediate sequitor of darkness.'[6]

Spanish society, Gándara thought, should be encouraged to embrace renewed values of striving, in practical ways, for improvement. Two of Felipe V's greatest servants exemplified the values he had in mind: José Patiño, born in Milán in 1666, and his subordinate and successor as supervisor of military and naval affairs, the Asturian José del Campillo y Cossío, born in Alles in 1693. If one work typified the kind of thinking that moulded Spanish economic policy in the period, it was the latter's *New System of Governance for America* (*Nuevo sistema de gobierno para la América*), written for the king in 1743 and published for the public's benefit in 1789. It belonged to a genre of works with similarly unequivocal titles, such as *What Is Wanted and Unwanted in Spain to Make Her What She Should Be instead of What She Is* (*Lo que hay de más y de menos en España, para que sea lo que debe ser y no lo que es*) of 1742, or *Spain, Awake!* (*¡España, despierta!*) of the following year. All these texts evinced a spirit reminiscent of the English projectors and Spanish *arbitristas* of an earlier age: a spirit of can-do, of dissatisfaction tempered by optimism, of invention responding to necessity. Their vision of a commercial and maritime future tempered hope with expectation.

After war service in the Mediterranean, Campillo was a commissary in Veracruz, transferring to active service in the convoys that accompanied Spanish mercury – vital for silver-refining – to the New World. Later, José Patiño sent him to survey a site for a new shipyard in Havana.[7] He oversaw the works there and launched *San Juan*, the first ship that the facility produced, before returning to Spain. From 1724 to 1733 he was charged with inspecting ships in Cantabrian yards, and then worked in the shipyards at Guarnizo. In 1741, two years before dying – probably of overwork – he was made assistant to Spain's equivalent of Lord High Admiral: in effect, he was in charge of all shipping, commercial and naval, throughout the monarchy.

In Campillo's informed judgement, everything was possible in the ports of the monarchy. They were 'brilliant, bustling places'. In picaresque novels, rootless mariners drifted through them – 'the jetsam of the seas', without friends, faith or fellow-feeling. Officials and entrepreneurs, ignored in fiction, bustled in the same streets and drank in the same taverns.[8] The monarch's grandeur could be measured along the coasts the empire touched.[9] Carlos III made paternal love for his people visible in public works that were, in total, more numerous and costly, Campillo reckoned, along the shores than inland.

Celebration of harbours and of the ingenuity of the engineers who created or enhanced them became routine in the archives, arts and letters of the time. Mariano Sánchez was an artist typical in his obsession, fortified by royal commissions, of studying ports in France and Portugal, as well as in Spain in the 1780s. His depiction of the shore as 'a document and teaching tool' expressed the favourable effects of legislation of 1778, which opened American trade to all peninsular ports. In 1802 the great statesman and Spanish *philosophe*, Gaspar de Jovellanos, enlivened his captivity in Mallorca, in Bellver Castle, after a fall from political grace, by enumerating, in his *Notes on Architecture* (*Memorias de arquitectura*), features that Sánchez depicted: grand civil and religious monuments; cathedrals; mercantile exchanges; defences; mills; floodplains; stacks of barrels ready for shipping; figures at work, hauling ropes or dragging cordage, fishing, binding, lading, and making fast; men and women caught forever in moments of activity: a 'busy, busy world'. Paintings of ports were celebrations of the industrious, evidence of the modernity of the monarchy.[10]

The Ports:
A *Tour d'Horizon*

In *Twenty-One Books Concerning Engines and Machines* (XXI *libros de los ingenios y las máquinas*), attributed to Pedro Juan de Lastanosa, and probably written in the 1560s, the author says:

> The crucial key to a town is its port, which serves to defend it from foes, feed it with provisions, and provide it with other goods. So it must cause no fear in merchants who may want to enter with very big ships and to whom it must be obvious that the location is safe.[11]

Such conditions were easier to state than achieve. Ships halted way offshore to avoid shallows and rocks. It took a long time to load and unload passengers and cargo via the sloops and tenders – typically big enough to hold perhaps 2 per cent of a merchantman's capacity – that plied back and forth between ship and shore.[12] The aim of every port authority was to monopolize loading and unloading. Engineers' responsibility for correcting what they saw as natural 'defects' was key. For the underwater foundations of moles, jetties and sea walls, wooden piles were laid, in default of traditional cement, with water-tight compartments, filled with hardcore, typically resting on rocks or stone blocks lowered into the water. As so often, the Romans provided an excellent model: wooden casks filled with stone, which they towed to where they were wanted, then sank. Such methods, if they were effective, were cheap.

Natural conditions required, in some cases, extemporized responses. In Cartagena de Indias, for instance, the famous Bocagrande Canal was closed in 1768 by means of a dam made in two sections: one on wooden pillars, bound by hoops and filled with stone, and the other supported by discarded masonry. Silting was among the most troublesome of natural occurences. Where moles or piers were built of stone, sand tended to accumulate in heaps or strands. Silting was the ultimate cause of Seville's derogation as the designated port for the Indies trade in favour of Cádiz. In Manila, the riverside port became unusable owing to silt, and Cavite arose to replace it – a *garfio* in the local lingo – that is, a settlement on a tongue of littoral sand. The Pasig River was dredged and canalized in an attempt to solve the problem, using mule-power to bring soil to the surface. In the 1770s, Havana Bay – 'a sea of almost undetectable tides' – was dredged by six vessels, mounted on pontoons, with barges alongside to load the yield and shift it elsewhere.

Nonetheless, ports were the links that kept the various parts of the Spanish monarchy in mutual touch. At local and regional levels, ports of cabotage were designated as *propios* – that is, belonging to particular routes, which were usually appropriations or adaptions of routes explored by Indigenous predecessors.[13] They acquired specialist engineers to build moles and quays in earnest when the customs officials arrived and settlements became 'strategic'. The highest category – the key ports or, as people said then, the 'throats' of the monarchy – were usually sited in great natural harbours and guarded by fortresses. We can take a *tour d'horizon* around the edges of Spanish America, visiting them, as it were, in turn.

A principal network can be defined, connecting, at first, Seville with Veracruz, Cartagena, Portobelo and Havana in the Caribbean, and Acapulco, Callao, Realejo and Panama on the Pacific coast. Buenos Aires, Montevideo, Valparaíso, Guayaquil, Campeche, San Blas, San Juan de Puerto Rico, Matanzas, Santo Domingo and others joined the network later, as they grew in dimensions and became elevated in status.[14] Their hinterlands are discernible in lading lists or 'maps of provenance of required provisions', such as that signed by Francisco de Tejada in December 1616, for a fleet bound for the Philippines. To feed a complement of 2,427 seamen and soldiers, over the eight months allowed for the voyage, stevedores had to load 9,941 quintals of hard tack, 2,051 of dried, salt fish, 1,267 of preserved meat, and 312 of rice; 1,503 pipes of wine and 95 of vinegar; 1,728 *arrobas* of oil, and 626 *fanegas* of beans and chickpeas. The measures were unstandardized, varying from place to place, but Tejada's tally amounted to 4,000 calories per person daily. Only 10 per cent, however, consisted of protein and no fresh supplies were available, except for the products of fishing at sea, which were usually relatively insignificant.[15] After the tedium, privations and uncertainties of an ocean crossing, arrival at a port must have been an experience of relief impossible nowadays to recover.

We can start our tour in Veracruz, 'the definitive port, the shopkeepers' city', the commonest mainland destination. As befitted the high risks of life in a precarious but profitable outpost, the mood in the city seemed always to teeter between exaltation and despair. In 1602 prophets there were actively awaiting the arrival of the Antichrist, 'the son of a very beautiful woman, born in the farthest part of Babylonia, named Ochenta, and impregnated by Satan'.[16]

In some ways, the Antichrist seemed already to have arrived. The Indies were a place of escape and therefore of frivolity, play and perdition. Veracruz was a sort of transatlantic mirror of Seville, a frontier boomtown bursting with vice. That was how Mateo de Alemán, author of the picaresque classic *Guzmán de Alfarache*, saw it: 'everybody's home turf, open for grazing; an inextricably knotted rope; an unfenced field, an unbounded world; a mother of orphans and a screen for sinners'. Inquisitors sought in vain for punishable sins in gaming dens, taverns and whorehouses, but, as a royal official told them, their efforts were in vain because 'the Antichrist had been there ahead of them.' In 1571 Fray Tomás de Mercado, author of the famous *Compendium on Contracts and Commercial Agreements* (*Suma de tratos y contratos*) used the same image slightly differently: 'In the Indies it is as hard to find a fair price as to catch the Antichrist or square the circle.' The 'throat and passage', as men said in 1599, from Seville to Mexico, might better be called, in global perspective, the western hemisphere's gateway between China and Europe, or the belly button or strategic centre of the Spanish monarchy. Merchants there handled silver, cochineal, hides, indigo, wool, dyes and exotic woods of the New World, and silks, painted screens, lacquer work, and porcelain from China and Japan. It was where European and African goods, such as wine, oil, wheat, mercury, iron, fine textiles, paper and steel tools arrived in America – not to mention the slaves imported under licence by resident and foreign merchants, mostly Portuguese.

Within the New World, the range of communications that centred on Veracruz extended way beyond New Spain, to Florida (San Agustín and Pensacola), the Caribbean (Havana, Puerto Rico, Jamaica, Santo Domingo) and southern Mesoamerica and Central America (Pánuco, Tampico, Tuxpan-Tamiahua, Puerto Caballos, Coatzacoalcos, Tabasco, Campeche and Yucatán). Reminiscent of Socrates' image of the Aegean surrounded by Greek cities, the ports that connected with Veracruz were like 'frogs around a pond'. Ninety per cent of the trade of New Spain passed through the city. Between 1561 and 1650, Veracruz controlled 36 per cent of the traffic of Spain's transatlantic convoys. In 1608 so many ships queued to enter the harbour that the ring-wall – the so-called Muro de las Argollas – could not accommodate them. In the surrounding decades, 407 ships anchored, comprising 95,000 tons in all. In the following decade the number of ships rose to 439 and the tonnage to 100,000. As the total shipping on the transatlantic route amounted to 977 vessels of a total of 216,000 tons, the proportion Veracruz handled can be seen to have attained 45 per cent. When a ship drew up at the quay, a landing licence had to be issued before goods were unladen and submitted for customs inspection and for review of the bills of lading the masters carried. Fraud, of course, was rife.[17]

If Veracruz dominated the wider region, Havana was preponderant within the Caribbean, and Cartagena de Indias was the emporium of South America. Our visit to Havana must await the section below on shipyards. As for Cartagena, while no other harbour on the Caribbean coast was as capable of taking in the largest ships, the place had serious disadvantages. It was located on a lee shore, so that sailings against the wind, towards the east, were problematic. Access to the central Caribbean was difficult and the prevalence of hideaways for pirates made the coast hazardous. The harbour entrance was protected with barriers of driven piles or chains, overlooked by forts, batteries, defensive walls and redoubts. Most supplies had to come via Cuba until the Canal del Dique improved communications with inland sources. Not far away, on the Venezuelan coast, La Guaira's later ascent to competitive status derived from the importance of its produce – cacao – and some natural assets: a deep bay, available fresh water and stone for construction. But there was no natural shelter to windward.

Nearby, at Puerto Cabello, the case of the Basque consortium known as the Real Compañía Guipuzcoana, which, from 1728, had a privileged role in trade with Venezuela, shows that private agencies could channel the empire's engineering input in the New World, albeit always under royal surveillance. Evidently, the location suited the cacao trade, but intervention by engineers was needed to make the port work. Before the company lighted on it, Puerto Cabello was little more than a village, under the guns of the fort of San Felipe, built to guard the bay in 1733. Swamps made the situation unhealthy, driving settlers inland, but the port was what counted. In a report issued in 1721 Pedro José de Olavarriaga wrote, 'The harbour should be valued as the best on its stretch of coast – and perhaps anywhere in the Americas: a key piece for the defence of the province.'[18]

The Guipuzcoan Company built a quay 58 metres (190 ft) long and 8 metres (26 ft) wide, along with storehouses, close to where the cacao grew, a bakery, and a cooperage facility. Because a sandbar just below the surface protected the harbour, the bay was so calm that it was said that you could tie a ship to its mooring with a strand of hair. A pier 77 metres (253 ft) long and 10 metres (33 ft) wide accommodated the heavily armed ships the company built for itself, mainly in its home province of Guipuzcoa, at shipyards in the port of Pasajes.

The business plan made sense: chocolate was so costly that a single cargo could recoup the entire expense of building a ship. *San Ignacio,* for instance, of 579 tons and with a crew of almost two hundred men, made its maiden crossing of the ocean in 1733, the first of twelve years of service. The yield amounted to 347 per cent of the cost of construction, and 123 per cent of that of outfitting and paying the crew.[19] The company exported a total of 2,979 tons of cacao that year. The scale of the operation and the short lifespan of the ships testify not only to the volume of production but to the demanding nature of the trade and, above all, its profitability – despite, as the Company's private regulations attest, the fact that

> it is the practice, on all our ships that arrive in an American port, to make presents of Spanish products to the governor, royal officers, warders, scribes, clerks, and commanders of the guard, and in Caracas to the lord bishop one cask of wine and another of vinegar, six small casks of olives, and two each of small and large capers, raisins, almonds, salmon, and tuna, and six of salt cod if there is any on board, with a flask of brandy or liqueur.[20]

In 1738 the military engineer Juan de Gayangos reported that Puerto Cabello could accommodate one hundred ships. The figure was probably realistic: some sources claimed it was big enough for 3,000. Olavarriaga described the port admiringly: the physical setting, the channels running a league across from east to west, the inner bays and the careening facilities suited to ships of up to ten or twelve fathoms of draft. The larger of the channels was big enough to hold the pirate-chasing frigates that were another of the Guipuzcoan Company's specialities. Four years previously, a trading post and warehouses had arisen, alongside offices, a sailyard, a bakery, an infirmary, quays and moles. Later, the erection of a 'royal pier' confirmed the growing prestige of the place. In 1774 it had 120 inhabited dwellings and more than 3,000 residents. The minimum sojourn for a merchant was reckoned to be of two months' duration but it was normal to stay for twice as long.

On the route north from here to New Spain, 'the quest for the perfect port' led to the establishment of Portobelo, Panama's 'point of connexion'.[21] The port that preceded it, Nombre de Dios, was abandoned towards the end of the sixteenth century because of the reefs that strew the approach and inhospitable hinterland of swampland and tangled forest. Francis Drake's incendiary raid in 1596 was the final, fatal blow. At Portobelo, 5 leagues to the west, the shore seemed perfectly configured, but the site was too unhealthy to keep most residents at home for longer than the twenty or thirty days of markets every year.[22] Construction of the customs house began in 1630. The story recalls that of Veracruz, occluded by uncertainty, shadowed by health threats, menaced with abandonment and disturbed by shifting patterns of settlement.

To the south, beyond the coasts dominated by Dutch and Brazilian rivals, Spain's next great port was Montevideo, a frontier post that gradually transformed into a naval and military base. Inland was Asunción, the great river port of the Paraguay, from where barges, toted or paddled, or propelled by a single sail, or little flotillas of canoes, or smacks or brigs for bigger cargoes, carried tobacco, yerba mate and hides to Buenos Aires. Customs records reveal moments in the history of the trade. In 1783, for instance, Juan Cuello took 2,926 arrobas of yerba mate, honey, peanuts, sugar and cotton from Asunción to Corrientes.[23] Cargoes of such dimensions demanded a lot of infrastructural investment.[24] Platforms – which gradually yielded to properly built docks – lined the shore. An adaptable Murcian, Antonio Sánchez, was one of the entrepreneurs responsible. He was the captain of his own trading vessels, an outfitter of boats, a carpenter, a forester and a captain of militia. From 1797 until his death in 1809 he ran the factory at Asunción that made cables and cordage. In 1801 he petitioned successfully for a salary: previously, the factory supervisor was paid piece-rates when work was on hand. His other activities continued.

In Buenos Aires, at the far end of the river route from Asunción, business boomed from 1802, when the viceroy, Joaquín del Pino, opened a new pier. The merchant community had appealed to the city council to fund the project, but received a dispiriting reply: 'this proposal cannot succeed, owing to bad design and location, and to the fact that consent is required from the owners of land that the builders must be able to access.'[25] A memo noted that the traffic from the river had to unload in the so-called port of Barracas, a league from the city, with much trouble and cost. The naval ministry, alarmed by the dissent, ordered del Pino to suspend work, but he shouldered the risk and promoted the common good. The engineer in charge of the work was the Mallorcan Martín Boneo, who had accepted every job that came his way: designing the bullring, supervising the police, installing street paving.

Still further south, efforts recurred at intervals to establish ports and settlement that would 'reduce' the land to Spanish domination, along the hard way south to the Strait of Magellan, which was never readily navigable, and Cape Horn. Antonio Pigafetta, Magellan's chronicler, had mentioned sites that seemed promising, such as San Julián, where the first circumnavigators wintered, and the capes at either end of the strait. Jesuits surveyed San Julián in 1745. Plans followed to occupy the site to pre-empt the British; however, they seized the place in 1766, during the Seven Years' War, only to be evicted in turn shortly afterwards.[26] In 1780, as part of a plan to make the Patagonian coast impregnable, Spain founded the new colony of Floridablanca. Officials, artisans, serving men, workers, small-scale traffickers and a small garrison constituted the population of 150 citizens.[27]

On the Pacific coast, Valparaíso was founded in 1556, to be designated eight years later as the chief port of the captaincy-general of Chile, and dubbed 'New Santiago of the Farthest Reach' (*Santiago del nuevo extremo*) – hardly a metaphor, as the outpost was the most remote in America, and it would be decades before Manila and Cavite appeared in the Philippines. For the export of grain, gold and copper, Valdivia and Talcahuano were subsidiary ports. Meanwhile, the discovery of silver at Potosí in 1545 had created demand for more openings to an increasingly global web of commerce. Arica in Chile, for example, exploded with life whenever mercury arrived from Huancavelica, or when a shipment of the same metal – with its almost alchemical power of turning silver ore into silver – came in from the mines of Almadén in Spain, or when a train of llamas brought silver from Potosí. The silver had to be transmitted to Callao to be loaded onto the Armada del Sur, the fleet that took it to Panama for the onward journey across the Isthmus to Portobelo.

Callao was always problematic from the engineers' point of view. The long jetty trapped sand and dammed the tide, causing the wall to erode. When the eighteenth century began, five breaches let the ocean in. The cosmographer Pedro Peralta Barnuevo hit upon a curious solution, with the grudging but effective help of a military engineer, Nicolás Rodríguez. They built a series of thick walls to channel the sands away from the danger points, creating artificial beaches. When the work was completed in 1727 the ruined wall could be restored. But they reckoned without the capricious environment: a terrible earthquake in 1746 tumbled much of their work into the sea.

Further along the route of our clockwise tour of the coasts lay Paita, one of the finest natural harbours in northern Peru. The Dominican friar Reginaldo de Lizárraga visited in 1589, describing it as a 'staging post for every ship bound from Lima for Panama and Mexico, and for those travelling in the opposite direction. Its soil is sandy. The few Indians who form the resident community have to procure fresh water in huge canoes from ten leagues away.'[28]

Further north still, in the province of Quito, Guayaquil was the major port. Lizárraga commented unfavourably on its fetid, unhealthy heat and the inaccessibility of the docks to big ships at low tide, requiring laborious transfers of goods and passengers by canoe. He also deplored the unremitting insects and the temerity of the abundant caimans, 'like crocodiles of the Nile – very big and clustered in such great numbers that I could watch the Indian oarsmen buffet them with their paddles to open a passage for the canoes to get through'.[29] Despite the disadvantages, the place was favoured with abundant local wood, a tradition of craftsmanship in canoe construction and proximity to excellent sources of cacao: hence the growing demand for facilities for shipbuilding, repair and careening, rope-making, and for exploiting the locally available pitch.

Further north, Panama awaited. Prior to Henry Morgan's pirate escapade in 1671, which obliged the removal of the port to its present location, 'Panama la vieja' was never a fully satisfactory site, owing to accumulations of mud and floating brush along the shore. Shipping – including the Manila galleon and merchantmen from New Spain – was obliged, in consequence, to anchor at Perico, a league away.

To protect the monopoly of the Manila galleon, the crown banned commercial sailings from New Spain to Peru for five years from 1631, later making the prohibition permanent. But it was 'a rule more honoured in the breach', under the pretext of carrying official personnel, urgent correspondence, vital mercury shipments or emergency relief. Accidents of navigation were a perennial source of excuses, as freak weather could carry ships to destinations remote from their intended routes. Still, intermediate ports along the central American coast benefited from the ban – none more so, perhaps, than Realejo, founded in the 1530s to be a terminus for transisthmian traffic but destined to play a quite different role, as a centre for the manufacture of specialized small ships, known as *costeños*. These were three-masted vessels built of the local variety of cedarwood, which is naturally resistant to termites and rot, and used for fishing and cabotage.[30] In 1743 one such ship left the port laden with ten lengths of Chinese silk 'stained with sea water', a variety of tableware, 24 rosaries of glass beads, loose glass beads and cheap beads of other kinds, tablecloths, a quantity of cinnamon, Nanking linen, razor blades, fake pearls, silks, combs, mattresses made in China, buttons of mother-of-pearl, coarse cloth from Cajamarca, and a consignment of metalwork crucifixes.[31] Globalization, evidently, was touching markets even in places where people were poor.

Acapulco was the target for most of the Manila galleon's wares, such as those recorded on the voyage of 1609: 'moiré silks; fine and ornate oil-painted screens; cutlery of every sort; multiple arrays of weaponry, including lances, curved blades and other curiously wrought items; writing sets; wooden boxes and cabinets, curiously lacquered and inlaid, and other bibelots to charm the eye'.[32] To Acapulco, Bernardo Balbuena, author of *Grandeza mexicana* (1604), dedicated these sonorous verses:

> Here Fortune's ever happy progeny –
> An eagle rampant for the city's ostentation –
> Silver and treasures, making harmony,
> From Spain and China, in yearly combination.

According to Balbuena, Acapulco was the Genoa, as Veracruz was the Venice, of America – the respectively east- and west-facing emporia of a narrow land.[33] Fray Andrés de Urdaneta, the friar-navigator to whom the exploration of the eastbound route across the Pacific is attributed, chose the site as 'expansive, secure, very healthful, and well supplied with sound water'. The Italian engineer Gemelli Careri praised Acapulco for 'the natural security of [its] harbour, which, curling like a snail, with a bottom of constant depth throughout the bay, holds ships as if in an enclosed patio, surrounded by very high hills, with trees at the shoreline to act as mooring'.[34] Old maps tend to emphasize the virtues of the location, secure and welcoming, like a spreading ceiba tree, to which the Manila galleon could be moored. Alexander von Humboldt, at the start of the nineteenth century, disagreed. He was always on the look-out for 'virgin' landscape and was disposed to despise human agency. For him the spot was ineptly chosen: 'I have seen few places in either hemisphere with an aspect, wilder, more ill adapted, and yet at the same time more romantic. The cliff face these rocks form is so abrupt that a ship of the line could scrape them as it passes safely.'[35]

The main defect was that ships at anchor in the road had to transfer passengers and cargo to boats for transhipment to where 'men wading chest-high in the water' would manhandle them onto the shore, while 'individuals who had disembarked were carried bodily between boat and shore'. The situation seemed unsatisfactory, and the warden of the fort, Rafael Vasa, put it right by commandeering the militia to build a pier by cutting and combining wooden pillars for the foundations and then hauling them into place, bent double, as he explained to Humboldt, 'like the peons we use to carry loads of stone'. The new jetty opened for business in 1782.

Repair and careening were the focuses of activity at Acapulco, once ships – always in need of attention after long voyages – had unloaded their wares. For the latter operation, the ship had to be hoisted, or 'mounted' in the sailors' lingo, on sand to be cleaned first on one side, then, after turning, on the other. Coastal patrol boats, highly vulnerable to the voracious tropical *teredos*, or shipworm, had to be careened every six months. At some ports, the topography was favourable, as at Santa Marta, where 'a small inner bay is available for careening'.[36] Expedients to cope with larger vessels included leaning one ship against another so as to raise part of the keel above the waterline. Sometimes ships did not survive the careening process, such as the frigate *San Sebastián*, in 1748, which was scrapped without attempt to get back across the Atlantic.[37] Even if the hull survived, the masts had to be dismantled with occasionally disastrous consequences. The engineers' solution was to build moles with walls at an angle, against which the ships could be tilted, or locks from which the water could be drained for careening and in which the ships could be refloated after repairs.

In 1791 the exploring expedition of Alejandro Malaspina – the climax and finale of the Bourbon monarchy's unsurpassed record of investment in scientific exploration – put into Acapulco for repairs (*Atrevida* in February and *Descubierta* the following month). Despite the laggardness of *Descubierta*, Malaspina ordered a thorough overhaul of hull, decking, rig and sails. They rubbed down the copper sheathing of the hull with esparto brushes. The pleasures of the port were sufficient to draw deserters, who, according to the straitlaced captain of the *Atrevida*, José Bustamante, infected the residents with fever, dysentery and venereal disease.[38] The health of the expedition, however, benefited from the provisions, barrels, timber, ironmongery, pitch and ballast the ships took on with a view to their voyage north to Alaska, to face conditions that tested the technology of the day to its limits.

The Shipbuilders

'Building ships is planting trees in the sea,' according to an old saying by Spanish nautical engineers. The oceans were new frontiers for Spaniards – hardly penetrated and probably never traversed before Columbus. Thereafter, demand for shipbuilding, careening, repairs, naval stockpiling and the manufacture of ships' munitions and stores made shipyards spring up relatively suddenly all around the growing empire.

Two conditions governed their siting: available specialized manpower and suitable natural resources, especially wood. The makings of sails and metal fixings and mountings could, after all, be shipped in from anywhere. New species of timber could be introduced, if necessary, even in unfamiliar climes. But the great bulk of the wood that went into the making of a ship had to grow locally. Guayaquil oak was thought to be of poor quality, but cinnamon, mangrove and the acacia-like *guachapelí* all served instead. Masts could be made of Antillean laurel. In New Spain and Florida, mainmasts of jalapa-wood were reputedly 'as good as Norwegian pine'.[39] In Cuba, mahogany, cedar, oak and the trees known regionally as *chicharrón, guaba, guayacán, jagua, majagua, ocuje, quiebrahacha, sabicú, yaba* and *yamagua* were all called on for different functions. Wood had to be cut a year and a half before construction began to allow time for seasoning.

Supply was plentiful, but so was demand – and not only for timber. For every ton of displacement, 10 metres (33 ft) of planks or 10 metres (66 ft) of logs were needed. A seventy-gun frigate, for instance, built in Ferrol in Spain in 1795 required 10,620 cubits of oak, 1,260 of beech, 120 of cedar, 6,700 of Spanish and 630 of imported pine.[40] In 1761–2 the Havana shipyard had eleven ships to build: eight of sixty and three of eighty guns. The job required 36,000 distinct pieces of wood of all sizes.[41] Lead or, from 1750, copper was needed to sheathe hulls. As a further preservative against rot, bitumen was in demand, usually made of a mixture of pitch, fat, fish oil, brimstone, coal dust and red lead. In Spanish America, rigging was of hemp in Chile, henequen in Yucatán and agave in the shipyards of Guayaquil. Other essential materials for chains and housings and fixings for masts and instruments included iron, tin and bronze. After every shipwreck, divers scavenged for such precious items. And of course most ships carried guns, which had to be manufactured or imported.

For shipbuilding and repair, even more than for the commercial purposes that were the business of all harbours, facilities had to be sheltered, defensible and deep-draughted to accommodate big ships. At Guayaquil, for example, large vessels had to put into the Isle of Puná for repairs, while smaller ones could stay at the main port. For ships were, in a sense, luxury products, high in cost and craftsmanship. Construction was both delicate and demanding, as the keel was pieced together, the ribs extended and the beams positioned to support the decking. When the skeleton of the hull was in place, means of propulsion – by oar, sail or both – were added. Every detail of the rigging was important to ensure the ship handled well. Safety and capacity were equally important, but hard to combine. The bigger the ship, the greater the risk of fatal corrosion or damage on the long voyages across vast distances and challenging environments. Captains and crews suffered comparable strain of other kinds. Tomás de Larraspuru, who led 34 fleets back and forth across the Atlantic between 1608 and 1632, held the record for stamina.[42] In consequence, facilities for the maintenance of ships and the refreshment of crewmen sprang up all over Spanish America.[43]

The need was obvious. As Pedro Menéndez de Avilés put it as early as 1556:

For the voyage to America, long and laborious as it is, we need the best ships possible. Instead, before being commissioned for the Atlantic, ships are deployed to the Levant and only sold in Seville when their owners feel they have little more life left in them. In the Indies, on the whole, they tend to scrape on rocks and undergo wastage, especially from infestation by the wood-devouring molluscs known as teredos. In Seville, masters will pay little more for a new ship than for an old one, in the expectation that since she will have to be scuttled in any case, she might as well be old. Typically vessels sail badly, cannot withstand artillery, and cannot support safely the cargoes with which they are laden.[44]

Indeed, according to the registers of Cádiz between 1778 and 1797, only 57 of the 725 ships were purpose-built for America, while 668 were second-hand vessels. Some arrived in ballast; some were sold after the owner's death or bankruptcy and others to pay their crews' arrears of wages. Some could barely float. Some were the prizes of piracy, some sold by the royal treasury as unfit for service. Sales in Havana as well as Cádiz included ships built in Spain, England, France, Britain's American colonies, Sweden, Venice, Ragusa, Denmark and Russia, as well as in La Guaira and Montevideo.[45]

The fact that merchants risked old ships in preference to new ones shows that they prioritized capital savings over long-term returns. The frequency of war and exposure to piracy deterred investment. The effect was to supply plenty of repair work for small, local shipyards in the New World. We should acknowledge, therefore, that these were probably more important overall for the success of the monarchy than the big centres of construction such as Havana, which has dominated the historical literature.

In the early years of the eighteenth century, the pace of shipbuilding in Havana slackened, though the port retained its prime importance as the vital staging post for transatlantic traffic. In the first three years of the eighteenth century, the shipyard produced two first-class ships, *Santa Rosa* and *Rubí*, but careening and repair occupied most of the capacity. From 1714, the appointment of a naval superintendent marked a new era. José del Campillo, who occupied the post from 1719 to 1725, was a transformative presence. He relocated the shipyard to the vicinity of the fortress, within the city limits, and launched *San Francisco* (1714), *San Juan Bautista* (1718), *Victoria* (1718), *Príncipe de Asturias* (1720), *Conquistador* (1723) and, in 1724, the fifty-gun *San Juan*, under the command of the Cuban Juan de Acosta.

Bernardo Tinajero de la Escalera, secretary of the Council of the Indies, thought Havana-built ships superior to their peninsular counterparts. 'If a new build from Vizcaya', he affirmed, 'can last, at best, ten years, one can rely on an Indies-built ship to serve for more than thirty.'[46] Other experts, including the scientific explorer Jorge Juan, were critical of the American-built product, perhaps because their standards of comparison were more influenced by the quality of some of the most impressive British prizes that Spanish fleets captured. But needs must: in 1751 the Marqués de la Ensenada demanded 125 new vessels, including 70 ships of the line and 25 frigates, within six years to bring the navy up to required strength.[47] Three years later, against Jorge Juan's advice, the naval ministry commissioned part of the programme from Havana.

Demand for timber there caused tension between shipbuilders and sugar-millers, who relied on it for fuel, but reason of state favoured the shipyards. The high reputation of American hardwoods strengthened the 'Cuban lobby' at court. In 1720 Francisco Guiral, governor of Guatemala, which supplied wood for masts, authored a memo in favour of transferring commissions to Havana.[48] Jerónimo de Uztáriz, the prestigious author of *Teórica y práctica de comercio y marina* (1724; Theory and Practice of Trade and Navigation) proposed, in a work that approximated to a comprehensive economic plan for the monarchy, that

the most secure, convenient and exploitable shipyard for the construction and launch of new ships is Havana, especially because, thanks to the advantage conferred by local cedarwood, tough oak and other woods of superior strength, such ships as, if built in Europe, last from twelve to fifteen years are good for thirty years if built over there. Moreover, in combat cedar has the additional benefit of absorbing shot without splintering. It will be of great service to His Majesty and an enhancement of his ships if all those destined for convoy service, or coastal defence, whether in the Windward fleet or elsewhere in the seas of the Indies, are built of the hardwoods produced in those regions and in their shipyards.[49]

Mexican silver, imperial policy and the commitment of the Havana elite to investment in industry combined to produce the ships the monarchy needed. Most of the navy's needs were supplied through private contracts. In 1713, for instance, the contractor Manuel López Pintado undertook to build ten ships to the design of Antonio de Gaztañeta, the default specialist and the navy's favourite. It was Gaztañeta who famously introduced the scientifically informed design for the *Incendio*, launched in 1726 with 58 guns. At about the same time two fifty-gun craft, *San Lorenzo* and *San Jerónimo*, made their debuts.

Juan de Acosta, who also busied himself with making gun carriages, as well as salvage and a little piracy on the side, took charge in 1732 of the construction of four new ships of the line, of 64 guns each. He got into trouble, however, for exceeding his brief, which did not extend to wood-cutting, raising finance or navigation. He completed work on *Africa*, but the new ship drew unfavourable assessments from the naval ministry. Problems with the wood supply recurred, with cutters exploiting the market to charge inordinate prices. Clearly, there was a crisis – but it was one of growth. In 1734, in accordance with the wishes of Lorenzo Montalvo, who was in charge of naval procurement, the government announced a competitive tender system for the construction of a new shipyard, to be known as La Tenaza, adjoining the Jesús María district immediately outside the walls, north of the bay. New naval storehouses would be part of the contract. In 1735 Acosta indicated that he would bid for a contract to build between eight and ten frigates of forty to fifty guns each, on condition that he was made 'commander and absolute master and governor' of the shipyard.

Relations with Montalvo could hardly have been worse. Acosta railed against his enemy's 'high-handed and insufferable conduct'. Montalvo had insinuated that ships could be produced more cheaply in Havana – a claim that provoked his rival's mirth. 'He has no idea', commented Acosta, 'of how to approach the means of making the shipyards work, nor does he have any knowledge, save of how to stain paper with ink, nor can he tell cedar, mahogany, or *sabicú* wood from a load of feathers.' Montalvo responded vociferously, accusing Acosta of charging 50,925 pesos for work that should only have cost 39,976. The crown prudently temporized, avoiding deciding between the rival systems of employing private contractors – costly but effective – and taking direct control of shipbuilding – cheaper but risky.[50]

After José Patiño died in 1737, Acosta's problems increased. The following year, he was told that new ships would have to carry seventy guns each, while costs would have to be frozen. In 1739 the War of Jenkins' Ear began against Britain, straining New Spain's finances. The Viceroy declared that the costs of defence and of subsidies would leave no money to spare for the three new ships that awaited completion in Havana. The Marqués de la Ensenada ignored the protest and called for fifteen new ships by 1742, of which ten would be built in Havana (three men-of-war of seventy guns, and seven frigates of between twenty and fifty guns each).

The decree coincided with what for Acosta was a disaster: in 1741 the crown signed a contract with the newly formed Real Compañía de La Habana, which aimed to follow for tobacco in Cuba the model that the Guipuzcoan Company had developed for cacao production in Venezuela. The terms granted the new company a monopoly of naval construction and equipment for ten years, including wood for shipbuilding and rations for the fleets. Acosta's misfortune was Havana's gain: in 1742 a further extension of the arsenal began, with a ring of strong walls and new facilities for proofing hulls. Two years later the Company delivered *Nueva Reina* and *Nuevo Fuerte*, ships of the line of seventy guns each, with artillery installed at La Carraca in Cádiz.

At first, production hardly faltered in Havana, where three seventy-gun vessels and two of eighty were commissioned in 1744. But the problems of obtaining raw materials and paying crews continued to multiply. In Venezuela, meanwhile, the Guipuzcoan Company combined shipbuilding with their core business in the cacao trade for an obvious reason – self-reliance for commerce and defence. The company's tobacco-trading counterpart in Havana could not operate in the same way. They were obliged to rely on the naval shipyard.[51] In 1748, when the Havana Company was in fairly grave financial difficulties, Ensenada notified the directors that he intended to build four ships a year – two each of eighty and seventy guns, respectively. The consequent limitations on capacity available for the private sector seemed daunting. At the request of a traders' committee, the king relieved Ensenada towards the middle of the following year of responsibility for the running of Havana's yard, when *Fénix*, *Rayo* and *Galicia* were lying unfinished. The future seemed uncertain.

In 1756, two years after Ensenada's dismissal from office, production was down to one large ship a year. Mateo Mullan, the Irish engineer who was in charge of La Carraca shipyard, wrote disparagingly of the output from Havana in 1760. He knew the ships because they routinely came to Cádiz to be finished off – not because there was anything wrong with them, but because fittings had to be conformable to current, mutable naval standards.[52] Mullan complained that they were troublesome vessels, difficult to steer and sometimes with imperfectly stable masts. English-style construction made ships easier to handle, with no tendency to buck; but Havana-built examples were very robust, perhaps – Mullan thought – because of the way in which the planking was fixed, and which peninsular shipyards duly adopted.

Catastrophe struck in 1762, when the city surrendered to a huge British task force after nine weeks' siege.[53] The invaders wrecked the shipyard and stripped it of all movable materials. Yet by the summer of 1763 the indefatigable Montalvo had it up and running again. Elevated to the rank of Conde de Macuriges, Montalvo became the 'patriarch of the shipyard'.[54] Still in charge of the navy after half a lifetime in the job, he was at last able to enjoy what he had always wanted – total command over the shipyard. In short order he floated three large new ships: *Astuto*, *Bizarra* and *Cazador*. Mullan, now a captain, undertook supervision of ship construction, to be succeeded on his untimely death by his son, Ignacio. In 1769 the landmark launching of *Santísima Trinidad*, the most celebrated product of the Havana shipyards, took place. At the time, the standard Spanish man-of-war had three decks, 74 guns and a crew of 549. *Santísima Trinidad* greatly exceeded that standard, with four decks and 120 guns, displacing nearly 5,000 tons. (Fatally holed at Trafalgar, she sank with over a thousand men.[55])

In 1770 Montalvo could express satisfaction that the yard had produced nine ships, bearing 452 guns in all, over three years. Thirty-nine vessels had been careened and repaired in the same period, but Montalvo considered that everything apart from major ship construction was a side issue. The wastage, as he saw it, of precious hardwoods on repairs, the problems of paying staff, even the building of frigates, were distractions. Recruitment for service at sea was another issue – met by matching the rewards to those enjoyed on service by land.

Montalvo's priorities were costly however, and from 1772 money was unmanageably tight: Pedro González de Castejón, new Director-general of Arsenals, imposed a restricted budget.[56] The American War of Independence deterred investment. Production eased. Montalvo's death in 1778 marked the end of an era. In 1780 only one ship was launched. The shipyard became paralysed, as costs of debt service, pay and timber rose, while budgets fell. From 1790 the wars provoked by the French Revolution made security for the shipyard unattainable. Between 1786 and 1793 only three ships were completed, all built by private contractors. The shipyards reverted to maintenance work until 1825, when the Spanish monarchy effectively abandoned its continental American empire.

In assessing the work of the Havana yards, one must acknowledge that 53 ships of the line had been built there, including 7 of the 12 three-deckers the Spanish navy commissioned. Of course, none of the work would have been possible without the imperial network that generated demand and ensured the supply of materials. The supporting role of other Spanish American shipyards, with their facilities for maintaining big ships and building small ones, was vital. Puerto Rico, Santo Domingo, Mayagüez, Chaguaramas and Puerto Cabello provided such support along the Atlantic edge.

Co-ordination between shipyards was key. From Puerto Cabello, for instance, in 1752, supplies, munitions and equipment, including two replacement masts of 24 and 25 metres (79 and 82 ft), respectively, were transferred to Pedro Messía de la Cerda's squadron in Cartagena. The sailmakers of Puerto Cabello purveyed pitch and sailcloth. The chandlers obtained nails and hoops for barrels. The Company provided the Venezuelan coastguard patrol boats with supplies for the complement of 491 officers and crew. The case of *San Antonio* demonstrates the value of the web of economic relationships. The ship had to be thoroughly overhauled in 1772 to protect a new project for developing fisheries in Cumaná. Officials of the Guipuzcoan Company oversaw the work; specialists came from far and wide: foreman, master stonecutter, blacksmith, lantern-maker, cooper, master sailmaker, chandler, provider of ballast, warehouseman and numerous workmen. A master carpenter assisted a royal naval officer in drawing up the certificate of seaworthiness and authorizing payment.

Other similar cases show how complex a matter it was to unite all the skills and resources shipyards demanded and, therefore, how hard it was to site and classify installations of different types and sizes. In Puerto Cabello the Guipuzcoan Company constructed small galleys to control smuggling and middle-sized craft, such as single-masted sloops, and mixed-use vessels of up to three masts. In 1777 the government considered the prospects of supplying sufficient timber from the Guyanas to turn the facility into a shipyard for major projects and even went so far as to order a sixty-gun man-of-war; in the event, however, the project had to be shifted to Pasajes, the main shipyard of Spain. The insuperable problems included the insecurity caused by war with Britain, local competition for the labour of wood-cutters, high local wages and the doubtful capacity of the harbour at Puerto Cabello. The problems of timber supply occupied many anguished pages of memoranda in naval circles. It could not be supplied locally in Venezuela: the dense coastal forests were a 'green barrier' against invaders and it seemed prudent to leave them intact.[57]

The Pacific Shipyards

On the Pacific coast, shipbuilders faced different problems. At Realejo, from the sixteenth century, abundant local timber, pitch and cactus for fibre ordained an industry that was specialized in construction with cedarwood, for vessels destined for cabotage. The biggest shipyard was at Guayaquil, serving a self-contained and prosperous regional network. In the 1730s Jorge Juan and Antonio de Ulloa pointed out its suitability for building big ships for trade and war. They noted that the local timber, sparsely knotted, smooth and resistant to rot, was excellent for hulls, and that cinnamon-, mangrove- and cassia-wood were available for keels. There was oak for plankage, and the twisted guayacan trees could provide pins and dowels; local cotton could provide sails; hemp could be brought from Chile for cordage, or local agave could serve for the purpose of smaller craft. For careening, coconut oil could help below the waterline, and, above, hulls could be painted with a solution of hemp.

In the Guayas estuary the shipyard resembled an assembly line, with discrete activities on different quays. While a vessel was undergoing repair, a jetty was erected on piles. When the work was complete, a movable ramp was raised, on which the craft was eased into the water. The military engineer Francisco de Requena, an acute observer, pointed out in 1770 that 'there is no permanent set-up – no construction docks with fixed ramps, no careening bays; yet Guayaquil is the only shipyard on the Pacific coast, except for small-scale affairs in Realejo in Central America or Concepción in Chile, where everyone engaged in commerce in the far south launches his vessels.'[58]

If the idea of establishing a royal shipyard, like Havana's, on the Pacific never materialized, it was in part because of financial and strategic obstacles, but also in part because the existing facilities did an adequate job. In 1777 Francisco Ventura de Garaicoa, director of the Guayaquil yard (an office founded in 1730), tendered a report to the viceroy at Bogotá, Manuel Flores: 335 men were employed in the shipyard, including 254 master carpenters and 81 specialist caulkers, not to mention wood-cutters and general workmen (who received wages partly in cash and partly in clothing, but also in other kind, including liquor, sometimes with riotous consequences). At about the same time, the repair-yard at Callao employed 175 men – 68 carpenters, 107 caulkers: the figure suggests a good deal of activity.

At Guayaquil, the workers oscillated between ship and shore, turning easily to work on buildings in the town at will. Almost all, by the time in question, were free Blacks or of mixed race, though there had been a time early on when whites and Native Americans had figured among them. Jobs were inherited: in a list of 169 specialists, only 39 family names appear.[59]

On the farther side of the Pacific, a similar situation prevailed. The Philippines needed permanent shipbuilding facilities. In 1619 a report recorded six ships in service for sailings to New Spain, one of Indian construction and the rest built in the Philippines. *Espíritu Santo*, constructed in Cavite, was seventy cubits long from prow to stern and displaced nearly 1,000 tons.[60] *San Felipe* and *Santiago* had been built at Albay and *San Juan Bautista* in Mindoro. *San Miguel*, from Cavite, measured 68 cubits in length – nearly 30 metres (100 ft). The Indian-built merchantman *San Laurencio*, launched in 1594, had three decks, a high poop and a raised forecastle, and measured 60 cubits in length, with a draught of 12 cubits and 19 cubits of depth of stowage. The relatively large size of such vessels is understandable: the Pacific was a more forgiving sea than the Atlantic, where trimmer design was better suited to the conditions, and costly finishing, for safety's sake, imposed relatively high costs per unit of displacement. The same report recorded the timbers used: *palo de María*, a low tree irregular in shape, was commended for extraordinary quality; *arguijo*, a tall, erect plant, recommended for keels, beams and, rather oddly, pumps; *laguán*, durable below the waterline and resistant to infestation; *banaba*, for lining the living quarters; and others, such as *guijo* and *dongón*, very tough and pale in hue. Iron and lead imported from China and Japan could be purchased in Manila for working by Chinese and Japanese smiths, who could turn an arroba of iron into nails overnight and who charged only 28 reales a month, plus a daily rice ration. Rigging could be spun from local plants known as *gemú* and *abacá*, which resembled hemp. The superb cotton of the Ilocos region served for sailcloth.

The siting of the shipyards was crucial. Cavite was 2 leagues from Manila, while Mindoro and Masbate were as far as 80 leagues away. Though Manila seemed distant from Seville or even Acapulco, it was well placed to receive excellent primary materials from China and Japan. The standard of local craftsmanship and the availability of design and technical skills from Spain constituted the basis of a potentially successful shipbuilding industry. *Nuestra Señora de la Victoria* and *San Francisco Xavier* were launched in 1655, *Nuestra Señora de la Concepción* in 1658 and *San Sabiniano* in 1663. A galleon named *Nuestra Señora del Rosario* is said to have been built in Cambodia by a Spanish master sent there with equipment and materials by the governor of the Philippines. The Khmer ruler received 40,000 pesos for the work, but demanded an extra 20,000 before he would allow the ship to sail. In the 1670s output declined, partly from fiscal motives: the greater the tonnage shipped, the greater the rebate payable on customs duties on arrival in Acapulco; but the new, officially imposed limit of 500 tons was routinely exceeded.

The 1720s saw a further reduction in the size of craft, partly owing to falling revenues in Manila and partly owing to the slimline designs advocated by Antonio de Gaztañeta.[61] But the construction of sloops, frigates and galleys for defence against Muslim pirates continued at a greater rate than ever, reflected in José González Cabrera Bueno's *Navegación especulativa y práctica* (Navigation in Theory and Practice), published in Manila in 1734. Chapter fifteen was devoted to naval construction, with 45 sections on hulls, masts, rigging, sailmaking and caulking for fighting ships. The Manila yard never seemed, however, to be able to supply adequate artillery for the ships built there. When the British attacked in 1762, the firepower of the ships in port was condemned as nugatory. Goods and passengers crammed the gunports. It would be rash to blame negligence or incompetence at the level of command. Insuperable problems arose from the complexity of a globally articulated system of supply, which placed impossible demands on those responsible for running it. At the beginning of the nineteenth century, the great naval historian José Vargas Ponce summed the situation up with nicely balanced nostalgia and lucidity:

Officers are required to know everything necessary to the operation of a ship – as it were, to breathe life into an inert and intricate
machine by means of extremely exacting mechanics; to govern
a floating city, encompassing a population with a great range of
conflicting demands; to pluck daily from the heavens data inaccessible from any other source; to struggle with the elements,
to bridle and tame them; to keep firm control of those disparate
tribes known as soldiers and sailors; and withal, if they are able
to master so many preliminary difficulties, to manage perfectly
every endeavour of war by land and sea.[62]

In short, the task was impossible. It was astonishing to see it done
at all.

7

THE PUBLIC SPHERE
Social and Economic Infrastructure

By thy great wisdom and by thy traffick hast thou increased
thy riches, and thine heart is lifted up because of thy riches.
(EZEKIEL 28:5)

'Palm-trees will not allow a man to wander among them with impunity,' wrote Goethe in *Elective Affinities* in 1809, 'and doubtless
his tone of thinking becomes very different in a land where elephants
and tigers are at home.'[1] The author was proffering homage to his contemporary fellow-countryman Alexander von Humboldt, renowned
as the 'prince of travellers', who had completed a scientific pilgrimage
through Spanish America and was now spending his time on diaries
and essays for publication. Humboldt drew a striking contrast between
the magnificence of tropical nature and the deficiencies of human
action. He has therefore become a hero for our ecologically conscious
age.[2] In his own day, though the public and the politicians welcomed
him wherever he went in Spain's dominions, he did not forbear to crit-
icize ill-planned settlements, barbarous habits and superstitious beliefs
in lines sometimes worthy of inclusion in the annals of the 'Black
Legend' of Spanish imperial iniquity. He formulated the notion of
Naturgemälde or 'canvas of nature' – the figureless plain, the unconquer-
able volcano, the virgin forest – against a vision of degenerate cities.
But he had, at best, an imperfect sense of how – thanks in large part
to the impact of the engineers – soil and landscape changed in Spanish
America in the half-century or so preceding his arrival.

He was by no means the first to differentiate a supposedly chaste
and untouched nature from its humanly recrafted simulacrum, or to
raise, inadvertently or by design, possible juridical presumptions. In his
Two Treatises of Government of 1689, John Locke echoed a long imperial

tradition when he used 'improvement' of land, by means of agriculture, to justify the appropriation of 'unexploited' territory from the poor English, Irish and Native Americans who occupied it purposelessly, and from rival empires who claimed it recklessly.[3] Longstanding disputes over far-flung lands drew potency from the fact that the Spanish Empire, from first to last, was a network of cities – with sparsely settled frontier zones invitingly dispersed among them.

The Replanted Habitation

To found cities, for sustenance and defence, on expanding frontiers was part of the tradition of the Reconquest in Spain. It required no strenuous or innovative thought to do the same in America.[4] Conquistadores, like most other migrants, tried to reproduce the feel of home, which for them typically included 'civility' (*civilidad, civitas*), a virtue that supposedly excluded disharmony. By electing town councillors, they 'created a depository of the polity' (*depósito de república*).[5] Their early settlements served to feed, refresh, direct and tax the Enterprise of the Indies. The earliest descriptions of cities or towns on Caribbean islands or in Tierra Firme are fairly uniform: on the scale of villages or hamlets, built of wood or mud, sustained by intensively cultivated gardens with fruit orchards and pens for livestock. Vineyards and olive groves were always planned in the hope of successful acclimatization, together with barns, pigsties, mills for flour and gunpowder, kilns for lime and tiles, quarries and the rudiments of a clothing manufactory – fulling mills for extracting the grease from fleeces.[6] In the high Andes, workshops focused on 'rushwork, sheepskins from native camelids, woollen serge and native clothing', while, in environments where cotton was abundant, spinners, weavers, carders and dyers congregated.[7]

With the conquest of Mexico in 1521, cities and the kernels of future cities became centres for the consolidation and spread of Spanish colonization. Within half a century, according to the criteria and calculus of Juan López de Velasco, chronicler and cosmographer, who compiled his data between 1571 and 1574, Spanish America contained 241 urban centres with 23,493 citizens – residents, that is, who headed households of at least half a dozen people. Of the capital cities of the constituent kingdoms and provinces, Santo Domingo had 500 citizens, Havana 60, San Juan de Puerto Rico 200, Caracas 55, Mexico City

3,000, Guatemala City 500, Panama 400, Santafé de Bogotá 600, Quito 400, Guayaquil 100, Cuenca 80, Lima 2,000, Cuzco 800, Santiago de Chile 375, La Paz 200, Potosí 400 and Asunción 300.[8]

Founding a city was always the culmination and usually the only retrospective act of justification following a 'discovery' or invasion. The procedure started with a rite of possession-taking, which comprised cutting branches, walking the bounds, seizing handfuls of soil, imbibing some water if there was any, and even uttering shouts to assert one's presence and alert rival claimants. A public scribe made a record of the actions. A herald proclaimed them. Masses, where priests were on hand, and the raising and implanting of large crosses accompanied the rituals, which concluded with the tracing of the outlines of the projected streets on the ground and the election of the first municipal council. From that moment the city possessed an inchoate infrastructure. Makers of streets, squares, aqueducts and fountains signified their intention to stay, though cities had to be, in a sense, portable. The citizenry might have to move to a new site in response to a bad original choice or some catastrophe, such as an earthquake, plague or attack by Indigenous peoples; in such cases, the polity kept its identity, name and council.[9]

The founding and growth of settlements had to conform to the crown's sprawling regulations: especially the 149 articles of the *Ordenanzas de descubrimiento, nueva población y pacificación* (Regulations for Discoveries, New Settlements, and Pacification – the affected euphemism for conquest) of 1573. The second part of the text set out required conditions: a healthy environment, with a good climate, under 'favourable stars and clear and benign skies, with consistently, unobstructedly pure, sweet air, and moderate temperatures neither excessively hot nor cold' (Art. 34). The city must be laid out 'with set-square and line' by a suitably qualified person, starting from the location of the main plaza, 'drawing the streets towards the main gateways and roadways, and leaving space for the extension of the built-up area in the same form, as the population increases' (Art. 111). Sites must be specified for the principal church and for a residence for a royal representative, a town hall, a customs house, a repair yard and hospitals, as well as premises for processing fish and meat and for tanning 'and other work that may yield offensive waste' (Art. 123).

The grid was commonly spoken of as a 'natural' layout, because it conferred obvious advantages in terms of controlling building line, density, orientation and hierarchy, while giving residents a sense of emotional security.[10] But it was not always easy to maintain, especially in the mining boomtowns.[11] Potosí, for example, never had a formal founding ceremony or a regular streetplan. When it made its unplanned appearance in 1545, everyone built his house where he liked. The first 94 dwellings were in the driest spots around a drained lake. Within eighteen months, 2,500 houses appeared, but there were no streets to connect them because there was no engineer or surveyor to lay them out. The outcome was an urban labyrinth, with shanties flung up slopes and over ravines for the conscripted native labourers, transient workers, royal officials and a mixed bag of adventurers. By the beginning of the seventeenth century Potosí had perhaps 160,000 inhabitants.[12]

The Infrastructure of Governance

Social and economic infrastructure in colonial towns was in the hands of the *cabildo*, the 'assembly of persons designated to govern the polity', to use the definition that was standard at the time, with two executive magistrates (*alcaldes ordinarios*) and a variable number of councillors. There was also scope for appointing technicians, who did not form part of the council, to such offices as those of supervisors, also called *alcaldes*, of works, sometimes specifically for works of defence. Quito had *alcaldes* to supervise tailors, hatters, saddlers and smiths. There was even an *alcalde* in charge of bullfights in Caracas. The inspector of weights and measures (*fiel ejecutor*) was normally charged with fixing the size of building plots and of properties in the hinterland. In Puerto Rico and Santiago de Chile, the same official was responsible for collecting fines imposed on malefactors and defalcators. Mexico City had *alcaldes* for sheep-grazing and the maintenance of the main tree-lined boulevard. The council of Caracas had a paid manager of church buildings to supervise their state of repair and decoration and see to the collection of their rents. There was a general clerk of works, whose role included providing for public buildings and recruiting the necessary labour. The constable watched over security. Mexico City and Caracas had designated administrators for hospitals.

Councils also appointed bell-founders and municipal clockmakers. If cities were to function as communities, synchronized activities were vital. Hernán Cortés commissioned Mexico City's first clock and installed it in the palace of a former Aztec paramount. Lima acquired one in 1549 and in Santafé de Bogotá the *audiencia* – royally appointed administrative and judicial body – ordered the installation of a clock in 1563. Jesuits had unsurpassed reputations as astronomers and custodians of time. In 1612 the council of Quito paid for the construction of a new bell-tower so that the chimes from the Jesuit School bell could be heard even in the furthest quarters of the city.[13]

Control of markets was crucial. That of Tlatelolco – which became, in effect, a suburb of Mexico City – was extremely busy. Cotton blankets and cacao beans – pre-Hispanic means of exchange – circulated alongside or drove out coins. Maize, tobacco and baskets were bartered for locally produced bread, hats, soap, guitars, candles and belts. Specialists in ironwork, hairdressing and cutlery had stands. Cultural exchange was conspicuous, with native tailors repairing and refashioning Spanish garments to give them new life: native consumers loved buttons. Healers abounded. Foodstuffs were copious, especially tortillas, maize cakes and other corn products, Spanish vegetables and pork.[14] In Quito towards 1800 there were 185 permanent shops dealing in food, thirteen stalls, thirty licensed outlets for alcohol and unnumbered other pop-ups and barrows – strong evidence of a lively market.[15] In Santafé de Bogotá, the council intervened to prevent shortages and hoarding. 'Has cacao gone up from 10 *reales* to 12?' asked the procurator, the official responsible, in 1802, 'and candles in the shops to 3 *reales* each? What justification can there be for the poor to be made to pay highly for articles of daily consumption? Hungry folk obliged to seek sustenance at crippling cost are likely to resort to crime.'[16]

The ingredients for bread – the inescapable staple of Spaniards, if not of indios – were enough to command a bureaucracy of their own. In Mexico City and Caracas, *alcaldes* were responsible for the warehousing and marketing of grain. Bakeries were foci of official anxiety. The normal procedure was for bakers to take the wheat they purchased to water-mills for grinding into flour but in Ubaté in New Granada in 1807, a native entrepreneur, Luis Pajarito, obtained a licence to construct a mill of his own to process locally grown grain – because, he claimed, the existing mill favoured rich clients and his own grain was imperfectly accounted for. With their millwheels formed of paddles and mounted on stone blocks, water-driven flour mills were common features of Spanish American landscapes from the sixteenth century. Every so often, millers would 'pick their teeth' – that is, re-point the grindstones to maintain their effectiveness. The miller's fee was a proportion of the grain he processed, known as his *maquila*, which was bigger in the dry than in the wet season. Variations in the availability of grains caused problems, not only from season to season but from biome to biome. In Veracruz, folk attributed to poor nourishment the supposed pallor of the inhabitants and the proverbial local lassitude, apostrophized as 'love of silver and fear of death'. The climate did not permit the usual seed plots and gardens to grace the city, which had to rely on imports.[17]

Getting a Grasp on Water

Water was, despite or because of its elusive character, the most fundamental of the materials that went into the making of a city and the ingredients that sustained its life.

The obstacles to achieving a well-distributed water supply were in most cases natural, not legal. There was no doubt in law that sweet water belonged to the crown and existed for the common use of all subjects. But there were areas of ambiguity, especially in relation to snow and snow-melt. In 1596, for instance, the council of Mexico City put the snows of the sierra up for auction, with licence to sell snow in the city for whoever met the reserve price. No buyers appeared. So the council added to the opportunity the sale of the monopoly in *aloja*, a popular summer beverage made of sugar-water and spices. This time interested parties did emerge. In Peru a similar system operated. In Chile on the other hand free access to highland snow or 'frozen waters' (*aguas congeladas*) in the local jargon was sacrosanct.[18] If water of the best quality flowed from the icy mountain tops, rainfall was highly esteemed, too, followed in order of preference by spring water and the yield of brooks, rivers, wells, seasonal melt, lakes and pools. It had to be channelled for critical purposes, including mills and factories and the basic essential of clean drinking water. To prevent contamination the council imposed severe fines on anyone who washed clothes 'or anything else' along the route of supply. In 1612 the penalty was two hundred strokes of the lash and the confiscation of the washed products.

The Spanish monarchy inherited some effective water-management systems from the indigenous past. Some of the hydraulic engineering that Spaniards found on arrival in the New World was spectacular. In aqueous parts of Mesoamerica, 'floating' plots or *chinampas*, dredged from lake bottoms for agriculture, obviated the need for irrigation or flood defences. Mexico City was criss-crossed with canals known as *acalotes*, of native construction, which bore thousands of canoes, laden with produce, to the central market places. Quito had garden plots called *camellones*, platforms of piled earth, dotted with basins for water; trenches that carried water over impressive distances, without using arched supports or syphon technology, demonstrated pre-Hispanic expertise in controlling the delivery of water. Native officials were well acquainted with the necessity for and means of keeping the water supply in order. In Santiago de Chile the native council was responsible for 45 irrigation channels in 1760, a figure that rose to 57 in 1810.

Despite the excellence of native systems for their own purposes, water management was an area in which Spanish engineers excelled. Many of the delivery systems they built still stand and still work, monuments to how the Spanish monarchy transformed the look of the empire and of how public works contributed to its strength. Conscious heirs of Frontinus, the great ancient authority on engineering, could exclaim with him, 'With such an array of indispensable structures, carrying so many waters, compare, if you will, the idle Pyramids or useless, though famous, works of the Greeks!'[19]

Santiago de Chile is a case in point. As well as the native-administered water supply, the city had the famous Maipo or San Carlos canal, which diverted water to the Mapocho River in order to ensure ample provision. Work on it began in 1742, encountering multiple hazards: problems with lining the ditches, the difficulties of a sharp incline and periodically ruinous earthquakes. Not until 1796, when Agustín Caballero drew up new plans in consultation with his fellow army engineer, Juan Garland, did successful operations resume. A section, formed of a trapezoidal cone, 31 kilometres (19 mi.) long, could carry 13 cubic metres (459 cu. ft) per second. In 1815 two other military engineers, Miguel María de Atero and Manuel Olagüer Feliú, completed a further section where 'you could see water flow through the cavity'.[20] Also in Chile, where the levels of rainfall were much inferior to those in the tropics, the problems of shunting water up slope were resolved at Colchagua with waterwheels up to 18 metres (59 ft) in diameter, drawing huge earthenware or metal buckets.

Some cities had plenty of water. Many thirsted. There were permanent artificial reservoirs, of which a good example was that of

San Ildefonso in Potosí, where water collected to work waterwheels at the mines. In growing settlements, however, cisterns and ponds had to be dug. Rainwater repositories, whether wells or tanks, tended to seep and let in impurities. A pre-Columbian filtration technique involved adding cactus stems and leaves to the water. In Arica and other places porous stones were used. Soon after the foundation of Santo Domingo, water flowed from the main well to the plaza mayor via a wheel-driven pump and a clay pipe; in 1544 a sewage system was planned ahead of the erection of a new district. In Havana the order of events was reversed. Growth superannuated the original system of wells and tanks until 1575, when engineer Francisco de Calona began to excavate a drainage system for washing effluent away, using water drawn by canal from the Almendares River, and for supplying public fountains. In 1591 the works, spanning 11 kilometres (7 mi.) from the riverbank to plaza de San Francisco, were complete. In New Spain, Quito, Peru and Venezuela, waterwheels raised water from wells, nourished aqueducts, supplied fountains and ditches, turned millstones and powered sugar mills and pumps in farms, factories and mines. In Mexico City and Caracas, designated *alcaldes* ensured a fair distribution of the water supply. At Santafé de Guanajuato, around 1749, tanks for collecting rainwater made an important contribution. In the same year, at the request of the council, the master-artisan Antonio Gordiano built the celebrated reservoir of La Olla, 20 metres (65½ ft) deep, adding another, called 'de los Santos', 12 metres (39 ft) deep, in 1788. Yet no comprehensive water supply was provided for the city. Water-carriers with their mules remained in service until the mid-nineteenth century.

Canals were the commonest means of bringing water from afar. Typically aligned at right angles to the rivers from which they drew, they usually had linings of wooden piles or planks at the side and thick stones on the bottom and were wide, shallow and with curved cross-sections to minimize flood damage. From 1530 a spring three-fourths of a league distant supplied the fountain in the main square of Mexico City with water 'clear, fine, and healthy' from Chapultepec, winding through canals, tunnels, archwork and tubing. Another spring at Ocholoposco could not be harvested because the gradient was insuperable: it was left for 'the local residents of Coyoacán to use, and the convent of Santa María de los Ángeles'.[21] In the desert region of northern New Spain canals were insurance against droughts and destructive flash-floods. They featured walls of double width, screens against evaporation, and even high flanking fences for extra protection. During the dry season, they could be detached from the river so that outflowed water could be separately preserved. Where nature permitted, water-bearing pipelines could be made of clay tubing, as at Santo Domingo, or of woods such as juniper, *guayamel* and cedar. Chapultepec's was of drilled limestone blocks. Some were lined with lead or coated inside with bitumen or *zulaque* – a mix of lime and brick with oil or fat, made waterproof with pigskins or oxhides. The enlightened engineer José Antonio de Alzate, a Mexican creole, sketched a project for a 'machine to drill wooden tubing for water pipes' in the hope of serving his country and his vocation. He got his inspiration from the work of a French army expert in hydraulics and ballistics, Bernard de Belidor.[22] In the South American cone, where water was abundant, there was little need for such inventive solutions. Water-carriers, wheeling huge carts stocked with jars to and from free-flowing rivers, long dominated the water supply of Buenos Aires and Montevideo.

Aqueducts were the costliest responses to problems of water supply, but the monarchy's servants rarely hesitated to build them when needed. Lima, relatively arid, was harder to supply. Riverside facilities along the Rímac were insufficient; so in 1565 a tax on meat was imposed to pay for an aqueduct to lead to the plaza mayor. Medical opinion had been decisive. Physicians opined that impurities in the water caused catarrh, quinsy and asthma, among other afflictions. In 1650 the original modest fountain was replaced with a baroque extravaganza, adorned with lions, griffins and allegorical scenes. In lesser squares the religious orders competed to erect taller, better, more capacious fountains, but the greatest of the water-supply works was the so-called Paseo de Aguas, a boulevard with a central canal with gardens and elaborate fountains, which opened in 1776, thanks to the efforts of Viceroy Guirior. Trujillo in Peru also had an aqueduct from the sixteenth century. It took water 11 kilometres (7 mi.) from the Moche River to a central deposit, from where channels extended to the plaza mayor, hospital and friary of San Francisco, feeding fourteen wells through gravel filters.

At Mexico City in 1571, work began on the drinking-water aqueduct of Santafe, comprising 904 arches, stretching over 3,908 metres (12,822 ft) in length, and rising, at its remotest point, over the dedicated washing-water aquifer at Chapultepec, where the temperature of the spring was 'too hot to touch'. In 1754 the historian and later official cosmographer of New Spain José Antonio de Villaseñor suggested that it would be worth erecting facilities 'which could serve for baths useful to restore the nerves, warm the bones of chilled bodies and promote copious sweating, which is known to be of great service to health'.[23] Cempoala and Otumba, meanwhile, shared a unique history. There, between 1543 and 1560, Francisco de Tembleque, an engineer from Toledo who had embraced a vocation as a friar, built an aqueduct 'in the Roman style' with only native manpower. An 8-kilometre (5 mi.) stretch reached Cempoala and an extension of fully 26 kilometres (16 mi.) more continued to Otumba, overleaping the precipitate ravine at Tepeyahualco by means of an arch 1,020 metres (3,346 ft) long, 17 metres (55½ ft) wide, and 38.75 metres (127 ft) high. The falsework, amazingly, was not of wood but mud.

Elsewhere in New Spain, at Querétaro, Juan Antonio de Urrutia, Marqués de Villar del Águila, solved the city's problems in 1738, contributing 60 per cent of the 124,791 pesos it cost to do so from his own pocket. From springs known as Los Ojos del Capulín, from the name of the wild cherry trees around it, an aqueduct 1 kilometre long brought the water required over 74 impressive arches, 23 metres (75 ft) high at the utmost point. Ten fountains and troughs supplied the domestic needs of all residents.[24] The aqueduct El Sitio, in Xalpa, which would attain a length of 50 kilometres (31 mi.), was designed to carry water from the rivulet known as El Oro to the Jesuits' hacienda over tiers of arches – four of them over a single depression 50 metres (164 ft) deep – and broad cuttings. The work was unfinished when the Jesuits were expelled in 1767, but completed in 1854. At Arizpe in Sonora circa 1782, Manuel Agustín Mascaró raised a canal on rounded pillars to link with the aqueduct he designed.

In New Granada, Santafe de Bogotá relied on a single large reservoir, until 1792, when another friar-engineer, the Capuchin friar Domingo de Petrés, from Valencia, was commissioned to build the aqueduct of San Victorino, with financial support from Viceroy Ezpeleta. He took water from the Arzobispo River, creating points where it could be tapped at San Diego, the foot of the hill of Monserrate, the Calle de los Tres Puentes, Las Béjares, Nieves square and the streets called Las Ánimas, Las Ranas, La Veleta and El Prado, before 'entering the square and emptying into the deep cistern', with its Doric finish, where, from 1803 onwards, industrious water-carriers gathered.[25] Dotted around the city were 34 spouts, taps, troughs and cisterns.

In the fullness of time, the modest original fountains that every-where marked major public spaces gave way to elaborate and sometimes extravagant public works of sculptural ostentation: flanked, at Salto del agua, for instance, by Solomonic columns, or like the so-called musicians' fountain at Tlaxapa, adorned with figures in niches playing violas and mandolins.

Draining Wetlands

If water was often scarce, it could, at times, also be excessive. It some-times bore disasters, which the biggest public works project in New Spain was undertaken to arrest. Though poets extolled the excellence of Mexico City's location, no verse could conceal the extraordinary problems, of which flooding was the most conspicuous. The inun-dations of 1553, 1580, 1604 and 1607 were followed by a soaking so thorough in 1629 that it provoked debate about shifting the site of the capital. The disaster was unsurprising, because the basic flood defences were as old as the city and each update had been insuffi-cient to remedy their issues. In 1555 Viceroy Luis de Velasco 'el viejo' mobilized 6,000 native labourers to build a barrier of wood and stone to keep the water at bay. He also ordered work to protect the main highways out of the city. A councillor, Ruy González, and a citizen, Francisco Gudiel, proposed an alternative plan: draining Lake Texcoco by means of a great ditch northward via Huehuetoca to the Tula River, beyond the central valley of Mexico and thence to the sea. The stone barrier, dedicated to St Lazarus, was completed, as we have seen, early in 1556.[26] In 1604, however, the rains were so heavy that the dynamic viceroy, the Marqués de Montesclaros, faced with collapsed build-ings and wrecked thoroughfares, resolved to remake the roads, raise the height of the aqueducts, refurbish the barriers and commit to the drainage project. Another flood in 1607 reinforced convictions that drainage was essential. The first stage, from Nochistongo to Huehuetoca, was ready by Easter 1608. Heinrich Martin – or Enrico Martínez, as he was called locally – was in charge of the work. German by birth, he was competent in surveying, cosmography, printing and astrology. His writings encompassed climate studies and researches in what we would now call the ecology of lakes. He put no fewer than 4,700 natives to work, constructing 13,079 metres (42,910 ft) of pipe-work, of which nearly half was above ground, dug to a depth of upwards of 11 metres (36 ft). For the rest, a tunnel of 1.5 to nearly 2 metres (5 to 6½ ft) wide and over 3 metres (10 ft) high was lit by 42 square skylights, whereby, Martínez explained, light entered. 'And earth is excavated by means of many curious and ingenious machines and devices'.[27] At maximum depth, the skylights were up to 44 metres (144 ft) deep, with the shallowest at 10 metres (33 ft). For nearly 1,000 metres (3,280 ft) the tunnel was lined with rough plaster, the rest with stone fixed with lime.

After the viceroy declared the drain open, two unforeseen consequences became apparent: sumps appeared, and production declined from *chinampas* (traditional Nahua) fields, dredged from the lake or flooded land. For years debate continued over both whether Martínez was right to dig the drain deeper in times of rain and what the right level was. Alonso Arias, an architect by formation, did not hesitate to condemn the whole project as useless, on the grounds that the tunnel was constructed on the basis of proportions far removed from those recommended by Vitruvius. He failed to mention that the Vitruvian figure would have demanded excavations of impractical depth and were anyway probably the result of scribal error.

Anxiety for the safety of the capital city of New Spain induced the Council of the Indies to commission a new expert, the Dutch expert in hydraulics Adriaan Boot, who demanded and received what he called good pay. Dignified with the title of 'royal engineer', Boot appeared before the viceroy in 1614 to undertake a leisurely inspection. His findings were clear. The plasterwork was deficient and the calculations of the depth of the work were based on errors. Boot's suggestion was to return to the former strategy of retaining the water behind a barrier. He proposed reinforcing the barriers, raising further the roadways and providing pumps, sluices, cranes and bridges to ease the effects of emergencies.

Experts called in for consultation refuted Boot's views and Martínez was confirmed in command. The sluice-gates in the barriers were raised to favour the cultivators of *chinampas*. The worst was yet to come. The 'great inundation' of St Matthew's Day 1629 'reduced the entire city to zero, leaving nothing unwrecked'. Some 30,000 indios died. The number of Spanish citizens fell to four hundred. Most of the urban area remained submerged until 1634, saving only the plaza mayor and those of El Volador and Santiago Tlatelolco. Victims who were spared ascribed their miraculous salvation to the Virgin of Guadalupe.

Desperate remedies were proposed, not least by the scribe of the city council, Fernando Carrillo, who suggested that every householder should surround his dwelling with a rubble fence, turning the streets into canals and the city into a sort of American Venice. Drainage re-emerged as the only viable solution. In 1630 the viceroy, the Marqués de Cerralbo, imposed a wine tax throughout New Spain – the first time the whole kingdom was taxed for the principal benefit of the capital (albeit not the sole benefit, as part of the proceeds was earmarked for the fortification of Veracruz).

Work on drainage resumed in Mexico City amid disturbing rumours of more sumps and subsidence and unapologetic demands from the Council of the Indies to relocate the capital to higher ground between Tacuba and Tacubaya. Martínez died in 1631, spared from the ignominy of seeing his plans deferred. Belatedly, in 1637, the incumbent viceroy commissioned a report on the case so far. He adopted the recommendation of the corps of engineers: to convert the main drain into a canal. In 1767 Ricardo Aylmer and Ildefonso Iniesta – army engineer and architect, respectively – argued for the final removal of what remained of the underground drainage system at Huehuetoca. The recommendation was carried out in 1788. Floods swept through the city again in 1792 and 1795, albeit less severely than formerly.[28]

The Bowels of Earth

Mines were as much a part of the economic infrastructure as communications and water supply. Pre-industrial capitalism was always unideological – for no one had yet thought of the ideology concerned – and so states could be and were entrepreneurs. The Spanish monarchy's key industry was mining, which was a royal prerogative, shared with individuals but with major operations reserved to the crown. Alluvial gold had been found in Columbus's day in the West Indies and later on a bigger scale in New Granada, where, on average, according to official returns, 4,063 pounds (1,843 kg) of gold dust were produced annually in the sixteenth century, 7,063 pounds (3,204 kg) in the seventeenth, amounting to 40 per cent of global output, and 9,375 pounds (4,252 kg) in the eighteenth.[29]

Silver, on the other hand, came from ore and demanded heavy investment, ruthless exploitation of labour and costly technical support. It needed the commitment of the state and the input of engineers.

By traditional methods, lead ore, on smelting at ferocious heat, would fuse, and oxidation would turn the lead into a granular residue. The natives of the Andean region used small, portable furnaces, called *huayras*. Especially after the discovery of veins of silver at Potosí in 1545, Spanish America became a laboratory of innovation in mining works. Production expanded thanks to the mercury-amalgamation technique, introduced in New Spain in 1555 and in Peru in 1571, which made low-quality ores exploitable. Mercury, brought at huge cost from Almadén in Spain and Huancavelica in Peru, became a crown monopoly in 1572. It was indispensable to silver production. The process saved on labour in the refineries – places, according to the beacon of Mexican enlightenment Francisco Javier de Gamboa, in 1761, 'of punishment for slaves, torment for martyrs, and vengeance for tyrants'.[30] The high cost of mercury ensured that the Indigenous methods were never wholly displaced, but without the new techniques operations on the scale and of the nature of those at Potosí would have been unthinkable.

Hydraulic engineering was key. Even in deserts mines required drainage, operated at Guanajuato, for instance, by waterwheels, or systems of pulleys drawn by teams of horses or mules. Syphons were also used, especially at Morán, in the central region of the viceroyalty, where, however, persistent flooding caused the works to be abandoned. In Mexico, the requisite high temperatures for smelting were obtained by hydraulically operated bellows – a system devised by Pedro Cornejo de Estrella in 1588.[31] In 1604 José Orozco Gamarra proposed a similar improvement for the Peruvian silver industry. He was a Spaniard who had married a granddaughter of the Inca Paramount Atahualpa; their son, Bartolomé Inga, made the journey to Spain to present the plan at court, with a proposal in code to preserve the secret.[32] Thenceforth, the indigenous system was discarded in favour of hydraulic bellows and a new procedure in which the ores were sieved and ground into powder for amalgamation with mercury. By 1597 New Spain had 406 silver refineries, of which water powered 167, while draught animals powered the rest. Fifty-nine of the hydraulic systems were at Pachuca and 36 at Taxco. In Zacatecas, on the other hand, the arid landscape demanded animal muscle-power.

Peru came to exceed Mexico in the scale and complexity of hydraulic mining operations. There were three water-operated engines for silver extraction at Oruro, whereas of the 96 in place at Micoypampa the greater part relied on water power. The flow of water to the refineries demanded the construction of a reservoir 5,000 metres (16,400 ft) above sea level at Cari-Cari. Natural repositories – lakes at San Lázaro, San Pedro and San Sebastián – were called into use. The La Ribera watercourse, 25 kilometres (15½ mi.) long, carried the water to the town, dividing the urban centre in two and requiring sixteen bridges in all to span it. Three further canals linked a network of eighteen reservoirs (to which three more were added in the seventeenth century). In a volcanic zone, reliance on reservoirs increased the hazards of breakage and floods, such as occurred in 1626, when seismic activity ruptured the Cari-Cari reservoir, releasing a torrent of stones and flood that smashed 32 refineries and damaged 34 more. Fray Diego de Mendoza blamed 'human greed, which looks only to its own interests, takes no care of the goods of others, and leads individuals to attend only to their own affairs, ignoring our shared responsiblity for putting harm to rights.' They were, however, all operating as normal again within a year.[33]

Ore was hard to pulverize. Early methods relied on thousands of indio feet, trampling over heated ore in long, lidded cases. Cold crushing was soon found to work as well, with the ore strewn on the flagstones of a courtyard for indios or, in Mexico, horses to stamp on. As the ore crumbled, water, salt and mercury were added while the trampling continued. At Potosí mechanization was a selective, gradual and always partial response to the difficulty of obtaining indio labour. Day and night, lumps of ore were pulverized under the sledgehammers of machines known as *almadenetas*, powered by hand or by pedals, as well as by water or draught animals. Weights dropped by gantries could replace sledgehammers. The resulting pulp was sieved to separate the powder suitable for amalgamation from the grains that had to be processed further in a grinding machine. In 1604 an ingenious friar, Álvaro Alonso Barba, introduced a 'hot' refining method: once reduced to powder, the ore was boiled in copper cauldrons with salt and mercury in a mixture, of which water formed 2 or 3 per cent. After three to twelve weeks' simmering, silver would gather at the bottom. Large amounts of mercury were necessary: quantities typically between five and eight times that of the expected yield of precious metal. Diminishing supplies therefore gradually shunted silver-extraction practices in favour of smelting, which American miners generally considered as suitable only for high-grade ore, but which a royal decree imposed as a universal procedure in 1784, in conformity with prevailing expert opinion in Europe. Almost immediately, however, research by Count

Ignaz von Born, director of the Natural History Museum of Vienna, shifted orthodoxy back in favour of Barba's method, albeit with an important proviso. Born speculated that cold rotation of the powdered ore in barrels could be a more energy-efficient and at least equally productive method of separating the silver. A royal commission of 1788 attempted to propagate the new technology at Potosí in 1788, but – owing to regional conservatism and perhaps to the peculiarities of American ores – without initial success. The rotating barrels were only gradually and grudgingly introduced, *faute de mieux*, in the course of the nineteenth century.[34]

Securing the Enlightenment

During the viceroyalty of Juan de Mendoza y Luna, Marqués de Monte-sclaros, in the early seventeenth century, Lima acquired its charming *alameda* – three handsome parallel avenues lined with eight rows of trees and with three central fountains. It was a sort of prefigurement of the enlightened city, of which Lima and Mexico City were the American paragons. Nonetheless, security needs remained paramount and the organization of the cities into quarters known as *cuarteles* – literally, garrisons – for police purposes reflected the frontier heritage.

In 1782 Mexico City encompassed 8 major and 32 minor police precincts, under the supervision of five officers attached to the criminal division of the court of *audiencia*, and one chief constable (*corregidor*) and the two magistrates (*alcaldes ordinarios*) who regularly formed part of the city council. Santiago de Chile contained four such precincts, as did Buenos Aires for the twenty administrative districts among which the city was organized. Caracas, Veracruz, Guadalajara and Quito had only civil districts – eight, four, and six each respectively, each with its own policing provisions. Querétaro's nine civil districts were distributed among three precincts. Lima at the time had four precincts, each under court-appointed magistrates, and forty districts with magistrates of their own: the whole structure covered 322 streets, 17 alleys, the plaza mayor, 6 minor squares and 6,841 dwellings with 8,222 entrances between them.[35]

Military engineers played decisive roles in creating what we might call the geography of security. Each precinct was supposed to house a military unit, quartered in four dormitories around an exercise yard; but lack of resources imposed less costly expedients – recourse to billeting in ostleries, religious houses, bivouacs and private homes and to public squares for parades and drill. In Mobile in Florida, from 1700 onwards, soldiers stayed in civilians' homes. In Santo Domingo military quarters were dispersed around the city and in Cartagena the city guard had rented houses up against the walls at its disposal. In Panama, the Mercedarians, Franciscans and Dominicans had to turn their churches over to the army whenever alerts boosted the size of the garrison. New barracks, however, were built at strategic spots in the late seventeenth and early eighteenth century: Cartagena, Valdivia, Santiago de Chile, Lima, Veracruz, New Orleans and Caracas.[36] For prisons, no semblance of uniformity prevailed. Short-term chastisement in stocks or under the lash served for many forms of delinquency. *Obrajes* – workshops to which delinquents were consigned to labour without pay – or exile to remote presidios or island penitentiaries such as Juan Fernández in Chile or San Lorenzo in Peru relieved the pressure on city gaols or police cells. The inquisition imprisoned its own penitents.

Around the mid-eighteenth century, although reformers depicted the Spanish American justice system as an ill-regulated Babel, the reality was dynamic, innovative and in some ways surprisingly efficient and developed apace in the decades that followed. Even in remote areas well-qualified magistrates were reviled in general but drew almost uniform praise as individuals. Pedro Galindo Navarro, for instance, spent his career in the late eighteenth and early ninetenth centuries amid the shabby poverty and lawlessness of the northern frontier of New Spain, never achieving his dream of a transfer to Mexico City but celebrated by successive superiors for the 'care and precision' of his work 'as a lover of justice'.[37] The paradigm – the way public administration was understood – was changing. Engineering was coming to be seen as a model for moulding civic and social life.

Engineers rallied to the cause of rational governance and to the aims of delivering the good life: one might almost say, 'the pursuit of happiness'. As the *Instruction* penned by the variously notorious and celebrated chief minister of the crown, the Conde de Floridablanca, put it in 1787, 'No one who is in the service of the state can unshoulder his responsibilities, nor impede the state's right to deploy his talents and merits.'[38] He might have had army engineers especially in mind when applying this precept in America and the Philippines. Between 1701 and 1720 the corps sent 18 of them to the colonies. From 1721 to 1768 the corresponding figure was 121; in the following two decades it rose to 183; between 1800 and 1808, another 61 arrived.[39] Once in the New World, they could rarely get away, so many and so diverse were the claims on their skills. Viceroys and governors conspired to keep them, coaxing them with laments, deceiving them with pretexts and impeding them with ineluctable commands. Félix Prosperi, whose term of appointment as an engineer, initially in Santo Domingo, in 1730 was for five years, was still in post 22 years later at the age of seventy, when nearly blind. Juan Garland was lucky to leave Chile in 1775 after ten years' service. He died on his way home.

For public buildings – the *mises en scène* of public life and the instantiations of the public sphere – military engineers built as fashion approved, in an academic, neoclassical style.[40] They were the designers and overseers of sets of government and viceregal palaces in Mexico City and Santafe de Bogotá, or military headquarters in Guatemala, and town halls and government buildings everywhere, including the post office in Havana in 1785 and the prison, courthouse, customs house and university of the new eighteenth-century regional capital at Guatemala City. They were builders of markets for fish, meat, food in general and, in cases such as that of the Mercado de San José in the Philippines, opened in 1783, textiles. They put up street-lights and sentry-boxes at city gates. They built hospitals at Comayagua, Mexico City and Santiago de Chile and cathedrals in Guatemala. They laid out recreational walkways and gardens. They erected foundries, mints, ironworks, laundries, bakeries and slaughterhouses.[41]

In all these activities they acted as public servants, albeit sometimes in collaboration with private enterprise, as when they helped build industrial workshops, which in the eighteenth century sometimes anticipated factory production, with different stages of manufacture located in complementary spaces.[42] Most of what the engineers built remained at public disposal, in the ownership of the crown. A signal instance was the neoclassical edifice erected in Mexico City between 1803 and 1807 to be the Royal Cigar and Cigarette Factory, where 5,000 men and 2,000 women wore uniforms to work.[43] Not far away, in 1781, making use of water from the aqueduct of Santafé, the military engineer Miguel Constanzó had designed a modern gunpowder factory, powered by water, to replace the rather risky and volatile munitions factory of Chapultepec, which had been working away since 1555. It was one of many, all blending sulphur, potassium nitrate and carbon in similar proportions and all more or less modelled on the state factory at

Villafeliche in Zaragoza. At La Laguna de Bay in Guatemala (1770) and in the Philippines (1773) the model was faithfully copied. In Lima by 1770 and in Santiago de Chile and Santafé de Bogotá at the beginning of the nineteenth century, it exerted influence, although old premises were available for adaptation.[44]

Linked with the gunpowder factories were workshops and foundries that introduced interesting new techniques for making guns. In Seville, where iron and steel guns were made, or La Cavada, in Santander, the main centre for bronze cannon, metals from the New World were under-valued, with a reputation for impurities that made manufacture complicated or risky, but engineers in the Indies worked at techniques for alloying and smelting that would overcome the problems. Cannon were made with varying degrees of success at establishments in Veracruz, Orizaba, Perote, Puerto Rico, Concepción and Santiago de Chile, where in 1768 Lorenzo de Arrau managed to cast five 24-pounders. At Cartagena de Indias, where demand was acute, the high level of nitrates in the atmosphere made iron gun-barrels split or crack.[45] Still, Cartagena had four hundred iron cannon of local manufacture in its arsenal in 1760. The protective layer of varnish with which guns were coated reacted poorly with the environment, and tended to peel or corrode. A writer in Lima, Pedro Antonio Bracho, recommended applications at intervals of three years of a mixture of pitch, wax and tallow in varying proportions according to local nitrate levels, but his recipe was of limited value. Experiments, sometimes with samples of bronze and iron imported from La Cavada and Seville, ended in the production of a satisfactory 'sticky, malodorous and viscous' coating in 1798.[46]

The Social Arena

The theatre and the bullring were places of socialization and armouries against a widely deplored menace: the 'relaxation' of manners. Fears of encroaching barbarism always animated frontier life and stimulated expenditure on supposed amenities of civilization. The first bullring in Lima, the Acho, opened in 1766 with a spectacle calculated to delight the public at every social level: a hecatomb of sixteen bulls. In Buenos Aires in 1783 Viceroy Vértiz decreed a playhouse, the proceeds of which would finance the foundling hospital. Previously, plays had been extemporized affairs, to which patrons came with chairs of their own, typically carried by slaves. The repertoire featured such piquant and challenging pieces as *Siripo*, by the journalist Manuel José de Lavardén, which told of the legendary passion of a native chief of that name for Lucía Miranda, the wife of the conquistador Sebastián Hurtado. *El amor de la estanciera* (The Love of the Rancher's Daughter) was the first work in the 'gauchesque' tradition that romanticized the cowboys of the Pampas. A stray firework from the patronal festivities of the neighbouring church of San Juan Bautista in 1792 put paid to the premises, but in May 1804 a new theatre opened with a performance of Voltaire's tragic appeal for religious tolerance, *Zaïre*. In Santiago de Chile the theatre suffered because of low prestige, deriving perhaps from its actors, who were all of mixed race, but Lima produced a diva in the great tradition of the stage in the person of 'Perricholi', as Micaela Villegas y Hurtado de Mendoza was known to her public. In 1776 her dalliance with Viceroy Amat became the subject of satire in the pasquinade against social pretension *Drama de dos palanganas* (The Clash of the Empty Vessels).[47]

In Mexico City there was no permanent bullring until that of San Pablo in 1815. Theatre, on the other hand, was established early and strongly. In 1753 Viceroy Revillagigedo opened the New Theatre, with capacity for an audience of 1,500. Groundlings stood behind the tier of seats, while other unfortunates occupied a gallery known as the chicken coop (*gallinero*), where a partition separated men from women. Above blue-and-white walls, mythological scenes decorated the ceiling. Balconies veiled with wrought-iron grills adorned the space. The season lasted from Easter Day to carnival the following February, with daily performances (except on Saturdays), concluding at ten or eleven in the evening.[48] Opposite the theatre, the Casa de Irolo was acquired as a training and rehearsal space for singers, dancers and musicians. In the mid-1780s Viceroy Bernardo de Gálvez donated a magnificent curtain for the proscenium and paid for improved facilities. As if in consequence, state regulation increased. Censors eyed scripts, programmes and scenery. Performers' reputations had to be spotless. Vendors were banned and audience members were forbidden to climb onto the stage. So, too, was the practice of dropping 'lighted tobacco and cigar stubs from the gallery with the all-too-common consequence of setting fire to the clothes and capes of occupants of the tier, benches, and standing room'.[49]

Theatre represented competition for coffee-houses, the earliest of which opened in Lima in 1771. In Mexico City the coffee-house of El

Tacuba opened its doors for the first time in 1785. Baths, cockpits, dance halls and courts for pelota – the fives-like game played with big basket-style gloves that make the pace of the ball fast and the size of the court enormous – were other rival places of diversion.

A constant appetite for news was a feature of the enlightened public sphere. Contrary to what is often supposed, a royal post system in private hands functioned between Spain and Spanish America from 1514, when Ferdinand the Catholic granted his counsellor Lorenzo Galíndez de Carvajal the exclusive right to carry mail to the Indies. No one who was 'not a member of the household or affinity' of the grantee could despatch any package, save for travellers' personal luggage and requisites. Of course, a good deal of correspondence escaped the system, as travellers whom the Galíndez family commissioned to carry official post could act undetectably as agents of anyone willing to confide in them. Galíndez's heirs retained his privileges until 1627 in Peru, where *chasquis* or native runners (whose name became officially naturalized as a Spanish word by fiat of the Real Academia de la Lengua in 1730) took letters to inland destinations. In 1633 the Conde de Oñate paid 10,000 silver ducats to take over the postal operation to New Spain.[50] Meanwhile, in New Granada, where no such monopoly existed, the public authorities ran the mail service.

The crown issued permits to private mail-handlers for these and other parts of the service, sometimes as a reward for other services, sometimes in return for cash. As the Conde de Campomanes observed in 1761 in *Itinerario de las carreras de postas del reino* (Routes of the Postal Services of the Realm), royally appointed postal operatives or *mandaderos del rey* enjoyed the privileges of not only being exempt from taxes and prosecution for minor offences, but entitled to bear arms and being eligible for election as town councilors. Broadly similar systems prevailed in other parts of the colonial world. (In 1639, for instance, Richard Fairbanks was designated as Boston's first postmaster, together with a monopoly of the sale of liquor; the post office was in a tavern he owned next to the harbour.[51]) From 1764, however, the state took over all postal operations to and in Spanish America, with a view to their importance for war and diplomacy. Henceforth a set of regulations, initially issued in the name of the Marqués de Grimaldi as 'Superintendent-general of mails and post' (*superintendente general de correos y postas*), specified procedures for a fleet of dedicated packet-vessels, on fixed routes and timetables, as well as the roles of employees and charges and tariffs.[52] The timetable stipulated the first day of every month for the departure of a mail boat from La Coruña for Havana on the so-called *carrera de La Habana* or Havana run. On arrival, post for New Spain and New Granada would transfer to vessels bound for Veracruz and Cartagena, respectively. A service to Buenos Aires was added in 1767, due to depart once a fortnight for Montevideo from La Coruña, with letters for Buenos Aires and the rest of the River Plate region, Chile and Peru.

An administrator general headed the system, under whom were regional heads and local delegates as well as sub-delegates. Handling was done by 'postal deputies' (*tenientes correos*), chosen from among candidates of good repute. They supervised carriers, selected by merit, who might be Spaniards, indios or individuals of any racial background, and who had the right to carry arms and to go anywhere without let or hindrance. Locations of post offices and staging posts were designated.[53] By land, the carriers, with the letters in leather saddlebags, carried passes stamped with the royal arms to deter attempts at restraint within or without the law. A representative disaster befell the carrier Francisco Cisternas one day in 1777, when his exhausted steed stumbled while fording the perilous Lontué River, south of Curicó, on the road to Concepción, in Chile. According to his own testimony, he rose, despite his injuries, from the water, clutching the documents in his mailbags, but the river bore them away.[54] Miraculously, a fisherman retrieved them at the river mouth. Cisternas resumed his journey, but a pitiless magistrate accused him of incurring his misfortune while drunk on *aguardiente*.

The exchange of correspondence was part of enlightened, literate society's crusading fervour in the quest for information. So were the 'Travellers' Guides' (*Guías de forasteros*) published from 1760. They featured almanacs with the phases of the moon, remarks on climate, festive calendars, a world-historical chronology, the birth dates of kings of Spain, assorted notes called *témporas*, which might include the names and whereabouts of officials and their departments, and even maps with commercial or other data.[55] The quest was for order as well as data. That is why in 1807 Ángel Antonio Henry, in charge of the post office of La Coruña, published with the Royal Stationery Office his *Directory for Addressing Letters from Spain to the Indies* (*Dirección general de cartas de España a sus Indias*). Exasperated with correspondents who addressed missives to 'Such and such a person in America' or, say, 'in Mérida' – as if there were not towns of that name in Extremadura, Venezuela and Mexico – he listed the routes from Spain to all the urban centres of the Spanish New World. What mattered, he wisely remarked, was that letters should reach their destinations.[56]

Gardening for Empire

'Desire to know the natural products that God has created for the benefit of man' was the inspiration for the work of José Quer y Martínez, according to his successor as head of the Royal Botanical Garden of Madrid.[57] King Ferdinand VI entrusted Quer with the establishment of the garden in 1755, because of the botanist's famed collection of plants from all over Spain, which he began to form as early as 1728, while he was a 33-year-old army surgeon, when a trip to Valencia acquainted him with avocados – exotica of American origin, bearing, like tomatoes and chocolate, a name of unmistakably Aztec origin. *Ahuacatl* in Nahuatl means 'scrotum': it is easy to see how the term came to be applied to the avocado plant. Quer's expeditions never went further than Italy or Oran. His research remained centred on Spain; but in inspiration and effect the garden he founded took on global significance. Transferred to its present site near the Prado in 1774, it became the nursery of the global monarchy and one of the grand ornaments of European science, forming the last link in a world-girdling chain of such gardens in Manila, Lima, Mexico City and the Canary Islands. At least in theory, samples of the plant life of every climate that the Spanish monarchy occupied could be centralized in a single place of research.

From Peru, for instance, in 1783, came 1,000 coloured drawings and 1,500 written descriptions of plants. Perhaps the most important collections were those of Hipólito Ruiz and José Pavón, whose expedition to Chile and Peru in 1777–88 allowed them to indulge their personal passion – the study of the healing properties of plants – and to produce the most complete study of quinine yet attempted.[58] Another prolific contributor was the uncontainable polymath José Celestino Mutis, who presided over scientific life in one of the heroic outposts of the Spanish Empire at Bogotá, in what is today Colombia, from 1760 until his death in 1808; at Mariquita he established a short-lived garden of acclimatization of his own, for the environments of the Andean region were so diverse – where climatic conditions contrasted up and down precipitous slopes, across vast altitudes and latitudes, and, with the incidence of sun and rain, from side to side of a single valley – that it required great pains to transplant specimens from one region to another. Insisting that America was 'recommendable' not only for its notorious mineral wealth but for 'trees, grasses, resins and balms of great promise for the improvement of health',[59] Mutis conceived and presided over the extension, from 1783 onwards, of work in New Granada along the lines Pavón and Ruiz had pioneered to the south.[60] All these sages and their many coadjutors were aware of 'unjust' and 'vulgar' foreigners' denunciations of Spaniards' alleged ignorance 'of how to use, publish, and systematize the veritable riches they possess in the New World'[61] and that such claims were part of Enlightened rivals' justifications for interfering in the Spanish monarchy and trying to wrest bits of it for themselves.[62] Spanish botanists had a long record of work in the field, going back in unsystematic fashion to Columbus's time and systematically to Philip II's patronage of efforts to assemble an American pharmacopoeia. The work of Francisco Hernández, compiled in New Spain in the 1570s, impressed and influenced European *érudits* for generations, in manuscript and partial editions, before its first complete edition in 1651. Further editions appeared at intervals until the last decade of the eighteenth century.[63] Ruiz explicitly cited Roman precedents for botanical research as an obligation of empire.[64] Imperial echoes helped make public spending – as we would now call it – on science under Carlos III and his successor higher, as Humboldt perceived, than in any other monarchy in Europe at the time.

The 'gardens of acclimatization', where exotic plants adjusted to unfamiliar environments, have been, perhaps, among historians, the most under-appreciated elements in the infrastructure of the Spanish monarchy, linking its spaces and spanning its oceans as thoroughly as any of the work of the explorers and engineers. They could gather useful specimens from an astonishing diversity of climes and make their flowers bloom together in scientific proximity. Plants acclimatized from one region could thrive in another, supplying the food of the empire, enlarging its areas of cultivation, replenishing its forests, informing its science and filling its pharmacopoeia. Thanks to global gardening – the cultivation, that is, of exotic specimens in gardens of acclimatization – transplanted species did more to enrich the Spanish homeland than the New World, but all were part of a network of what historians call ecological exchange, which was one of the most conspicuous features of the environmental history of the early modern world. Until about 1500, for perhaps 150 million years or so, from the moment when Pangaea – the unified world landmass – split, and the continents began to drift apart, a divergent pattern of evolution had made the life forms of the various continents ever more different from one another. Relatively suddenly, by the scale of the long preceding period, the pattern went into reverse, when Earth-girdling travel and a mixture of deliberate and unconscious transplantation of plants, animals and bacteria substituted a new trend, in which the life forms of different continents began to be swapped. Convergence succeeded divergence as evolution's dominant trend. It became possible to grow and breed plants and animals in environments that had never seen their like before. Products migrated between hemispheres, across previously impassable barriers of climate and expanses of ocean. So did people. So did pests. As an example of human impact on evolution, nothing comparable had happened since the first farmers began speciation and hybridization in the service of 'unnatural selection' – breeding new species for human use. Nor would human agency affect evolution so radically again until the late twentieth century, when genetic modification made it possible to defy natural selection altogether.[65]

Huge transformations in humans' relationship with the environment accompanied the early modern exchanges of biota. First, climate underwent global fluctuations: the 'Little Ice Age' was in progress for most of the period and revived briefly at its end, though temperatures generally took an upward turn in the eighteenth century. Second, in direct consequence, human settlement changed both its range and its nature, invading new ecological frontiers on an unprecedented scale: farming grasslands, felling forests, climbing slopes, reclaiming bogs, penetrating game preserves and deep-sea fisheries, expanding and founding cities, turning deserts into gardens and gardens into deserts. This was part of a drive for resources and energy sources in an increasingly populous and competitive world. For animal furs, fats, proteins, migrating fish and wandering whales, hunters ransacked previously unmolested wild zones. The exploration and exploitation of new frontiers created an illusion of abundance that inspired ecological overkill; yet imperialism also had positive environmental effects, as colonialists came, in some cases, to see themselves as custodians of 'tropical Edens', preparing the way for a revived respect and even reverence for nature in the eighteenth-century West.[66] The care of forests demanded and received constant attention.

The Spanish monarchy, which covered a wider range of environments than any previous empire, was especially adept in promoting transfers of useful biota, and unwittingly instrumental in exchanges of harmful ones. It is tempting to pick out the well-documented introductions of life forms as the highlights of the story, or focus on the legends of heroes who bore life-changing new foodstuffs across the oceans. Christopher Columbus is fairly credited with a lot of 'firsts'. From his first ocean crossing in 1492, he brought back descriptions and samples of New World plants, including pineapple and cassava or manioc. On his second transatlantic voyage in 1493, he took sugarcane to the island of Hispaniola – but let it grow wild. Pigs, sheep, cattle, chickens and wheat made their first appearance in the New World on the same occasion. Other heroic firsts are the subjects of legends or fables. Juan Garrido, a Black companion of Cortés, supposedly first planted wheat in Mexico.[67] The story of Sir Walter Raleigh, the sixteenth-century poet, courtier, historian and pirate, introducing potatoes to England is false but has an honoured place in myth.[68]

The real, though unwitting, heroes, however, are surely the plants and animals themselves, which survived deadly journeys and successfully adapted to new climates, sometimes – in the case of seeds – by accident, with little human help. They travelled in the cuffs or pleats of the clothing of carriers who didn't know they were there, or were caught in the fabric of cloth bales and sacks.[69] And, in combination with global warming, the transmission of food plants – partly by accident, partly by luck and partly through the gardens of acclimatization – hugely increased the world's ability to sustain large populations, not only because the total amount of food energy available in any one place increased as food sources multiplied and new eco-niches became available for settlement and exploitation, but because diversification of crops liberated the people who adopted them from dependence on unique staples and therefore from vulnerability to blights. The ecological exchange was part of the essential framework of the population explosion that followed and has been sustained ever since.

8

HEALTH INFRASTRUCTURE
Hospitals and Sanitation

But unto you that fear my name shall the Sun of righteousness
arise with healing in his wings; and ye shall go forth, and grow up
as calves of the stall. (MALACHI 4:2)

The reports of famine were greatly exaggerated, as far as Lord
Curzon could see, peering from the flocked and curtained seclu-
sion of his private railway carriage. Britain's viceroy of India was
self-deluded. Out of sight, the bodies were piling up, their bones poking
through skin tightened by starvation. Partly as a result of Curzon's
cost-cutting policies, at least a million subjects of the Raj died in 1899
in the last of a series of famines that had claimed at least 10 million
Indian lives since 1877.[1] The failure was chiefly but not solely moral.
To function in accordance with their own characteristic objectives,
empires have to conserve resources – especially of manpower – on
which depend levels of production, of taxation and of efficiency in
war. The most abject of failures is the failure to keep the subject
population alive.

For the Spanish in America as for the British in India demographic
disaster was palpable. Typically, within a generation's span, native
populations declined by up to 90 per cent on contact with the newcomers. 'The breath of a Spaniard' was proverbially fatal. Debate is
inexhaustible over the lethal effects of culture shock, demoralization,
maltreatment and violence. Clearly, however, it was contrary to
Spaniards' interests and policy for the people on whom they relied for
tribute and labour to perish. Unlike the English in North America,
whose economy could dispense with Native Americans in favour of
settlers and slaves, and who could in consequence exterminate or expel

entire populations in unregretted profligacy, Spaniards needed their
natives and resented the unhelpful fragility of Indigenous lives. They
were the unwilling spectators of holocausts inflicted by disease. Smallpox was almost certainly, by a large margin, the biggest killer. But any
pathogen, however mild its effects in the Old World, could scythe
through unimmunized indigenes.

While unaccustomed pathogens killed natives, unfamiliar environments were injurious or lethal to Spaniards and other European
migrants overseas. Migration was injurious to health. Settlers in the
New World had to endure pains of acclimatization to a new ambiance,
where accustomed elements of diet were often hard to come by, and life
harder than at home. Conquistadores suffered from altitude sickness
in ranges higher and more precipitate than any they had ever seen;
from agues and exhaustion in tropics simultaneously wetter and hotter
than any they previously knew; from anaemia induced by the protein-
deficient pap natives gave them to eat; from the withdrawal symptoms
ineluctable in a hemisphere without wine; and from venereal afflictions equally ineluctable in a hemisphere full of sexual opportunities.[2]
At high altitudes in Peru, Carrion's disease smothered the bodies of
Pizarro's followers with warts.[3]

The effects diminished over time. Conquistadores' creole descendants did not have to make the same adjustments. The native survivors of
intruder-borne plagues passed their immunity on to future generations.
Colonies, however, remained unhealthy places, scattered with gimcrack
boomtowns where disease incubated and subject to the stresses
economic and social change imposed. Natives might be wrenched
from familiar lifeways and homes to exposure in new niches, in mines,
ranches, haciendas, piggeries and industries previously unknown, such
as sugar refining and silk-weaving. And while creoles grew ever more
robust, more newcomers were always arriving and struggling with the
shock of unfrequented latitudes and climes. In some ways, environmental change worked against the interests of colonists' health. In
regions where sugar planting and ranching coexisted in tropical conditions, mosquito-borne diseases multiplied. A conspicuous consequence
was the rampant mortality that ripped through the ranks of the armies
Spain sent to confront rebels. *Aedes Aegypti* – the malaria mosquito
– killed far more Spaniards than Simón Bolívar's followers could
account for.[4]

Healing Arts

Early modern medicine was ill-equipped to cope. Doctors were as likely to kill as to cure.[5] The theory of humours dominated medical education until well into the nineteenth century. Most treatment, in consequence, was at best irrelevant. Dietary adjustments – Galenic medicine's favourite remedy – were rarely attuned to the problems they were meant to cure. Blood-letting, a standard expedient, weakened patients. Surgical hygiene relied more on luck than judgement. Contagion and infection were blamed on exhalations and 'odours'. The Laws of the Indies enjoined that hospitals for diseases deemed contagious must be located at a safe remove from other habitations. When lepers were admitted to the specialized facility in Cartagena, the law required the authorities to have all the patients' belongings transferred there, too, 'so that with this precaution the disease shall not affect other people'.[6] The chapel was commonly the biggest building in a hospital, as prayers were at least as likely to be efficacious as the attentions of doctors. The chapel in the Hospital de San Lázaro in Barquisimeto, Venezuela, which had been founded by the local priest, Pedro del Castillo, in 1565, to serve general purposes, not lepers, was nearly twice as big as the entire area occupied by patients.[7] The Peruvian satirist Juan del Valle y Cañedes captured the caprice of professional care by likening physicians to earthquakes – 'a dangerous tremor, a licensed Vesuvius' – except that 'the doctor kills more quietly.'[8]

It is possible that the Spanish Empire impacted negatively on health care, at least to begin with, by disrupting indigenous traditions and persecuting native healers or *curanderos*. Jesuits, as we shall see, were sympathetic to traditional healers and made use of them in their missions; in the mid-1650s the order withdrew entirely from the business of attempting to extirpate idolatry, partly out of awareness that shamans were serviceable allies.[9] The need to appropriate native experts, not only in health care but in the service of the altar and the maintenance of Christian places of worship, was acute in much of the overseas monarchy, where priestly manpower was always in short supply.[10] Yet the prejudice against 'popular' culture that convulsed godly elites in Europe,[11] and victimized traditional healers on the eastern side of the Atlantic, was intensified in the New World, where paganism was a more conspicuous and recent or current presence. The apparatus of State and Church was, on the whole, hostile to shamans, who were the custodians of pagan traditions, and who typically doubled as medicine men or wise women in the care of the sick.[12]

Magic and science always shade into one another: both are attempted means of controlling nature. The dividing line was blurred throughout the colonial period, and it was not always easy for inquisitors and extirpators of idolatry to tell the difference between pharmacy and fantasy. Coca in Peru, for instance, was used in both healing and divination. Extirpators were willing to allow the former, but often in practice curtailed it in the effort to stamp out paganism. Excessive bathing and sweating aroused comparable suspicions in Mexico, as did the use of marijuana, which might serve properly medicinal or dubiously psychotropic purposes.[13] In Yucatán, shamans condemned for idolatry in the seventeenth century administered cures of obviously suspicious character, involving chants, incantations, talismans, figurines, fragments of hair and spells written on paper, but also applied traditional Indigenous pharmaceutical remedies, including ants, armadillo skins, chocolate and herbs that the clergy suspected as magical because European herbaria failed to recognize them.[14]

The famous case of Juan Básquez in Lima in 1710 illustrates the problems.[15] The healer's accuser was a Spanish priest who had paid him the compliment of consulting him, but who emerged dissatisfied with the treatment prescribed. Básquez's case demonstrates toleration of Indigenous healing, as well as its limits. The repertoire of curative substances he deployed – including blood, saliva and a range of plant and animal substances unacknowledged in Spanish pharmacopoeia – contributed to the ban the inquisitors imposed on his practice; Bethlemite brethren, however, who were prominent in hospitaller work, were made responsible for his good conduct; so he may have remained involved indirectly as a sort of medical consultant.

The effectiveness of the shamans' cures may have been limited, but probably not much less so than those of physicians and surgeons trained in Europe before the Scientific Revolution, and perhaps not until the rise of the germ theory of medicine in the nineteenth century. The therapeutic effects of confidence in one's doctor are a function of cultural circumstances. American placebos should have been no less helpful, in principle, than European equivalents. Shamans were unencumbered by humoral theory. Their knowledge of their own store of pharmaceutical substances must have been superior to that of newcomers. Clients seem to have valued their ministrations. A famous illustration in the Florentine Codex – a Nahuatl version of Bernardino de Sahagún's sixteenth-century compilation of 'Aztec' traditions – shows smallpox victims under the attention of Indigenous carers, with not a Spaniard in sight.

Of course, Spanish healers had novelty value that could trump the appeal of familiar medicine. A spectacular instance was that of the extraordinary adventurer Alvar Núñez Cabeza de Vaca's own elevation to the rank of native holy man, if his autobiography is to be believed.[16] His American career began when he was a royal nominee in the ill-starred reconnaissance of Florida in 1528. Cast away on the Texas coast in the debacle of the expedition, he led a party of survivors – two fellow Spaniards and a resourceful Black slave – on a seven-year odyssey, via enslavement by hostile natives and adoration by friendly ones, to safety in New Spain. On arrival, he was clad in skins, long-bearded and with waist-length hair. Not only did he look like a holy man, he also behaved like one. To the astonishment of the Spanish slavers who met him on the frontier, over a thousand Indigenous followers accompanied him. His own narrative of his adventures is unsurpassable, a gripping tale whose spell no historian of the episode can escape. It was a remarkable achievement to reach Mexico at all, picking a path across potentially lethal country possibly amid murderous enemies. To have emerged as the head of what seems to have been an extraordinary, almost messianic, mass movement of Indigenous people was a staggering outcome. How did he do it?

Alvar Núñez's own explanation was providential. God procured his survival by a miracle and endowed him with strange graces – like a Siegfried with a supply of dragon's blood or a Samson with an abundance of curls – in order to help bring the Indigenous peoples he met to Christianity. In particular, God gave him powers of healing. At first, our hero relied on the rudimentary medical knowledge of one of his Spanish companions to swap cures for kindnesses along the road. One night, however, the small expedition's resident physician cried off, and Cabeza de Vaca was left to handle one of the most difficult cases the party had encountered: the patient, according to local opinion, was already dead. Alvar Núñez made the sign of the cross over the body, and imitated Indigenous physicians by blowing breath over it. In the first of his many supposed miracles, the corpse revived, ate, strolled and chatted. Other, less advanced victims of ailments, whom Alvar Núñez treated later that day, 'had become well and were without fever and very happy'.[17] For the autobiographer, the miracles became evidence of validation by a higher authority, like the battlefield deeds of prowess asserted by conquistadores in the statements of merits with which they plied the crown in search of offices and titles.

Black healers also supplemented medical manpower, though some of them, too, fell foul of Inquisitorial suspicions of the abuse of divination and magic under the guise of healing. It is doubtful, however, whether Spaniards and Blacks combined could have replaced the Indigenous health-care manpower they threatened to displace. Outside major centres of population, where, as we shall see, Church and State made extensive provision for the care of sick indios, health care for Indigenous people was subject to two great principles: first, in the Spanish Empire, that religion was the only aspect of the native culture that the state was deeply concerned to modify; and second, as the historian David Arnold formerly proposed, European empires generally did not prioritize Indigenous medicine as a set of practices with which to meddle.[18] In rural fastnesses, there was little option, for indigenes and settlers alike, but to confide in native medicine and, if anything, it seems that the tolerance and in some places the encouragement of traditional healers from colonial authorities grew towards the end of the period. In Paraguay, despite repeated, but unavailing, attempts to garner funds for a hospital 'for the assistance of the poor', Bishop Manuel Antonio de Torre complained of the 'ridiculous cures' of wise women, who were patients' almost unique recourse.[19] In 1799 the viceroy of Mexico Miguel José de Azana declared, 'no prohibition against *curanderos* providing aid to the sick in Indian communities . . . Ignorant though they are they have more experience and knowledge than everyone else.'[20] In Caracas the university and medical establishment supplicated throughout the period for the suppression of *curanderos* – not only on suspicion of heterodoxy but on the grounds that their monopoly of business deterred potential medical students; yet the need for professionally untrained but cheap and popular 'practical' healers never abated. 'I have determined', the king declared, establishing an inspectorate of the medical profession in the city in response to local petitioners in 1777, 'that, because of the shortage of physicians as reported in the city of Caracas, the continued presence of some of the more able, better-behaved of the *curanderos* be allowed, and that they should be listed and examined and approved by a specially appointed committee.'[21]

As always with cultural encounters, therefore, change was imperfect. Colonial health structures did not involve the displacement of Indigenous tradition with intruded practices, but a blending of existing, arriving and innovative procedures. Insights into the state of colonial pharmacy and medicine on a remote frontier come from the work of Pedro de Montenegro, a Jesuit in the province of Paraguay who compiled a tract on ethnobotany in 1710 and dedicated it to Our Lady of Sorrows. Though well meant, the dedication was hardly encouraging. Sorrow was the likeliest outcome of the medical ministrations of missionaries at the time. Until near the end of the seventeenth century, there were not even any qualified physicians in the Jesuit missions. Montenegro was among the first to have any relevant experience, though it is not clear that even he had a medical degree. Born in 1663 he worked in the Hospital General in Madrid before his reception in the Order. In 1702 he transferred to be the nurse and surgeon to the perhaps 3,000 indios of the Misión de los Santos Mártires de Japón, high above the course of the Uruguay River in what is now Argentina. He died there in 1728. No memorials remain among the few tumbled stones that mark the spot.

In 1705, according to the preface to his tract, he attended to some of the mission indios who fought for Spain in the conquest of the Colonia da Sacramento – the formerly Portuguese stronghold at the mouth of the River Plate, tending 'various perforations of the breast by spears and shot'.[22] He could not do them much good. Such science as he knew was out of date even by the standards of his day. He accepted not only the Galenic theories common to most doctors at the time but also the assumptions that disease originated from 'vegetative force' and the spontaneous generation of parasites – intestinal worms, for instance, from the excess of 'malos humores'. He believed in the efficacy of astral influences, and thought that the herb he called *güembe* was 'procreated by the Sun' under the influence of Mars and gathered earth on its roots owing to the emanations of the Moon, 'and that is why it is so poisonous when it is gathered under a waxing moon'.[23]

At the time the Jesuits had no hospitals or pharmacies in any of their missions in the region of the Paraná (though they did in the Mojos area of Upper Peru, where they also maintained a presence, and in the River Plate zone there was a *botica* or dispensary in Buenos Aires and another in Córdoba from early in the seventeenth century).[24] The Jesuit College of San Pablo in Lima had a *botica* that not only dispensed remedies locally but despatched them to order all over Spanish South America.[25] The situation improved gradually. Five missions in his region had pharmacies by 1768; in the interim, however, as Montenegro explained, local plants, selected and applied according to traditional native knowledge, had to serve. Montenegro's pharmacopoeia was composed entirely of locally available plants, with a glossary in Tupi-Guaraní. 'Finding myself as I did in these lands in America,' he wrote, 'without a store of medicaments and without any pharmacist to hand, I acknowledged myself therefore obliged to become a compiler of pharmaceutical information.' Ethnobotanical remedies saved his own life on three occasions from wounds or symptoms classical Western medicine deemed irremediable. The plants he listed and illustrated 'are true medicines with potential to effect cures'.[26] The Jesuit medics seem to have learned more from their *curuzyaras*, or native assistants – who, of course, were usually shamans or their descendants and might, in less propitious circumstances, have been suspected as perpetuators of paganism – than the other way round.

Though religious orders ran them, missions should be classed as part of the infrastructure of the Spanish Empire – heavily subsidized and expensively defended at the royal treasury's cost. In the seventeenth century the maintenance of missions accounted for over half the crown's costs in New Mexico. But, despite investing in health care and infirmaries, missions' usefulness in promoting good health was limited. For long periods, they struggled to keep their inhabitants alive. As Jesuits in Florida in 1570 avowed, many indios were used to a foraging life and 'to take them out of it is like death to them.'[27] As a Franciscan complained, 'as soon as we bring them round to a Christian and community way of life . . . they fatten, sicken, and die.'[28] Culture shock – sharpened by the floggings that were missionaries' favoured form of discipline, for their congregations as well as for themselves – restrained population growth.

Nevertheless, even in the remote outposts of the Paraná, missions did contribute to public health. Not only did they organize, distribute and deploy native personnel – there was, at least in theory, a *curuzyara* approved by the clergy in every village in the reductions, the Jesuit pueblos – but they maintained high standards of hygiene and sanitation. They generally dug dedicated cemeteries in churchyards or nearby plots, instead of cramming putrescent, malodorous remains under church floors. Mission drainage systems were relatively well engineered. Under the Jesuit reductions majestic sewers up to 2 metres (6½ ft) high flowed with water from tanks above ground.[29] The volume of food production surely did more for welfare generally than any amount of cack-handed medical care. In California, wrenching the people out of nomadism, the missions provided new crops – wheat, grapes, citrus, olives. In 1783 they produced 22,000 tons of grain, a total that rose to 37,500 in 1790, and 75,000 by 1800. By the time the secular authorities seized it in 1834, Fr Junípero Serra's model mission of San Gabriel had 163,578 vines and 2,333 fruit trees as well as abundant livestock.[30]

The Healthy Environment

Missions, of course, were on the fringes of the monarchy, with limited access to professional wisdom and up-to-date medical knowledge. But even in the cities that were the showpieces of colonial civilization, notions of what we now call public health were rudimentary at the start of our period. In mines and slaughterhouses, and around middens and cemeteries, prevailing theory ascribed pollution to 'corrupt air' caused by exhalations and miasma. Sewerage was hit-and-miss: Buenos Aires had none throughout the colonial period; Havana's sewage was discharged into the bay, where it accumulated. Potable water was the object of heroic efforts of engineering. In the 1570s the Augustinian friar Diego de Chaves undertook one of the first great engineering schemes to provide clean water and disease-free fisheries in his Indigenous parish at Yuririapúndaro (the name means lake of blood in Otomí) in Guanajuato. He built a canal to replace the stagnant local lake with a continual supply of fresh water from the Lerma. A plan of 1580 shows the town dominated by the Augustinian house and surrounded by contentedly grazing livestock – cattle with curling horns, and horses and asses bent to the turf.[31]

Street cleaning was the responsibility of residents until well into the eighteenth century, when governments began to see it as a task only the state could administer. Peru had no public street-cleaning service until the first dust-carts appeared in the streets of Lima in 1792. Four years later, when the city still had only six refuse carts, Hipólito Unánue denounced the foul air that rose from filthy streets. In Mexico, when the Marqués de Revillagigedo arrived as viceroy in

1789, he found that between the cleanings that occurred at intervals of two years Mexico City's canals emitted 'rotten exhalations' because they were clogged with filth, running with excrement and scattered with dead dogs that the night watch killed after curfew. Locals used the cathedral atrium as a latrine and the fountains as washtubs for bodies and clothes, while 'mischievous boys' flung in dead animals and other refuse. A flood caused by a severed water pipe spread the contents of a street-centre sewer.

The newcomer introduced nightly refuse collections in 36 carts and daily street-cleaning routines, including the compulsory sweeping and sprinkling of street-fronts by householders or other property owners. He laid sweepable pavements and lit them with lamps every four or five blocks to deter malefactors. He imposed hefty fines for fouling and banished pigs and cows from the streets or at least controlled the access of livestock to public city thoroughfares. Contemporary observers, from the *protomédico*, or general medical supervisor, Diego García Jove, to Vicente Cervantes, the head of the city's botanical garden, were unanimous in approving the effects, which included a conspicuous improvement in public health. The measures were hard to sustain, however, at least to the standards of fastidious citizens. Less than a year into the viceroyalty of Revillagigedo's successor, the Marqués de Branciforte, Pedro Basave complained that it was 'a nauseous, suffocating experience' to walk through the streets.[32]

In the seventeenth and eighteenth centuries, urban planners' usual recourse was to construct *alamedas* – leafy parks or broad boulevards where citizens could take the air. Many grew to magnificence. Mexico City's, with its ranks of elms, surrounding canal and central fountain, was opened in 1592 and by 1625 evoked a famous description by Thomas Gage of the daily parade of 2,000 coaches through cool glades, accompanied by horseborne gallants and pretty slave girls swathed in white mantillas 'like flies in milk'.[33] *Alamedas* came to represent, for colonial engravers, the accomplishments of Enlightened elegance for which the city was famed. Provincial towns echoed the problems and solutions of the capitals. Veracruz had an *alameda* from early in the seventeenth century, and in 1766 six new fountains, fed by lead pipes, enhanced it. But the revenues of the town, according to a report of 1771, could not meet the charges of 12,000 to 14,000 pesos a year for cleaning the streets and clearing the latrines.[34] Fresh air was always sought as a preventive and a remedy: Humboldt praised the engineer Antonio

Barreiro for improving the health of Acapulco by opening a cut in the mountainous hinterland to let in the breeze.[35]

Hospitals

If the *alameda* seems an oblique device for confronting colonial ill health, the hospital was, at least, more direct if only doubtfully more effective. Hospitals were only for the poor. The rich had physicians attend them in their own homes, but hospitals formed the infrastructure of health care for everybody else. For indios, slaves, rankers in armies and fleets, and the poor white flotsam that the vagaries of life flung onto the streets and beaches, they provided refuge, rest, food, prayer and nursing – all of which contributed more to recovery from hurt and harm than the ministrations of the physicians whom hospitals commonly employed. 'The rich get no better treatment in their homes than the poor in this hospital,' declared an encomiast of Mexico City in 1554, referring to the Hospital de la Concepción.[36] In 1541 Charles V ordered that there should be 'hospitals in every pueblo of Spaniards and indios . . . where the poor and sick may be cured'.[37] This laudable intention was easier to proclaim than to realize, but by 1627, when Vázquez de Espinosa wrote his *Descripción de las Indias*, most places with more than 300 Spanish residents had some sort of hospital. Mexico City had 30 to serve some 100,000 inhabitants.[38] Over the history of the Spanish global monarchy as a whole, Francisco Guerra catalogued over 1,000 hospitals throughout the overseas dominions, not counting mission facilities.

The big demands that hospitals placed on the state were financial. The seriously injured, sick or dying were cared for, usually largely at public expense or at the cost of endowments in land, rents, tribute, shares of taxes, or cash, in which the crown or colonial authorities participated. Financial expedients – which, as we are about to see, were many and various – were always playing catch-up with costs. Hospitals typically ran at a loss. Lima's main hospital, for instance, never seems to have had a deficit of less than 5,000 pesos in any recorded year. The records for 1786–90 show staggering annual losses of 43,000 pesos.[39] In the same city, the Hospital de la Caridad, founded by a confraternity in 1559, served the needs of female patients, employing native nurses in exchange for clothes and dowries; despite this economical plan, the trustees spent 20,000 pesos in 1637, although income amounted only to 6,000.

By no means negligible, of course, was the contribution of foundations established entirely or largely at the expense of private benefactors. Cortés provided the endowment of the hospital he founded in Tenochtitlán in 1521. In the long run, Lima's most impressive hospital, the Hospital de San Andrés, grew out of the initiative of the priest Diego Molina, who began collecting alms for the care of poor, sick Spaniards in 1552. The modest buildings that resulted were replaced on a grand scale thanks to the generosity of Viceroy Andrés Hurtado de Mendoza, who supplied 17,000 of the 19,000 pesos required. In 1586 the hospital treated an average of 90 patients per diem. From 1597 it had 2,500 inmates and 20 staff. By 1620, according to the Carmelite encomiast Vázquez de Espinosa, it could 'compete with the best in the world' and resembled a small town, with its five hundred beds, separate madhouse and 'a quantity of slavers of both sexes for the service of the poor'.[40]

A disciple of Thomas More, Mexico's indefatigable judge Vasco de Quiroga, who became, in 1536, an equally indefatigable bishop, founded, particularly for the treatment of sick natives, hospitals in Mexico City and Michoacán as kernels of what he called *repúblicas de hospital* – health centres, we might say today, to attract communities with schools, orphanages and workshops. His fellow judge, Sebastián Ramírez de Fuenleal, helped with the funding. The scope of alms in hospital finance is illustrated – amusingly, in hindsight, albeit obliquely – by the prosecution in 1620 of the suspiciously well-named Pedro Pecador, who pocketed the donations he solicited for the hospital of Santo Domingo, founded in Lima in 1593: the court recovered 400 pesos from him.[41]

In New Orleans, in the last major province to join the Spanish monarchy with the cession of most of Louisiana from France in 1763, La Charité had opened in 1736 with a legacy left by a sailor. In 1744 a French governor added to the endowment with a private gift. Under Spanish administration, following the destructive earthquake of 1778, the hospital reopened under the new advocation of San Carlos, but despite the obvious appeal to the namesake king it still relied on private endowments, granted by the mega-philanthropist Andrés Almonester y Roxas, a notary and office-holding pluralist whose commercial opportunities for self-enrichment made him a fortune, which he devoted to enhancing the town with charitable foundations.[42]

Normally, indeed, institutions of government stepped in to supplement private charity from public funds. A remarkable instance was that of the hospital of San Nicolás de Bari – the oldest in Santo Domingo – originally a private philanthropical enterprise by a Black woman who, of her charity, from 1503, looked after sick people in her hut. The governor granted her legatees the rents of six stone houses in order to continue her work. In 1519, with the aid of these funds and private subscriptions, the hospital was rebuilt in stone. A confraternity formed to administer it and, in 1574, successfully resisted takeover by royal nominees. By 1586 capacity had risen to seven hundred beds. In 1698 the necessity of refinancing could no longer be deferred and a royal subsidy of 83,000 pesos paid for the care of military, naval and governmental personnel. In 1700 the hospital merged with the projected – but frustrated – local institution intended for foundlings, for which, in 1696, the king had made provision that proved inadequate: 2,000 pesos for the building and 600 pesos, to be raised from vacant encomiendas, to pay for personnel. The money was lamentably deficient for the purpose but represented a useful addendum to the resources of San Nicolás. On a grander scale, the Hospital de Santa Ana in Lima started in 1549 with private donations, which royal subventions augmented – notably in 1553 in the form of 2,000 pesos a year from the fines levied by judges with a further 400 pesos from the royal treasury, because, as the king acknowledged, 'it is very necessary that in that city . . . there be created a hospital where poor indios can be cured.' In 1618 more than 12,000 pesos came to the hospital via rents and 500 pesos in the form of alms, while the *Real Patronato*, the crown's share of tithes, contributed 3,000.[43]

Gradually, the *Real Patronato* progressively took over responsibility for hospitals originally of private foundation. In 1622, for instance, the Hospital de San José de Gracia for indios passed into public control – a prime example of the way in which colonial society relied on the collaboration of Indigenous notables, since the infirmary´s native founders in 1586 included heirs of Hernando de Tapia, who had been one of the key mediators of power in Tenochtitlán under Cortés and under the first two viceroys. The Hospital de San Lázaro, founded with private funds by the president of the *audiencia* of Guatemala, Alvaro de Quiñones y Osorio, in 1638, lasted only two years before the crown stepped in, handing the funding over to the *patronato* and the care to the Order of San Juan de Dios. The Hospital de San Francisco de Paula in Havana was at first entirely dependent on the legacy of a former canon of the cathedral, albeit augmented by a round of new donations in the eighteenth century and, by 1730, a share of the royal entitlement to tithes.[44]

In practice, *patronato* funds became the principal resource for health care in colonial territories. The hospital dedicated to Nuestra Señora de los Remedios in Santiago de Cuba began in 1523, endowed at royal command and with episcopal reluctance by rents assigned by the bishop and supplemented with a share of the *patronato*. Even so, it was never viable, despite occasional hand-outs from subsequent, more generous successors in the see. In 1740 the governor complained that it could serve no more than fifteen patients at best. In 1754 the Bethlemite Order took it over. In 1544 Charles v assigned 600 pesos de oro for hospitals in Cuba, but the cathedral chapter never released the money. The twenty beds of the Hospital de San Felipe y Santiago, founded by the king in Havana in 1597, were supposed to be maintained from *patronato* funds, but foundered until the Order of San Juan de Dios took over in 1603. The military hospital at San Agustín in Florida, dedicated – perhaps rather inauspiciously for a wilderness at the edge of empire – to Nuestra Señora de la Soledad, was established in expectation of ample *patronato* funding. But the position was insecure. Franciscans deputed from mission work kept it going by their labour, and an attempt to transfer the burden to the Order of San Juan de Dios failed in 1682. During the Seven Years' War costs were met by means of compulsory deductions from soldiers' pay and a charge on patients of 1 real a day – somewhat reminiscent of the 'co-pay' with which, in the United States today, patients must top up insurance companies' outlay.[45]

In other cases the intervention of crown, council or cathedral chapter shored up private hospitals with shaky finances, without completely displacing existing frameworks. In Lima in 1680, mine-owners started a facility for their sick workers: the Hospital de la Concepción. Black confrères of the Confraternidad de la Limpia Concepción looked after the patients, but the owners levied a peso on each mineworker's wage every year at Christmas to help meet costs. The confraternity and, presumably, the workers resented the levy and in 1684 induced the crown to step in with funds from the *patronato*, enhanced by a charge of 12 and a half pesos against the owner of every slave who received treatment. Revenues remained insufficient, however, and a reorganization of 1686 introduced a new pattern: 1 and a quarter pesos a week from every mine-owner, and annual contributions from workers of 2 pesos for married men and 1 peso from bachelors. The Hospital de la Resurrección in Comayagua in the mountains of what is now Honduras, proved equally hard to pay for. From its inception as an episcopal foundation in 1650 it relied on infusions of alms. The finances remained precarious even after the transfer of costs to the charge of the *patronato*, and in 1793 charges were introduced for the treatment of soldiers: in effect, the solution amounted to support by the crown on an ad hoc basis.[46]

In the early years of the empire, the encomienda system, which supported conquistadores with tribute or labour services due from indios, also provided for hospitals. The Hospital de la Concepción, founded in 1511 as the first in Puerto Rico, had one hundred *encomendados*, or individuals liable for tribute, to cover the cost of its handful of beds – between half a dozen and a dozen at various times – until 1523, when the re-siting of the city created the opportunity for a new system, more in line with the gradual or fitful shift away from the use of the encomienda as an instrument of royal policy. Thenceforth private endowments kept the institution going, with voluntary labour supplied by a confraternity, until 1701, when responsibility shifted to the royal *patronato* – the crown's share of tithes. A further rebuilding in another new location in 1772 was at public expense.[47] The foundation of the Hospital Real de Indios in Mexico City was facilitated by grants of indio labour from Chalco, a community obliged by royal orders of 1576 and 1580 to cut wood for scaffolding for building and repairs and supply twenty carriers to deliver it.[48]

Lotteries were fairly common methods of financing hospitals, and should probably be classed as state contributions, as they involved the alienation of a right that might otherwise have benefited the royal treasury. Lottery revenues were especially useful in making up the shortfalls that hospitals frequently experienced as a result of taking more cases than their endowments could support. The hospital of San Pedro, for instance, in Mexico City, had a good record in admitting some 6,000 patients a year on average over a period of some twelve decades; it enjoyed an income of a little under 40,000 pesos in 1811, but expended 48,510. A lottery made up the difference. In 1765 the crown added 1,000 pesos from a lottery to the endowment of the Hospital de los Pobres founded by Francisco Ortiz Cortés, a former precentor of Mexico City's cathedral, though alms-giving was also vital for ongoing finance.[49]

Royal authorities deflected a wide range of other revenues into the hands of hospital trustees. Mexico's Hospital Real de Indios in the late eighteenth century garnered a total of 40,000 pesos a year, including a direct annual grant of 1,000 pesos from the royal treasury, 8,225 pesos from the profits of the theatre and 23,000 from the tribute which indios formerly owed to the cathedral but which the crown diverted by decree in 1763.[50] The Hospital de San Andrés in Lima enjoyed the right of licensing cockfights. That of Nuestra Señora de Atocha in Lima and the foundling hospital in Buenos Aires received – like, as we have seen, Puerto Rico's Concepción – the local monopolies of the right to print or to license presses. Anchorage fees were also important. The San Lázaro hospitals of Cartagena and Havana received them. In Panama, the Hospital de San Sebastián, founded in Portobelo in 1597 by Governor Alonso de Sotomayor, relied on the royal treasury to pay for medicines, beds and staff wages until 1759, when anchorage fees were assigned, supplemented by alms raised by the Confraternity of the Holy Spirit. A routine shortfall remained, met by charges on the crown of 2 reales for every soldier treated, and 1 real per patient on the owners of hospitalized slaves. Among foundations supported from fines levied by the courts and assigned by the crown was the Hospital de la Caridad, Havana. In the same city, the sale of the galley shipyards paid for the Hospital Militar at Philip II's command in 1597.[51]

Among assigned crown revenues, *escobillas* – literally, sweepings, the residue of the smelting of precious ores – formed a big part of the financial basis of care in, for instance, the Hospital de la Caridad in Santiago, Hispaniola. When Charles V granted a charter to the Hospital de San Sebastián in Cartagena de Indias in 1534, he envisaged that *escobillas* would pay for it. At the royal court the officials responsible had overlooked the fact that Cartagena had no mines. To replace the non-existent *escobillas*, the hospital received a share of fines levied in local judgements from 1538; in 1560 a share of the state's income from intestate deaths was added; occasional top-ups from the royal treasury helped make up remaining deficiencies. Despite the rather desperate nature of these measures the hospital turned over 1,000 patients annually by 1612, when the Order of San Juan de Dios took it over. *Escobillas* were more plentiful in Lima, where they supplied, with help from a share of fines and from numerous donors, much of the 100,000 maravedíes a year that Charles V envisaged for the foundation of Nuestra Señora de la Concepción in 1537.[52]

Episcopal and clerical foundations were, in effect, paid for from the public purse, out of the share of tithes owed to the royal treasury under the arrangements by which the papacy confided care of the church to the crown. The system involved mind-boggling accounting. Half the tithes of any diocese went to the bishop and chapter, for distribution at their discretion; some of their share commonly went to health care in foundations or temporary initiatives of their own. The remaining 50 per cent of the tithes were divided into nine equal portions, of which two went to the crown for the upkeep of public works, including hospitals; four were for the churches of the diocese. Of the remaining three parts, half went on the costs of amplifying and maintaining the cathedral buildings, and half (less 10 per cent deducted for any hospital the chapter might have under its own control) on hospitals generally. In effect, therefore, 18.61 per cent of tithes were available for public works under the aegis of bishop and chapter and 9.15 per cent for other public works. The crown could alter the standard distribution from time to time as needs arose.[53]

Staffing Health Care

Colonial municipal councils (or *cabildos* in Spanish) usually took part in the provision of hospital care, normally in partnership with other entities, including the church, the crown, confraternities and individual benefactors. In partial consequence, quarrels over jurisdiction were normal, even after 1565, when, by royal decree, *cabildos* enjoyed formal control of all the hospitals they founded. In 1574 the crown attempted to take over all hospital administration by decree, but opposition by the wide range of existing trustees doomed the effort.

From the examples so far reviewed, the role of religious orders and confraternities in providing hospital care is apparent. In some of the cases in which such organizations were involved, they provided nursing and medical attention, in others they took over the administration of the hospital concerned and contributed to funds or shouldered responsibility for collecting dues assigned by public authorities. According to legislation proclaimed in 1541 – the same as decreed the objective of establishing a hospital in every centre of population – and repeated in 1630, religious orders could only administer hospitals, not own them or their incomes, as 'ministers and helpers of the hospitals and their poor'.[54] According to a tally of 1774, the Order of San Juan de Dios

– the largest single purveyor of hospital and hospice care – had 36 hospitals in its keeping in Mexico, with a total of 1,316 beds. Between 1768 and 1773, 129,983 patients passed through their doors. If the records that the order kept are reliable, 9,829 patients died. The order's portfolio included, from 1608, the Hospital de San Bartolomé for Indian mineworkers in Huancavelica, and the pocket-sized Hospital de la Vera Cruz in Guadalajara, formerly run by a resident confraternity, which had occasionally received short-term help from the crown. The religious of San Juan de Dios took over the sixteen beds in 1606. The oldest religious order founded in the New World, the Hermanos de Nuestra Señora de Belén, operated refuges for the poor in much of central America and, from 1672, the Hospital del Carmen in Lima, budgeting for 12 reales a day for food: the viceroy paid twelve days' food costs a year and his wife added a thirteenth. The Dominicans were entirely responsible for hospitals in Manila for most of the colonial period.[55]

Where provision overlapped, or where hospitals competed to serve the same constituencies, or where the distribution of funds was glaringly irrational, compromises gradually emerged as a result of negotiations between town councils, the local church authorities, interested confraternities or religious orders, private benefactors and representatives of the crown. In Puebla, the Hospital de San Juan Letrán had an endowment in part from the *cabildo* and in part from the Blacks' Confraternity of the Cristo de la Expiación, and relied on supplementing funds by collecting alms, while San Pedro, the rival hospital, was maintained by the cathedral chapter. It took nearly a hundred years to sort out their respective terrains, with San Pedro, from 1645, dealing with male patients, while San Juan Letrán became exclusively for women.[56] From 1538, the city council of Santo Domingo paid 100 pesos a year for the salary of the director of the hospital de la Rinconada.[57] In Lima, the Hospital de San Andrés, founded in 1546, had five hundred beds under a doctor paid from the funds of the *cabildo*. In 1549 the archbishop endowed the Hospital de Santa Ana for indios and that of San Bartolomé for Blacks. The hospital of the Confraternidad de la Caridad was founded in accordance with the confrères' broad mission in 1552, but came to specialize in the treatment of Spanish women and girls. In Mexico City in the 1770s and '80s Archbishop Alonso Núñez de Haro supervised a rationalization that brought the new general hospital, dedicated to San Andrés, into existence. Installed in the building vacated by the suppression of the Jesuits, it was perhaps the most impressively equipped medical facility in the New World, growing to a capacity of 1,000 beds, with a pharmacy of legendary dimensions and theatres for dissections and autopsies. Among the institutions the archbishop suppressed and incorporated was the Hospital de Amor de Dios, which specialized in venereal diseases, and had enjoyed lavish royal and archiepiscopal sponsorship, including the assignment of *Real Patronato* funds, rents owed to the cathedral, and the crown's income from the town of Ocuituco in Morelos.[58]

The Medical Professionals

As well as building hospitals, engineering amenities and organizing hygiene, the state contributed to public health by regulating medical practice, at least in towns, where *cabildos* often contended with crown appointees to license practitioners and punish quacks. The first *protomédico* – the official responsible for examining and inspecting doctors and apothecaries – of Mexico City, Pedro López, in 1527, was a nominee of the *cabildo*, whose job of examining and controlling medical practitioners resembled navigation in 'multitudinous seas'. Understandably, the remote edges of the monarchy attracted charlatans and expellees from guilds at home. The *cabildo* stumbled between short-lived appointments even after 1570, when the king elevated Francisco Hernández to the office, with nominal responsibility throughout New Spain; but the latter's tenure seems to have been a means of providing him with a salary rather than the city with an arch-physician, as his energies were mainly devoted to the botanical researches the crown demanded of him. If Hernández ever interfered in the management of medical affairs he left no trace of it in the records. The breadth of his remit in competition with local supervisors only increased the overall confusion and multiplied opportunities for fraudulent interlopers, who 'practise[d] medicine without fear of God our Lord and without the bachelor's degree'.[59] In 1585 the viceroy named an impressive newcomer to the office. Luis de Porras was a Salmantine 'professor' and former physician of the Royal bedchamber. He was literally armigerous, since he arrived with four swords and his own firearm. But the *cabildo* rejected him on the grounds that its own right to appoint *protomédicos* was inviolable. Lima meanwhile experienced no similar problems of conflicting jurisdiction. The first inspector of medical practices, Hernando de Sepúlveda, arrived in 1537 with a royal commission.

The scope for medical regulation was, in any case, limited by practical considerations: the shortages of qualified personnel, the rivalries between religious foundations and lay physicians, the problems of verifying quacks' claims, the reliance on traditional healers and on surgeons who often had little formal education and who sought the work as a means of escape from slavery, poverty and social restrictions. No medical degree courses were available, even in Mexico and Peru, until well into the seventeenth century, and the numbers of qualified individuals were never equal to demand. In 1791, for instance, 56 surgeons served Lima's approximately 60,000 people.[60] More than forty of them were Blacks or mulattos. Nor could the *protomédicos* easily enforce their discipline. A conspicuous case in Mexico City in 1791 involved the unqualified provider of surgery Manuel de San Ciprián, who, refusing to close one of his two barber's shops, fled from the hired swordsman of the *protomédico* to the viceroy, claiming that he was being persecuted for refusing to pay a bribe.[61]

Physicians, in any case, were usually only for the rich. But efforts to provide free or almost free medical attention for the poor in the colonies brought doctors into the sphere of public health. As early as 1511, Gonzalo Velloso, royally appointed surgeon in Santo Domingo, was commissioned to treat slaves and indios at public expense. Provision, however, was never very systematic. Sooner or later, as the historian John Tate Lanning observed, 'Every Spanish American city had some kind of public doctor, but . . . the institution was never precisely the same in any two places.'[62] Doctors' oaths usually included an undertaking to serve the poor as an obligation of the works of mercy, and a reputation for compliance with the oath in this respect could be an advantage in competition for salaried positions.

In 1553 Dr Juan de Alcázar, the first recipient of a medical degree from the University of Mexico, announced that he would offer free treatment to poor patients – apparently as part of his campaign to win appointment as *protomédico*. But it was not until the early seventeenth century, when the lamentable state of health in the public gaol forced the *cabildo* into action, 'that anything approaching systematic medical care for the poor in Mexico City came into being'. The council then began to provide salaried posts for the relief of the indigent. From 1607 to 1643 six physicians, eight druggists, six surgeons, three bonesetters, three phlebotomists and one oculist were maintained at public expense.[63]

In Lima the *cabildo* started paying for a doctor to treat the poor in the Spanish hospital in 1552 and at that of the indios not more than three years later. Funds were always begrudged, however, and the *cabildo* frequently suspended payments, arguing that hospitals could meet such costs from their endowments.[64] Quito encountered a lot of trouble in finding and keeping public physicians, despite the willingness of the *cabildo*, from the 1570s, to lay a levy on taxpayers for the purpose. When they did find a doctor, they could not always rely on him to treat the poor when richer pickings were available. The doctor Francisco Meneses, for instance, in 1610, was reproved because he would 'only treat those who [could] pay him'.[65] Even where successful, efforts to improve the health of the poor were not entirely disinterested: the reasons for the campaign by the *audiencia* president, Juan Jorge Villalengua y Marfil, to get Quito's poor off the streets and into the poorhouse was the conviction that they spread disease.[66]

Beyond the provision of medical facilities and the regulation of care, public policy contributed to health through the engineering of urban hygiene and sanitation and through initiatives to combat the spread of disease. State institutions took responsibility for enforcing quarantine in time of plague, regulating the hoarding and distribution of grain in time of famine, and promoting inoculation and vaccination, when medical science made such new techniques available. The eradication of smallpox was the goal of the immunization campaigns of the late eighteenth century, often with dramatic impact. In Chile, for instance, the epidemic of 1769 killed a third of infected patients. By the time the disease struck again in 1774 local savants had inoculated five hundred people, all of whom survived. In Guatemala, over the next two decades, José Felipe de Fores led a campaign that achieved 14,000 inoculations. Only 46 of his patients died in the epidemic of 1796. Public authorities were not always committed to such efforts, which relied on heroic pioneers, but when vaccination technology became available in the early years of the eighteenth century the unanimity with which Church and State supported it was remarkable. As in other areas when public vaccination campaigns were mounted, secular prejudice has blamed the clergy of the Spanish monarchy for obscurantism and obstruction, whereas in reality bishops were vital in urging compliance and local clergy generally tireless in turning out their congregations and often in undertaking the work of vaccination themselves.[67] Exemplary cases encouraged public response. Even before the great Vaccination Expedition sponsored by the crown arrived in America, with the aim of touring the colonies and spreading the technique, Alejandro Arboleys, the personal physician of the viceroy of Mexico, vaccinated the viceroy's son along with five orphans *pour encourager les autres*. On the French model, juntas were established to keep up the work: first in Mexico City, consisting of eight laymen known for 'zeal in public welfare', with six doctors, the senior councillor and the city attorney.[68]

How did the health infrastructure serve the state? Obviously it helped keep troops in the field and seamen aboard ships. It helped to project the image of a benevolent king, who, in the tradition of the *speculum regis*, was alert to his people's welfare. It contributed to the demographic buoyancy of the colonies. Although missions have a mixed record – excoriated for insensitivity to Indigenous cultures, or for narrowly religious priorities, or for the selective moral failings of some of their ministers – the demographic evidence proves that, after the initial shocks that all colonial contacts caused, they succeeded in nourishing and nurturing growing populations. The official records suggest that hospitals, too, were relatively effective in conserving lives. In 1793 over 4,500 patients passed through Santa Ana, Lima. Only 421 deaths were recorded. Surviving registers from the main hospital of Mexico City between 1777 and 1781 show throughput of nearly 3,500 patients in an average year. In 1793 there were 4,372, of whom 295 died on the premises. In the spell for which records are complete, from 1768 to 1773, the Order of San Juan de Dios treated 1,785 patients, of whom 252 died in their care. The figures may be misleading: dying patients may have been discharged once the hospitals despaired of them. But even if the efficacy of colonial health care seems, in hindsight, to deserve commendation, were subjects more loyal in consequence? Did they appreciate the relative benignity of the Spanish monarchy in the relevant respects, compared with rival empires? It would be rash to assume too much. In 1582 the Corregidor of Otavalo complained that the resources of the Hospital de la Caridad – including more than 4,000 head of sheep – were wasted for want of patients: 'There's not an indio,' he wrote, 'who, having fallen ill, is willing to go there for a cure, because he holds it certain that if he enters he will then die.'[69]

9

THE MISSIONARY FRONTIER
Missions as Infrastructure

I have not hid thy righteousness within my heart; I have declared thy faithfulness and thy salvation: I have not concealed thy loving kindness and thy truth from the great congregation. (PSALM 40:10)

The long walk across mountains and through jungle started in Andamarca, one of the highest and most remote outposts of the Spanish Empire. After sixteen days' journey in 1590, Nicolás Mastrillo, the future Jesuit Provincial who was then a rookie on his first mission, had experienced almost every environment the Andes had to offer, from the thin air and piercing cold of the high valleys to the tough, lush growth of the approach slopes. His first letter home, addressed to his confrères back in his Andalusian house of study, recounted his adventures with boyish, breathless enthusiasm for all the hardships and dangers he experienced, as he travelled in search of unevangelized indios with an experienced fellow priest, and a native boy to serve as a rather hit-and-miss interpreter. When at last they found a small party of potential neophytes, they sat down to share a meal, communicating by smiles and gestures. Everything seemed to go splendidly, with the hosts reciprocating the Jesuits' delight in their company. Suddenly, however, a chief whom Mastrillo called Liquiti arrived with a group of interlopers, inducing a dangerously darkened mood. 'These are not fathers,' Mastrillo understood Liquiti to say with a scowl, 'but Spaniards in disguise.' Almost equally suddenly, the atmosphere changed again, this time for the better, as the chief reconsidered. 'No,' he decided, 'they must be real fathers, because they are sharing our food.' Evidently, the gulf in good manners between the Jesuits and the secular Spaniards with whom the indios came in contact was so vast that the natives could not conceive that the two types of foreigner belonged to the same nation.[1]

In one way, Mastrillo's letter shows how precarious the Spanish monarchy was, for the document never reached its destination. Captured at sea by English pirates, it reached the hands of crown agents who scoured it for intelligence before leaving it to languish among the State Papers in Britain's National Archives, where it still lies. But, more germane for present purposes, the letter also shows how missionaries played a part in forming and maintaining the monarchy independently of the networks – of warriors, settlers and traders – that spread over the Spanish Empire. They were engineers of empire in a literal sense, designing churches, dwellings, infirmaries, mills, storehouses, schoolrooms, stables, corrals and all the dependencies of their busy communities, supervising the building of bridges and roads (usually constructed and maintained by the joint efforts of the linked communities), laying out irrigation systems and water supplies, digging ditches, erecting defences, constructing the forges, lasts, rope-walks and machinery necessary for supporting the artisans they trained and for producing goods, sometimes on what can only fairly be called an industrial scale, and even, in some cases in remote regions, setting up armouries to produce extemporized, ersatz firearms of their own invention, such as the gun-barrels of reed or hollowed wood that native militias used to repel slavers. Appealing in 1713 for public funds to support his work in the forested eastern flanks of the Andes, the Franciscan Fernando de San Joseph summed up the work: the missionaries cleared trails a hundred leagues long and built 'bridges over the large, fast-flowing rivers', promoting 'the expansion of new dominions'.[2] Missions extended the infrastructure of empire in remote and frontier regions, beyond the reach of Spain's effective military mastery, where religious replaced or supplemented the routine personnel and institutions of government. Indeed, in a widespread or at least recurring opinion among members of religious orders, the business of empire was best left largely or entirely to missionaries. Two contexts help to explain their view.

First, it is worth recalling that power struggles between churches and states disfigured the early modern period, especially in the West. The Reformation was, at one level, a secular bid for control of the clergy. Where the Church withstood takeover by governments, clerical hierarchies struggled to preserve social influence, especially by tightening marriage discipline and asserting a monopoly over the regulation of family life. The distribution of the fruits of clerical taxation, the extent of lay interference with ecclesiastical appointments, the role of church courts and the amount of property tied up in religious foundations were other more or less constant sources of tension. In the New World, clerical–secular rivalry was exacerbated, because control over a precious economic resource was at stake: the labour of indios, partly because religious orders wanted to appropriate Indigenous manpower for their own purposes, and partly because they wanted to protect natives from over-exploitative lay masters. An episode from Chucuito in the mid-sixteenth century illustrates the point vividly. Scholars were long baffled by the extraordinary size and numbers of the churches the Dominican friars erected in the region in the space of a couple of decades; in the 1980s, however, the architectural historian Valerie Fraser solved the problem by discovering a series of Dominican submissions to the crown, in which the friars explained that they were unable to comply at once with royal orders to hand their indio labourers over to the secular authorities on the grounds that they were engaged in church building.[3] The communities in the area soon had more churches than they knew what to do with, but maintained the evasive expedient in order to keep workers out of rapacious hands. Meanwhile, of course, all the usual Church–State conflicts continued over control of the sources of wealth and power.

Second, the only way in which Spain's rulers consistently and determinedly wanted to change the empire they ran – at least until secular values took over much of the elite in the eighteenth century – was religious. Economic exploitation was, of course, a necessary part of the relationship between metropolis and empire, but the purpose of introducing new economic activities was rather to generate wealth than change Indigenous culture: on the contrary, in most of Mesoamerica, the Andean zone and the Philippines, production of traditional products by existing means was one of the constant features that threaded the pre-colonial and colonial eras together, in contrast to the more radical economic interventions typical of English, Dutch and Portuguese imperialism in the Americas. Most other forms of culture were left intact in Spanish-ruled regions. Local political elites stayed in place: though there were changes of personnel, they nearly always happened within the same groups, and usually within the same dynasties, as was normal in a composite monarchy such as Spain's. Efforts to displace native languages were sporadic, at most. In disputes among natives, courts continued to uphold traditional laws and customs, except where they conflicted with Christianity. To replace paganism with Catholicism, on the other hand, was the one objective that really mattered, partly because it was genuinely, conscientiously espoused at and in the heart of the monarchy, and partly because the legitimacy of the Spanish conquest depended on fulfilling the papal commission to spread the faith. For some clergy, especially in the Franciscan Order, where millenarianism was rife, the opportunity the New World represented was truly sacred: a chance to recreate an apostolic church, dedicated to poverty and charity, evincing the purity and sanctity of which mendicants had dreamed, delivering the 'Age of the Holy Spirit' prophesied by generations of Franciscan 'spirituals'. Such hopes made their task of evangelization urgent and the presence of secular Spaniards as tiresome as any thorn in the flesh.[4]

The Effectiveness of Missions

Scholarship has exposed all the deficiencies and failures of missions as means of spreading faith and inculcating allegiance: they were incubators of diseases; they exacerbated plagues by introducing livestock that were reservoirs of infection; their methods of evangelization were often superficial – Dominicans, especially, were often critical of Franciscans for inattention to dogma, and Jesuits for tolerating dubious areas of pre-Christian Indigenous cultures. Physical abuse was the obverse of efforts to maintain discipline with insufficient manpower, and scourging – devolved for the sake of priestly decency to native or Black intermediaries – was the standard remedy for every ill. Rebellions were, if not common, recurrent and some orders seemed to welcome them as opportunities for martyrdom. It is worth observing, however, that missions were, on the whole, surprisingly successful in drawing recruits and harnessing affections. Franciscans in the remote areas of the forested eastern flanks of the Andes, where they launched missionary efforts in the eighteenth century, seem to have benefited from the control of precious salt supplies and the judicious bestowal of steel tools.[5] But the loyalty they inspired seems inexplicable in balance-sheet terms. The researcher Cameron Jones has uncovered what he calls 'a preference' for the missionaries, feeding them through famines and dying to defend them against pagan assailants.[6]

The claim that secular intruders hampered evangelization had a lot of strong evidence and stronger opinion on its side. The notion that the sinfulness of lay Spaniards set the indios bad examples was among the themes of Dominican homilies at least as early as 1511, when Fray Antonio de Montesinos – a preacher as small, noisy and uncompromising as St Paul – uttered his famous sermon against Spanish rapacity, inspiring the young Bartolomé de Las Casas, the future voice of humanity in the empire, to dedicate his life to the protection of indios. In 1517 similar scruples led the crown to hand government of the American dominions to a commission of three Jeronimite friars. In 1522 Las Casas, who by then was formally charged by the crown with defence of indios against injustice and maltreatment, launched his first scheme for liberating natives from excessive impositions by transferring some of their responsibilities for production to Spanish peasant immigrants. One of his unremitting complaints was that the *conversación* – close contact, that is – of lay intruders was inimical to the conversion of the crown's native subjects and destructive of their souls. His next big project, launched in 1537, was for a colony in Guatemala he called 'La Vera Paz', from which all lay people were to be entirely excluded. The Dominicans eventually found the colony unmanageable without help from Spanish soldiers, but the ideal of an empire of love, unencumbered by worldly purposes and uncorrupted by secular presence, continued to tug at clerical sensibilities. Against this background, the role of missions as forges of empire is intelligible.

In most places the religious found in practice that they could not manage without secular help and, in particular, without armed force to protect them. The Dominicans gave up in La Vera Paz after the martyrdom in 1556 of the author of a vast theological summa in Quiché – the longest work in any indigenous language of the Americas. The Jesuits massacred at Chesapeake in 1571 had refused soldiers, as did the Franciscans who perished at San Sabá in 1758. The Jesuits who manned the first mission in the Pacific island of Guam in 1668 were guests of a local chief, who, in a classic demonstration of the stranger-effect, gave the land for a church. They tried to do without Spanish troops and to exclude lay Spaniards, but the martyrdom of their leader in 1672 provoked a violent Spanish conquest.[7] Indeed, Jesuits' valorization of martyrdom was almost heretical in its intensity, recalling the lust for self-immolation that St Augustine condemned in the Donatists, and may have contributed to risks they undertook.[8] Their mission among the Guaycurú in the 1590s failed so miserably that they turned to thoughts of compulsion by 'fire and sword'.[9] Nonetheless, three regions in America stand out as mission fields where the foundations of Franciscans and Jesuits effectively took the place of imperial structures and – as it were – kept the empire going with little or no secular input: Florida, California (outside the presidios discussed above) and the inner frontier of Spanish South America in the basins of the Amazon and Paraguay river systems.

Florida was first. 'In future,' claimed Pedro Menéndez de Avilés in 1565, seeking to tempt his king into investing in the conquest of what is now the southeast United States, 'Florida will render much wealth to Your Majesty and, in value to Spain, will greatly exceed New Spain and even Peru.'[10] His words proved delusive. Indeed, the entire project for colonizing Florida rested on false assumptions and in particular on wildly wishful mental constructions of the geography of the imperfectly explored hemisphere. Menéndez de Avilés had chosen Santa Elena as the site of Florida's first Spanish settlement because he mistakenly thought it to be near the mythical 'land of Chicora', vaunted by an earlier explorer, and only about 1,255 kilometres (780 mi.) from the Mexican silver mines of Zacatecas: in reality the distance was about 2,900 kilometres (1,800 mi.), with the Mississippi in between. Viceroy Luis de Velasco thought the colony could be close enough to Mexico to be supplied by cattle drives and planted unworkable and short-lived garrisons along the supposed route.[11]

By about 1619, when Fray Luis Jerónimo de Oré wrote his *Account of the Martyrs in the Provinces of La Florida*, the truth was obvious. 'One cannot hope', the friar averred to Philip's successor, 'for any temporal gain from the many thousands Your Majesty spends in sustaining the soldiers in the presidio, and the number of religious engaged in preaching the law of Christ.'[12] The newly acquired province had no resources that Spaniards thought worthy of exploitation; the coast from the Chesapeake southward was of interest only because its bays commanded the Gulf Stream route from the Caribbean to the zone of westerly winds in the North Atlantic that took ships back to Spain; the sole reason to occupy the coast was to keep it out of the hands of foreign 'pirates'. Florida was a 'loss leader' in the imperial economy.

The monarchy's willingness to pay the costs of Franciscan missions in what are now northern Florida and southern Georgia is often attributed to royal piety; but Oré's text helps to show that the friars gave good value for the king's cash. Compared with soldiers, Franciscans were cheap to maintain, relatively dispensable and of high propaganda value as martyrs. In Oré's summing-up, 'they pay for their keep.' In its day, his rough-hewn compilation of materials circulated in manuscript and functioned as a conduit of the texts it unites into the historiographical tradition. Now it provides a quarry of wonderful anecdotes of sacred sufferings and hair-raising escapes. The work is full of instructive data on the friars' struggles with concubinage, their notions of sanctity and martyrdom, their methods of evangelization, their animadversions on native 'superstitions' (which strikingly resembled the 'popular culture' of talismans, taboos and unscientific treatments that godly meddlers harried in Europe in the same period), their outraged response to the menace of English pirates and their modest expectations of miracles. Oré cannot forbear to mention a dog that died after daring to profane a martyred friar's body; the vultures prospered by showing greater respect or perhaps better taste. The long list of martyrs Oré praised was, in one respect, deceptive: despite high turnover in apparently precious clerical manpower in the early decades of the enterprise, Florida represented a stunning success story for Spain. Native chiefs sought legitimation from representatives of the Spanish crown from as early as the late 1560s. In the late seventeenth and eighteenth centuries, when English competitors tried to suborn or intimidate Indigenous communities into a new allegiance, the loyalty of most natives to a monarchy that lacked resources to defend or reward them adequately was remarkable. The missionaries did the monarchy's work. After describing some gruesome martyrdoms of the 1580s, Oré described the surprising turnaround: 'It was God's will, though, that little by little these difficult conditions were eased so that today the Indians consider it a great honor to be Christians. In fact they pursue those who are not and insult them, so the religious are now faced with defending these *hanopiras*,' as they called the recalcitrant pagans.[13]

The missions should, perhaps, be commended not for working well, but rather (like the empire of which they formed part) for working at all. From the 1590s onward Franciscans established foundations on the Georgia coast and inland in Timucua and Apalachee; like pagan kings in late antique and early medieval episodes of evangelization, indio leaders seem readily to have seen ways of using the friars, sometimes as legitimators of their own claims to authority, sometimes as advisors and technical experts, and sometimes as mediators with a transcendent source of power, but compliance was unreliable and normally contingent on payola in the form of doles of European goods or material help against other native peoples. In the interior, the Spanish Empire came to rely on unfortified and largely ungarrisoned missions, which were viable as long as no one disputed them in arms. Even then, they tended to be economically precarious and feeble as agents of Christianization. One of the Jesuits who launched the Santa Elena mission summed up the difficulties in a letter to Menéndez in 1570. Seasonal migrations interfered with evangelization, so that 'in order to obtain fruit in the blind and sad souls of these provinces, it is necessary first of all to order the Indians to come together and live in towns and cultivate the earth.' However,

> it must be done rightly, as our Lord commands, neither by compelling them nor with a mailed hand. And this for two reasons: the first that they have been accustomed to live in [the present] manner for thousands of years, and to take them out of it is like death to them; the second, that even were they willing, the poverty of the soil and its rapid exhaustion will not admit of it . . . Unless this is done, although the religious remain among them for fifty years, they will have no more fruit than we in our four years among them, which is none at all, nor even a hope, nor the semblance of it.[14]

Still, the Franciscans who took over from the Jesuits made huge investments of effort and manpower. By 1675 they had nine missions at intervals on the Florida coast from San Agustín northward almost as far as modern Savannah, while 26 more stretched inland to beyond the Apalachicola River. Most had a few dozen indios. There were 150 at Santa Catalina, the largest and northernmost. The westernmost missions, however, were rebellious and unsustainable. Such security as they enjoyed ended in the late seventeenth century, when French and English adventurers began infiltrating Georgia and western Florida respectively, from Mississippi and Carolina.

In 1670 a treaty fixed the frontier with Anglo-America a little south of Charleston. English slavers, however, never respected it. Between 1680 and 1706 most Georgia missions collapsed, albeit temporarily, as a result of English incursions, culminating in 1704 in the raid led by James Moore, former governor in Charleston, who destroyed missions and burned the missionaries at the stake, enslaving 4,000 women and children, and killing most men. 'I never heard', Moore reported, 'of a stouter or a braver thing done.'[15] The Franciscan provincial likened the English to 'hungry wolves' who slaughtered Indians until 'the grass turned red with the blood of the poor'.[16]

A measure of the balance of success and failure of the missions is that indios showed a remarkable partiality for Spanish ways, even beyond the missionaries' reach. In the 1740s a visiting Jesuit found to his surprise that people at the mouth of the Miami River in Florida spoke Spanish, which trade had spread in their direction.[17] In the 1770s William Bartram, the deft botanical artist and plant hunter who was irrepressible in seeking species to catalogue, noticed that Creeks and Seminoles 'manifest a predilection for the Spanish customs' and language.[18] In a pattern often repeated in the later history of Native American relations with 'white' empires, self-seeking native factions would defy their own leaders, infringe treaties and abuse weapons the Spaniards gave them to make war at will. Still, by the time the Seven Years' War broke out in 1756, almost all the Indigenous peoples of Florida were, with varying degrees of enthusiasm, allied or submissive to Spain. They generally realized that Spain would befriend them, the United States betray them. In June 1784, Alexander McGillivray, the Creek chief whose father was a Scots trader, signed a treaty with Spain, promising that 'the crown of Spain will gain and secure a powerful barrier . . . against the ambitious and encroaching Americans.'[19]

The Jesuits

As custodians of the Spanish frontier, the Franciscans were equalled or excelled by the Society of Jesus. The Jesuits were not, when they first arrived in Spanish America in the 1560s, concerned to establish permanent missions of the sort run by the orders that preceded them. Rather, they introduced methods of evangelization proper to the Counter-Reformation era and ethos in which they originated and thrived, organizing itinerant spiritual blitzes in existing parishes. In 1580, however, encouraged by the viceroy of Peru, who saw them as potential agents of empire, they turned to projects of colonization beyond spiritual conquest, 'attracting' desert and forest indios to agrarian ventures and settled lives. In part, no doubt, their recruitment efforts got help from the fact that indios in their care were usually exempt from having to provide labour or pay tribute owed, in other circumstances, to Spaniards, while the Jesuits themselves abjured personal service.

They began to visit unevangelized areas, in the spirit of the journey of Nicolás de Mastrillo, described at the start of this chapter, and to set up pueblos, which, in effect and where the natives were disposed to accept their leadership, the missionaries came to govern. Such was not always the case: in the sierra of Santa Cruz, for instance, which they adopted as one of their first mission fields, they had to make painful compromises with indigenous values and culture, tolerating and even condoning the practice of cruel torture and enslavement of captives in local warfare.

Like the Franciscans, they could never be absolutely sure of their recruits' loyalty and had to put up with secessions from the communities they founded, back into the familiar forests and foraging that represented, for malcontents in the reductions, an alternative paradise of relative leisure and freedom. Failures triggered desertions – not so much the occasional defeats by slavers and invaders from Brazil, which tended to make the reductions appealing as relatively secure; more disturbing were plagues. They bedevilled every community receptive to European vectors of unfamiliar pathogens or to Indigenous people who were making the perilous adjustment to sedentary agriculture among tilled fields and flocks of invasive species. After plagues struck the new Paraguayan missions of Loreto and San Ignacio in 1618, the priests were all too aware of fugitives who took to the woods for 'merry bouts of drinking out of a priest's skull'.[20] Other indios had their own ways of coping with the downside of mission life. Martin Dobrizhoffer, whose sensitive, vivid tales of life in South America the empress Maria Theresa of Austria loved to hear at her court, where he latterly became a sort of pet Scheherazade, witnessed the fatigue among indios unaccustomed to wielding axe and plow, their 'bodies bathed in sweat and burning with heat'. They exclaimed, '*La yvichigui*, now my blood is angry,' and relieved their anger by blood-letting, watching 'the blood sprouting for some time with pleased eyes'.[21]

In some of the remotest frontiers, however, deep down the drainage areas of the rivers Amazon, Paraguay and Paraná, missionaries encountered indios who evinced the phenomenon best designated as the 'stranger-effect' – a culture of acceptance and even veneration of strangers, who were welcomed as objective arbitrators and holy men. The initiative for founding missions came at least as often from indio chiefs who saw the advantages of Jesuit patronage as from the religious themselves. Without support from Spanish troops, Jesuit missionaries repeated the extraordinary feats of kinds all religious orders reported with equal credibility wherever local cultures were favourable: dethroning idols with impunity, replacing them with Christian altars and scourging recalcitrant shamans. It is tempting to suspect that chiefly supporters were only too pleased to see shamanic authority subverted. The phenomenon which, in the British Empire, David Cannadine dubbed 'ornamentalism'[22] may have contributed: according to Dobrizhoffer, the eighteenth-century evangelist of the warlike, horseborne, unquenchably bibulous Abipones of Paraguay, most Guaraní shared Spaniards' 'foolish mania' for formal honours and loved to receive the titles and signs of rank with which the Jesuits rewarded friendship.[23]

The divisions among indio peoples were also propitious from a missionary point of view. Towards the end of the seventeenth century, for instance, among the valley-dwelling victims of highlanders' slave-raids in the remotest interior of Bolivia, the peoples known to Spaniards as Chiquitos welcomed the Jesuits, perhaps because they saw the priests as potential protectors against depredations by raiders from the nearby mountains, or secular Spanish slavers or Brazilian *bandeirantes* (whose slaving incursions sustained much of the economy of Brazil at the time) alike.

The Jesuits' early descriptions of their hosts seem calculated to justify the indios' subordination, stressing the irregularity and savagery of their wandering, foraging lives, their inattention to spiritual values, their dedication to passing pleasures, their nakedness, the fluidity of their sexual couplings, the rudimentary nature of their educational practices and their supposed lack of 'civility' in the form of institutions of government recognizable as such from a European perspective. On the other hand, the Jesuits were equally sensitive to evidence of the natives' potential for conversion, especially in their love of music and their talent for friendship and charity. The project on which the newcomers embarked was therefore not only to teach them Christianity, but to reorganize their entire society, imposing settlement, substituting agrarianism for foraging, introducing schools and enforcing social life and worship in conformity with Christian teachings, while subjecting everyone to a system of government in which the missionaries were at the top.[24]

In consequence of these conditions, reductions became highly productive and populous enterprises. In Chiquitos, they eventually embraced 24,000 indios, specializing in the production and export of honey on a vast scale, but including a peasantry devoted to cultivating maize as a staple, and well-trained artisans in every craft necessary to supply the colony with the means of what the Jesuits classed as civilized life. Missions sufficiently close to arteries of communication might have other economic specialities: at Yapeyú, the cash crop for export was mate; many missions exported hides. 'And so the indios live now,' the Jesuits of Chiquitos reported,

> in circumstances very different from those that formerly pre-vailed. They have everything needful to sustain life. They no longer go naked but have clothes of their own. They have houses to dwell in, under a government that sees that that they do their work. Nor do they wander any more hither and yon across the mountains.[25]

Proof of the Jesuits' economic effectiveness is the cupidity it aroused in secular administrators and, occasionally, bishops, who tended to assume that the conspicuous prosperity that distinguished the Jesuits' enterprises must be the result of unconscionable methods of exploitation or secret sources of wealth. Genuinely, however, it seems to have been the result of the efficiency from which the Jesuits were able to make profits and plough them back into the soil and fabric of the missions. The governor of Buenos Aires who admitted in 1683 that 'they do not accumulate beyond what is strictly necessary' seems to have grasped their methods accurately.[26]

In one respect, the Jesuits departed radically from previous missionary ideals and, indeed, from their own initial inclinations: they organized their own armies. Their early efforts to practise non-violence were impressive. In 1631 Antonio de Montoya, a prolific founder of reductions, evacuated over 10,000 indios from regions vulnerable to slavers in rafts and on foot to a new Canaan, 1,125 kilometres (700 mi.) distant along the Paraná, over rapids and around waterfalls in the teeth of slaver hostility: more than half the evacuees died.[27] In the circum-stances, military measures were unavoidable. In 1637 Jesuit ex-soldiers began to drill native militias to repel the *bandeirantes*. In a series of canoe-borne battles along the Acaragua River in 1640–41 St Francis Xavier 'guided the bullets' from reed-barrelled guns wrapped in oxhides under the talented Guaraní captain Ignacio Abiaru.[28] Repeatedly from the 1670s indio forces, armed with bolas, lances, slings and arrows tipped by iron from the mission forges, accompanied by their commissariat in the form of droves of cattle, intervened to defend or extend the Spanish frontier onwards, and defended their own lands against slavers and invaders. In Chiquitos the Jesuits created a formidable militia that contributed, for instance, three hundred warriors for defence against a Portuguese onslaught in 1727, four hundred towards a punitive expedition against assailants of a nearby mission in 1729, and 1,000 in 1761, when the region was threatened by pagan Guaycurú indios. In 1762–3 the fifteen missions of Paraguay collectively sent 6,000 armed men to help Spain recover the east bank of the Río de la Plata from the Portuguese.[29]

The Mission Life

As feats of engineering, the Jesuit missions were admirable, especially in Paraguay, where, typically, despite the undermining efforts of burrowing ants, which the builders ever deplored, they acquired paved and arcaded streets, in a period when such urban and urbane embellishments were rare everywhere. Planners chose elevated ground where possible, so that rain and sewerage would flow into the nearest river, and usually diverted streams to sluice out the latrines. The standard urban model, applied almost everywhere in defiance of peculiar environmental conditions, had a plaza, about 37 square metres (400 sq. ft), at its heart, centred on a statue of Our Lady or the saint in whose honour the settlement was named. Together with the church, the priests' dwelling, built around a central courtyard, occupied one side of the square. Warehouses, full of mate, cotton, grain and other necessities of indio life, adjoined it, with workshops alongside. Beyond the church there was usually a house of refuge for widows and orphans – 'a good, strong, commodious house', according to instructions drawn up in 1715, 'where widows and orphans can be taken in' as well as, in an addendum that shows that mission residents were not immune from a hankering for the forest life, 'the wives of those who have fled the pueblo'.[30] The cemetery – of which, as we have seen, Jesuits were pioneers in the effort to remove the health hazard of putrescent remains seeping from graves in church interiors – was behind the church and planted typically with oranges, palms and cypress.

From the square radiated streets of equal lengths, lined with dwellings for individual indio families. Each had a corral for keeping a variety of domestic fowls. The dogs and cats – in Paraguay each household usually had three or four of each – shared the living quarters of about 5 or 6 square metres (59–65 sq. ft), behind oxhide doors, within walls of adobe, under roofs of straw. As time went on, however, the Jesuits gradually replaced the adobe with stone and the straw with tiles – imported, at first, from Potosí, but increasingly, from 1714 onwards, produced in their own workshops. In 1714 the Provincial ordered construction suspended on all other projects in order to provide indios, working eight- or fifteen-day shifts, with decent homes in stone 'with such care that it should not be necessary to tear down and rebuild or repair every year'.[31] The results are still visible in, for example, the red stone homes that survive from the great days of the Reducción de Santiago.

The almost oppressively uniform planning, the inflexibility of the standard model, the way the pueblos took shape as Jesuits regimented indio workers to realize projects conceived in priestly imaginations – all the features of the engineering of the reductions seem to prefigure the paternalism of early industrial bosses who built utopias to house their workforces in Pullman, Illinois, or Port Sunlight, Merseyside, and similar urban experiments. Indeed, in urbanism and government alike, the Jesuit style is often called paternalistic. It was, in a sense, literally paternal, as the commonest image Jesuits used of their indio charges was of children – a term evocative of natural subordination, tractability and Edenic innocence in the sense of ignorance of sin: all the qualities the missionaries wanted to see. Some missionaries' accounts of their experiences demonstrate impatience with natives' alleged obstinacy and the invincibility of their ignorance: the Tupi lexicographer Juan Felipe Betterndorf in the mid-seventeenth century and Juan Daniel a hundred years later registered roughly the same degree of dissatisfaction. Backsliding and apostasy evoked frequent lamentations with denunciations of wily shamans manoeuvring to conserve their power. There were always intractable pagans looking on, unmoved, at the missionaries' efforts. 'The barbarians', reported a

Jesuit correspondent in 1675, 'behold the Christian funeral ceremonies with curiosity – because the rites differ in many ways from their own – in myopic paganism.'[32]

On the whole, however, evidence of the effectiveness of Jesuit missions is overwhelming. Readers can perceive the alchemy of cultural hybridity between the lines, for instance, of Dobrizhoffer's musings on the prodigious argot of communities who spoke, he thought, 'neither correct Spanish nor correct Guaraní', but a kind of creole patois in which both tongues were mixed. Hybrid religion, of course, would never satisfy Jesuit evangelists. Some of the evidence that they genuinely and deeply converted their charges relies, of course, on interested testimony, like that of Marcial de Lorenzana, who reported in 1610 that it was unnecessary to awe indios by demonstrating healing powers or induce them by spiritual bribes: rather, he specialized in prayer and laying-on of hands to obtain converts. His reduction, he wrote to his superior,

> goes daily from strength to strength in every way, and indio men and women turn up very willingly at our new settlement. Since my return here their enthusiasm has grown and they tell me that they have become aware of how much I love them. More and more people are arriving, evincing desire for baptism; we are losing no more lives to the plague; those baptized *in articulo mortis* have recovered. Their devotion to the Gospel is great and they say that when a priest lays hands on their heads he heals them in a way they feel immediately. Those who have two wives are leaving them and they are doing other things that tend to show their incipient fear of God.[33]

Unreliable as the Jesuits' boasts sometimes sound, the records of baptisms, deaths, marriages and confessions show that Christian practices did accumulate, and the Jesuits' annual reports strike believable notes, precisely because their triumphs are often equivocal. The 1637–9 report, for instance, mentions the expulsion of a congregant for 'morally deviant' behaviour, his consequent suicide and the dissection of his body by wild beasts: 'A horrible example of divine justice,' the reporter remarks, 'which left everyone shocked and promoted the careful conservation of good customs.' The same document praises the natives for awareness of sin and the commendable severity of their countermeasures:

> They say the rosary every day, whip themselves, and wear sack-cloth for a week at a time. They talk to women with their eyes lowered, as the Jesuits do, and go to confession regularly. They are also the most diligent of guardians over each other's sins, admonishing the guilty party and making a report to the mission-aries . . . Before letting themselves be seduced by sin . . . they seek to master their passion with bodily scourgings . . . With doleful voices the women and children invoke God's mercy, responding mutually in chorus. The men go out and the women come in, disciplining themselves with no less feeling than the men.[34]

For a while, the crown endorsed Velasco's original opinion that remote frontiers could be devolved to Jesuit rule. In 1608 a royal decree confirmed that Paraguay beyond the existing borders of the monarchy was to be acquired by evangelization alone, unaided by military forces. Further decrees exempted reduction residents from all tributes and services, other than those required by the Jesuits. The reductions became victims of their own success, in two respects. First, sedentarism affected the residents as it always does when first introduced among mobile populations, creating eco-niches for diseases to which large numbers of unimmunized people succumbed. The missions never fully overcame the hazards of plague, despite sedulous measures; nor did they ever monopolize indio affections: unnumbered thousands of natives preferred their traditional ways of life. Nevertheless, the Jesuits attracted many scores of thousands into their fold – over 140,000, by their own count, at the height of the operation in 1732. Secular admin-istrators suspected that the Jesuits manipulated the census to avoid the modest poll tax the order paid.

In any case it was irksome to the secular authorities to have so many productive souls beyond the reach of their exactions for labour, taxation and military service. Slavers resented the effectiveness with which Jesuits organized native militias. The Portuguese in Brazil beheld covetable territories that the Spanish crown had little material interest in retaining. Jesuit paternalism could be represented as what we should now call cultural insensitivity or, more pejoratively, racism. The autonomy the Jesuits enjoyed was denounced by their enemies as lèse-majesté, their economic efficiency as cupidity, their discipline as tyranny. Rival orders accused them of 'putting their sickle into our ripening corn'. Their insistence on distributing all the fruits of residents' labour equitably across the community exhibits, according to the observer's inclination, the grandeur or grind of communism. The walls with which they enclosed their settlements served to keep indios in or enemies out, as the commentator prefers. The Jesuits' detractors did not want for causes of complaint or opportunities for invention.

Meanwhile, the world around the missions changed. For images that contrast the mood of the Enlightenment with the preceding era in the Spanish monarchy, one can hardly do better than call to mind the royal palace that the Bourbons built in Madrid with the Escorial, which embodies the ethos of the preceding Habsburg dynasty, as interpreted by Philip II. The Escorial is a monastery, enclosing a palace. The site was selected to demonstrate the supremacy of God, manifest in the way the pinnacles of nature in the surrounding mountains dominate the dome and spires. The royal bedchamber overlooks the chapel, with a privileged view of the Most Holy Sacrament, of which the Habsburgs were, by papal commission, hereditary guardians. The kings whose images line the sky above the chapel are not kings of Spain, but of ancient Israel. In the grand halls and salons of the Madrid palace, divine images also throng the paintings by Tiepolo that adorn the ceilings, but they are images of Roman gods. The Spanish monarchy always bore two models in mind: the Kingdom of God and the empire of Rome. But the former dominated until the eighteenth century, when the latter took over. Classicism and secularism were part of the ideological toolkit of the Enlightenment.

So, accordingly, was anticlericalism, which affected the Jesuits at least as much as any arm of the Church. In 1759 Portugal expelled the order and confiscated its property. Between 1764 and 1773 the order was abolished in most of the rest of the West. Some of the allegations against the reductions were utterly fantastic: the much-repeated suspicion that the Jesuits' missionizing was a front for the concealment of secret mines of gold and silver; that they bewitched their indio victims into submission, and that their methods of punishment – which, in common with contemporary standards, in the absence of a prison service, relied heavily on the scourge – amounted to sadistic abuse. Others were more plausible: that Jesuit government was authoritarian and Jesuit discipline unenlightened.

The controversy over the balance of propriety and iniquity in Jesuit behaviour was, however, irrelevant to the fate of the order. The balance of power in the struggle between Church and State shifted decisively statewards in the eighteenth century. The Jesuits – for their militancy, tenacity, power, wealth, social influence and preference for a universal vision over the priorities of states and nations – were everywhere the secularizers' principal target. For lay servants of the Spanish crown, one of the Jesuits' most offensive privileges was the way they modified the *patronato* – the power over ecclesiastical appointments that the popes resigned to the monarchs. The Jesuits retained the right to nominate their own office-holders or, at worst, submit a short list from which the secular authorities were bound to make the final choice.[35] In South America, they were the obvious sacrifice for the crown to make in pursuit of a territorial accommodation with Portugal.

The adjustments of the frontier in Portuguese favour, with consequent suppression of missions, began in 1750. At intervals over the following decade, Jesuits sometimes encouraged indio armed resistance and even took active roles in leading it, boosting the arguments of secularizers who alleged that the erection of a priestly republic was a treasonous secession from the empire in an attempt to arrogate sovereignty to the Order. In any case, the missions were wiped out in a murderous rationalization of a previously vague border – an example of Enlightenment idealism at its worst.[36] In 1760, the year in which the Jesuits founded the last of their missions, the crown decreed their expulsion. When the decree was enforced in America in 1767, the Jesuits yielded without resistance and almost without demur. Within a generation, the indio communities had dispersed and dwindled almost to nothingness. Now only ruins remain – like the 'bare, ruin'd choirs' that Shakespeare remembered in Reformation England, 'where late the sweet birds sang'. In surviving fragments in the mission church of La Trinidad in southern Paraguay, the singers and musicians can still be seen, carved in the act of indulging the shared love of music of the Jesuits and their charges. At San José de Chiquitos, where the forests the Jesuits knew have been slashed and burned and reduced to dry scrub, four broad stone facades fill the east side of the plaza mayor: their false fronts contain the only dressed stone for many miles. Behind the structure are wood and mud under tin roofs, still housing the Madonnas and Archangels that the Jesuits left with their departure.[37]

The Franciscans

While the role of missions dwindled on the Paraguay and Paraná rivers, they came into their own, albeit under Franciscan rather than Jesuit auspices, in California. In some ways, Upper California, though colonized two centuries later than Florida, resembled the earlier colony: another outpost that seemed to promise little profit at the time, but which had to be seized for strategic reasons – control of the Acapulco current, in California's case, just as Florida conferred control of access to the Gulf Stream. In the late 1760s, José de Gálvez, sent from Spain to impose reforms on the government in New Spain, decided to pre-empt English, French and Russian rivals by securing the reputedly fine harbours along the California coast. The decision came at a bad time for recruiting manpower. By expelling the Society of Jesus, the crown had deprived itself of some of its most effective frontiersmen. At the time, Baja California was virtually a Jesuit republic, resembling the former state of Paraguay. In 1768 Gálvez turned to the Jesuits' usual understudies, the Franciscans.

Junípero Serra arrived to head the Franciscan effort in that same year, mortifying his flesh with undergarments of bristles or wire and a programme of unsparing self-flagellation. His brief was not only to occupy the former Jesuit missions, but to extend Spain's reach northward at least as far as Monterey, to counter the Russian threat and keep the great natural harbours of California out of the hands of other powers. A march of 400 kilometres (250 mi.) led him to San Diego. Naval and military expeditions took an agonizingly long time to find Monterey but located an even better harbour further north at San Francisco in the process. So both had to be occupied.

The natives responded to the Franciscans with indifference in some places, violence in others. The enterprise seemed doomed – and almost perished for want of commitment in New Spain. Yet Serra followed the 'call of so many thousands of pagans who are waiting in California on the threshold of holy baptism . . . on a road the principal end of which was the greatest honour and glory of God'.[38] Serra's determination was extremely heroic, or perhaps extremely foolhardy. Lay explorers helped, especially Juan de Anza, who developed land routes to New Spain and mapped the interior as far as the Rockies and Utah Lake, and naval commanders, especially Juan Francisco de Bodega y Quadra, who charted the coast of Pacific North America and made it safe for Spanish shipping. Within a few years of Serra's first efforts, California began to look viable.

By the early 1780s, a string of economically precarious missions threaded from San Diego to San Francisco, where an annual ship was the only contact with the rest of the Spanish monarchy. They converted the environment as well as its inhabitants, wrenching the people out of nomadism, producing new crops – wheat, grapes, citrus, olives – from the soil. In 1783 the missions produced 22,000 tons of grain, a total that rose to 37,500 in 1790 and 75,000 by 1800. Serra also founded veritable industries. San Gabriel had looms and forges and made woodwork, bricks, wheels, carts, plows, yokes, tiles, soap, candles, earthenware, adobe and leather shoes and belts. The productivity of the mission economy could be measured by the contribution of 134 pesos San Gabriel made to the cost of the Spanish commitment to the War of American Independence. (The eleven families living in the newly founded town of Los Angeles raised 15 pesos.)

Ranching on mission land grew even more spectacularly. The Franciscans had only 427 head of cattle in 1775. Between 1783 and 1790 their holdings in horses, mules and cattle grew from 4,900 to 22,000; other livestock increased from 7,000 to 26,000. By 1805 they had at least 95,000 head all told. San Gabriel alone counted 12,980 cattle and loaned out a further 4,443 cattle to lay colonists, along with 2,938 horses and 6,548 sheep. In 1821 the mission had 149,730 cattle, 19,830 horses and 2,011 mules.[39] In terms of head of kine per mission resident, the total represented 1.3 per person in 1785, and 7.3 in 1820.

The friars also exploited the potential for trading furs with Yankee merchants, who made laborious voyages around the South American cone to take advantage of the opportunity in the 1790s. William Shaler of Connecticut, who visited in 1804 on a trading venture from Canton, China, drove satisfactory bargains by advancing supplies for the missions against delivery of furs. His journal revealed how,

> for several years past, the American trading ships have frequented this coast in search of furs, for which they have left in the country about $25,000 in specie and merchandise ... The missionaries are the principal monopolizers of the fur trade, but this intercourse has enabled the inhabitants to take part in it.[40]

Even more remarkable than their economic success was the missions' record in boosting their own populations. They survived the terrible demographic disaster that ensued in California as in all the other places where European intrusions exposed Indigenous people to unaccustomed diseases. Indios achieved unprecedented prosperity under Franciscan tutelage, with the advantages of the new food sources – animals and crops – that the Franciscans introduced and the extra muscle power of the mules, oxen and horses that arrived from New Spain. The effect, however, as a Franciscan complained, was that 'as soon as we bring them round to a Christian and community way of life ... they fatten, sicken, and die.'[41] But because the missions spread, attracted indios and privileged the active population, who were least likely to succumb to disease, the overall numbers of mission denizens grew. When Serra died, there were 4,650 indios in the missions. In 1790 mission indios numbered 7,500. The total rose to 13,500 in 1800. By 1821, when Mexico succeeded the Spanish monarchy in taking responsibility for California, there were, on average, over 1,000 indios in each of the twenty missions, while the numbers of Indigenous people more widely continued to decline.[42] By the same date, the colonial population had risen to over 3,000.

The missionary enterprise achieved these transformations amid the usual conflicts between the friars and the lay authorities. Soldiers' outrages made the friars work harder, provoking a hostile alliance among formerly divided local tribes. Felipe de Neve, governor of California from 1779 to 1782, was indifferent to piety, steeped in the anticlericalism of the Enlightenment, and jealous of the friars' successes. He was at odds with Serra from the first, taunting him with the threat of secularization of mission lands, and reminding the friars that their missions were revocable royal grants, conceived as temporary and destined to revert to civil jurisdiction when their work was done.[43] In other words, the friars' reward would be deprivation. Neve challenged the Franciscans' right to confirm baptized indios and accused the friars of disobedience, immeasurable pride and unspeakable artifice. He ignored missions in his plans for future colonization.

He also cast doubt on the efficacy of the conversions. All evangelization involves compromise with the neophytes' cultures and traditions. The friars tended to be suitably strict where sex was concerned, locking up young mission girls at night,[44] but were more indulgent about what they considered to be indifferent traditions, including dancing and traditional healing.[45] Hugo Reid, a Scot who settled in Los Angeles in 1832 and profited locally from secularization of Church property by the Mexican government, thought the indios of San Gabriel

> have at present two religions – one of custom and another of faith. Hell . . . is for whites, not for Indians, or else their fathers would have known it. The Devil, however, has become a great personage in their sight; he is called Zizu and makes his appearance on all occasions. Nevertheless, he is only a bugbear and connected with the Christian faith; he makes no part of their own.[46]

That judgement was self-interested and insensitive to the supple variety of Catholic devotion. Certainly, however, the friars had to struggle continually against natives' intractability or indifference. When San Gabriel was founded, indios 'made themselves so scarce', according to one of Serra's helpers, that over a few months 'one hardly saw a single indio.' The locals, he reported, 'moved to another site far away from us'.[47] In 1775 Fernando Rivera y Moncada, captain of Baja California, reported a rebellion at the mission of San Diego de Alcalá, in which Fray Luis Jaume was martyred, because the indios 'wanted to live as they did before'.[48] In October 1785 the green-eyed sorceress Toypurina launched a rebellion at San Gabriel, because, she declared, 'I hate the padres and all of you, for living here on my native soil . . . for trespassing on the land of my fathers.' When natives took up arms in several California missions in 1824, their shamans relied on amulets and talismans to prevail against the Spaniards.[49]

The alternative course for failed or flinching rebels was to run away from the missions. As a typical missionary put it: 'Let the more intelligent Indians be asked why they run away and they will reply: ". . . Naturally we want our liberty and want to go hunt for women."' But the testimony of recaptured runaways from Dolores near San Francisco in 1797 concentrates on hunger and fear of excessive punishment as reasons for flight.[50] In 1801 Fray Fermín Lasuén explained how malcontents would claim to be 'hungry' and ask to go to the mountains for a week to hunt. The hunger was rather for a way of life than for food, which was usually available in abundance in the missions. 'I said to them with some annoyance,' the friar continued,

'Why, you make me think that if one were to give you a young bull, a sheep, a bushel of grain every day you would still be yearning for your mountains and your beaches.' The brightest of the Indians who were listening to me said, smiling and half-ashamed of himself, 'What you say is true, Father.'[51]

The friars' only recourse was to flogging or chaining, sometimes applied in frustration or despair. Serra acknowledged, 'I am willing to admit that in the infliction of the punishment . . . there may have been inequalities and excesses on the part of some fathers.'[52] Fray Esteban Tapis of the Santa Barbara mission explained that the lash or the stocks were used to punish sexual misconduct or a second offence of running away, while shackles were applied for a further offence, for 'such are the chastisements which we inflict, in keeping with the judgment with which parents punish their own beloved children'.[53] In 1806 a mission indio, Julio César, recalled a further hazard from the caprice of lay supervisors who inflicted punishments without reference to the priests: 'We were at the mercy of the administrator, who ordered us to be flogged whenever and however he took a notion.'[54]

Mission life was, in its way, as hard for the friars as for the indios. The Franciscans, wrenched from their familiar environments and ways of life, facing superhuman demands in hostile surroundings, struggled to contain common temptations with excesses of discipline. César spoke of how Fray José María Zalvidea 'struggled constantly with the devil . . . He constantly flogged himself, wore haircloth, drove nails into his feet.'[55] From time to time missionaries succumbed to problems of sexual incontinence, drink and spasms of lunacy.

As if they were not sufficiently unsparing themselves, missionaries suffered under *flagella Dei* in the form of secularizing officials. Church–State tensions were always interfering with the efficient running of the empire and disturbing its peace. In California, governor Felipe de Neve's policies were characteristic. Liquidation of missions in Texas began in the 1790s, sometimes because of their success in creating Indigenous Christianity. In 1792, for instance, the Franciscan provincial reported that the mission of San Valero had accomplished its task. All the indios were Christians and 'no pagans remain within 150 miles.' The mission could be wound up.[56] For missions were costly, dwindling assets. Though the California missions grew throughout the colonial era, the difficulties of sustaining the enterprises were obvious elsewhere.

The South American reductions, as we have seen, did not long survive the expulsion of the Jesuits. By 1781, the mission of San Juan Bautista – something of a flagship among the Texas missions – which had baptized 1,434 indios up to 1761 and typically held 300 native residents at a time, was down to a total of 169, only 63 of whom were under instruction. By the 1820s all the Texas missions were in decline in terms of numbers of neophytes. Their waning depleted their image: achievements that look creditable in hindsight seemed disappointing at the time.

Still, *si monumentum requiris, circumspice*. The network of missions that lined the under-resourced frontiers of the monarchy may not have satisfied secular criteria of effectiveness; nor, except in some Jesuit areas, were they competent against external enemies. But they did win the allegiance of hundreds of thousands of subjects; they harnessed resources for the monarchy, even if the return was modest, and kept them out of foreigners' hands; and they did the job for which they were designed: they made indios not into mock-Spaniards but into real, if often idiosyncratic, Catholics. They served the crown's only fixed purpose: to spread the Catholic faith. For the rest, Spanish rulers were content to leave Indigenous culture – economies, languages, communal traditions, local and regional polities – intact. In terms of the political theory on which the monarchy rested, however unsoundly in its enemies' opinions, the missions legitimized the Spanish presence. Today, their legacy is under threat from Protestant interlopers, secularism and the folly or weakness of the Catholic hierarchy, but most of the descendants of the people they evangelized still uphold the faith they taught.

10

THE LAST CENTURY
Engineers in the Aftermath
of Empire

For I will diminish them, that they shall no more rule over the nations. (EZEKIEL 29:15)

In 1960 Lucian Freud headed to the Goya Museum at Castres to look at a painting that fascinated him. He wanted to create character studies, 'not mere likenesses', and Goya's work set his standard. He especially admired Goya's collective portrait of shareholders of the Real Compañía de Filipinas (Royal Company of the Philippines), of 1815, which, Freud said approvingly, captured complete nullity – represented 'absolutely nothing'.[1] The work belongs in the tradition of what might be called Spanish 'anti-portraiture' from Velázquez's *Las Meninas* (Maids of Honour) to Goya's own devastatingly candid royal family group, *Familia de Carlos IV*: moral as well as physical delineations of regal vacuity. King Ferdinand VII appears amid the company's directors, who, enveloped in shadow, seem to ignore him while they talk among themselves or stare into space, apparently clueless as to why they are there or whether it matters. The only light enters via an open doorway at one side, illuminating, as the focal point of the painting, a figureless patch of floor in a way perhaps better suited to the depiction of a funeral. The painter's message is clear: the only future worth living lies outside, where the air is fresh, beyond the darkness of dim monarchs and dull cliques.[2]

The nineteenth century has, since Samuel Smiles, been hailed as the age of engineers, who stamped and shaped it.[3] But continuities with the previous century deserve to be acknowledged. Frank Safford's classic work on the history of Colombia, *The Idea of the Practical* (1976), referred to a 'neo-Bourbon' period, from 1821 to 1845, undifferentiated in key respects from the late colonial era and spanned by uninterrupted intellectual dynasties. José Manuel Restrepo, author of the *Map of the Coasts of Colombia* (*Carta corográfica de la República de Colombia*), which has remained influential since its appearance in 1825, was the intellectual successor of Vicente Talledo, who died in Madrid in 1820 – an army engineer of Cantabrian provenance, whose work in the design of barracks, bridges and batteries included the remarkable *Map of the Coasts of New Granada* (*Mapa corográfico del Nuevo Reino de Granada*) of 1814.[4] As Safford noticed, the modernizing, 'techno-scientific' programmes of the post-independence era, devoted to 'useful knowledge' for the fledgling republic, often unfolded under the aegis of the same engineers, mathematicians, cartographers and pilots as previously, or their designated successors.[5]

In any case, empires do not typically fall all of a sudden. Spaniards lost the wars of independence but continued to be active overseas in the nineteenth century.[6] Under successive, mutually antagonistic governments, policy was uniform: to hold on to what remained of the empire and craft an increasingly uniform system of administration for the overseas territories.[7] A single directorate were created for the empire in 1847, and became, in 1863, a ministry responsible for all territories. Until the debacle of 1898, Cuba, Puerto Rico, the Philippines and the islands of the Carolinas, Marianas and Palaos remained in Spanish hands.[8] The Dominican Republic returned to Spanish allegiance from 1861 to 1865. Equatorial Guinea was part of the empire until 1968 and Spanish Sahara until 1975. In all these territories Spanish engineers' work never ceased, as much recent research has shown. Engineers were essential personnel. The economy and flexibility they brought to their tasks seem, in retrospect, astonishing in their effects – connecting continents and bringing to Spain's overseas possessions an aura of belated efficacy.

The Spanish monarchy's first railway, for instance, and, by most counts, the world's seventh, was in Cuba, stretching 29 kilometres (18 mi.) from Havana to Bejucal, opened on 19 December 1837, some years after a Sevillan resident in London, Marcelino Calero, had suggested introducing the new method of transport to the island. The first accident occurred the following year, when a bull maddened by the alarming steam whistle bumped the locomotive *Villanueva* off the tracks. Also in Havana, on 1 November 1877, the fire brigade answered the first telephone call in Spanish territory. The local postmaster,

Enrique Arantave y Bellido, packed up a couple of the new instruments, obtained from the United States, and sent them straight off to Madrid, where the design was copied and improved in time for Christmas.[9] On the far side of the world, in the Philippines, where semaphore telegraphy had operated since 1836, an electric cable linked Manila to Hong Kong from 1880.[10]

Despite these innovations, Anglo-Saxon critics never stopped raging against Spanish technical incompetence and the 'decadence of the Latin races' compared with the supposedly exclusive talent for mechanics and mathematics that British, Germans and North Americans exhibited. Yankee filibusters and imperialists in search of excuses for seizing Spanish or formerly Spanish territory joined with Protestant or anticlerical forgers of the 'Black Legend' of Spanish moral inferiority, fantasist crafters of sensationalist fiction about the Inquisition, and racist maligners of Moors', Jews', gypsies' and Native Americans' supposed adulteration of Spanish blood. For some 'thinkers' – who were rather smatterers and sciolists – the 'Spanish soul' was better attuned to arts and letters than science and technology.[11] In one respect Spain was imperfectly equipped: new devices, such as railways, oil-fired engineering and electricity, required protocols and discourse that did not yet exist in the Spanish language. Some proposed a solution: a good technical dictionary with Spanish equivalents for imperfectly naturalized foreign terms. Ramón Arizcún, the inspector-general of the army corps of engineers, called for a 'clean-up' of language ('la elegancia de palabras depuradas') – instead of which, he complained in horrorstruck tones, the influence of English and French infected the lexicon with neologisms and barbarisms.[12] Still, Spain needed and got industrializing technology, like most of the rest of the Western world, for reasons of state and war as well as of commerce, finance, education and culture.[13]

The Professional Framework

Public works remained part of the practice of the state, but two changes shifted some responsibility and action towards the private sector: in 1841, beyond peninsular Spain, compulsory appropriation of property in the public interest was abolished, and a new era opened in consequence. Meanwhile, civil engineers encroached on what had been largely a preserve of military and naval professionals.

Until 1866, military engineers remained largely in charge of public works in overseas territories. Thereafter, local committees staffed by civil engineers increasingly took over.

The expansion of engineering education outside the armed services facilitated the change. A royal ordinance of 1803 called for more institutions for training engineers. In 1821 a school combining training in the military and civil branches of the profession had been founded, to be divided in 1825 into one establishment for marine engineers and another for construction and hydraulics. The School of Mines was set up in Madrid in 1835 and that of Forestry and Agriculture in 1843. 'To know is to do. He who does not do does not know,' declared the founder and first head, Bernardo de la Torre.[14] Not long previously, in 1841, a school of civil engineering had reopened. In 1847 publication began of the celebrated *Memorial de Ingenieros* (Engineers' Almanac), with 'articles and news of importance for the art of war in general and to the profession of engineers in particular'. In 1850 the Royal School of Arts (Real Conservatorio de Artes) became the Royal Industrial Institute (Real Instituto Industrial) and began training engineers. The responsibilities of the Ministry of Development (Ministerio de Fomento), established the following year, included supervision of industrial, commercial and architectural education, as well as commissioning local roads and telegraph poles. The year 1854 saw the creation of corps of forestry engineers, thanks to the viable numbers of graduates in the field. Schools of telegraphy, agriculture and, in 1868, topography followed, with admission accessible to women from 1880. There were designated corps of railway and landscape engineering from 1896 and 1900, respectively.

Changes of government did not displace responsibility for oversight from the Ministry of Development, but each field acquired a supervisory board of experts – a sort of lay clerisy – who exercised vigilance over every area of specialization.[15] Admissions and promotions – subject to strict rules of seniority – in the various corps were in the hands of committees on which the relevant government ministries were represented. In nineteenth-century Spain, engineers were part of the armoury of state and the vanguard of the nation.[16]

The long preponderance of military engineers in overseas territories was the result not of official prejudice in their favour, though they had the right to engage in private work if their duties to the state permitted. Rather, it was their availability that preserved their monopoly and often brought them work in the private sector or secondment to railway construction. Until the 1860s a large number of them were always surplus to military needs. They worked as supernumeraries on contracts or commissions from government ministries, or hung around in the hope of some enduring appointment.[17] There were two hundred qualified men in the corps in 1820. In 1828 during the absolutist terror, when a deservedly liberal reputation tainted engineers in general, their numbers fell by 65 per cent. In 1846, 80 men were newly commissioned, but only 31 received guaranteed salaries. Until 1875, the numbers in the lists exceeded the salaried positions in the service. There were about four hundred in the corps in the 1890s. On emerging from training, a military engineer entered a world of great mobility of labour. To earn a living, places as instructors in military academies or secondment to public works, especially in the colonies, were common means of recourse. It seemed as if the state could furnish a well-instructed profession but not take advantage of it.

Despite, therefore, the increased specialization in engineering education, graduates had to be flexible in undertaking varied work. Mariano Albó, one of the exiles of the purge of 1823, took to architecture in Gibraltar before returning to Madrid in 1833, where the Real Academia de San Fernando – the artists' organization that still exercized responsibility for all kinds of design – waived the rules to enable him to work for the town council. In 1859 captain of engineers Juan Bautista Orduña obtained official leave to go to Havana as municipal architect, where he also took on, perhaps in a voluntary capacity, the role of commander of the fire brigade. Shortages of civil engineers and the high cost of meeting their 'salaries, emoluments, and accommodations' led military engineers to redeployment in road building in Cuba, the Philippines and elsewhere.[18] Some took permanent jobs in public works – such as that of Director of Public Works in Guinea under the Ministry of State – on secondment to civil ministries. Civil engineers had a nominal monopoly of work in ports, but their military counterparts were often subcontracted to carry it out. In 1902 the military engineer Eduardo Gallego complained at a ruling from the Council of State on the grounds that he could see no justification for 'the exclusive competence granted to civil architects in public and private construction, or in the design and execution of roads, bridges, canals, water supply systems for health and hygiene, public fountains, re-landscaping, industrial uses of water, water supply regulators and electrical installations'.[19]

It is possible that Gallego, who himself became an entrepreneur and founded a private engineering firm, protested too much. A superior officer of his, general of engineers José Marvá y Mayer, saw civilians and military professionals as collaborators in the service of society and the creation of wealth. At the Congress of the Association for Progress in the Sciences (Congreso de la asociación para el progreso de las ciencias) in 1909, he argued that the role of an engineer combined technical and social responsibilities as an intermediary between capital and labour. In a free-enterprise system, the general averred, engineers could provide 'empirically based reflections and evidence concerning the labour conditions imposed by mechanization'.[20]

For engineers born in the colonies – of whom, according to the lists of 1892, there were only three Cubans, two Puerto Ricans and one Filipino – the situation was easier to understand. In Cuba, for instance, industrialization was under way from 1832, when the Royal Commission on Development (Real Junta de Fomento) was formed and coal and steam began to transform production and transport. The commission remained active until 1854, investing the proceeds of taxes and tolls.[21] Among the employees was the military engineer Carlos Benítez, controller of the Sabanilla railroad, who designed lighthouses, bridges and buildings and advised on the construction of a port at Matanzas.[22] His colleague, Francisco de Albear y Lara, a Cuban by birth, was of transcendent importance. He was in charge of public works on the island from 1847. His military accomplishments included the cavalry barracks at Trinidad, the battery of La Pastora, gunpowder stores and defensive watchtowers. He left his mark on the civil sphere by building warehouses for the treasury, a chamber of commerce, a pier, a botanical garden, a school of agriculture and the religious house of the Trinitarians in Havana. In 1848 he assumed the directorship of the post office. He found time for planning the railroad from Macagua to Villa Clara, amplifying the quays at Cienfuegos, and saving the capital from malaria, yellow fever and dysentry by building a new water supply system to replace the turbid, polluted water formerly brought from the river Chorrera or Almendares.

Water for Growth

Albear's work covered the full range of engineers' efforts with infrastructure. But the water supply – always crucial – grew in importance with the demands of industrialization and demographic growth. Between 1831 and 1835 the Conde de Bagaes and Nicolás Campos had collaborated in bringing into service an aqueduct named in honour of Fernando VII, drawing the waters of the Almendares into a reservoir for purification through filters of sand and carbon. From there the water was pumped to Havana through a pipe 42 centimetres (16½ in.) broad from where other pipes distributed it across 7.5 kilometres (4½ mi.) in distance, and over 22 metres (72 ft) of altitude. It was not enough. In theory, it was supposed to supply 40,000 cubic metres (1.4 million cu. ft) a day but never achieved much more than one-tenth of the envisaged output in practice. A total of 895 tanks and 2,976 wells supplemented the supply. In 1861 Albear tackled the first phase of his project, dedicated to sustaining the flow of the Almendares River and preserving the high-quality output of the springs of Vento. By 1865 the foundations of a great new reservoir were complete. In 1878 the first of the new supply flowed through to Havana. The outstanding work to complete distribution wasn't completed until 1892.

The island's second city, Matanzas, got an aqueduct of its own in 1872, thanks to the skill of a Mexican engineer, Juan Francisco Bárcena, and the capital supplied by local businessmen. The water came from a spring at Bello, 14 kilometres (8½ mi.) away.[23] In San Juan de Puerto Rico, another military engineer, Juan Manuel Lombera, designed an aqueduct with hydraulic pistons raising the level of the water, following a method of Jean-Michel Montgolfier's devising, which he had seen in Philadelphia.

The Philippines, meanwhile, was also the scene of an important experiment in aqueduct design. Francisco de Carriedo, a soldier of Cantabrian origin who became mayor of Manila, left 10,000 pesos in his will for the construction of an aqueduct. Innumerable impediments intervened and the structure only began to supply water in 1882, to a design by a civil engineer, Genaro Palacios y Guerra, who built an underground gallery 160 metres (525 ft) long and 1.7 metres high to draw water from the San Mateo River. Filtered through porous wood, the water rose by means of steam pumps to a reservoir from where gravity brought it to the city. The supply was abundant: 8,000 cubic metres (282,517 cu. ft) a day. But it required extensive infrastructure: a tunnel 3,290 metres (10,795 ft) long, 29 vertical shafts, a syphon 400 metres (1,312 ft) long to cross the ravine known as El Ermitaño, bridges, galleries, pipework and two underground reservoirs, each of 56,000 cubic metres (1.98 million cu. ft) in capacity, at San Juan del Monte, Manila's highest hill.

At Jolo the skilled military engineer Carlos de las Heras built an aqueduct 1.5 kilometres (just under a mile) long from a dam purpose-built on the stream known as La Sultana to three fountains of coral in the city's central square and another in another square. The Chinese trading community contributed 96 barrels of Portland cement, transported from Singapore; the bricks came from Borneo; iron pipes 10 centimetres (4 in.) in diameter came from the auction of a bankrupt local sugar mill. The 2,590 inhabitants of Jolo now had the benefit of at least 60 litres of water a day and had no longer to rely on costly supplies from Chinese water-carriers.[24]

Embellishing Cuba

All over the residual empire, but especially in Cuba, sugar boomed. It was a genuinely industrial sector, largely mechanized early in the second half of the century: the first centrifuge to separate the sugar arrived in 1849 at La Amistad at Güines.[25] The advances of sugar, measurable in the amount of labour it absorbed, transformed the 'pearl of the Antilles'. Between 1511 and 1762 about 60,000 Africans arrived in Cuba. In 1791 there were 85,000, in 1817 that number had risen to 199,000, and by 1841 the African population had reached 436,000. Increasing numbers of slaves favoured the growth of the white population, too. The big promoter of white colonization was José Antonio Saco, a Cuban campaigner for autonomy within the Spanish monarchy and against annexation by the United States. In 1862 he presented a case against slavery and the power of the sugar barons, recommending diversification into the production of rice, oranges and indigo. Fifty-seven per cent of the white population was engaged in farming at the time.[26]

Population growth required improved communications. Between 1792 and 1800 no fewer than eighty new towns appeared, demanding roads, canals and access to international routes. From 1796 to 1802 the Conde de Mopox – the Havana native Joaquín de Santa Cruz

– headed the Royal Commission of Guantánamo (Real Comisión de Guantánamo) with three objectives in mind: to build roads, to bring water from the Günes hills, where, decades later, a railroad would run, and the resettlement of Guantánamo Bay.[27]

Change was most intense in Havana (as, in the Philippines, in Manila). As in the chief remaining imperial sub-capitals, where new developments recalled the viceregal splendours of Mexico City and Lima, marking a further link between the eighteenth and nineteenth centuries, creole elites embraced or accepted empire and their taste reflected it in frankly baroque exhibitionism. Public works erred on the side of extravagance, exhibiting wealth, power and a desire to be recognized for metropolitan civility. Obsession with the display of 'good taste' shaped the public sphere, the civic infrastructure and a hinterland landscaped to evince the happiness and harmony of a picture postcard.

In the 1870s Samuel Hazard visited Havana from the United States and praised the generosity of one munificent citizen, compared with the meanness of his rich fellow-countrymen:

[In] the centre of the Paseo is the beautiful Glorieta, and fountain of India, surrounded by noble palmas reales [the iconic trees, sacred to voodoo priests but revered by all Cubans]. The fountain is a work of considerable beauty, carved out of Carrara marble, and erected at the expense of the Conde de Vill Nueva. It is one of the most beautiful of public fountains . . . and is an example which some of our millionaires, who hoard their money to no earthly good, would do well to follow in beautifying their native cities.[28]

The Fountain of India in the Paseo de Extramuros was inspired by the Cibeles Fountain of Madrid. Another son of the city, Claudio Martínez de Pinillos y Ceballos, whose responsibility for the island's finances made him the governor's number two, brought another lion-guarded fountain, the work of Giuseppe Gaggini, from Italy at his own expense in 1836 to stand in the equally prominent Plaza de San Francisco. He competed with the governor, Miguel Tacón, to endow the city with grand public works. Tacón, a veteran of the wars of independence of the mainland republics, also commissioned a fountain from Italy in 1836 – depicting Neptune and erected at the entrance to the port, as if to direct commerce seaward in allusion to one of the conflicting strands in island politics: the merchants and officials wanted to encourage an outward, imperial perspective against the introspectiveness of some creole planters and liberals.

In exchange for a monopoly of the sale of fish, Tacón induced the Catalan slave trader Francisco Martí y Torrens to finance a modern fish market within the city walls, complete with refrigeration unit and tank for live fish.[29] By the same means – granting a monopoly to a trusted partner for a limited term – Tacón obtained a new market in the main square, the Plaza de Fernando VII. It was built like a medieval cloister, with the shops in the aisles and living quarters for stall-keepers above. Smaller and, to his mind, more up to date was the market built in the Plaza del Cristo, with a rectangular plan and vaulted interior, along the lines of Faneuil Hall in Boston, Covent Garden in London and the former Les Halles in Paris. Tacón caused something of a sensation by decreeing yet another new market outside the walls, to be known as the 'Steam Market'. This prefiguring of the department stores of the future measured 120 metres long by 92 wide (394 × 302 ft), over two floors, with direct access from outside to shops 'for every product, craft and service'. Food was sold in the interior spaces, under vaults and between pillars, on tiled floors. 'There are few better examples,' an observer averred, 'even in Paris or London. Water for cleaning and for consumption by large numbers of users comes from an elegant stone fountain with four spouts, located between the galleries and the meat section.'[30]

Tacón also arranged for the construction of a theatre and a boulevard, named after him and interspersed with five ornamental fountains surrounded by majestic poplars and pines. Mercedes Santa Cruz y Montalvo, the cosmopolitan Condesa de Merlín, daughter of the Conde de Mopox, returned to her native Havana for two months in 1840, as the widow of the ambitious and implacable French warrior Cristophe Antoine Merlin, who had sacked Bilbao in 1808. In her account, published in epistolary form in three volumes in 1844, she captured the atmosphere:

At six o'clock all the voiturettes are waiting at the doors of the houses for the ladies, hatless and with flowers in their hair, and the dress-suited gentlemen with their sticks, waistcoats and white trousers, all dressed to perfection, to parade along the

Paseo de Tacón to the lovely boulevards where – whether through
indolence, fastidiousness or pride no one goes on foot.[31]

Beyond the walls an avenue of Tacón's construction extended for
1.6 kilometres (1 mi.) across sixteen suburban districts. Here too was
a place for the denizens of 'elegant Havana' to see and be seen. In 1863
the demolition of the walls facilitated the integration of the suburbs
into the growing city. From 1842 a horse-drawn omnibus served the
population, succeeded in 1859 by a tramway with branch lines, capable of supporting 36-seater carriages. The Spanish entrepreneur José
Domingo Trigo operated the concession, taking the opportunity to
develop the El Carmelo district, which became part of El Vedado. The
tramlines were electrified at public expense in 1897. At the beginning
of 1898 Mariano de la Torre, Marqués de Santa Coloma, petitioned to
open 18 kilometres (11 mi.) of electric railroad, divided between five
lines joining different parts of the city.[32]

Echoes in Manila

The progress of Havana seemed to inspire Manila. Landscaping,
streetscapes, monuments – even the style of mapping and the design
of documents were full of echoes. Manila had long nourished, since
1595, imperial self-perceptions as the 'capital' of the archipelago and
as the 'Rome of the Far East' ('la Roma de extremo oriente'), from
where Catholicism spread.[33] The shock of the brief British occupation in 1762, however, induced a period of cautious, defensive
vigilance, behind the eight heavily guarded gates in the encircling
walls. Until 1852 the gates were locked every night.

The kernel of the city was small: a grid of seventeen well-paved
streets, dominated by official and ecclesiastical buildings and the
University of Santo Tomás, the oldest in Asia, founded in 1611.
Beyond, most of the remaining 80 per cent of the population resided in
huts of wood or fibre – journeymen, company employees and the operatives of a vast fleet of canoes. Lines of division by class or ethnicity
were less marked than in most Asian cities. The Chinese quarter
bordered the Pasig, stirring fear and resentment by their commercial
nous and record of rebellion. Around 1880 the colony was 40,000-
strong in Manila, with 60,000 more in the rest of the archipelago,
running most of the retail sector and crafts. In the calle del Rosario, in

the Binondo district, women of mixed Chinese and native extraction staffed most of the Chinese-owned shops, cheek by jowl with white traders from Spain and elsewhere, who constituted no more than 5 per cent of the total population of the city. For dairy products the Tondo district was dominant. The tobacco factory was in Mesig. Around the governor's palace in San Miguel clustered sugar and timber mills, while cordage workshops and printers predominated in Sampaloc. Malate housed a lot of scribes and seamstresses.[34]

When the flag was lowered for the last time in Manila in August 1898, telephone, telegraph and railway lines were in place; there was a cable service to Hong Kong, and the steamships to Spain via Suez took less than a month.[35] A huge programme of modernization had transformed the archipelago, especially since 1875, when the restoration of the monarchy brought a period of political stability. From 1882, moreover, the government pursued a modest policy of integrating Spanish Micronesia – the Carolinas, Marianas and Palaos – despite tempting offers from an increasingly expansionist Japan to purchase the lot.[36] Recent research has challenged the old orthodoxy that the Spanish Pacific stagnated until the United States took over. On the contrary, the gap between conception and execution – between what citizens and administrators wanted and what the empire provided – narrowed as the engineers did their work. Today, surviving achievements of the era are conspicuous.[37]

Distance has done most to craft Manila's image in Europe and America.[38] After the curtailment of the galleon route to Acapulco in 1821, communications with the wider world depended on ships from Cádiz rounding the Cape of Good Hope. From the 1840s, Spaniards bound for the Philippines usually made use of British ships as far as India or, from 1858, of the new rail route from Alexandria to Suez. In 1859 the traveller Máximo Cánovas, bored with shipboard company, contented himself with reading about and observing such 'sea monsters' ('monstruos marinos') as dolphins and whales.[39] The opening of the Suez Canal in 1869 made a huge difference. French vessels plied the new route, but from 1871 there was the Spanish line, Olano, Larrinaga & Cía, headquartered in Liverpool. In 1880 the Marqués del Campo obtained a concession and subsidy to run a direct service to Manila.

The last stage of the journey took passengers amid the shallows, storms and dangerous currents of the Strait of Java. Those looking to economize shipped on sailing vessels that would round Africa via the Cape; they would see no land during their five or six months at sea. Those arriving in Manila could hardly avoid passing through installations designed or modified by Ildefonso de Aragón y Abollado, an army engineer from Cádiz, of restless spirit and unvarying efficiency. In 1800 he was arrested for insulting the military governor of Lérida (Lleida), and was transferred, understandably enough, to the Philippines two years later. He stayed until 1827, in charge of the local engineering corps, eluding repeated orders to return by appealing to the engineer's standard excuse: the unceasing sequence of emergencies. In the year of his arrival he submitted plans for twenty boathouses at the fort that guarded the passage of the Pasig 'to keep the gunboats'.[40] In 1804, rapidly diagnosing an obvious but unmet need for reliable and suitable manpower, he created a corps of workmen at the disposal of the engineering unit in Manila. He specialized in bridges.

Notable examples of his work include the wooden structure on stone pillars across the Pasig, built in 1814; another, of 1804, with two arches and wooden decking, at San Antonio Abad; the Las Piñas bridge, of 1803, just outside the homonymous village, arching almost 6 metres (20 ft) across the oddly named 'Tripa de gallina' stream; and the Sampaloc bridge over a floodplain. He started a topographical archive in 1818, where he housed his many maps and views, his plans of the artillery park and the arsenal at Cavite, the customs house, cemeteries, defences and his sketches for bridges over the Parián, where the Chinese colony resided, as well as his descriptions of the provinces of Tondo, Luzón and Pampang. He helped to found the Real Sociedad Económica de Manila. His indefatigability was astonishing. In 1816 he drew up the plans for the 200,000-peso tobacco factory and warehouse at Binondo. The Manila galleon was still plying its trade and the islands remained dependent on Mexican silver. Yet a sense of economic and political renewal was already in the air.[41] Life was no longer to be spent waiting for the galleon between its sailing in June and its uncertain return, punctutated only by the annual arrival of Chinese junks in March.

In 1887 Manila had 157,062 inhabitants. As the end of the nineteenth century approached, Manila was the third city of the Spanish world, after Havana and Barcelona. In *El filibusterismo* of 1891, José Rizal contrasted the old city within the walls, 'the home of presumptuous nullity', with the suburbs.[42] The booming market in China for the tobacco, coffee, sugar, foodstuffs (especially rice but also such high-value specialities as sea cucumber, sharks' fins and birds' nests), exotic woods and rope fibres from the Philippines had stimulated the economy. The bourgeoisie had broken into the Chinese opium trade.[43] Businesses connected with the development of infrastructure were thriving: the Compañía General de Tabacos de Filipinas; the shipping companies; Pinillos Izquierdo y Cía.; the railroads; the electric light provider, Sociedad de Luz Eléctrica. The Azucarera La Carlota was big in sugar; as was the Luis Garriga Company in the export of rope-work, Hermanos Borri y Escolta in food exports and the Compañía de Colonización de Mindanao, formed by a group of forestry engineers in 1889, in the exploitation of forest products.

Roads and Road Bridges

As in Spain, a road-building frenzy hit the overseas colonies even at the height of the railway craze, which proved more complementary than competitive. One of the first priorities for the Commission for Development (Junta de Fomento), formed in Cuba in 1834 to mobilize private sector investment in exchange for alienated revenues and tolls, was to extend the road network. The sugar boom, which mobilized dubiously qualified technicians, landowners, convict labourers, slaves and wage-earners in a common endeavour, created the opportunity. In 1830 free Blacks were given the option of compounding for debts or crimes by working on the roads. Fears ensued that these dangerous gangs might have an evil influence on peasants and slaves by drawing them into vagrancy.

A problem that defied solution was the lack of plans for the maintenance of public works in general and of roads in particular. In 1831 Rafael Quesada, the chief surveyor to the Board of Agriculture (Junta de Agricultura), observed that 'while we persist in the folly of not thinking beyond today, there will never be an adequate transport system, and one might as well bury treasure in the fields.'[44] José Antonio Saco, the eloquent Cuban statesman, learned one thing from John McAdam, the Scot who invented macadamization: water undermines roads. But the method of construction Saco recommended failed to reflect McAdam's principles: Saco thought roads should be elevated above grade, with gutters alongside to drain the water away.[45] Debate in Cuba over whether to use aggregate or blocks, and of what dimensions, for road building became almost as intense as between partisans and critics of railroads or of independence versus autonomy (of whom Saco was one).[46]

As a road-builder, in partial consequence, the development commission was a failure. Critics complained that it had achieved only 2 leagues of new roads at a cost of 3 million pesos in 36 years. The railways, as we shall see, set the pace in subsequent decades. In 1856 new 'Ordinances for the conservation and regulation of roads' appeared but, as Captain General José Gutiérrez de la Concha noted with evident annoyance in 1850, resistance to innovation was palpable. The need to surface a road, he pointed out, should not cause stupefaction in those responsible.

The situation had improved by 1865. The royal highway across the island stretched 1,450 kilometres (900 mi.), east to west from Baracoa to Mantua. In the best stretches it was as much as 10 metres (33 ft) wide. In others, according to critics, it looked more like a cattle track than a proper road. Secondary roads branched from it to settlements all over the island, but most roads were local – about 80 per cent of the total. The sugar barons' private interests, which rarely served any other constituencies' interests, determined the routes. Floods, bad weather and construction failures impeded them. As stone became increasingly common for bridge building, costs and technical complexities multiplied. Albear approved wood as the material for new bridges at Bacuranao (1848) and Las Vegas (1853). For the Bridge of Alcoy, over the Luyanó River in Havana, the civil engineer in charge, the Frenchman Jules Sagebien, who was seconded to the army corps of engineers first as a subaltern and then as a volunteer, decided on a wooden superstructure of low arches on stone pillars to support the greatest possible width. He also built the clock tower of the church Guanabacoa, and in Havana, where he ultimately settled with his Canarian wife and ten children, he built the seafront warehouses of Casa Blanca in 1848. Ten years later he built the metereological observatory and in 1861 was in charge of the building of the Tacón Theatre. The sickness of one of his children obliged him to return to France, where he reputedly pined away in nostalgia for Havana.

Matanzas, where Sagebien spent much of his time, is known as the city of two bridges ('la ciudad de los puentes'). Two rivers, the San Juan and the Yumurí, surround the town centre and flow into the bay.[47] When the sugar harvest was in, Matanzas was the second busiest port on the island and the precious product had to be carried at peril through fords in saddlebags and buckboards. At a spot aptly called 'El tumbadero' ('the tumbler'), on the Canímar River, Sagebien proposed a stone bridge. The San Luis River acquired a wooden-superstructured bridge on stone pilings, like so many colonial examples. In 1849 an iron, three-arch bridge for Bailén was designed by the captain of engineers, Carlos Benítez. To fix the stone supports he devised a six-horsepower steam hammer. Despite his acquaintance with iron bridges he did not generally recommend them in Cuba because of high costs and exposure to corrosion. He favoured a combination of stone supports, sound wooden superstructures, and iron for the railings, especially as maintenance was so hard to arrange: 'In France and England maintenance costs begin on the day construction ends – which is why the bridges remain as new. We neither maintain nor restore them.'[48] Not even the most rigorous maintenance routines in the world would have saved his beloved bridge at Bailén in 1870, when a terrible hurricane destroyed it.

Not far away, in Puerto Rico, the influence of Cuban experience was irresistible and the effects of the sugar boom evident: around 1850, the island had 257 water-driven sugar mills and 211 operated by oxen.[49] The improvement of the road sytem was a primary objective. Among engineers posted to Puerto Rico the Navarrese Evaristo Churruca was noteworthy. He served as inspector general from 1870, and attracted fame as the designer of Bilbao's celebrated suspension bridge. He arrived in 1867 among sixteen new appointees, of whom eight went to Cuba and five to the Philippines.[50] He built bridges at Bayamón, Caguas and Mayagüez and restored many of the buildings toppled in the earthquake of 1867, including the churches of Guayama and Humacao. He proposed the lighthouse of El Morro de San Juan and produced a plan for improving the harbour. Also commendable was Miguel Martínez de Campos y Antón, born in Madrid in 1839 and top of the graduation class of 1860, who drew up plans for a range of projects for harbour improvement, highways and local roads, and bridges of iron and wood.

In 1891 the engineer Eduardo Cabello reckoned that the island had 235 kilometres (146 mi.) of highway 'in a reasonable state of repair' and a further 54 kilometres (33½ mi.) under construction. In 1897 Baldomero Donnet was less sanguine. Shortage of money, materials and manpower, exacerbated by torrential rains, had restricted the

road-building programme. Of a proposed 880 kilometres (547 mi.) only
230 of them (143 mi.) were complete, and 30 kilometres (18½ mi.)
more were under construction. His solution was to settle for hard earth
road surfaces, supplemented with cheap narrow-gauge railways. In
1898 the central highway led 134 kilometres (83 mi.) across the island
from north to south, from San Juan almost as far as Ponce, via Río
Piedras, Caguas, Cayey, Aibonito, Coamo and Juana Díaz. A final
section between Arecibo and Ponce awaited completion. Remarkable
viaducts included those at Aguadilla, on the way from Utuado to
Arecibo, 36 metres (118 ft) long, and at Arecibo, of 45 metres (148 ft).
Both were the work of the civil engineer José María Sáinz.

Roads in the Philippines

In the 7,000 islands of the Philippines, rushing rivers, precipitate
mountains, typhoons, tropical rains and the occasional earthquake
made road building no less problematical. Cabotage and river travel
were the obvious recourse in regions that were short of capital, manpower and materials for roads and where horseflesh was rare and
demand for transport wavering and seasonal. Plans for roads arose
from time to time: general schemes in 1868, 1875 and 1897, and another
designed specifically to help administrators and clergy to get about.

Public works strained finances. In 1869 import duties on construction materials, including iron and dredging equipment, were abolished.
Engineers tried to eliminate or circumvent the costly bureaucratic
enquiries that delayed work and raised expectations, as at Bucay in
1880, when commissioners kept forty workmen, two foremen and two
native scouts idle for four months at local expense without coming to a
decision about the route of a projected road. Work – whether by public
authorities or contractors – had to be paid from the public purse
because offers of tolls failed to attract investors. Traffic was insufficient
or unpredictable. Railway technology had an adverse effect on road
building. The architect Genaro Palacios recommended rail as the basis
for internal communications. Rails cost 25,000 pesos per kilometre
and roads only 14,000, but railroads offered private investors a prospect of return. In the interstices of the rail system, Palacios suggested,
provincial and local authorities could provide basic roads.

Even as late as 1897, on Luzón there were only three roads designated as first-class – that is, fully surfaced, properly drained, decently

maintained and reasonably wide. The first united Manila with Laoag, 545 kilometres (338 mi.) to the west. The others led to Aparri, 565 kilometres (351 mi.) away, in the north, and Albay, 486 kilometres (301 mi.) to the south. Of second-class roads, the example that stretched over 44 kilometres (27 mi.) in the east of the island to Morong, attracted general approval. Local roads bore only two-wheeled vehicles and tended to be unusable during rains. A plan was under consideration to extend the road system northwards for 70 kilometres (43 mi.) from Dagupan to Baguío via the Benguet Valley, with the aim of cutting the laborious journey of three days on horseback to seven or eight hours, but the surveyors in charge, José Cavestany and José Herbella Zóbel, were captured by insurgents on 3 September 1898. The U.S. administration, which classed 1,596 kilometres (992 mi.) of roads in the Philippines as first-class, took over and completed the project.[51]

Meanwhile, conditions such as the remoteness of the colony and its relative unattractiveness to investors slowed the transition from military to civil personnel. The effects on bridge-building were notable. Of 124 projects in the Philippines during the nineteenth century, only 14 were executed by civil engineers.[52] Newly arrived specialists, trained in civilian schools, tended to think of stone, brick or iron for bridges, but the cheap option the army favoured – wooden superstructures on stone supports – generally prevailed. The availability of hard tropical timber made truss bridges the commonest form: 'ugly but solid' ('feo, pero sólido') was said of the example built with four struts at Tabucán by a civil engineer, Damián Quero, in 1876. In 1855 the military engineer Nicolás Fernández, who had served in Puerto Rico, proposed to span the Pasig at Manila with tubular iron trusses, 75 metres (246 ft) long and perched on decorative neo-medieval supports, with a supplementary swing bridge. The project received the official go-ahead in 1860 but was abandoned after a severe earthquake three years later. Suspension bridges, with steel cables and flat causeways, began to appear. The model was the toll bridge over the Pasig between Quiapo and Arroceros, opened with much fanfare on 4 January 1852: it was 110 metres (361 ft) long and 7 metres (23 ft) wide. Also over the Pasig was the wooden bridge in two sections made by a civilian, Eduardo López Navarro, in 1863. Known as the Puente de la Convalescencia, it collapsed in 1890. The swing bridge called the Puente de España, designed by Casto Olano and opened in 1876, proved more durable, built of struts and trusses of varying lengths and supported by piles.

Railways

Governor Miguel Tacón, who ran Cuba from 1834 to 1852, was no railway enthusiast, dismissing what he thought was a faddish mode of transport. But the railway age was irresistible. As early as 1831, bullfights vacated the main square of Havana to make room for a railway station, housing a small locomotive that took passengers for joy-rides around the square.[53] The promoters hoped to make money from what was no more than a piece of showmanship, but they were aware that their technology had wider potential applications.

The previous year a commission had reviewed the possibility of laying a railroad from Manila to Güines and along the coast to Matanzas.[54] Two years later plans for the first line were in place, retracing the route of a canal proposed in 1801 by military engineers Félix and Francisco Lemaur. The promoters raised a loan in London at 6 per cent in 1834. They bought rails and engines modelled on Stephenson's *Rocket* and laid the lines over gravel beds 15 centimetres (6 in.) deep and sleepers made not of wood but of leather at intervals of 3.6 metres (12 ft). On the queen's saint's day in 1837 the stretch from Havana to Bejucal was declared open. The rest, as far as Güines, 45 kilometres (30 mi.) away, followed the year after. The new facility cut the cost of transporting sugar by 70 per cent. Competition from beet sugar, which already accounted for 10 per cent of global production, was an irresistible stimulus.

With military engineers Francisco Lemaur and Manuel Pastor as advisors, a Rail Commission (Junta de Caminos de Hierro), composed of members of the chamber of commerce and the city council, set about planning a network. The gauge was fixed at 1,435 metres (4,708 ft), though there were apparently arbitrary exceptions. Specialists were hired from the United States: Alfred Kruger and the father-and-son team, Benjamin Wright and Benjamn Jr. In 1839 a second, 28-kilometre (17 mi.) stretch opened via Cárdenas as far as Montalvo, under the direction of engineer Manuel José de Carrerá y Heredia, whose father, a veteran of the wars of independence, had retired to Cuba after surrendering to Venezuelan rebels in 1823. Carrerá became the controller of the Sabanilla line in 1850, and designed many of the installations that graced Cuba's railways, including the station at Matanzas, halts and shelters for passengers in styles ranging from neoclassical through neogothic to mock-oriental, and stores, postboxes, signalmen's huts, cabins for crossing-keepers, workshops, offices and lodgings for operatives.[55]

The needs and siting of sugar mills meant that rail lines tended to run parallel to rivers, often requiring transport by cabotage from river mouth to port. Passenger traffic was slight at first. In 1842 the Development Commission of Cuba sold the system to a consortium of sugar-owners, the Havana Railroad Company (compañía de caminos de hierro de La Habana). Trains and canes were perfect partners. But the next development took the lines beyond the existing sugar-producing area towards a new frontier of settlement: the Júcaro line, 50 kilometres (31 mi.) long, planned by the celebrated Alfred Cruger, began operations in 1844 and opened up Cárdenas for sugar planting. A line between the copper mines at Santiago del Prado and a loading quay at the port of Santiago de Cuba started up in the same year. Sagebien's design included a rotating loading system, in which trucks full of copper were emptied and then filled with machinery, coal or tools for transport elsewhere. Draught animals worked the mechanism. By 1851, when the United States bought up half the island's sugar, 558 kilometres (347 mi.) of railroad were in place. That extent had doubled by 1868, under 21 operating companies (the operators of the Cárdenas and Júcaro lines merged in 1853 to eliminate competition).

Ten years of war against the insurrectionists from 1868 to 1878 delayed development of the railways, but in the following twenty years 532 kilometres (330 mi.) were added. The system remained, however, a patchwork of disconnected parts, perhaps because hostile landowners and the interests of navigation companies combined to frustrate the construction of a central, connecting railroad across the island. The army's was the strongest voice in favour of the project, yet it did not prove powerful enough.

For Puerto Rico in 1874 the colonial ministry ordered a study of the prospects of a coastal railway to link the urban centres to areas of production of coffee, tobacco and sugar. The mountainous interior was left out of account. Three years later Leonardo de Tejada, a civil engineer, completed a preliminary survey and the project was put out to tender. But little interest ensued and the first section, 10 kilometres (6 mi.) long in the west of the island, was not opened until 1881. In 1891, 73 kilometres (45 mi.) of track were laid between Martín Peña and Arecibo. Seven years later, 240 kilometres (149 mi.) were in operation, with a further 12 kilometres (7 mi.) under construction and 217 kilometres (135 mi.) at the planning stage.

In the Philippines, where, in 1875, Eduardo López Navarro drew up a scheme for a railway system in Luzón, official dispositions in favour of railways prompted a British-led consortium, Barry, Brenon and Peralta, to come up with a scheme, with demands for guarantees that competition would be fairly adjudged and concessions granted for a long term.[56] They envisaged 1,730 kilometres (1,075 mi.) of track would be laid. In 1885 the British Manila Railway Company began work on a line from Manila to Dagupan with a 99-year concession and a government guarantee of a return of 8 per cent per annum. At almost 7.9 million pesos, the final costs exceeded the budget by 63 per cent. The railroad opened in 1892, with a truss bridge on iron supports, at Pampanga. The objective was not so much to carry passengers as to facilitate access to Manila for regional produce, especially rice and sugar, but passenger services made a significant contribution, with four classes of accommodation. Profits were divided fifty–fifty between the company and the treasury. Shortly afterwards an entrepreneur, Jacobo Zóbel, joined the engineer Luciano Bremon and Adolfo Bayo, a banker, in the Transit Company of the Philippines (Compañía de tranvías de Filipinas) to build 16 kilometres (10 mi.) of track connecting Manila with Malabón in the north.[57] The network spread, taking in mining concessions and, in Mindanao, a line reserved for military purposes.

Telegraph lines multiplied alongside the railways. Spain got its first telegraph line in 1852 and the following year the military engineer Manuel Portillo erected Cuba's first from Havana to Batabanó; he also started a school of telegraphy and fixed the charges for sending messages. The Philippines, as we have noted, had a semaphore system from 1836, when José María Peñaranda, governor of Albay and veteran of campaigns against Muslim pirates, established a system of signals among the forts that defended his province against the 'Moors' of Masbate. Governments in Madrid regarded it as a priority to link the archipelago to Spain by cable. The only practical route was via Hong Kong. Beginning in 1869 the lines were strung from Manila to Punta Santiago and Cape Bolinao. A telegraphy school opened in 1872 and by 1876 more than 1,000 kilometres (621 mi.) of wires were in place. The international connection went out to public tender, and British competitors won.[58] On 2 May 1880, the first cable from the Philippines reached Spain. The text conveyed to King Alfonso XII the salutations of his 6 million Filipino subjects 'with love, loyalty, and reverence' ('con amor, lealtad y veneración').

Harbours and Lighthouses

In 1882 a typhoon wrenched the lighthouse of San Nicolás from its perch on the island of Corregidor, in Manila Bay, into the sea, with the loss of the adjoining keepers' house and its thirteen denizens. It had been built only six years previously by civil engineer José Echevarría using the latest design from Europe: a metal frame secured to the ground by pinions. The method served in Cádiz or Corunna, but not in volcanic environments or on shifting sands.[59] On perilous coasts, where navigation was tricky and landmarks unfamiliar, the need to work at improving harbour access, building quays and erecting lighthouses was unremitting.

From 1845, Havana had the benefit of a jetty, about 140 metres (460 ft) long, built by military engineer Juan María Muñoz and supported with a double row of piles on the sharp slope to the shore. A wall and a platform with mooring rings completed the work. Seven more piers followed. Matanzas, where from 1819 a steam service operated to Havana every Thursday, with return the following Sunday, was screened by a sand bar that obliged ships to anchor in the middle of the bay. In 1848 military engineers Carlos Benítez and José Pérez Malo solved the problem with a mechanical dredger of their own design. Benítez proposed, in addition, an artifical harbour between two huge sea walls. New moles appeared at Casilda, Jagua Bay and other spots along the coast.

In the Philippines a Public Works Commission (Junta de Obras) was established for the port of Manila in 1880, making possible the enlargement of formerly cramped facilities by the addition of a new outer harbour. In 1883, thanks to the indefatigability of Eduardo López Navarro, whose repeated spells of service made him the most accomplished engineer in the islands in the last decades of the century, the work was finished, with the opening of a sheltered anchorage 2 kilometres (just over a mile) to the south of the mouth of the Pasig, and an additional protective sea wall 335 metres (1,100 ft) long, rising 4.5 metres (14½ ft) above sea level. Summoning every available man and machine to the task, another civil engineer, José

García Morón, replaced the stone flanges with blocks of absorbent masonry compound.

López Navarro's speciality was lighthouses. Harbours were of little use without lights to guide ships to them. The approach to Manila was enhanced by a light at San Nicolás. In 1846 the Trade Commission (Junta de Comercio) commissioned a lighthouse on the north bank of the Pasig estuary, with a stout, tapering tower (which survived earthquakes in 1852 and 1863). The adjoining dwelling housed a keeper and family 'habituated to obedience and discipline' ('acostumbrada a la obediencia y la disciplina') – usually old soldiers or seamen.[60] Eight lamps of English manufacture kept the light burning, backed with parabolic reflectors and 560 mirrors. The fear that approaching vessels would misidentify shore lights of various kinds remained constant until Fresnel lenses replaced the reflectors. In 1868 López Navarro improved the Pasig estuary lighthouse by enlarging the upper chamber and installing a lighting system designed by the Parisian firm of Barbier, Bernard & Turenne, with three lamps and an eight-sided lantern under a copper cover. Operating from 1870, it could send a beam out over a distance of between 14 and 16 kilometres (9–10 mi.), at 16.25 metres (53 ft) above sea level. Other similar establishments could be seen in the Philippines. In Luzón, on the Isle of Cabra, 72 kilometres (45 mi.) southwest of Manila Bay, a giratory lighthouse began emitting its beam on the night of 1–2 May 1889, using a mercury bath to lubricate the rotation. At Melville, on the Joló sea, civil engineer Guillermo Brockman designed a similar structure on an octagonal stone tower. In 1893 Baldomero Donnet drew up a meticulous survey: he counted nineteen lighthouse and fifteen harbour lights in the Philippines, with two more under construction.

What Filipinos call typhoons are hurricanes in Havana. A perfectly cylindrical tower, such as that built at the fort of El Morro at Havana in 1845, was best for resistance to wind. Military engineer José Benítez chose that form for the Colón Lighthouse, 51.8 metres (170 ft) tall and equipped with Fresnel lenses, alongside the treacherous Bahama Channel. In 1868 Cuba had twelve working lighthouses and in 1876 a plan for studding the entire coast with light was approved. On Puerto Rico, meanwhile, the entrance to the harbour of San Juan acquired a lighthouse in 1846. Thirty years later Evaristo Churruca's last project there was to replace it with a new, Fresnel-equipped facility.

A Forest Coda

On 17 April 1917, a mail steamer bound for the Philippines from Cádiz struck a mine off Cape Town and sank with its seventy passengers and one hundred crew. The choice of route in preference to the Suez Canal had been made precisely in order to elude the fortunes of war. Among the victims was the Sevillan explorer, geologist, ethnographer, cartographer and – by training – mining engineer Enrique D'Almonte y Muriel, who had done more than any other individual to map the Spanish Empire. He was on his way to Manila, ostensibly to complete his work on the lands and peoples of the East Indies. The likelihood is that he was on a secret mission. No one was better fitted for one. As a fellow explorer, Emilio Bonelli, remarked, D'Almonte could remember every name and resist every hardship.[61] He had lived in the Philippines from 1880 to 1898 and in Guinea from 1900 to 1912. He spent two further years in Western Sahara. His experience in Spain's colony at Río Muni led him to propose a railway across the continent from the river mouth at Puerto Iradier to the Indian Ocean. He took part in negotiating boundaries with neighbouring European colonies, challenging the Germans in Cameroon on every point. He insisted on the importance of the value of the forests of the drainage area of the Muni as part of an overall vision of the Spanish Empire, anticipating what became official policy in the 1920s. In 1900 a frontier treaty with France seemed to set the seal on Spain's claims in the region, which a naval expedition had first affirmed in 1858.[62]

D'Almonte's fame – deserved on his merits but enhanced by his mysterious death – exceeded that of the predecessor who influenced him profoundly: Sebastián Vidal y Soler, a forestry engineer from Barcelona. Vidal arrived in the Philippines in 1872 as inspector general of the Bureau of Forestry, founded in 1863, and head of the Plants and Forests Statistical Commission (Comisión de Flora y Estadística Forestal), which collected 2,060 specimens and ran the botanical garden of Manila. In the following decade, when his malaria permitted, Vidal undertook studies in Mindanao. He wrote a handbook for the forestry service. A colleague, Ramón Jordana, was the author of a report on the produce of publicly owned forests (*Memoria sobre la producción de los montes públicos de Filipinas*).

Their careers captured an epoch of transition from the old regime, in which functionaries ruled the forests, to the new, in which engineers held sway. Rejecting Edenic notions of tropical nature, Vidal and Jordana adopted a scientific approach to the investigation, delimitation, exploitation and conservation of forest resources.[63] They reckoned that of the 19 million hectares (46.95 million ac.) of forest in the Philippines, exploitable resources covered 9 million (22.2 million ac.). They believed that the prospects were far better than in Cuba, where the demands of timber and sugar production had been devastating, but they found plenty of evidence of levels of destruction that they deemed dangerous. 'The forest never fully recovers from swidden cultivation,' opined Vidal, referring to the slash-and-burn technique that prevailed in pre-colonial times. His death in Manila in 1898 was a great loss.[64]

His judgement on the Cuban situation was accurate. In 1852, 40 per cent of the island was covered in forest; in 1923 the corresponding figure was 16 per cent. Timber had gone for fuel in sugar refineries – 'fell and clear', as the practice was called – or left for the cutters to harvest for their own benefit ('fell and leave'). Ramón de la Sagra – the wealthy anarchist who was also an accomplished botanist and one of the island's most admired intellectuals – spoke of the sugar business as 'cultivation by rapine' ('cultivo de rapiña'). In 1859 a son of local landowners, Francisco de Paula Portuondo, became the first Cuban graduate in forestry engineering. Conservation measures introduced in 1876 had scant effect. 'Everything remains to be done,' was the unquestionable judgement of an official report.[65]

Everything remained to be done in environmental conservation, and much in almost every other respect. Yet, over the entire range of infrastructure throughout the Spanish global monarchy, a great deal had been accomplished. The measure of the state's priorities and the engineers' efforts is the long list of public works, distributed throughout the foregoing pages, serving the peace, civilization, health, sustenance, defence, settlement, communications, productivity, evangelization and commerce of the subject communities that constituted the empire. Spaniards often compared themselves unfavourably as imperialists with the Romans on whom they modelled their policies and whose emphasis on engineering they echoed. Rome's empire lasted, by most methods of reckoning, for a thousand years longer than Spain's. But if one allows for the acceleration of change, it was no discreditable achievement to keep so vast and diverse an empire going for so long in the unpropitious circumstances of the modern world. Would it have been possible without the investment in public well-being that infrastructure represented, or without the allegiance which that investment bought from key communities and collaborative elites?

REFERENCES

All translations of foreign-language sources into English are by the authors,
unless otherwise stated.

Introduction: Making Empire Work

1 Percy B. Shelley, 'Ozymandias', *Poetry Foundation*, 1817, available at www. poetryfoundation.org, accessed 7 May 2020.
2 James Bieri, *Percy Bysshe Shelley, a Biography: Exile of Unfulfilled Renown, 1816–1822* (Newark, NJ, 2005), pp. 55ff.
3 Angela Miller, 'Thomas Cole and Jacksonian America: The Course of Empire as Political Allegory', *Prospects*, XIV (1989), pp. 65–92; Louis L. Noble, *The Course of Empire: Voyage of Life, and Other Pictures of Thomas Cole*, NA (New York, 1853), pp. 177–8.
4 F. Fernández-Armesto, *Civilizations* (London, 2004), p. viii.
5 Karl Wittfogel, *Oriental Despotism: Comparative Study of Total Power* (New York, 1957); K. W. Butzer, *Early Hydraulic Civilization in Egypt* (Chicago, IL, 1956).
6 J. B. Pritchard, ed., *Ancient Near Eastern Texts Relating to the Old Testament* (Princeton, NJ, 1969), p. 409.
7 Stanley D. Walters, *Water for Larsa* (New Haven, CT, 1970), pp. 33–5.
8 Sabine MacCormack, *On the Wings of Time: Rome, the Incas, Spain and Peru* (Princeton, NJ, 2007), pp. 5–12 and 274; Anthony Grafton et al., *New Worlds, Ancient Texts: The Power of Tradition and the Shock of Discovery* (Cambridge, 1995); John H. Elliott, *El viejo mundo y el nuevo (1492–1650)* (Madrid, 1990), pp. 21–7.
9 John Peter Oleson, ed., *Building for Eternity: The History and Technology of Roman Concrete Engineering in the Sea* (Oxford, 2014); Mathias Döring, *Römische Häfen, Aquädukte und Zisternen in Kampanien:*

Bestandsaufnahme der antiken Wasserbauten (Darmstadt, 2007).
10 John Peter Oleson, ed., *The Oxford Handbook of Engineering and Technology in the Classical World* (Oxford, 2008), pp. 1–9.
11 Justine Christianson and Christopher H. Marston, eds, *Covered Bridges and the Birth of American Engineering* (Washington, DC, 2015); Jessica B. Teisch, *Engineering Nature: Water, Development, and the Global Spread of American Environmental Expertise* (Chapel Hill, NC, 2011).
12 Pierre Chaunu, 'Les routes espagnoles de l'Atlantique', *Anuario de estudios americanos*, XXV (1968), pp. 95–128.
13 F. Fernández-Armesto, *Millennium* (London, 1995), p. 228.
14 C. Verlinden, *Koloniale Expansie in de 15de en 16de Eeuw* (Bussum, 1975), pp. 35ff.
15 Guillaume Gaudin and Pilar Ponce Leiva, 'Introduction au dossier: El factor distancia en la flexibilidad y el cumplimiento de la normativa en la América Ibérica', *Les Cahiers de Framespa*, XXX (2019), pp. 1–10.
16 R. Hakluyt, *Discourse of Western Planting*, ed. D. B. and A. M. Quinn (London, 1993).
17 C. R. Boxer, 'Piet Heyn and the Silver Fleet', *History Today*, XIII/6 (June 1963), pp. 398–446.
18 Helen Rawlings, *The Debate on the Decline of Spain* (Manchester, 2012).
19 H. Kamen, *Spain in the Later Seventeenth Century* (London, 1980), pp. 67–105.
20 P. Hämäläinen, *The Comanche Empire* (New Haven, CT, 2008); S. Ortelli, *Trama de una gurerra inconveniente: Nueva Vizcaya y la sombra de los apaches (1748–90)* (Mexico City,

2007); F. Fernández-Armesto, *Our America* (New York, 2014), pp. 65–9.

21 Thomas E. Chávez, *A Moment in Time: The Odyssey of New Mexico's Segesser Hide Paintings* (Albuquerque, NM, 2012).

22 John L. Kessell, *Mission of Sorrows: Jesuit Guevavi and the Pimas* (Tucson, AZ, 1970).

23 M. A. Goldberg, *Conquering Sickness* (Lincoln, NE, 2016); D. Weber, *The Spanish Frontier in North America* (New Haven, CT, 1992), p. 341.

24 Fernández-Armesto, *Millennium*, p. 192.

25 Weber, *The Spanish Frontier in North America*, pp. 228–9.

26 Ibid., pp. 300–304.

27 D. Monroy, *Thrown among Strangers* (Berkeley, CA, 1993), p. 21.

28 Thomas E. Chávez, *Spain and the Independence of the United States* (Albuquerque, NM, 2002), p. 32; Gabriel Paquette and Gonzalo M. Quintero Saravia, eds, *Spain and the American Revolution: New Approaches and Perspectives* (New York, 2020), pp. 7–11.

29 Diego Barros Arana, *Historia general de Chile*, vol. VII (Santiago, 2001), p. 51.

30 Gwyn A. Williams, *Madoc: The Making of a Myth* (Oxford, 1979), p. 146.

31 F. Fernández-Armesto, 'Inglaterra y el Atlántico en la Baja Edad Media', in *Canarias e Inglaterra a través de los siglos*, ed. A. Bethencourt Massieu (Las Palmas, 1995), pp. 11–28.

32 Mary W. Helms, *Ulysses' Sail: An Ethnographic Odyssey of Power, Knowledge and Geographical Distance* (Princeton, NJ, 1988), pp. 131–71.

33 F. Fernández-Armesto, 'The Stranger-Effect in Early Modern Asia', *Itinerario*, 24 (2000), pp. 80–103.

34 G. Fernández de Oviedo, *Historia general y natural de las Indias*, Bk V, ch. 3.

35 Ian Caldwell and David Henley, 'The Stranger Who Would Be King', *Indonesia and the Malay World*, XXVI (2008), pp. 163–75.

36 Federico Navarrete, *Historias mexicas* (Mexico City, 2018), pp. 223–9.

37 F. Salomon and G. L. Urioste, eds, *Huarochirí Manuscript: A Testament of Ancient*

and Colonial Andean Religion* (Albuquerque, NM, 1991).

38 M. Restall, *Maya Conquistador* (Boston, MA, 1998), pp. 144ff.

39 Geoffrey McCafferty, 'The Cholula Massacre: Factional Histories and Archaeology of the Spanish Conquest', in *The Entangled Past: Integrating History and Archaeology*, ed. M. Boyd et al. (Calgary, 2000), pp. 347–59.

40 Gregorio Mora-Torres, ed., *Californio Voices: The Oral Memoirs of José María Amador and Lorenzo Asisara* (College Station, TX, 2011), p. 63.

41 R. Alan Covey, *How the Incas Built Their Heartland* (Ann Arbor, MI, 2011), p. 63.

42 Kenneth R. Wright, Jonathan M. Kelly and Alfredo Valencia Zegarra, 'Machu Picchu: Ancient Hydraulic Engineering', *Journal of Hydraulic Engineering*, CXXIII (1997), pp. 838–43.

43 J. Hyslop, *The Inka Road System* (New York, 1984); C. Morris and D. E. Thompson, 'Huanuco Viejo: An Inca Administrative Center', *American Antiquity*, XXXV (1970), pp. 344–62.

44 Pablo Alzola y Minondo, *Las obras públicas en España: estudio histórico* (Bilbao, 1899), p. 597; Manuel Díaz-Marta, 'La ingeniería hidráulica española en América', *Cuatro conferencias sobre historia de la ingeniería de obras públicas en España* (Madrid, 1987), pp. 109–48; Nicolás García Tapia, *Del dios del fuego a la máquina de vapor: la introducción de la técnica industrial en Hispanoamérica* (Valladolid, 1992), p. 64; Ignacio González Tascón, *Ingeniería española en ultramar, siglos XVI–XIX*, 2 vols (Madrid, 1992), p. 748; Ramón María Serrera Contreras, *Tráfico terrestre y red vial en las Indias españolas* (Barcelona, 1992), p. 335; Luis García Ballester, ed., *Historia de la ciencia y de la técnica en la corona de Castilla*, 4 vols (Valladolid, 2002); Manuel Silva Suárez, ed., *Técnica e ingeniería en España*, 9 vols (Zaragoza, 2004–19); María Antonia Colomar and Ignacio Sánchez de Mora, *Cuatro siglos de ingeniería española. siglos XVI–XIX* (Madrid, 2019): Biblioteca virtual 'La

ciencia y la técnica en la empresa americana', Fundación Ignacio Larramendi-DIGIBIS, presentación de Xavier Agenjo Bullón, www.larramendi.es.

45 Gaspar Pérez de Villagrá, *Historia de la Nueva México*, ed. M. Encinias et al. (Albuquerque, NM, 1992), pp. 124–6.

46 Rodolfo Segovia, *El lago de piedra: la geopolítica de las fortificaciones españolas del Caribe* (Bogotá, 2006), pp. 11–13.

1 Enter the Engineers: Amateurs and Professionals in the Making of Infrastructure

1 Vicente Casals, *Los ingenieros de montes en la España contemporánea (1848–1936)* (Barcelona, 1996), p. 7.

2 Quoted in Horacio Capel, 'Remediar con el arte los defectos de la naturaleza. La capacitación técnica del cuerpo de ingenieros militares y su intervención en obras públicas', *Antiguas obras hidráulicas en América. Actas del Seminario de México, 1988* (Madrid, 1991), pp. 508–11.

3 Clarence Glacken, *Traces on the Rhodian Shore: Nature and Culture in Western Thought from Ancient Times to the End of the Eighteenth Century* (Berkeley, CA, 1990), pp. 461–2.

4 Francisco de Ajofrín, *Diario del viaje que por orden de la sagrada congregación de Propaganda Fide hizo a la América septentrional en el siglo XVIII* (Madrid, 1958), vol. I, pp. 75–6.

5 Niall Ferguson, *Empire: How Britain Made the Modern World* (London, 2007), p. 1.

6 John Darwin, *El sueño del imperio. Auge y caída de las potencias globales, 1400–2000* (Madrid, 2012), p. 53.

7 Mark Elvin, *The Pattern of the Chinese Past* (Stanford, CA, 1973), pp. 298–315.

8 Ferguson, *Empire*, pp. 1–2.

9 Guillermo Céspedes del Castillo, *América hispánica (1492–1898)* (Barcelona, 1983), p. 60.

10 Nicolás García Tapia, *Ingeniería y arquitectura en el renacimiento español* (Valladolid, 1990), pp. 46–53.

11 Alicia Cámara Muñoz, 'La profesión de ingeniero', in *El renacimiento. Técnica e ingeniería en España*, ed. Manuel Silva (Zaragoza, 2004), pp. 158–61.

12 Nicolás García Tapia, 'La fábrica del sitio', in *Madrid, ciencia y corte*, ed. Antonio Lafuente and Javier Moscoso (Madrid, 1999), p. 80.

13 Jose Manuel Lucía Mejías, 'Un personaje llamado Miguel de Cervantes: una lectura crítica de la documentación observada', *Cuadernos AISPI*, V (2015), pp. 24–5.

14 Miguel de Cervantes Saavedra, *El celoso extremeño*, ed. Florencio Sevilla (Alicante, 2001), p. 138.

15 Alicia Cámara Muñoz, 'La profesión de ingeniero. Los ingenieros del rey', in *Técnica e ingeniería en España*, vol. I: *El Renacimiento* (Zaragoza, 2004), p. 134.

16 Juan Agapito y Revilla, *Los abastecimientos de aguas de Valladolid* (Valladolid, 1907), p. 23.

17 Alicia Cámara Muñoz, *Fortificación y ciudad en los reinos de Felipe II* (Madrid, 1998), p. 128.

18 José Vicente Rodríguez, 'Mariano Azzaro de Clementis', *Diccionario biográfico español*, Real academia de la historia, http://dbe.rah.es/biografias/19482/mariano-azzaro-de-clementis, accessed 30 May 2020.

19 Juan Miguel Muñoz Corbalán, *Los ingenieros militares de Flandes a España (1691–1718)* (Madrid, 1993), pp. ii and 153.

20 Bernal Diaz Del Castillo, *Historia verdadera de la conquista de Nueva España* (Madrid, 1984), p. 103.

21 Manuel Lucena Giraldo, *A los cuatro vientos. Las ciudades de la América Hispánica* (Madrid, 2006), p. 93.

22 María Luisa Laviana Cuetos, *Guayaquil en el siglo XVIII. Recursos naturales y desarrollo económico* (Seville, 1984), p. 261.

23 Bernabé Cobo, *Historia del Nuevo Mundo* (Madrid, 1964), pp. i and 121.

24 Alexander von Humboldt, *Ensayo político sobre el reino de la Nueva España* (Paris, 1836), pp. v and 166.

25 Alfredo Castillero Calvo, *La vivienda colonial en Panama* (Panama City, 1994), pp. 134–5.

26 Vicenta Cortés Alonso, 'Tunja y sus vecinos', *Revista de Indias*, XXV (1965), pp. 99–160.

27 Francisco de Solano, *Cuestionarios para la formación de las relaciones geográficas de Indias, siglos* XVI–XIX (Madrid, 1988), pp. 99–111.

28 Manuel Lucena Giraldo, 'Defensa del territorio y conservación forestal en la Guayana (1758–1793)', in *El Bosque Ilustrado. Estudios sobre la Política Forestal Española en América* (Madrid, 1991), p. 144.

29 Ignacio González Tascón, *Ingeniería española en ultramar, siglos* XVI–XIX (Madrid, 1992), p. 33.

30 Luis Javier Cuesta Hernández, 'Alonso García Bravo', *Diccionario biográfico español*, Real academia de la historia, http://dbe.rah. es/biografias/48900/alonso-garcia-bravo, accessed 30 May 2020.

31 González Tascón, *Ingeniería española en ultramar*, p. 300.

32 Alfonso Muñoz Cosme, 'Instrumentos, métodos de elaboración y sistemas de representación del proyecto de fortificación entre los siglos XVI y XVIII', in *El dibujante ingeniero al servicio de la monarquía hispánica. siglos* XVI–XVIII, ed. Alicia Cámara Muñoz (Madrid, 2016), pp. 18–21.

33 Fray Luis de Olod, *Tratado del origen y arte de escribir bien* (Gerona, 1766), p. 89.

34 González Tascón, *Ingeniería española en ultramar*, p. 67.

35 Ibid., p. 71.

36 Joseph Antonio Portugués, 'Real Ordenanza e Instrucción dada en San Lorenzo el 4 de julio de 1718 para los ingenieros, y otras personas', in *Colección general de las ordenanzas militares, sus innovaciones y aditamentos* (Madrid, 1765), VI, pp. 756–70.

37 González Tascón, *Ingeniería española en ultramar*, p. 90.

38 Nicolás García Tapia, 'La ingeniería', in *Historia de la ciencia y de la técnica en la corona de Castilla*, ed. José María López Piñero (Valladolid, 2002), III, pp. 437–45.

39 María Portuondo, *Ciencia secreta. La cosmografía española y el Nuevo Mundo* (Madrid, 2013), p. 39.

40 Antonio Sánchez, *La espada, la cruz y el padrón. Soberanía, fe y representación cartográfica en el mundo ibérico bajo la monarquía hispánica, 1503–1598* (Madrid, 2013), p. 303.

41 Ibid., pp. 126–7.

42 Mauricio Nieto Olarte, *Las máquinas del imperio y el reino de Dios. Reflexiones sovre ciencia, tecnología y religión en el mundo atlántico del siglo* XVI (Bogotá, 2013), p. 43.

43 Ernesto Schäffer, *El consejo real y supremo de las Indias* (Madrid, 2003), II, pp. 319–27.

44 José Luis Casado Soto, 'Entre el Mediterráneo y el Atlántico. Los barcos de los Austrias', in *Guerra y sociedad en la monarquía hispánica: política, estrategia y cultura en la Europa moderna (1500–1700)*, ed. Enrique García Hernán and Davide Maffi (Madrid, 2006), I, p. 880.

45 Nieto Olarte, *Las máquinas del imperio y el reino de Dios*, p. 155.

46 González Tascón, *Ingeniería española en ultramar*, p. 271.

47 José Sala Catalá, *Ciencia y técnica en la metropolización de América* (Aranjuez, 1994), pp. 41ff.

48 Tamar Herzog, *Frontiers of Possession: Spain and Portugal in Europe and the Americas* (Cambridge, 2015), p. 257.

49 Benito Jerónimo Feijóo, *Teatro crítico universal* (Madrid, 1779), p. 314.

2 The Oceanic Scaffolding: Maritime Communications

1 J. H. Parry, *The Spanish Seaborne Empire* (Berkeley, CA, 1990). The work was part of a series on 'civilizations' edited by J. H. Plumb, and the title was adapted for works on the Dutch and Portuguese 'seaborne' empires. It is not clear whether Parry or Plumb proposed the use of the term.

2 Charles Verlinden, 'Les Origines coloniales de la civilisation atlantique', *Journal of World History*, I (1953), pp. 378–92.

3 F. Fernández-Armesto, *Civilizations* (London, 2000), pp. 455–84.

4 F. Fernández-Armesto, *The World* (Upper Saddle River, NJ, 2011), pp. 434–61.

5 Geoffrey Parker, *The Army of Flanders and the Spanish Road* (Cambridge, 2004), pp. 70–90.

6 Agustín Palau Claveras and Eduardo Ponce de León, eds, *Ensayo de bibliografía marítima española* (Barcelona, 1943), p. 461.

7 UK National Archives, SP 94–5, f.25: letter from Pedro Vitoria, Santa Marta, to an unnamed official in Cartagena, 23 May 1595.

8 Greg Bankoff, 'Aeolian Empires: The Influence of Winds and Currents on European Maritime Expansion in the Days of Sail', *Environment and History*, XXIII/2 (2017), pp. 163–96.

9 F. Fernández-Armesto, *Pathfinders: A Global History of Exploration* (Oxford, 2006), pp. 35–6.

10 Edward Wilson-Lee, *Memorial de los libros naufragados. Hernando Colón y la búsqueda de una biblioteca universal* (Barcelona, 2019), p. 239.

11 *Colección de documentos inéditos para la historia de Ultramar* (Madrid, 1886), II, p. 109.

12 Ibid., 2nd series, (Madrid, 1861), II, p. 261.

13 Pierre Adam, 'Navigation primitive et navigation astronomique', in *Vie Colloque Internationale d'Histoire Maritime: Les aspects internationaux de la découverte océanique au quinzième et seizième siècles* (Paris, 1966), pp. 91–110.

14 F. Fernández-Armesto, *Amerigo: The Man Who Gave His Name to America* (New York, 2007), pp. 74–8.

15 Samuel E. Morison, *The European Discovery of America: The Southern Voyages* (Oxford, 1974).

16 Rolando A. Laguardia Trías, *El renigma de las latitudes de Colón* (Valladolid, 1974), pp. 13–17, 27–8.

17 F. Fernandez-Armesto, 'Maps and Exploration in the Sixteenth and Early Seventeenth Centuries', in *History of Cartography*, III, part 1, ed. D. Woodward (Chicago, IL, 2007), pp. 738–70.

18 Ibid.

19 Eugenio de Salazar, *Cartas de Eugenio de Salazar, vecino y natural de Madrid, escritas a muy particulares amigos suyos* (Madrid, 1866), pp. 53–5.

20 José M. Oliva Melgar, 'La metrópoli sin territorio: ¿Crisis del comercio de indias en el siglo XVII o pérdida del control del monopolio?', in *El sistema atlántico español*, ed. C. Martínez Shaw and J. Oliva Melgar (Madrid, 2005), pp. 19–75.

21 Marcus Rediker, *Villains of All Nations: Atlantic Pirates in the Golden Age* (Boston, MA, 2004), pp. 38–53; Jody Greene, 'Hostis Humani Generis', *Critical Inquiry*, XXXIV (2008), pp. 683–705.

22 J. H. Elliott, *Empires of the Atlantic World: Britain and Spain in America, 1492–1830* (New Haven, CT, 2006), p. 224.

23 M. Lucena Giraldo, *Organización y Defensa de la Carrera de Indias* (2003).

24 Jan Pieter Heije, 'Een triomfantelijk lied van de Zilvervloot', Klassieke Nederlandstalige literatuur in elektronischer edities, Project Laurens J. Coster, https://cf.hum.uva.nl/dsp/ljc/heije/zilver.htm, accessed 7 May 2020.

25 Oscar H. K. Spate, *The Spanish Lake* (Canberra, 2004), pp. 58–82.

26 R. Vaughan Williams and A. L. Lloyd, eds, *The Penguin Book of English Folk Songs* (Baltimore, MD, 1959), p. 163.

27 John Fisher, *Commercial Relations between Spain and Spanish America in the Era of Free Trade, 1778–1796* (Liverpool, 1985), pp. 92–115.

28 Lutgardo García Fuentes, *Los peruleros y el comercio de Sevilla con las Indias, 1580–1630* (Seville, 1997), p. 28.

29 Pierre Chaunu, *Séville et l'Atlantique*, VIII, part 1 (Paris, 1959), pp. 96–7.

30 William Barr and Glyn Williams, eds, *Voyages to Hudson Bay in Search of a Northwest Passage*, 2 vols (London, 1993–4), II, p. 171.

31 Fernando López-Ríos Fernández, *Medicina naval española en la época de los descubrimientos* (Madrid, 1993), pp. 109–10.

32 Fernanda Molina, 'La sodomía a bordo: sexualidad y poder en la Carrera de Indias (siglos XVI–XVII)', *Revista de Estudios Marítimos y Sociales* (2010), III, pp. 9–21.

33 *Cartas de Eugenio de Salazar*, p. 40.

34 Ibid., pp. 47–52.

35 Ibid., p. 44.

36 Ibid., p. 45.

37 Ibid., pp. 40–41.

38 *Colección de documentos inéditos para la historia de España*, 112 vols (1842–95), here vol. LXXXI (1883), p. 194.

39 Antonio M. Bernal, *España: Proyecto inacabado* (Madrid, 2005), pp. 281–3.

3 Making Ways: Landward Communications

1 Pablo Alzola y Minondo, *Historia de las obras públicas en España* (Madrid, 1899), pp. 298–9.

2 Francisco Javier Rodríguez Lázaro, *Las primeras autopistas españolas (1925–1936)* (Madrid, 2004), p. 303; Jimena Canales, *A Tenth of a Second: A History* (Chicago, IL, 2007), p. x.

3 'When people could not resort to exact methods of measuring and cartographic representation, concepts of territoriality had to be fundamentally different to our modern understanding. Occasionally one even gets the impression as if there had been no territorial concept at all, but only hierarchies between officials and inhabitants of settled places. This conclusion would be premature, though, because of course there was territorial thinking, even if less in terms of a concrete spatial concept of social organization or political unity as we usually imagine it.' Werner Stangl, 'Scylla and Charybdis 2.0: Reconstructing Colonial Spanish American Territories between Metropolitan Dream and Effective Control. Historical Ambiguities and Cybernetic Determinism', *Culture and History Digital Journal*, IV/1 (2015), p. 3.

4 Xavier Gil, 'City, Communication and Concord in Renaissance Spain and Spanish America', in *Athenian Legacies: European Debates on Citizenship*, ed. Paschalis M. Kitromilides (Florence, 2014), pp. 217–18.

5 Tomás Manuel Fernández de Mesa y Moreno, *Tratado legal y político de caminos públicos y posadas* (Valencia, 1755), p. 134.

6 Juan de Castellanos, *Elegías de varones ilustres de Indias* (Madrid, 1847), IV, pp. 53, 58, 63.

7 José Oviedo y Baños, *Historia de la conquista y población de Venezuela* (Caracas, 1967), p. 225.

8 Castellanos, *Elegías de varones ilustres de Indias*, p. 68.

9 Fray Tomás de Mercado, *Tratos y contratos de mercaderes* (Salamanca, 2015), p. 3.

10 Gil, 'City, Communication and Concord', pp. 202–3.

11 Serge Gruzinski, *La ciudad de México: una historia* (Mexico City, 2004), p. 323.

12 Gil, 'City, Communication and Concord', p. 199.

13 Fernando Cobos, 'Metodología de análisis gráfico de los proyectos de fortificación', in *El dibujante ingeniero al servicio de la monarquía hispánica, siglos XVI–XVIII*, ed. Alicia Cámara Muñoz (Madrid, 2016), p. 120.

14 John Luke Gallup, Alejandro Gaviria and Eduardo Lora, *Is Geography Destiny? Lessons from Latin America* (Washington, DC, 2003), pp. 3–5.

15 Ignacio González Tascón, *Ingeniería española en ultramar, siglos XVI–XIX* (Madrid, 1992), p. 411.

16 Carl Langebaek Rueda, *Los herederos del pasado: indígenas y pensamiento criollo en Colombia y Venezuela* (Bogotá, 2009), II, p. 41.

17 González Tascón, *Ingeniería española*, p. 444.

18 Emanuele Amodio, 'Relaciones interétnicas en el Caribe indígena: una reconstrucción a partir de los primeros testimonios europeos', *Revista de Indias*, LI (1991), pp. 51–193, 595; Sofia Botero Páez, 'Redescubriendo los caminos antiguos desde Colombia', *Bulletin de l'Institut français d'études andines*, XXXVI (2007), pp. 347–8.

19 John Hyslop, *Qhapaqñan, el sistema vial incaico* (Lima, 1992), p. 78; Carl H. Langebaeck, 'Los caminos aborígenes. Caminos, mercaderes y cacicazgos: circuitos de comunicación antes de la invasión española en Colombia', in *Caminos reales de Colombia* (Bogotá, 1995), pp. 37–41.

20 González Tascón, *Ingeniería española en ultramar*, pp. 441–2.

21 'Este camino de los incas es tan hermoso como el de Aníbal en los Alpes, que pone

admiración verlo.' Bernabé Cobo, *Historia del Nuevo Mundo* (Seville, 1892), III, p. 266.

22 Ramón María Serrera Contreras, *Tráfico terrestre y red vial en las Indias españolas* (Barcelona, 1992), pp. 134–7.

23 Pablo Fernando Pérez Riaño, *La cabuya de Chicamocha. Su trascendencia en nuestra historia* (Bogotá, 2012), pp. 16–19.

24 'Debe el rey mandar labrar los puentes e las calzadas, e allanar los pasos malos.' 'Apostura y nobleza del reino es mantener las calzadas y los puentes, de manera que no se derriben ni deshagan.' María Luisa Pérez González, 'Los caminos reales de América en la legislación y en la historia', *Anuario de estudios americanos*, LXVIII (2001), pp. 35–6.

25 Nicolás García Tapia, 'La ingeniería', in *Historia de la ciencia y de la técnica en la corona de Castilla*, ed. José María López Piñero (Valladolid, 2002), p. 448.

26 Geoffrey Parker, *Felipe II* (Barcelona, 2010), p. 482.

27 *Recopilación de leyes de los Reinos de Indias* (Madrid, 1841), II, Bk 4, Título 17, pp. 130–33.

28 *Teoría y leyes de la conquista* (Madrid, 1979), ed. Francisco Morales Padrón, p. 497.

29 Arndt Brendecke, *The Empirical Empire: Spanish Colonial Rule and the Politics of Knowledge* (Berlin, 2016), p. 17.

30 Bk IV, title XVI, law 1 of the *Recopilación* of 1681.

31 Pérez González, 'Los caminos reales de América', p. 43.

32 Serrera Contreras, *Trafico terrestre y red vial*, p. 27.

33 David J. Robinson, *Mil leguas por América. De Lima a Caracas, 1740–1741. Diario de don Miguel de Santisteban* (Bogotá, 1992), p. 71.

34 María Luisa Pérez González, 'Los caminos reales de América', pp. 51–2.

35 Francisco de Ajofrín, *Diario del viaje que por orden de la sagrada congregación de Propaganda Fide hizo a la América septentrional en el siglo XVIII* (Madrid, 1958), I, p. 137.

36 Sergio Ortiz Hernán, 'Caminos y transportes mexicanos al comenzar el siglo XIX', in *Los ferrocarriles de México. Una visión social y económica* (Mexico City, 1989), pp. 1247–8.

37 José Omar Moncada Maya and Irma Escamilla Herrera, 'Diego García Conde, un militar español en la transición al México Independiente', *Revista de Indias*, LXXVI/267 (2016), pp. 459–61.

38 Serrera Contreras, *Tráfico terrestre y red vial*, p. 31.

39 Jesús Ruiz de Gordejuela Urquijo, *Vivir y morir en México. Vida cotidiana en el epistolario de los españoles vasconavarros, 1750–1900* (San Sebastián, 2011), p. 65.

40 '"barrancos eternos, rodeando ríos y traspasando montañas llega uno más muerto que vivo al término del viaje", castigado pese a que su propósito era "trabajar, sufrir y distraerse de todo vicio."' Serrera Contreras, *Tráfico terrestre y red vial*, p. 46.

41 'presidio volante, al que se destinarán todos los vagos, todos los ociosos, y todos los delincuentes del reino por más o menos tiempo, según gradúen sus sentencias los tribunales.' Ibid., p. 61.

42 Clarence H. Haring, *El comercio y la navegación entre España y las Indias en época de los Habsburgo* (Paris, 1939), p. 211.

43 Alfredo Castillero Calvo, *El descubrimiento del Pacífico y los orígenes de la globalización* (Panama City, 2013), pp. 83–6.

44 Serrera Contreras, *Tráfico terrestre y red vial*, p. 74.

45 Alfredo Castillero Calvo, 'Panama en la historia global', *Boletín de la Real Academia Sevillana de Buenas Letras*, XLIV (2015), pp. 104ff.

46 José Luis Mora Mérida, 'Ideario reformador de un cordobés ilustrado: el Arzobispo y Virrey don Antonio Caballero y Góngora', in *Andalucía y América en el siglo XVIII: actas de las IV Jornadas de Andalucía y América*, ed. Bibiano Torres Ramírez and José J. Hernández Palomo (Seville, 1985), vol. II, pp. 254–5.

47 Emanuele Amodio, Rodrigo Navarrete and Ana Cristina Rodríguez Yilo, *El camino de los españoles* (Caracas, 1997), pp. 33–4.

48 Secundino-José Gutiérrez Álvarez, *Las comunicaciones en América* (Madrid, 1992), pp. 277–8.

49 Arístides Ramos Peñuela, 'Los caminos al río Magdalena', *Credencial*, 287 (2013), p. 98.

50 Serrera Contreras, *Tráfico terrestre y red vial*, p. 103.

51 Katherine Bonil-Gómez, 'Free People of African Descent and Jurisdictional Politics in Eighteenth-Century New Granada: The Bogas of the Magdalena River', *Journal of Iberian and Latin American Studies*, XXIV (2018), pp. 189–90.

52 Bernardo Ward, *Proyecto económico* (Madrid, 1982), pp. 284–5.

53 Manuel Lucena Giraldo, '¿Filántropos u oportunistas? Ciencia y política en los proyectos de obras públicas del Consulado de Cartagena de Indias, 1795–1810', *Revista de Indias*, LII (1992), p. 635.

54 Jorge Juan and Antonio de Ulloa, *Relación histórica del viaje a la América Meridional* (Madrid, 1748), I, p. 286.

55 Antonio Vázquez de Espinosa, *Compendio y descripción de las Indias occidentales* (Washington, DC, 1948), p. 348.

56 Ibid., p. 348.

57 Serrera Contreras, *Tráfico terrestre y red vial*, p. 118.

58 Antonello Gerbi, *Caminos del Perú: Historia y actualidad de las comunicaciones viales* (Lima, 1943), p. 1.

59 Sebastián Lorente, *Escritos fundacionales de historia peruana*, ed. Mark Turner (Lima, 2005), pp. 23, 294ff.

60 John Hyslop, *Qhapaqñan: El sistema vial inkaico* (Lima, 1992), pp. 78ff.

61 Gerbi, *Caminos del Perú*, p. 31.

62 Concolorcorvo, *El lazarillo de ciegos caminantes. Desde Buenos Aires hasta Lima, 1773* (Buenos Aires, 1942), p. 112.

63 Ibid., p. xvii.

64 Serrera Contreras, *Tráfico terrestre y red vial*, pp. 242–7.

65 Enriqueta Vila Vilar, *Hispanoamérica y el comercio de esclavos. Los asientos portugueses* (Seville, 1977), p. 139.

66 Acarete du Biscay, *An Account of a Voyage up the River d la Plata, and thence over Land to Peru with Observations on the Inhabitants, as well Indians and Spaniards* (London, 1698).

67 Serrera Contreras, *Tráfico terrestre y red vial*, p. 179.

68 Ibid., p. 183.

69 Enriqueta Vila Vilar, *Hispanoamérica y el comercio de esclavos: Los asientos portugueses* (Seville, 1977), p. 139.

70 Gutiérrez Álvarez, *Las comunicaciones en América*, p. 289.

4 Troubled Waters: Along and Across Internal Waterways

1 T. Wilder, *The Bridge of San Luis Rey* (New York, 1928), p. 15.

2 Luis Moya Blanco, 'Arquitecturas cupuliformes. El arco, la bóveda y la cúpula', in *Curso de mecánica y tecnología de los edificios antiguos* (Madrid, 1987), p. 99.

3 Fray Diego de Ocaña, *Un viaje fascinante por la América hispana del siglo XVI* (Madrid, 1969), p. 268.

4 Ignacio González Tascón, *Ingeniería española en ultramar, siglos XVI–XIX* (Madrid, 1992), p. 592.

5 Alexander von Humboldt, *Ensayo político sobre el reino de la Nueva España* (Mexico City, 1984), p. 195.

6 Pablo Fernando Pérez Riaño, *La cabuya de Chicamocha. Su trascendencia en nuestra historia* (Bogotá, 2012), p. 112.

7 Inca Garcilaso de la Vega, *Comentarios reales* (Mexico City, 1984), p. 109.

8 José de Acosta, *Historia natural y moral de la Indias* (Madrid, 1954), p. 194.

9 Antonio Vázquez de Espinosa, *Compendio y descripción de las Indias occidentales* (Washington, DC, 1948), p. 467.

10 Jorge Juan and Antonio de Ulloa, *Relación histórica del viaje a la América meridional* (Madrid, 1978), I, p. 576.

11 Geoffrey Parker, *El ejército de Flandes y el camino español, 1567–1659* (Madrid, 1976), pp. 121–2.

12 Rommel Contreras, 'El puente Urrutia de Cumaná', in *Documento de trabajo* (Cumaná, 2013), pp. 2–4.

13 Conde de Cabarrús, *Cartas (1795)* (Madrid, 1990), p. 67.

14 Dirk Bühler, 'La construcción de puentes en las ciudades latinoamericanas como empresa de ingeniería civil que refleja las necesidades comunales y su impacto sobre el espacio urbano y social: Puebla, Lima y Arequipa', in *Historia social urbana. Espacios y flujos*, ed. Eduardo Kingman Garcés (Quito, 2009), p. 105.

15 Manuel Lucena Giraldo, *Historia de un cosmopolita. José María de Lanz y la fundación de la ingeniería de caminos en España y América* (Madrid, 2005), pp. 106–13.

16 González Tascón, *Ingeniería española en ultramar*, p. 556.

17 Ibid.

18 José Omar Moncada Maya and Irma Escamilla Herrera, 'Diego García Conde, un militar español en la transición al México independiente', *Revista de Indias*, LXXVI/267 (2016), p. 461.

19 Ramón Serrera Contreras, *Tráfico terrestre y red vial en las Indias españolas* (Barcelona, 1992), pp. 34–7.

20 Alba Irene Sáchica Bernal and María del Rosario Leal del Castillo, *El puente del común. De obra pública a monumento nacional* (Bogotá, 2015), p. 68.

21 Sergio Mejía Macía, *Cartografía e Ingeniería en la Era de las Revoluciones. Mapas y obras de Vicente Talledo y Rivera en España y el Nuevo Reino de Granada, 1758–1820* (Madrid, forthcoming), pp. 182–4.

22 González Tascón, *Ingeniería española en ultramar*, p. 587.

23 Ibid., p. 588.

24 Richard Henry Stoddard, *The Life, Travels, and Books of Alexander von Humboldt*, (New York, 1859), pp. 170–73; 'Noticias del viaje del padre jesuita Manuel Román al descubrimiento del caño Casiquiare (1744)', in *Viajes a la Guayana ilustrada. El hombre y el territorio*, ed. Manuel Lucena Giraldo (Caracas, 1999) pp. 44–9.

25 Felipe Fernández-Armesto, *The Americas: A Hemispheric History* (London, 2003), p. 75.

26 Neftalí Zúñiga, *Pedro Vicente Maldonado. Un científico de América* (Madrid, 1951), pp. 184–94.

27 I. González Tascón et al., *Obras hidráulicas en América colonial* (Madrid, 1993), pp. 343–5.

28 Félix de Azara, *Memorias sobre el estado rural del río de La Plata en 1801* (Madrid, 1847), p. 51.

29 Manuel Lucena Giraldo, 'Una obra digna de romanos. El canal del dique, desde su apertura hasta la independencia', in *El río Magdalena* (Bogotá, 2014), p. 94.

30 González Tascón, *Ingeniería española en ultramar*, p. 463.

31 J. Herráez de Escariche, 'D. Pedro Zapata de Mendoza, gobernador de Cartagena de Indias', *Anuario de estudios americanos*, III (1946), pp. 377–9; Francisco de las Barras de Aragón, *Documentos referentes al Canal de Navegación construido en 1650 entre Cartagena de Indias y el río de la Magdalena* (Madrid, 1931).

32 Expediente sobre el Canal del Dique (1647–63), Archivo General de Indias (AGI), Santa Fe, NM, p. 199.

33 H. Capel et al., *Los ingenieros militares en España: siglo XVIII* (Barcelona, 1983), p. 229.

34 Expediente sobre el Canal del Dique, p. 199.

35 Ibid., p. 236.

36 Testimonio de las diligencias ejecutadas en virtud de Real Cédula de S. M. Sobre la abertura del nuevo dique del río de la Magdalena (1725–7), AGI, Santa Fe, NM, p. 376.

37 José Ignacio de Pombo, *Manifiesto del Canal del Dique*, Cartagena (10 July 1797); Antonio Ybot León, *La arteria histórica del Nuevo Reino de Granada. Cartagena-Santa Fe, 1538–1798* (Bogotá, 1952), pp. 367–72.

38 González Tascón, *Ingeniería española en ultramar*, p. 433.

39 G. Mack, *The Land Divided: A History of the Panama Canal and Other Isthmian Canal Projects* (New York, 1944), pp. 40–47.

40 Alfredo Castillero Calvo, *La ruta interoceánica y el Canal de Panama* (Panama City, 1999), pp. 35ff.

41 Celestino A. Araúz, 'Un sueño de siglos: El Canal de Panama', in *Tareas* (Panama City, 2006), p. 123.

42 Robert S. Weddle, *Changing Tides: Twilight and Dawn in the Spanish Sea* (College Station, TX, 1995), p. 111.

43 Oskar H. K. Spate, *The Spanish Lake* (Canberra, 2004); Rainer F. Buschmann, Edward R. Slack Jr and James B. Tueller, *Navigating the Spanish Lake: The Pacific in the Iberian World, 1521–1898* (Honolulu, HI, 2014), p. 3.

44 Gabriel Paquette and Gonzalo M. Quintero Saravia, eds, *Spain and the American Revolution: New Approaches and Perspectives* (New York, 2020), pp. 7–11.

45 'Derrotero de un viaje de Portobelo a Nicaragua y de regreso por la ruta de Costa Rica por el alférez y subteniente de milicias José de Inzaurrandiaga', in *Documentos históricos* (San José, 1990), pp. 29–43; E. Fonseca Corrales et al., *Costa Rica en el s. XVIII* (San José, 2003), pp. 210–11; Julian Andrei Velasco, 'Viaje de Portobelo a Nicaragua realizado por don Don José Inzaurrandiaga en 1779 y su descripción del obispado de León de Nicaragua', *Boletin de la AFEHC*, LII (2012).

46 Mack, *The Land Divided*, pp. 98–9.

47 'Derrotero de un viaje de Portobelo a Nicaragua'; Fonseca Corrales et al., *Costa Rica en el s. XVIII*, pp. 210–11; Velasco, 'Viaje de Portobelo a Nicaragua'.

48 N. Bas Martín, *El cosmógrafo e historiador Juan Bautista de Muñoz* (Valencia, 2002), pp. 132–4.

49 Miles P. Duval, *Cadiz to Cathay: the Story of the Long Struggle for a Waterway across the American Isthmus* (Stanford, CA, 1940), p. 18.

50 Carlos José Gutiérrez de los Ríos, conde de Fernán Núñez, 'Repuesta a la memoria antecedente', Real Academia de la Historia (Madrid), sig. 9-6039 (2), ff. 20v.–32.

51 Memorial dirigido al conde de Floridablanca por D. Ramón Carlos Rodríguez, representante de D. Joaquín Antonio Escartín, relativo a la apertura de un canal de comunicación entre el mar del Norte y el del Sur en América, proyectado por éste. AHN ESTADO, 2923, exp. 472. http://pares.mcu.es/ParesBusquedas20/catalogo/show/12692354, accessed 7 December 2020.

52 'Proyecto de Don Joaquín Antonio Escartin', Real Academia de la Historia (Madrid), 9-6039 (2), ff. 3–9.

53 M. de la Bastide, *Mémoire sur un nouveau passage de la Mer du Nord au Mer du Sud* (Paris, 1791), pp. 25ff.

54 Fernán Núñez, 'Repuesta a la memoria antecedente', ff. 20v.–32.

55 H. G. Miller, *The Isthmian Highway: A Review of the Problems of the Caribbean* (New York, 1929), p. 8.

5 The Rings of Stone: Fortifying the Frontiers

1 *The Memoirs of Philip de Commines*, ed. A. R. Scoble (London, 1884), II, p. 77.

2 Fernando Cobos Guerra, 'Ingenieros, tratados y proyectos de fortificación. El trasvase de experiencias entre Europa y América', in *El patrimonio fortificado. Cádiz y el Caribe: una relación transatlántica*, ed. Pilar Chías and Tomás Abad (Alcalá de Henares, 2011), pp. 175ff.

3 Ramón Paolini, 'Fortificaciones españolas en el Caribe: Panama, Colombia, Venezuela y Cuba', in *El patrimonio fortificado*, ed. Chías and Abad, pp. 348–9.

4 Juan Manuel Zapatero, *Historia de las fortificaciones de Cartagena de Indias* (Madrid, 1979), p. 21; Rodolfo Segovia Salas, 'Cartagena de Indias. Historiografía de sus fortificaciones', *Boletin Cultural y Bibliográfico*, XXXIV–XXXV (1997), pp. 6–14; José Antonio Calderón Quijano, *Las fortificaciones españolas en América y Filipinas* (Madrid, 1996), pp. 335–47.

5 K. Deaghan, 'Strategies of Adjustment: Spanish Defence of the Circum-Caribbean Colonies, 1493–1600', in *First Forts: Essays on the Archaeology of Proto-Colonial Fortifications*, ed. Eric Klingelhofer (Leiden, 2010), pp. 17–40, at p. 20.

6 José Antonio Calderón Quijano, *Historia de las fortificaciones en Nueva España* (Madrid, 1984), p. 357.

7 José Antonio Calderón Quijano, *Las defensas indianas en la Recopilación de 1680* (Seville, 1984), pp. 32–48.

8 Ross Hassig, *War and Society in Ancient Mesoamerica* (Berkeley, CA, 1992), p. 65.

9 Richard J. Chacón and Rubén G. Mendoza, *Latin American Indigenous Warfare and Ritual Violence* (Tucson, AZ, 2007), p. 19.

10 David Webster, 'Lowland Maya Fortifications', *Proceedings of the American Philosophical Society*, CXX (1976), pp. 361–71.

11 R. Bradley, 'Reconsidering the Notion of Fortaleza Kuélap', www.researchgate.net (2015), accessed 6 August 2018.

12 H. W. and J. E. Kaufmann, *Fortifications of the Incas, 1200–1531* (Oxford, 2006).

13 John H. Parry and Philip M. Sherlock, *A Short History of the West Indies* (New York, 1986), p. 36.

14 Ramón Gutiérrez, *Fortificaciones en Iberoamérica* (El Viso, 2005), p. 29.

15 Ray F. Broussard, 'Bautista Antonelli: Architect of Caribbean Defence', *The Historian*, I/4 (August 1988), pp. 507–20, at p. 508.

16 Felipe Fernández-Armesto, *The Spanish Armada: The Experience of War in 1588* (Oxford, 1988), pp. 260–70.

17 Luis Gorrochategui, *Contra Armada. La mayor victoria de España sobre Inglaterra* (Barcelona, 2020), pp. 261–5.

18 'atrasado y empeñado por la cortedad del sueldo.' Gutiérrez, *Fortificaciones*, p. 25.

19 Sergio Paolo Solano, 'Pedro Romero, el artesano: trabajo, raza y diferenciación social en Cartagena de Indias a finales del dominio colonial', *Historia Crítica*, LXI (2016), p. 155.

20 Gutiérrez, *Fortificaciones*, p. 204.

21 Calderón, *Fortificaciones*, p. 395.

22 Gutiérrez, *Fortificaciones*, p. 35.

23 Emilio José Luque Azcona, *Ciudad y poder: la construcción material y simbólica del Montevideo colonial* (Seville, 2007), p. 159.

24 Ibid., pp 87–90.

25 Alfredo Castillero Calvo, 'Fortificaciones del Caribe panameño', in *El patrimonio fortificado*, ed. Chías and Abad, p. 416.

26 Deaghan, *Strategies of Adjustment*, p. 53.

27 Calderón, *Fortificaciones*, p. 393.

28 Gutiérrez, *Fortificaciones*, p. 75.

29 Bernardo de Balbuena, *Siglo de oro en las selvas de Erífile* (Madrid, 1821), p. 55.

30 Gutiérrez, *Fortificaciones*, p. 152.

31 Antonio Sahady Villanueva, José Bravo Sánchez and Carolina Quilodrán Rubio, 'Fuertes españoles en Chiloé: las huellas de la historia en medio del paisaje insular', *Revista INVI*, XXVI (2011), pp. 133–65.

32 Gutiérrez, *Fortificaciones*, p. 340.

33 Luque Azcona, *Ciudad y poder*, pp. 161–5.

34 'el mantener las plazas sin medios no es obra de hombres, sino solo de Dios.' Calderón, *Fortificaciones*, p. 64.

35 Ibid., pp. 49–72.

36 Gutiérrez, *Fortificaciones*, p. 147.

37 Broussard, 'Antonelli', p. 511.

38 Juan Marchena Fernández, 'Sin temor de Rey ni de Dios: violencia, corrupción y crisis de autoridad en la Cartagena colonial', in *Soldados del Rey. El ejército borbónico en América colonial en vísperas de la independencia*, ed. Allan J. Kuethe and Juan Marchena Fernández (Castellón, 2005), I, pp. 45ff.

39 María Antonia Durán Montero, *Lima en el siglo XVII* (Seville, 1994), pp. 87–8; Juan Gunther Doering and Guillermo Lohmann Villena, *Lima* (Madrid, 1992), pp. 125–7.

40 Rodolfo Segovia, *El lago de piedra: la geopolítica de las fortificaciones españolas del Caribe* (Bogotá, 2006), p. 27.

41 'abierta sin defensa ninguna y dessarmada.' Calderón, *Fortificaciones*, p. 360.

42 Gutiérrez, *Fortificaciones*, pp. 42, 86, 191; Segovia, *El lago de piedra*, p. 15.

43 Gutiérrez, *Fortificaciones*, p. 31.

44 Gustavo Placer, *Los defensores del Morro* (Havana, 2003), pp. 11–26.

45 Segovia, *El lago de piedra*, p. 50.

46 Tamara Blanes Martín, *Fortificaciones del Caribe* (Havana, 2001), pp. 81–4; Gutiérrez, *Fortificaciones*, pp. 45, 118.

47 Carlos Flores, 'Fortificaciones españolas en el Caribe: México, Guatemala y Honduras', in *El patrimonio fortificado*, ed. Chías and Abad, pp. 275–6.

48 Gutiérrez, *Fortificaciones*, pp. 75, 92.

49 Calderón, *Fortificaciones*, pp. 366, 376–8.

50 'baluarte de las Antillas, protectora del Golfo de México, guardián ... de las flotas.' Milagros Flores, 'Fortificaciones españolas en el Caribe: La Florida y Puerto Rico',

in *El patrimonio fortificado*, ed. Chías and Abad, p. 222.

51 Calderón, *Fortificaciones*, p. 245.

52 John R. McNeill, *Mosquito Empires: Ecology and War in the Greater Caribbean, 1620–1914* (Cambridge, 2010), pp. 137ff.

53 For illustrations of Veracruz and San Juan, see Jorge González Aragón, Manuel Rodríguez Viqueira and Norma Elisabethe Rodrigo Cervantes, eds, *Corpus urbanístico: fortificaciones costeras de México en los archivos españoles* (Mexico City, 2009), pp. 40–114.

54 René Javellana, *Fortress of Empire: Colonial Fortifications of the Spanish Philippines, 1565–1898* (New York, 1997), pp. 25ff.; Pedro Luengo, 'La fortificación del archipiélago filipino en el siglo XVIII. La defensa integral ante lo local y lo global', *Revista de Indias*, LXXXVII (2017), pp. 741–2.

55 Isacio Pérez Fernández, *O. P. , Fray Toribio Motolinía, O.F.M., frente a Fray Bartolomé de las Casas, O. P. : estudio y edición crítica de la carta de Motolinía al emperador (Tlaxcala, a 2 de enero de 1555)* (Salamanca, 1989), pp. 66–80, 236.

56 Max L. Moorhead, *The Presidio: Bastion of the Spanish Borderlands* (Norman, OK, 1975), pp. 10–11.

57 Thomas H. Naylor, Charles W. Polzer et al., eds, *The Presidios and Militia of the Northern Frontier of New Spain*, 2 vols in 3 parts (Tucson, AZ, 1986), vol. II, part I, p. 260.

58 Ibid., pp. 335–65.

59 Ibid., pp. 512–27.

60 Quijano, *Las defensas indianas*, p. 54.

61 Moorhead, *The Presidio*, p. 163.

62 Naylor, Polzer et al., *The Presidios and Militia*, vol. II, part I, pp. 261–78.

63 Ibid., II, pp. 465–71.

64 Vito Alessio Robles, ed., *Brigadier Pedro de Rivera: Diario y derrotero de la visita a los presidios de la América septentrional española* (Málaga, 1993), pp. 111–16.

65 Ibid.

66 Naylor, Polzer et al., *The Presidios and Militia*, vol. II, part II, p. 473.

67 Gabriel Curiel Defossé, *Tierra incógnita: el noreste novohispano según Fray Juan Agustín Morfi, 1673–1779* (Mexico City, 2016), p. 70.

68 Naylor, Polzer et al., *The Presidios and Militia*, vol. II, part I, p. 287.

69 'estuviese en continuo movimiento en toda aquella tierra.' Ibid., p. 145.

70 Ibid., p. 303.

71 Lawrence Kinnaird, ed., *The Frontiers of New Spain: Nicolas de Lafora's Description 1766–68* (Berkeley, CA, 1958), p. 44.

72 Ibid., p. 19.

73 Ibid., pp. 23, 30, 61.

74 David Weber, *Bárbaros: Spaniards and Their Savages in the Age of Enlightenment* (New Haven, CT, 2005), p. 183.

75 Felipe Fernández-Armesto, *Our America: A Hispanic History of the United States* (New York, 2014), p. 67.

76 D. J. Weber, *The Spanish Frontier in North America* (New Haven, CT, 1993), pp. 228–9.

77 Moorhead, *The Presidio*, p. 243.

78 Jack S. Williams, 'San Diego Presidio: A Vanished Military Community of Upper California', *Historical Archaeology*, XXXVIII (2004), pp. 121–34.

79 Maynard Geiger, 'A Description of California's Principal Presidio, Monterey, in 1773', *Southern California Quarterly*, XLIX (1967), pp. 327–36.

80 Roberto L. Sagarena, 'Building California's Past', *Journal of Urban History*, XXVIII (2002), pp. 429–44.

6 On the Waterfront: Ports and Shipyards

1 Juan Marchena y Justo Cuño Bonito, 'Preámbulo: el buque ⁀ mo unidad de análisis', in *Vientos de guerra. Apogeo y crisis de la Real armada (1750–1823)*, ed. Juan Marchena and Justo Cuño Bonito (Madrid, 2018), vol. II, p. 18.

2 Christopher Storrs, *The Resilience of the Spanish Monarchy, 1665–1700* (Oxford, 2006), p. 63.

3 Fernando Rodríguez de la Flor, *El sol de Flandes: Imaginarios bélicos del siglo de oro* (Salamanca, 2018), vol. I, pp. 281–94.

4 José Ramón Carriazo Ruiz, *Tratados naúticos del renacimiento* (Salamanca, 2003), pp. 190–92.

5 Storrs, *The Resilience of the Spanish Monarchy*, pp. 104–5; José Pérez Magallón,

'Prólogo, y notas sobre las fuerzas navales españolas', *Magallánica*, IV (2018), pp. 7–8, accessed 4 January 2021.

6 Miguel Antonio de la Gándara, *Apuntes sobre el bien y el mal de España* (Madrid, 1988), p. cxxii.

7 Agustín González Enciso, 'Les Infraestructures: le développement des chantiers navals et des arsenaux', in *La Real Armada: la marine des Borbons d'Espagne au XVIIIe siècle*, ed. Agustin Guimerá and Olivier Chaline (Paris, 2018), pp. 100–114.

8 Delphine Tempère, 'Vida y muerte en alta mar: pajes, grumetes y marineros en la navegación española del siglo XVII', *Iberoamericana*, II (2002), p. 117.

9 Felipe Pereda and Fernando María, eds, *El Atlas del rey planeta: la 'Descripción de España y de las costas y puertos de sus reinos' de Pedro Texeira (1634)* (Hondarribia, 2002), pp. 74–7.

10 Daniel Crespo Delgado, 'Mar de la ilustración. El sueño de un mundo nuevo', in *Una mirada ilustrada: los puertos españoles de Mariano Sánchez*, ed. Pedro Navascués Palacio and Bernardo Revuelta Pol (Madrid, 2014), pp. 117–18.

11 Dolores Romero Muñoz and Amaya Sáenz Sanz, 'La construcción de los puertos: siglos XVI–XIX', in *Puertos y sistemas portuarios (siglos XVI–XX)*, ed. Agustín Guimerá and Dolores Romero (Madrid, 1996), p. 185.

12 Manuel Nóvoa, 'Los puertos y su tecnología durante el siglo', in *Proyección en América de los ingenieros militares. Siglo XVIII* (Madrid, 2016), p. 454.

13 Emanuele Amodio, 'Relaciones interétnicas en el Caribe indígena: una reconstrucción a partir de los primeros testimonios europeos', *Revista de Indias*, LI (1991), pp. 51–193 and 581–9.

14 Juan Antonio Rodríguez-Villasante Prieto, 'Geopolítica para América en el siglo XVIII. El sistema portuario para el control del territorio', in *Proyección en América de los ingenieros militares. Siglo XVIII*, pp. 96–7.

15 Thomas Calvo, *Espadas y plumas en la monarquía hispana. Alonso de Contreras y otras vidas de soldados* (Madrid, 2019), pp. 129–30.

16 Antonio García de León, *Tierra adentro, mar en fuera. El puerto de Veracruz y su litoral a sotavento, 1519–1821* (Mexico City, 2014), p. 469.

17 Ibid., p. 479.

18 Gerardo Vivas Pineda, *La aventura naval de la Compañía guipuzcoana de Caracas* (Caracas, 1998), p. 237.

19 Ibid., pp. 62–3.

20 Ibid., p. 55.

21 Alfredo Castillero Calvo, *Portobelo y el San Lorenzo del Chagres: Perspectivas imperiales, siglos XVI–XIX* (Panama City, 2016), I, pp. 20ff.; Alfredo Castillero Calvo, 'El comercio entre Panamá y China en los comienzos de la globalización: evidencias de la cultura material', *Investigación y Pensamiento Crítico*, VIII (2018), pp. 58–62.

22 Enriqueta Vila Vilar, 'Las ferias de portobelo: apariencia y realidad del comercio con india', *Anuario de estudios americanos*, XXXIX (1982), p. 281.

23 Isabel Paredes, 'La carrera del Paraguay a fines del siglo XVIII', *América Latina en la historia económica*, XXI (2014), p. 74.

24 Ibid.

25 Javier Barrientos Grandón, *Joaquín del Pino y Rozas, un virrey del río de La Plata* (Madrid, 2015), pp. 135–6.

26 María Ximena Senatore, *Arqueología e Historia en la Colonia Española de Floridablanca, Patagonia* (Buenos Aires, 2007), p. 31

27 Marcia Bianchi Villelli, Silvana Buscaglia and María Marschoff, 'Trapitos al sol. Análisis de textiles de la colonia española de Floridablanca (Patagonia, siglo XVIII)', *Intersecciones en Antropología*, VII (2006), p. 3; María Laura Casanueva, 'Inmigrantes tempranos: maragatos en la Patagonia argentina. Las cuevas del Fuerte Nuestra Señora de El Carmen', *Revista Española de Antropología Americana*, XLIII (2013), pp. 118–19.

28 Ignacio González Tascón, *Ingeniería española en ultramar, siglos XVI–XIX* (Madrid, 1992), p. 108.

29 Fray Reginaldo de Lizárraga (1545–1615), *Descripción breve del reino del Perú, Tucumán,*

Río de la Plata y Chile (1605), p. 46, available at www.cervantesvirtual.com.

30 David R. Radell and James J. Parsons, 'Realejo: A Forgotten Colonial Port and Shipbuilding Center in Nicaragua', *Hispanic American Historical Review*, LI (1971), pp. 298–302; Guadalupe Pinzón Ríos, 'Frontera meridional novohispana o punto de encuentro intervirreinal: el espacio marítimo entre Nueva España y Guatemala a partir de sus contactos navales', in *A 500 años del hallazgo del Pacífico. La presencia novohispana en el Mar del Sur*, ed. Carmen Yuste López and Guadalupe Pinzón Ríos (Mexico City, 2016), p. 349.

31 Pinzón Ríos, 'Frontera meridional', p. 357.

32 Alberto Baena Zapatero, 'Reflexiones en torno al comercio de objetos de lujo en el Pacífico. siglos XVII y XVIII', in *A 500 años del hallazgo del Pacífico*, ed. López and Pinzón Ríos, p. 226; Gustavo Curiel, 'De cajones, fardos y fardillos: reflexiones en torno a las cargazones de mercaderías que arribaron desde el Oriente a la Nueva España', ibid., pp. 196–8.

33 Es todo un feliz parto de fortuna/ Y sus armas un águila engrifada/ De tesoros y plata tan preñada/ Que una flota de España, otra de China/ De sus obras cada año va cargada. José Antonio Calderón Quijano, 'Nueva cartografía de los puertos de Acapulco, Campeche y Veracruz', *Anuario de estudios americanos*, XXV (1968), p. 516.

34 Ibid., p. 518.

35 Myron J. Echenberg, *Humboldt's Mexico: In the Footsteps of the Illustrious German Scientific Traveller* (Montreal, 2017), pp. 3–4.

36 Antonio Julián, *La perla de la América, provincia de Santa Marta* (Bogotá, 1980), p. 229.

37 Vivas Pineda, *La aventura naval*, p. 254.

38 Andrés Galera Gómez, *Las corbetas del rey. El viaje alrededor del mundo de Alejandro Malaspina (1789–1794)* (Bilbao, 2010), p. 71.

39 Juan Carlos Cádiz and Fernando Duque de Estrada, 'La construcción naval: las instalaciones en tierra', in *Puertos y fortificaciones en América y Filipinas* (Madrid, 1985), pp. 109–10.

40 Erich Bauer Manderscheid, *Los montes de España en la historia* (Madrid, 1980), pp. 167–8.

41 José Manuel Serrano, 'El astillero militar de La Habana durante el s. XVIII', in *Vientos de guerra. Apogeo y crisis de la Real armada, 1750–1823*, ed. Juan Marchena and Justo Cuño (Madrid, 2018), vol. III, p. 351.

42 Pablo E. Pérez Mallaína, 'Generales y almirantes de la carrera de Indias. Una investigación pendiente', *Chronica Nova*, XXXIII (2007), p. 289.

43 José Luis Casado Soto, 'Barcos para la guerra: soporte de la Monarquía Hispánica', *Cuadernos de Historia Moderna*, Anejos, XLVII (2006), pp. 30–35.

44 Esteban Mira Caballos, *Las armadas del imperio. Poder y hegemonía en tiempo de los Austrias* (Madrid, 2019), pp. 82–5.

45 Marina Alfonso Mola, 'Navegar sin botar. El mercado de embarcaciones de seguna mano en la carrera de Indias (1778–1797)', *Jahrbuch für Geschichte Lateinamerikas*, XXXIV (1997), pp. 156–7.

46 Serrano, 'El astillero militar', p. 321.

47 María Baudot Monroy, '"Navíos, navíos, navíos". La política naval de Julián de Arriaga. El periodo de los grandes cambios: 1750–1760', in *Vientos de guerra. Apogeo y crisis de la Real armada (1750–1823)*, ed. Juan Marchena and Justo Cuño Bonito (Madrid, 2018), vol. I, p. 116; Agustín González Enciso, 'Les infrastructures: Le développement des chantiers navals et des arsenaux', in *La Real Armada*, ed. Guimerá and Chaline, pp. 100–114.

48 Antonio Bethencourt Massieu, 'El Real astillero de Coatzacoalcos (1720–1735)', *Anuario de estudios americanos*, XV (1958), p. 373.

49 Serrano, 'El astillero', pp. 323–4.

50 Ibid., pp. 324–40.

51 Ibid., p. 343.

52 Mauricio Nieto Olarte, *Las máquinas del imperio y el reino de Dios* (Bogotá, 2013), pp. 261–4.

53 Elena A. Schneider, *The Occupation of Havana: War, Trade, and Slavery in the Atlantic World* (Chapel Hill, NC, 2018), pp. 124ff.

54 Serrano, 'El astillero', p. 357.

55 José Gregorio Cayuela and Ángel Pozuelo Reina, *Trafalgar: Hombres y naves entre dos épocas* (Barcelona, 2004), pp. 140–47, 333.

56 Julián Simón Calero, 'Construcciones, ingeniería y teóricas en la construcción naval', in *Técnica e ingeniería en España. El siglo de las luces. De la ingeniería a la nueva navegación*, ed. Manuel Silva Suárez (Zaragoza, 2005), p. 600.

57 Manuel Lucena Giraldo, 'Defensa del territorio y conservación forestal en Guayana (1758–1793)', in *El Bosque Ilustrado. Estudios sobre la Política Forestal Española en América*, ed. Manuel Lucena Giraldo (Madrid, 1991), pp. 142–5.

58 María Luisa Laviana Cuetos, 'La Maestranza del astillero de Guayaquil en el siglo XVIII', *Temas Americanistas*, IV (1984), p. 26.

59 Ibid., p. 32.

60 Iván Valdez-Bubnov, 'Comercio, guerra y tecnología: la construcción naval para la carrera de Filipinas (1577–1757)', in *Comercio, guerra y finanzas en una época en transición (siglos XVII–XVIII)*, ed. Antonio José Rodríguez Hernández, Julio Arroyo Vozmediano and Juan A. Sánchez Belén (Valladolid, 2017), p. 241.

61 Francisco Fernández González, 'La construcción naval en la real armada entre 1750 y 1820', in *Vientos de guerra. Apogeo y crisis de la Real armada, 1750–1823*, ed. Juan Marchena and Justo Cuño (Madrid, 2018), vol. I, pp. 531–2.

62 José Vargas Ponce, *Elogio histórico de D. Antonio de Escaño* (Madrid, 1962), p. 13.

7 The Public Sphere: Social and Economic Infrastructure

1 Johann Wolfgang Goethe, *Elective Affinities* (Santa Fe, NM, 2003), p. 307.

2 Nicolaas A. Rupke, *Alexander von Humboldt: A Metabiography* (Chicago, IL, 2008), pp. 185–6.

3 Tamar Herzog, *Frontiers of Possession: Spain and Portugal in Europe and the Americas* (Cambridge, 2015), pp. 120–21.

4 Manuel Sánchez García, *Granada desgranada. Raíces legales de la forma urbana morisca e hispana* (Bogotá, 2018), pp. 141–9.

5 Xavier Gil, 'City, Communication and Concord in Renaissance Spain and Spanish America', in *Athenian Legacies: European Debates on Citizenship*, ed. Paschalis M. Kitromilides (Florence, 2014), pp. 196–204; Jorge Díaz Ceballos, 'New World Civitas, Contested Jurisdictions and Intercultural Conversation in the Construction of the Spanish Monarchy', *Colonial Latin American Review*, XXVII/1 (2018), p. 33.

6 Ignacio González Tascón, *Ingeniería española en ultramar, siglos XVI–XIX* (Madrid, 1992), p. 397.

7 Jorge Juan and Antonio de Ulloa, *Noticias secretas de América*, ed. Luis Javier Ramos Gómez (Madrid, 1985), vol. II, pp. 219–27.

8 Manuel Lucena Giraldo, *A los cuatro vientos. Las ciudades de la América Hispánica* (Madrid, 2006), p. 90.

9 Alain Musset, *Ciudades nómadas del Nuevo mundo* (Mexico City, 2011), pp. 29–40.

10 Sophia Greaves and Andrew Wallace-Hadrill, eds, *Rome and the Colonial City: Rethinking the Grid* (Oxford, 2022).

11 Luisa Durán Rocca, 'La malla urbana en la ciudad colonial iberoamericana', *Apuntes. Instituto Carlos Arbeláez Camacho para el patrimonio arquitectónico y urbano*, XIX (2006), pp. 117–18.

12 Kris Lane, *Potosí: The Silver City that Changed the World* (Berkeley, CA, 2019), pp. 92–117.

13 'Contribución del cabildo de Quito a la adquisición de un reloj público', Quito, 13 de enero de 1612. Francisco de Solano Pérez-Lila, ed., *Normas y leyes de la ciudad hispanoamericana, 1601–1821* (Madrid, 1996), vol. II, pp. 35–6.

14 Serge Gruzinski, *La ciudad de México. Una historia* (Mexico City, 2004), pp. 335–7.

15 Manuel Lucena Salmoral, 'Las tiendas de la ciudad de Quito, *circa* 1800', *Revista*

Ecuatoriana de Historia, IX (1996), pp. 126–35.

16 Cecilia Restrepo Manrique, *La alimentación en la vida cotidiana del Colegio mayor de nuestra señora del Rosario, 1653–1773. 1776–1900* (Bogotá, 2012), p. 131.

17 Joseph M. H. Clark, 'Environment and the Politics of Relocation in the Caribbean Port of Veracruz, 1519–1599', in *The Spanish Caribbean and the Atlantic World in the Long Sixteenth Century*, ed. Ida Altman and David Wheat (Lincoln, NE, 2019), pp. 189–210.

18 Javier Barrientos Grandón and Claudia Castelleti Font, 'De las nieves y su disciplina jurídica en el derecho indiano', *Revista de Historia del Derecho Privado*, VI (2006), pp. 65–9.

19 Frontinus, *The Stratagems: The Aqueducts of Rome*, trans. C. E. Bennett, ed. M. B. McElwain (Cambridge, 1925), pp. 357–9.

20 'Antecedentes y documentos de la apertura del canal', in *Informe o noticia histórica sobre la apertura del canal de Maipo: formaciónyi progresos de la sociedad* (Santiago, 1859), VI, p. 9, www.memoriachilena.gob.cl/602/w3-article-80836.html, accessed 24 February 2021.

21 José Antonio de Villaseñor y Sánchez, *Suplemento al Theatro americano (La ciudad de México en 1755)*, ed. Ramón María Serrera (Mexico City, 1980), p. 136.

22 González Tascón, *Ingeniería española en ultramar*, p. 235.

23 Villaseñor, *Suplemento al Theatro americano*, p. 155.

24 Dolores Romero Muñoz et al., *Obras hidráulicas de la ilustración* (Madrid, 2014), p. 189.

25 María Clara Torres, Hugo Delgadillo and Andrés Peñarete, 'Obras en Bogotá', in *Fray Domingo de Petrés en el Nuevo Reino de Granada* (Bogotá, 2012), p. 59.

26 José Sala Catalá, *Ciencia y técnica en la metropolización de América* (Aranjuez, 1994), p. 41.

27 Henrico Martínez, *Repertorio de los Tiempos e Historia Natural desta Nueva España* (Mexico City, 1606).

28 *Documentos relativos a la desecación del valle de México*, ed. Ana María Calavera (Madrid, 1991), pp. 113ff.

29 Alfredo Castillero Calvo, *Los metales preciosos y la primera globalización* (Panama City, 2008), p. 37.

30 Elías Trabulse, *Ciencia mexicana. Estudios históricos* (Mexico City, 1993), p. 103.

31 Ernesto Shäfer, *El consejo real y supremo de las Indias* (Salamanca, 2003), vol. II, p. 375.

32 Jorge Cañizares-Esguerra, 'Bartolomé Inga's Mining Technologies: Indians, Science, Cyphered Secrecy, and Modernity in the New World', *History and Technology*, XXXIV (2018), pp. 61–5.

33 González Tascón, *Ingeniería española en ultramar*, p. 315.

34 Tristan Platt, 'The Alchemy of Modernity: Alonso de Barba's Copper Cauldrons and the Independence of Bolivian Metallurgy', *Journal of Latin American Studies*, XXXII (2000), pp. 1–54, at pp. 16ff.

35 Alfredo Moreno Cebrián, 'Cuarteles, barrios y calles de Lima a finales del siglo XVIII', *Jahrbuch für Geschichte von Staat, Wirtschaft und Gesellschaft Lateinamerikas*, XVIII (1981), pp. 102, 143.

36 Juan Marchena and Carmen Gómez Pérez, *La vida de guarnición en las ciudades americanas de la ilustración* (Madrid, 1992), pp. 152–66; José Omar Moncada Maya, 'El cuartel como vivienda colectiva en España y sus posesiones durante el siglo XVIII', *Scripta Nova*, VII (2003), pp. 146–7.

37 Charles R. Cutter, *The Legal Culture of Northern New Spain, 1700–1810* (Albuquerque, NM, 1995), pp. 56–7, 80–105.

38 *Gobierno del señor rey D. Carlos III, o Instrucción reservada para dirección de la junta de Estado* (Paris, 1838), pp. 240–41.

39 Horario Capel, Joan Eugeni Sánchez and Omar Moncada, *De Palas a Minerva: la formación científica y la estructura institucional de los ingenieros militares en el siglo XVIII* (Barcelona, 1988), p. 322.

40 Fernando Rodríguez de la Flor, 'El imaginario de la fortificación entre el barroco y la ilustración española', in *Los ingenieros militares de la monarquía hispánica*

en los siglos XVII *y* XVIII, ed. Alicia Cámara Muñoz (Madrid, 2005), pp. 47–50.

41 Horacio Capel Sáez, 'Ciencia, técnica e ingeniería en la actividad del cuerpo de ingenieros militares: su contribución a la morfología urbana de las ciudades españolas y americanas', in *El siglo de las luces. De la ingeniería a la nueva navegación*, ed. Manuel Silva Suárez (Zaragoza, 2005), pp. 359–62.

42 Aurora Rabanal Yus, 'Arquitectura industrial borbónica', in *El siglo de las luces. De la industria al ámbito agroforestal*, ed. Manuel Silva Suárez (Zaragoza, 2005), pp. 97–105.

43 María Amparo Ros, 'La Real Fábrica de Puros y Cigarros: organización del trabajo y estructura urbana', in *Ciudad de México: Ensayo de construcción de una historia*, ed. Alejandra Moreno Toscano (Mexico City, 1978), p. 49.

44 González Tascón, *Ingeniería española en ultramar*, pp. 385–7.

45 Manuel Gámez Casado, 'Cañones al óleo. Una alternativa para la artillería de Cartagena de Indias a fines del siglo XVIII', *Gladius*, XXXVIII (2018), p. 165.

46 Ibid., pp. 171–2.

47 Gregorio Weinberg, 'Tradicionalismo y renovación', in *Buenos Aires, Historia de cuatro siglos*, ed. José Luis Romero and Luis Alberto Romero (Buenos Aires, 2000), vol. I, pp. 102–4.

48 Juan Pedro Viqueira Albán, *¿Relajados o reprimidos? Diversiones públicas y vida social en la ciudad de México en el siglo de las luces* (Mexico City, 1987), p. 70.

49 Gruzinski, *La ciudad de México*, p. 123.

50 Clarence H. Haring, *El comercio y la navegación entre España y las Indias en época de los Habsburgo* (Paris, 1939), p. 39.

51 Winifred Gallagher, *How the Post Office Created America: A History* (New York, 2016), p. 13.

52 Rocío Moreno Cabanillas, 'Cartas en pugna. Resistencias y oposiciones al proyecto de reforma del correo ultramarino en España y América en el siglo XVIII', *Nuevo Mundo, Mundos Nuevos* (2017), pp. 18–19.

53 Cayetano Alcázar, *Historia del correo en América* (Madrid, 1920), pp. 23–74;

Sylvia Sellers-García, *Distance and Documents at the Spanish Empire's Periphery* (Stanford, CA, 2013), pp. 16–17; Nelson Fernando González Martínez, 'De los "chasquis" de Nueva España: la participación de los indios en la movilización de correo y la reforma del aparato postal novohispano (1764–1780)', *Indiana*, XXXIV (2017), pp. 103–4.

54 'se levantó del agua con los pliegos en la mano metidos en unas alforjas, el río se los quitó': José Araneda Riquelme, 'Las reformas de los correos en la ruta del sur de Chile. Instituciones, actores e historias (1768–1777)', *Nuevo Mundo, Mundos Nuevos*, http://journals.openedition.org/nuevomundo/70235; DOI: https://doi.org/10.4000/nuevomundo.70235.

55 Lina Cuéllar Wills, 'Territorios en papel: las guías de forasteros en Hispanoamérica (1760–1897)', *Fronteras de la Historia*, XIX (2014), p. 180.

56 Ángel Antonio Henry, *Dirección General de Cartas de España a sus Indias: no sólo según el orden geográfico general, sino por el particular que rige en el ramo de Correos* (Madrid, 1807), vol. I, p. 34.

57 Casimiro Gómez Ortega, *Elogio histórico de Don Joseph Quer* (Madrid, 1784), p. ii.

58 A. R. Steele, *Flowers for the King: The Expedition of Ruiz and Pavón and the Flowers of Peru* (Durham, NC, 1964).

59 Olga Restrepo Forero, 'José Celestino Mutis: el papel del saber en el Nuevo Reino de Granada', *Anuario Colombiano de Historia Social y de la Cultura*, XIX (1991), pp. 47–99, at p. 63.

60 J. A. Amaya, *Celestino Mutis y la expedición botánica* (Madrid, 1986).

61 Gaspar Xuarez's preface to H. Ruiz, *Flores Peruvianae et Chilensis Prodromus* (Rome, 1797), p. iii.

62 Rainer Buschmann, *Iberian Visions of the Pacific Ocean, 1507–1899* (New York, 2016), pp. 188–9.

63 Silvia Renzi, 'Writing and Talking of Exotic Animals', in *Books and the Sciences in History*, ed. M. Frasca-Spada and N. Jardine (Cambridge, 2000), pp. 151–67.

64 Hipólito Ruiz, *Flores Peruvianae et Chilensis Prodromus* (Rome, 1797), p. ix.

65 Felipe Fernández-Armesto, *1492: The Year the World Began* (New York, 2010), pp. 3–4.

66 Richard H. Grove, *Green Imperialism: Colonial Expansion, Tropical Island Edens and the Origins of Environmentalism, 1600–1860* (Cambridge, 1995).

67 Matthew Restall, 'Black Conquistadors: Armed Africans in Early Spanish America', *The Americas*, LVII (2000), pp. 171–205.

68 Redcliffe N. Salaman, *The History and Social Influence of the Potato* (Cambridge, 1985), p. 148.

69 Alfred W. Crosby, *The Columbian Exchange: Biological and Cultural Consequences of 1492* (New York, 2003), pp. 64–76.

8 Health Infrastructure: Hospitals and Sanitation

1 Mike Davis, *Late Victorian Holocausts* (London, 2001), pp. 163–4.

2 H. Figueroa Marroquín, *Enfermedades de los conquistadores* (San Salvador, 1957), pp. 11–47.

3 Suzanne A. Alchon, *Native Society and Disease in Colonial Ecuador* (Cambridge, 2002), pp. 20–21.

4 John R. McNeill, *Mosquito Empires: Ecology and War in the Greater Caribbean, 1620–1914* (Cambridge, 2010), pp. 267–87.

5 David Wootton, *Bad Medicine: Doctors Doing Harm since Hippocrates* (Oxford, 2006), pp. 2–3.

6 'para que con esta precaución no passe el contagio a otros.' *Recopilación de leyes de los Reinos de las Indias* (Madrid, 1681), Bk 4, Título 17, f. 18v.

7 Francisco Guerra, *El hospital en Hispanoamérica y Filipinas, 1492–1898* (Madrid, 1994), p. 390.

8 Adam Warren, *Medicine and Politics in Colonial Peru* (Pittsburgh, PA, 2010), pp. 15–16.

9 Kenneth Mills, 'The Limits of Religious Coercion in Colonial Peru', *Past & Present*, 145 (November 1994), pp. 84–121, at p. 90.

10 Mario Polia and Fabiola Chávez Hualpa, 'Ministros menores del culto: shamanes y curanderos en las fuentes españolas de los siglos XVI–XVII', *Antropológica*, XII (1994), pp. 7–48, at pp. 7–10.

11 Peter Burke, *Popular Culture in Early Modern Europe* (Aldershot, 2009), pp. 12–15.

12 Fernando Cervantes, *The Devil in the New World* (New Haven, CT, 1994), p. 60.

13 Joseph A. Gagliano, 'Coca and Popular Medicine in Peru: An Historical Analysis of Attitudes', in *Spirits, Shamans and Stars: Perspectives from South America*, ed. D. L. Browman (The Hague, 1979), pp. 39–54; G. Aguirre Beltran, *Medicina y magia: el proceso de aculturación en la estructura colonial* (Mexico City, 1963), pp. 113ff; Linda A. Newsom, 'Medical Practice in Early Colonial Spanish America: A Prospectus', *Bulletin of Latin American Research*, XXV (2006), pp. 367–91; Nicholas Griffiths, 'Andean Curanderos and their Repressors: The Persecution of Native Healing in Late Seventeenth and Early Eighteenth-Century Peru', in *Spiritual Encounters: Interactions between Christianity and Native Religions in Colonial America*, ed. Fernando Cervantes and Nicholas Griffiths (Birmingham, 1999), pp. 185–97; Noemí Quezada, 'The Inquisition's Repression of Curanderos', in *Cultural Encounter: The Impact of the Inquisition in Spain and the New World*, ed. Mary E. Perry and Anne J. Cruz (Berkeley, CA, 1991), pp. 37–57.

14 Ryan A. Kashanipour, 'A World of Cures: Magic and Medicine in Colonial Yucatán', PhD thesis, University of Arizona, 2012, pp. 192–3.

15 Kenneth Mills, *Idolatry and Its Enemies: Colonial Andean Religion and Extirpation, 1640–1750* (Princeton, NJ, 1997), pp. 259–62.

16 Andrés Reséndez, *A Land So Strange: The Epic Journey of Cabeza de Vaca* (New York, 2007), pp. 133ff.

17 Ibid.

18 David Arnold, ed., *Imperial Medicine and Indigenous Societies* (Manchester, 1988), p. 14.

19 Fernando Aguerre Core, 'El ramo de 'hospital' y la atención de la salud en el

Paraguay durante la segunda mitad del s. XVIII', PhD thesis, University of Arizona, Tucson, 2019, available at www.academia. edu, p. 17.

20 Kashanipour, 'A World of Cures', pp. 187–8.
21 Emanuele Amodio, 'Curanderos y médicos ilustrados: la creación del protomedicato en Venezuela hacia finales del s. XVIII', *Asclepio*, LXIX (1997), pp. 95–129, at p. 124.
22 Carmen Martín Martín and José Luis Valverde, eds, *La farmacia en la América colonial: el arte de preparar los medicamentos* (Granada, 1995), p. 28.
23 Ibid., pp. 49–50.
24 Ibid., pp. 23–5.
25 Luis Martin, *The Intellectual Conquest of Peru: The Jesuit College of San Pablo, 1568–1767* (New York, 1968), p. 102.
26 Martín Martín and Valverde, eds, *La farmacia en la América colonial*, pp. 94–5.
27 Woodberry Lowery, *The Spanish Settlements: Within the Present Limits of the United States: Florida, 1562–1574* (New York, 1905), p. 354.
28 F. Fernández-Armesto, *Nuestra América* (Madrid, 2014), p. 132.
29 Martín Martín and Valverde, eds, *La farmacia en la América colonial*, p. 26.
30 David Weber, *The Spanish Frontier in North America* (New Haven, CT, 1991), p. 263.
31 Ignacio González Tascón, *Ingenería española en ultramar, siglos XVI–XIX* (Madrid, 1992), pp. 260–61.
32 John T. Lanning, *The Royal Protomedicato: The Regulation of the Medical Profession in the Spanish Empire* (Durham, NC, 1985), pp. 352–8.
33 Thomas Gage, *The Traveller* (Woodbridge, 1758), vol. I, p. 49.
34 Francisco González de Cosío, *Historia de las obras públicas en México*, vol. I (Mexico City, 1971), p. 278.
35 González Tascón, *Ingenería española en ultramar*, p. 262.
36 Guerra, *El hospital en Hispanoamérica y Filipinas*, p. 55.
37 Warren, *Medicine and Politics in Colonial Peru*, p. 20.
38 Guerra, *El hospital en Hispanoamérica y Filipinas*, p. 55.

39 Ibid., p. 432.
40 Ibid.
41 Ibid., pp. 221–2, 447.
42 Ibid., p. 193.
43 Ibid., pp. 68–75, 433.
44 Ibid., pp. 348, 102.
45 Ibid., pp. 95–6, 188–9.
46 Ibid., pp. 291, 349.
47 Ibid., p. 78.
48 González Cosío, *Historia de las obras públicas en México*, vol. I, p. 245.
49 Ibid., p. 194.
50 Ibid., p. 175; Eusebio Buenaventura Belena, *Recopilación sumaria de los autos acordados de la Real Audiencia y Sala del Crimen de Esta Nueva Espana, y Providencias de su Superior Gobierno* (Mexico City, 1787), vol. I, p. 374.
51 Guerra, *El hospital en Hispanoamérica y Filipinas*, pp. 45, 96, 104, 366.
52 Ibid., pp. 371–3, 430.
53 González de Cosío, *Historia de las obras públicas en México*, vol. I, p. 171.
54 Ibid., pp. 176–7.
55 Guerra, *El hospital en Hispanoamérica y Filipinas*, pp. 459, 541–3.
56 Ibid., p. 225.
57 Warren, *Medicine and Politics in Colonial Peru*, p. 20.
58 Guerra, *El hospital en Hispanoamérica y Filipinas*, p. 229.
59 Lanning, *The Royal Protomedicato*, pp. 24–7, 60, 145, 29.
60 Warren, *Medicine and Politics in Colonial Peru*, p. 8.
61 Lanning, *The Royal Protomedicato*, pp. 184, 286–7.
62 Warren, *Medicine and Politics in Colonial Peru*, p. 19.
63 Lanning, *The Royal Protomedicato*, pp. 32–3, 44, 201–2.
64 Ibid., p. 36.
65 Ibid., p. 38.
66 Cynthia E. Milton, *The Many Meanings of Poverty: Colonialism, Social Compacts, and Assistance in Eighteenth-Century Ecuador* (Stanford, CA, 2007), p. 160.
67 Sean P. Phillips, 'Pox in the Pulpit: The Catholic Church and Smallpox in France,

1724–1836', PhD thesis, University of Notre Dame, 2016.

68 Warren, *Medicine and Politics in Colonial Peru*, pp. 371–80.

69 Guerra, *El hospital en Hispanoamérica y Filipinas*, pp. 413, 433.

9 The Missionary Frontier: Missions as Infrastructure

1 Felipe Fernández-Armesto, *Philip II's Empire: A Decade at the Edge: The Hakluyt Society Annual Lecture* (London, 1999), p. 17.

2 Cameron D. Jones, *In Service of Two Masters: The Missionaries of Ocopa, Indigenous Resistance, and Spanish Governance in Bourbon Peru* (Stanford, CA, 2018), p. 35.

3 Valerie Fraser, *The Architecture of Conquest: Building in the Viceroyalty of Peru, 1535–1635* (Cambridge, 1990), pp. 25ff.

4 G. Baudot, *Utopie et histoire au Méxique* (Toulouse, 1977); J. Phelan, *The Millennial Kingdom of the Franciscans in the New World* (Berkeley, CA, 1970), pp. 118ff.; A. Milhou, *Colón y su mentalidad mesiánica en el ambiente franciscanista español* (Valladolid, 1983), pp. 8ff.

5 Jones, *In Service of Two Masters*, pp. 25–6.

6 Ibid., p. 28.

7 Francis X. Hezel, 'From Conversion to Conquest: The Early Spanish Mission in the Marianas', *Journal of Pacific History*, XVII (1982), pp. 115–37.

8 Luke Clossey, *Salvation and Globalization in the Early Jesuit Missions* (Cambridge, 2008), pp. 81–3, 125–6.

9 Magnus Mörner, *The Political and Economic Activities of the Jesuits in the La Plata Region: The Habsburg Era* (Stockholm, 1953), p. 66.

10 Eugenio Ruidíaz y Caravia, *La Florida: su conquista y colonización por Pedro Menéndez de Avilés* (Madrid, 1893), vol. II, p. 104.

11 David Weber, *The Spanish Frontier in North America* (New Haven, CT, 1992), pp. 67–72.

12 Luis Jerónimo de Oré, *Account of the Martyrs in the Provinces of La Florida*, ed. Raquel Chang-Rodríguez and Nancy Vogeley (Albuquerque, NM, 2016), p. 148.

13 Ibid., pp. 100, 120.

14 Woodberry Lowery, *The Spanish Settlements within the Present Limits of the United States: Florida, 1562–1574* (New York, 1905), p. 354.

15 Weber, *The Spanish Frontier*, p. 42.

16 John J. TePaske, *The Governorship of Spanish Florida, 1700–63* (Durham, NC, 1964), p. 197.

17 Weber, *The Spanish Frontier*, p. 304.

18 Ibid., p. 300.

19 Ibid., p. 282.

20 Philip Caraman, *The Lost Paradise* (London, 1975), p. 37.

21 Martin Dobrizhoffer, *An Account of the Abipones, an Equestrian People of Paraguay* (London, 1822), p. 35.

22 David Cannadine, *Ornamentalism: How the British Saw Their Empire* (Oxford, 2001), pp. 3–10.

23 Dobrizhoffer, *An Account of the Abipones*, p. 101.

24 Cecilia Martínez, 'Las reducciones jesuitas en Chiquitos. Aspectos espacio-temporales e interpretaciones indígenas', *Boletín Americanista*, LXXI (2015), pp. 133–54.

25 Werner Hoffmann, *Las misiones jesuíticas entre los Chiquitanos* (Buenos Aires, 1979), pp. 153–4.

26 George O'Neill, *Golden Years on the Paraguay* (London, 1934), pp. 134–6.

27 John E. Groh, 'Antonio Ruíz de Montoya and the Early Reductions in the Jesuit Province of Paraguay', *Catholic Historical Review*, LVI (1970), pp. 501–33.

28 John Hemming, *Red Gold* (London, 1978), pp. 266–71.

29 Caraman, *The Lost Paradise*, p. 255.

30 Ibid., pp. 132–42.

31 Ibid., p. 136.

32 Eliane C. Deckmann Fleck, 'From Traditional Practices to Reduction Practices: Rituals of Healing, Grief and Burial at the Jesuit-Guarani Reductions (Jesuit Province of Paraguay, 17th Century)', *Espaço Ameríndio*, V (2011), pp. 9–44.

33 Pablo Pastells, *Historia de la Compañia de Jesús en la provincia de Paraguay*, 9 vols (Madrid, 1912), vol. I, p. 163.

34 Eliane C. Deckmann Fleck, 'From Devil's Concubines to Devout Churchgoers:

Women and Conduct in Transformation (Jesuit-Guarani Reductions in the Seventeenth Century)', *Estudos Feministas*, XIV (2006), pp. 617–34.

35 O'Neill, *Golden Years on the Paraguay*, p. 131.

36 See Charles Maier, *Once within Borders: Territories of Power, Wealth, and Belonging since 1500* (Cambridge, 2017), pp. 25ff.

37 Richard Gott, *Land without Evil* (London, 1993), pp. 150–51.

38 Ibid., p. 24.

39 Douglas Monroy, *Thrown among Strangers: The Making of Mexican Culture in Northern California* (Berkeley, CA, 1993), p. 66.

40 William Shaler, 'Journal of a Voyage between China and the North-West Coast of America, made in 1804', *American Register*, III (1808), p. 153.

41 F. Fernández-Armesto, *Nuestra América* (Madrid, 2014), p. 132.

42 Weber, *The Spanish Frontier*, pp. 263, 282.

43 Monroy, *Thrown among Strangers*, p. 107.

44 Ibid., p. 61.

45 Ibid., p. 50.

46 Robert F. Heizer, ed., *The Indians of Los Angeles County: Hugo Reid's Letters of 1852* (Los Angeles, CA, 1968), pp. 74–6, 101–2.

47 Ibid., p. 102.

48 Robert F. Heizer and Alan F. Almquist, *The Other Californians: Prejudice and Discrimination under Spain, Mexico and the United States to 1920* (Berkeley, CA, 1971), p. 40.

49 T. Blackburn, 'The Chumash Revolt of 1824: A Native Account', *Journal of California Anthropology*, II (1975), pp. 225–7.

50 Heizer and Almquist, *The Other Californians*, pp. 8–9.

51 Ibid., p. 48.

52 J. A. Sandos, *Converting California* (New Haven, CT, 2008), p. 70.

53 E. B. Webb, *Indian Life at the Old Missions* (Los Angeles, CA, 1952), p. 49.

54 Heizer and Almquist, *The Other Californians*, pp. 87–9; R. H. Jackson and E. D. Castillo, *Indians, Franciscans, and Spanish Colonization: The Impact of the Mission System on California Indians* (Albuquerque, NM, 1995); J. Sandos, *Converting California:*

Indians and Franciscans in the Missions (New Haven, CT, 2004); S. Hackel, *Children of Coyote, Missionaries of Saint Francis: Indian–Spanish Relations in Colonial California, 1769–1850* (Chapel Hill, NC, 2005).

55 Monroy, *Thrown among Strangers*, p. 25.

56 B. Leutenegger and M. B. Habig, 'Report on the San Antonio Missions in 1792', *Southwestern Historical Quarterly*, LXXVII (1974), pp. 487–98.

10 The Last Century: Engineers in the Aftermath of Empire

1 'I went to see it and it is really of absolutely nothing': Michael A. Codding, ed., *Tesoros de la Hispanic Society of America* (Madrid, 2017), pp. 314ff.; Jean-Louis Augé, 'L'Assemblée de la Compagnie royale des Philippines, 1815', https://musees-occitanie.fr.

2 Emilio La Parra, *Fernando VII un rey deseado y detestado* (Barcelona, 2018), pp. 15–35.

3 Samuel Smiles, *Lives of the Engineers* (London, 1862), pp. iii, vff.

4 Sergio Mejía, *Cartografía e ingeniería en la era de las revoluciones. Mapas y obras de Vicente Talledo y Rivera en España y el Nuevo Reino de Granada (1758–1820)* (Madrid, forthcoming), pp. 97, 449.

5 Frank Safford, *El ideal de lo práctico. El desafío de formar una élite técnica y empresarial en Colombia* (Medellín, 2014), pp. 197–252.

6 Leandro Prados de la Escosura, 'La pérdida del imperio y sus consecuencias económicas', in *La independencia americana. Consecuencias económicas*, ed. Leandro Prados de la Escosura and Samuel Amaral (Madrid, 1993), pp. 253–5.

7 María Dolores Elizalde Pérez-Grueso and Xavier Huetz de Lemps, 'Imperios, comunidades e historia social filipina', in *Filipinas, siglo XIX. Coexistencia e interacción entre comunidades en el Imperio español*, ed. María Dolores Elizalde Pérez-Grueso and Xavier Huetz de Lemps (Madrid, 2017), pp. 9–39.

8 María Dolores Elizalde, 'El Pacífico del siglo XIX', in *A 500 años del hallazgo del Pacífico. La presencia novohispana en el Mar*

del Sur, ed. Carmen Yuste López and
Guadalupe Pinzón Ríos (Mexico City,
2016), pp. 390–93; Rainer F. Buschmann,
Iberian Visions of the Pacific Ocean, 1507–1899
(Basingstoke, 2014), pp. 2–3.

9 Jesús Sánchez Miñana, 'Del semáforo al
teléfono: los sistemas de telecomunicación',
in *El ochocientos: de las profundidades a las
alturas*, ed. Manuel Silva Suárez (Zaragoza,
2013), pp. vii–viii, 84.

10 José María Fernández Palacios, 'España
y Filipinas en la expansión telegráfica a
Ultramar: el cable submarino entre Manila
y Hong Kong', *Revista Española del Pacífico*,
XXIII (2010), p. 131.

11 David Marcilhacy, *Raza hispana.
Hispanoamericanismo e imaginario nacional
en la España de la restauración* (Madrid,
2010), pp. 115–16.

12 Cecilio Garriga Escribano and Francesc
Rodríguez Ortiz, 'Lengua, ciencia y técnica',
in *El ochocientos: de los lenguajes al patrimonio*,
ed. Manuel Silva Suárez (Zaragoza, 2011),
pp. vi, 111.

13 Jürgen Osterhammel, *The Transformation of
the World: A Global History of the Nineteenth
Century* (Princeton, NJ, 2014), pp. 710–24.

14 'Saber es hacer. El que no hace, no sabe':
Erich Bauer Manderscheid, *Los montes de
España en la historia* (Madrid, 1980), p. 519.

15 Miguel Alonso Baquer, *Aportación militar
a la cartografía española en la historia
contemporánea* (Madrid, 1972), pp. 199–200.

16 Vicente Casals Costa, *Los ingenieros de
montes en la España contemporánea, 1848–1936*
(Barcelona, 1996), pp. 251–2.

17 Manuel Silva Suárez, 'Presentación sobre la
institucionalización profesional y académica
de las carreras técnicas civiles', in *El
ochocientos*, ed. Manuel Silva Suárez, pp. v,
21–8.

18 Ignacio J. López Hernández, 'El cuerpo
de ingenieros militares y la Real Junta de
Fomento de la isla de Cuba: obras públicas
entre 1832 y 1854', *Espacio, Tiempo y Forma*,
VIII (2016), p. 490.

19 José Ignacio Muro Morales, 'Ingenieros
militares en España en el siglo XIX'.
www.ub.edu/geocrit/sn/sn119-93.htm.

20 Ibid.

21 López Hernández, 'El cuerpo de ingenieros
militares', p. 487.

22 Ignacio J. López Hernández, 'Carlos
Benítez y los puentes de la ciudad cubana
de Matanzas en 1849', *Laboratorio de Arte*,
XXVI (2014), p. 302.

23 Ignacio J. López Hernández, *Ingeniería
e ingenieros en Matanzas: defensa y obras
públicas entre 1693 y 1868* (Madrid, 2019),
vol. I, p. 200.

24 Ibid., p. 200.

25 Ibid., p. 377.

26 Consuelo Naranjo Orovio, 'La otra Cuba:
colonización blanca y diversificación
agrícola', *Contrastes*, XII (2001–3).

27 María Dolores González-Ripoll Navarro,
*Cuba. La isla de los ensayos. Cultura y sociedad
(1760–1815)* (Madrid, 1999) pp. 25ff; *Real
Comisión de Guantánamo a la Isla de Cuba
(1796–1802)*, Biblioteca virtual de polígrafos,
Fundación Ignacio Larramendi. DOI: http://
www.larramendi.es/es/consulta_aut/registro.
do?id=62617, accessed 11 March 2021.

28 Paul B. Niell, 'Rhetorics of Place and
Empire in the Fountain Sculpture of
1830s Havana', *Art Bulletin*, XCV (2013),
pp. 440–64.

29 Miguel Ángel Castillo Oreja, 'El
abastecimiento y la creación de nuevos
espacios públicos en la Habana del Siglo
XIX', *Quiroga*, V (2014), p. 35.

30 Ibid., p. 40.

31 Styliane Philippou, 'La Habana del siglo
XIX: todo lo sólido se desvanece en el
aire', *Quiroga*, V (2014), p. 116; Consuelo
Naranjo Orovio and María Dolores
González-Ripoll Navarro, 'Perfiles del
crecimiento de una ciudad: La Habana a
finales del siglo XVIII', *Tebeto. Anuario del
Archivo Histórico Insular de Fuerteventura*,
V/I (1992), pp. 236–8.

32 Philippou, 'La Habana', p. 118.

33 Xavier Huetz de Lemps, 'La capitalidad de
Manila y el archipiélago filipino a finales
del siglo XIX', in *De la isla al archipiélago en el
mundo hispano*, ed. Xavier Huetz de Lemps,
Françoise Moulin-Civil and Consuelo
Naranjo Orovio (Madrid, 2009), p. 90.

34 Julio Pérez Serrano, 'Características de la población de las Islas Filipinas en la segunda mitad del siglo XI', in *La crisis española del 98: aspectos navales y sociológicos* (Madrid, 1998), p. 15.

35 José María Fernández Palacios, 'De la aventura incierta al placer de viajar en el siglo XIX: la evolución de las comunicaciones navales entre España y Filipinas a través del relato de los viajeros', *Revista Española del Pacífico*, XXIV (2011), p. 106.

36 Guillermo Martínez Taberner, 'Comercio intra-asiático y dinámicas inter-imperiales en Asia oriental: el Japón Meiji y las colonias asiáticas del imperio español', *Millars*, XXXIX (2015), p. 125.

37 Dídac Cubeiro Rodríguez, 'Comunicacións i desenvolupament a Filipines: De l'administració espanyola a la nord-americana (1875–1935)', PhD thesis, Universidad Pompeu Fabra, 2011, pp. v, 419–24.

38 Guillermo Gaudin and Pilar Ponce Leiva, 'Introduction au dossier: el factor distancia en la flexibilidad y el cumplimiento de la normativa en la América Ibérica', *Les Cahiers de Framespa*, XXX (2019). http://journals.openedition.org/framespa/5553, accessed 19 February 2019.

39 Máximo Cánovas del Castillo, *Noticias históricas, geográficas, estadísticas, administrativas de las Islas Filipinas, y de un viaje á las mismas por el Cabo de Buena-Esperanza, y regreso á España por la China, la India, la Arabia, Egipto, Malta y Gibraltar* (Madrid, 1859).

40 Juan Carrillo de Albornox y Galbeño, Diccionario biográfico electrónico (DB-e) de la Real Academia de la Historia, https://dbe.rah.es/biografias/68318-ildefonso-de-aragon-y-abollado, accessed 4 August 2023.

41 Manuel Pérez Lecha, 'Los últimos años de la Nao de China: pervivencia y cambio en el comercio intercolonial novohispano-filipino', *Millars*, XXXIX (2015), p. 50.

42 Jose Rizal, *El filibusterismo: Continuacion de Noli me tangere. Novela filipina* (Barcelona, 1911), I, p. 183.

43 Ander Permanyer Ugartemendia, 'Una presencia no tan singular: españoles en la economía del opio en Asia oriental (1815–1843)', *Millars*, XXXIX (2015), p. 81.

44 Secundino José Gutiérrez Álvarez, *Las comunicaciones en América* (Madrid, 1992), p. 291.

45 Ignacio González Tascón, *Ingeniería española en ultramar, siglos XVI–XIX* (Madrid, 1992), pp. 659–60.

46 Ibid., p. 664.

47 López Hernández, *Ingeniería e ingenieros en Matanzas*, pp. 212–17.

48 Ibid., p. 262.

49 Lizette Cabrera Salcedo, *De los bueyes al vapor: Caminos de la tecnología en Puerto Rico y el Caribe* (San Juan, 2010), pp. 92ff.

50 Fernando Sáenz Ridruejo, 'Ingenieros de caminos en Puerto Rico, 1866–1898', *Anuario de Estudios Atánticos*, LV (2009), p. 315.

51 Cubeiro Rodríguez, 'Comunicacións i desenvolupament', p. 317.

52 María Isabel Piqueras Villaldea, *Las comunicaciones en Filipinas durante el siglo XIX: Caminos, carreteras y puentes* (Madrid, 2002), p. 229.

53 González Tascón, *Ingeniería española en ultramar*, p. 664.

54 Antonio Santamaría, *Historia de los ferrocarriles de Cuba, 1830–1995* (Madrid, 1992), pp. 294–5.

55 Rolando Lloga, 'La arquitectura asociada a los ferrocarriles en el occidente de cuba (1837–1898)', *Quiroga*, V (2014), pp. 91ff.

56 Carmen Navasquillo Sarrión, 'Gobierno y política de Filipinas, bajo el mandato del general Terrero (1885–1888)', Doctoral proposal, Universidad Complutense, 2002, p. 427.

57 Cubeiro Rodríguez, 'Comunicións i desenvolupament', p. 283.

58 Fernández Palacios, 'España y Filipinas en la expansión telegráfica a Ultramar', p. 143.

59 González Tascón, *Ingeniería española en ultramar*, p. 632.

60 Miguel Ángel Sánchez Terry, *Faros españoles de Ultramar* (Madrid, 1992), p. 75.

61 José Antonio Rodríguez Esteban and Alicia Campos Serrano, 'El cartógrafo Enrique D'Almonte, en la encrucijada del colonialismo español de Asia y África', *Scripta Nova*, XXII (2018), p. 13.

62 Juan Carlos Guerra Velasco and Henar Pascual Ruiz-Valdepeñas, 'Dominando la colonia: cartografía forestal, negocio de la madera y apropiación del espacio en la antigua Guinea Continental española', *Scripta Nova*, XIX (2015), p. 4; Agustín R. Rodríguez González, 'Prólogo a una colonia: la estación naval de Guinea (1858–1900)', *Cuadernos de Historia Contemporánea*, CCXLIV (2003), pp. 237–46.

63 Richard H. Grove, *Green Imperialism: Colonial Expansion, Tropical Island Edens and the Origins of Environmentalism, 1600–1860* (Cambridge, 1995), pp. 474ff.; J. Prest, *The Garden of Eden* (New Haven, CT, 1981), pp. 38ff.

64 Susana Pinar, 'Sociedades económicas e ingenieros de montes en Filipinas. Sobre el aprovechamiento forestal durante el periodo de administración española', *Revista de Indias*, LIX/216 (1999), pp. 417–38, at p. 434.

65 Vicente Casals Costa, *Los ingenieros de montes en la España contemporánea* (Barcelona, 1996), p. 371.

ACKNOWLEDGEMENTS

We are grateful to the family of Don Rafael del Pino y Moreno and to the Foundation that he established and which bears his name for support for this book, both moral and material. Without a grant from the Foundation our research would have been impossible and our time unavailable. We have to thank, in particular, Don Rafael's daughter, Doña María del Pino y Calvo-Sotelo, President of the Foundation, and her colleagues on the Board of Trustees, and Don Vicente Montes, Director of the Foundation, and all the staff, for their unfailing interest and help. We are also grateful to the publishing teams at Penguin Random House in Spain and Reaktion Books in the Anglophone world for their sensitive and insightful work on our manuscripts. Our colleagues and students – Manuel Lucena Giraldo's at the Consejo Superior de Investigaciones Científicas and IE University, Madrid, and Felipe Fernández-Armesto's at the University of Notre Dame – were characteristically kind and forbearing. The defects of the present book have survived despite all their help and are the result only of the authors' failings.

PHOTO ACKNOWLEDGEMENTS

The authors and publishers wish to express their thanks to the following sources of illustrative material and/or permission to reproduce it:

Images © Alcazar de Sevilla: p. 163; Archivo General de Indias: pp. 162, 163, 164, 165, 166, 167, 169, 170, 171, 172, 173, 174, 175, 176; Archivo General de Simancas: p. 160; Biblioteca Central de Marina, Madrid: cover (top), p. 168; Biblioteca del Palacio Real (Madrid): p. 166; Bibliothèque Nationale de France: p. 173; CEDEX-CEHOPU: p. 165; Madrid, private collection: cover (bottom), p. 161; Ricardo Sanchez Rodriguez: pp. 86, 87, 120.

INDEX

Page numbers in *italic* refer to illustrations